D1273743

300 YEARS OF AMERICAN SEATING FURNITURE

Pl. 1—*Windsor seating furniture installation at the Yale University Art Gallery; Mabel Brady Garvan Galleries.*

300 YEARS OF AMERICAN SEATING FURNITURE

Chairs and Beds from the Mabel Brady Garvan and Other Collections at Yale University

PATRICIA E. KANE

NEW YORK GRAPHIC SOCIETY *Boston*

Library of Congress Cataloging in Publication Data

Kane, Patricia E
300 years of American seating furniture.

Includes bibliographies and index.
1. Chairs—United States—Catalogs. 2. Beds and bedsteads—United States—Catalogs. 3. Yale University. I. Title.
NK2715.K36 1975 749'.3 75-9097
ISBN 0-8212-0678-8

First Edition

New York Graphic Society books are published by Little, Brown and Company. Published simultaneously in Canada by Little, Brown and Company (Canada) Limited.

Printed in the United States of America

Contents

Pl. 2—*Wainscot chair, Connecticut, 1640–1660 (no. 1).*

Foreword

THIS BOOK is the fourth in a series begun in 1965 to record, identify, and interpret Yale's collection of American arts. The first, *American Pewter—Garvan and Other Collections at Yale,* with an introduction by Graham Hood, was published simultaneously as a special issue of *The Yale University Art Gallery Bulletin* and as a book in 1965.

One thousand forty-three pieces of seventeenth-, eighteenth-, and nineteenth-century silver are recorded in the second publication, *American Silver—Garvan and Other Collections in the Yale University Art Gallery,* 1970. Written and brought to completion by Kathryn C. Buhler and Graham Hood, this monumental two-volume work makes available forty years of research which was begun in 1930 by John Marshall Phillips, the first Curator of the Mabel Brady Garvan Collection, and carried on by him until his death in 1953.

In 1973 the publication of American furniture at Yale began with *The American Clock, 1725–1865—The Mabel Brady Garvan and Other Collections at Yale University.* Patricia E. Kane was co-author with Edwin A. Battison of the Smithsonian Institution. With its many large photographs of the clock movements and detailed descriptions, it was a step forward in clock catalogues.

The present book, *300 Years of American Seating Furniture,* includes objects acquired over a long period because of their historical interest to the University, objects collected and given to the Yale University Art Gallery, and objects acquired for the furnishing of University buildings.

The first gift of record to Yale's furniture collection is a seventeenth-century chest over drawers given to the University in 1800 by a now unknown donor. In 1829 Abraham Bishop, Jr., gave ten of the finest Massachusetts Chippendale side chairs (no. 98) to the Yale Library; an armchair (no. 97) from this original set of twelve chairs was given in 1955 by Maria Trumbull Dana. Of special significance is a caned chair (no. 34) first owned by the Reverend James Pierpont, a founder of Yale and pastor of the First Church of New Haven. This chair, which was preserved in the library for many years, was transferred to the Art Gallery in 1969. In 1841 the Reverend John E. Bray gave an oak wainscot chair (no. 1) believed to have been owned and used by the Reverend Abraham Pierson, who in 1701 became rector of the Collegiate School (now Yale University) in Saybrook, Connecticut. This chair in recent years has been used for the inauguration of Yale's presidents. The University also owns a fine upholstered armchair (no. 207) and side chair (no. 135) once owned by Ezra Stiles, President of Yale from 1778 to 1795.

The nucleus of Yale's collection was given in the 1930's by Francis P. Garvan, Yale '97, in honor of his wife, Mabel Brady Garvan. As reported in *The New York Times* on June 22, 1930, he dreamed of "educating America" in her native arts. But Mr. Garvan was far ahead of his time, and now, forty years later, the ground-swell of interest and enthusiasm of the 1970's may bring reality to his hopes.

Following Mr. Garvan's example, C. Sanford Bull gave a part of his collection to Yale in 1949. In Mr. Bull's gift was a splendid Rhode Island scroll-back side chair in the Queen Anne style (no. 122) and several regional examples of Connecticut chairs made in small Connecticut towns. In 1954 Charles Stetson gave the University two elegant pieces of the Federal period, a couch (no. 222) and a sofa (no. 225). The New Haven collector Olive Louise Dann bequeathed to Yale in 1962 some of the finest American seating furniture. Her Philadelphia easy chair (no. 214), camel-back sofa (no. 224) and superb lolling chairs in both Queen Anne and neo-classical styles are outstanding. They bespeak the taste of the connoisseur, as do two great chairs (nos. 62 and 252) given by Mr. and Mrs. David Stockwell—one, a fine Philadelphia side chair in the Queen Anne style and the other a bentwood rocker purchased at the Centennial Exhibition in Philadelphia.

As noted above, some furniture included here was bought for the many new buildings designed for Yale. Indeed, the chairs acquired for this purpose during the past century add interest and breadth to this study. Usually such furniture acquired for everyday use has been contemporary, but when the Department of Statistics established its offices in the Dana House (24 Hillhouse Avenue) in 1964, Professor Francis Anscombe and his staff acquired antique chairs and sofas appropriate for the period of the house.

In the Foreword to *The American Clock, 1725–1865*, I wrote, "As plans developed in the late 1950's for the publication of the Garvan and Related Collections of American Arts it was determined to bring all of the collections scattered about the country back to New Haven for study, research, and restoration. This task was undertaken by Meyric Rogers, who, after a distinguished career as Curator of American Decorative Arts at the Art Institute of Chicago, was named Curator of the Garvan and Related Collections in 1958." Mr. Rogers brought together in the Garvan Furniture Study—located in the basement of what was then the Yale University Press building—some seven hundred pieces of furniture. There, preliminary cataloguing and the first steps toward publication were begun about 1960 by Mr. Rogers and John Kirk, then Assistant Curator. Many observations in this book are based on their notes, descriptions, and conclusions made before Mr. Rogers retired in 1964 and before Mr. Kirk resigned in 1967 to accept the directorship of the Rhode Island Historical Society. Subsequently Mr. Kirk included studies of a number of Yale pieces in his exhibition catalogue, *Connecticut Furniture, Seventeenth and Eighteenth Centuries,* and his books, *Early American Furniture* and *American Chairs: Queen Anne and Chippendale.*

Following her appointment as Assistant Curator in 1968, Patricia E. Kane, under the direction of Professor Jules Prown (then Curator), continued the studies of the clock and furniture collections to prepare them for publication. The result is a new kind of book on American furniture. Structural details of a large number of closely related but variant chairs have been closely scrutinized. The woods have been determined by microscopic analysis. Minute details are described to encourage study of style and of craft methods employed in the making of useful objects for everyday use. Breaks and repairs, scars and replacements, are noted. Because of the size and range of the collection, which is especially rich in objects owned by the common man, the study covers a fair cross-section of American seating furniture made between 1670 and 1970. Some of the chairs shown are very beautiful. Others represent common solutions to the need for seats.

Miss Kane brings to each object a probing eye and an open mind. She has visited many museums, small historical societies, and private collections seeking documented counterparts to establish the origin of Yale's objects. Her findings are summed up in cogent remarks on each piece. There she weighs each bit of information, explains the basis of her attributions, and comments on the source of the design or the skill of execution or the quality of materials—be they mellowed wood or shiny new steel. We hope the diversity of the collection will lend importance and usefulness for the historian interested in the wide range of artifacts used by early Americans and for the present-day collector seeking information about vernacular objects as well as masterpieces.

The publication of this book has been made possible by Mrs. Francis P. Garvan, dedicated and long-time friend of American Arts at Yale. We thank her.

Charles F. Montgomery

Acknowledgments

MANY PEOPLE have expended time and effort on the creation of *300 Years of American Seating Furniture,* and their contributions are gratefully acknowledged. Fine photographs add a great deal to art publications. For this one, Charles Uht took the majority of the excellent black and white prints; his photographs are supplemented by those of Joseph Szaszfai and of E. Irving Blomstrann, who is also responsible for the color plates of the individual pieces of furniture. Color photographs of the Mabel Brady Garvan Galleries are the work of Norman McGrath.

My own task began with the draft left by John T. Kirk, formerly Assistant Curator of the Garvan and Related Collections of American Art, when he resigned that post to become Director of the Rhode Island Historical Society. Fernande E. Ross, then editor of the furniture catalogue, offered valuable assistance familiarizing me with the philosophy of the catalogue and preparing basic information on the objects. I am also grateful to Jules D. Prown and Theodore E. Stebbins, Jr., for their guidance (1968–70). To Roger Howlett and Elton Wayland Hall thanks are owed for their help in completing condition reports and in measuring objects. Arnold Cowmeadow of the Yale School of Forestry and Environmental Studies, Gordon Saltar, and the U.S. Forest Products Laboratory in Madison, Wisconsin, prepared the microscopic identifications of the furniture woods. Florence M. Montgomery, former Curator in charge of Textiles at the Henry Francis duPont Winterthur Museum, lent her expertise and her time in choosing appropriate reproduction textiles for the new upholstery. Joseph LiVolsi is responsible for the fine new upholstery in which some of the objects appear. Credit is also due Emilio Mazzola, cabinetmaker with the Yale furniture collections from 1960 to 1972, and Peter Arkell, the present furniture conservator, for the fine state of repair of the collection.

Many museums and individuals have offered invaluable assistance in locating related examples. I would like to acknowledge the help of staff members of the Henry Francis duPont Winterthur Museum in particular: Charles Hummel, Nancy Goyne Evans, Karol Schmiegel, and the staff of the Decorative Arts Photographic Collection. Thanks are also extended to Frances Gruber of The Metropolitan Museum of Art; David B. Warren of the Bayou Bend Collection of the Museum of Fine Arts, Houston; the Art Institute of Chicago; the Detroit Institute of Arts; the Henry Ford Museum, Dearborn, Michigan.

In an attempt to understand more accurately the variety of regional styles, particularly in rural seating furniture, the collections of a number of New England museums and historical societies were examined. In particular I would like to thank J. Peter Spang III of Historic Deerfield, Inc., Deerfield, Massachusetts; John F. Page of the New Hampshire Historical Society, Concord, New Hampshire; Henry Maynard of the Wadsworth Atheneum, Hartford, Connecticut; Melvin E. Watts of the Currier Gallery of Art, Manchester, New Hampshire; James L. Garvin of Strawberry Banke, Inc., Portsmouth, New Hampshire; and Hulda M. Payson of the Essex Institute, Salem, Massachusetts. All these people took time from their busy schedules to allow me to study the large furniture collections under their charge. I would also like to extend thanks to the following individuals and institutions for allowing me to study their furniture, much of which had histories of ownership in the upper Connecticut River Valley: Mrs. Doheny H. Sessions of the Porter-Phelps-Huntington House, Hadley, Massachusetts; the Historical Society of Greenfield, Massachusetts; the Amherst Historical Society in Amherst, Massachusetts;

Lewis A. Shephard of the Mead Art Building, Amherst College; Juliette Tomlinson of the Connecticut Valley Historical Museum, Springfield, Massachusetts; the Ramopogue Historical Society, West Springfield, Massachusetts; the Storrowton Village Museum, Westfield, Massachusetts; the Longmeadow Historical Society, Longmeadow, Massachusetts; and the Northampton Historical Society, Northampton, Massachusetts.

For the opportunity to study their collections in eastern Massachusetts I would like to extend my gratitude to the Historical Society of Old Newbury, Newburyport; The Society for the Preservation of New England Antiquities, Boston; the Boxford Historical Society, Inc.; the Concord Antiquarian Society; the Gore Place Society, Waltham; the Fairbanks House, Dedham; the Jackson Homestead, Newton; the Historical Society of Watertown; and the Dorchester Historical Society. In Connecticut I have enjoyed having the privilege of studying and photographing the furniture of the Lyman Allyn Museum, New London; the Connecticut Historical Society, Hartford; the Stanton House, Clinton; the Henry Whitfield Museum, Guilford; the Dorothy Whitfield Historic Society, Guilford; the Litchfield Historical Society and Museum; the Madison Historical Society; the Eells-Stow House, Milford Historical Society; the New Haven Colony Historical Society; the Keeler Tavern Preservation Society, Inc., Ridgefield; the Stratford Historical Society; and the Wilton Historical Society. I would also like to thank the firm of Israel Sack, Inc.; Joseph Butler, Curator of the Sleepy Hollow Restorations, Inc.; Dean A. Fales, Jr.; and Esta J. Astor; of the Maine Historical Society, for their help.

When the curatorial staff of the Garvan and Related Collections of American Arts began to plan the new Mabel Brady Garvan Galleries with the firm of Chermayeff & Geismar Associates in 1972, we acknowledged that our American collections at Yale must include objects of the late nineteenth and twentieth centuries. For their assistance in working toward the inclusion of nineteenth-century furniture from various parts of the University in this catalogue I would like to thank members of the offices of President Kingman Brewster and of the University Treasurer, John Ecklund. Professor Francis Anscombe of the Department of Statistics also allowed us to include the furniture purchased for the Dana House, offices of the Department of Statistics. The task of compiling information about the newly acquired modern furniture was carried forward by Nancy Curry Bavor, Linda Cohen, and Elaine Piraino.

The help of those who read parts of the manuscript, Benno Forman, Jill Mitchell, Elaine Piraino, Rita Reif, Lila Freedman, and Robert Trent, was invaluable. I would like to thank especially Charles F. Montgomery, Curator of the Garvan and Related Collections, for his careful reading of the entire manuscript, for his thoughtful, provocative questions, and for his constructive criticism. The typing of the manuscript, including many revisions, has been very conscientiously carried forth by Marion Sandquist. In the monumental task of transforming typescript and photographs into a finished book I was privileged to have a dedicated editor, Betty Childs, who was always kind, firm, and helpful. I am also indebted to Klaus Gemming, the designer, for shaping the reams of photographs and the complex text into pleasing and meaningful patterns.

The collections of American furniture at Yale University offer a unique opportunity to observe great numbers of objects ranking from the finest to the ordinary. We have attempted to set forth their various qualities and features clearly and faithfully.

P. K.

INTRODUCTION

Chairmaking in America

THE MANUFACTURE OF CHAIRS, like all the industries in America, has undergone revolutionary changes in the past three centuries, evolving from a small-scale handcraft operation to a vast, highly mechanized industry. Radical changes occurred in the way chairs were designed, executed, and merchandized.

In colonial America the foundation of the craft was the apprenticeship system, a part of the cultural baggage inherited from England. The system developed differently in America, however, for there were no guilds as there were in England to regulate the trades. In England the specialized branches of the furniture-making business, the turners, joiners, and upholsterers, had each established its own trade organizations, known as a company, fellowship, or guild;[1] the cabinetmakers, newer specialists in the furniture industry, organized their own separate society by about 1750. The role of the English companies was essentially to supervise the training and to certify the ability of the practitioners of the crafts, to insure that the quality of goods produced was maintained, and to supply security and mutual assistance for their membership.

In America, on the other hand, where the original settlers had to establish for themselves the basic forms of governmental order, the regulation of apprenticeship came under the jurisdiction of civil authorities and not under masters of the individual trades. A boy was usually apprenticed at the age of fourteen for a period of seven years. Advertisements by furniture makers often included notices to the effect that apprentices of that age were sought: "Wanted by said Stackhouse [a Hartford, Connecticut, windsor chairmaker] one or two likely lads 14 or 15 years old, as apprentices to the above business."[2] The typical form of indenture stated that the apprentice

> shall his said Master . . . faithfully serve, his secrets keep, his lawful Commands gladly every where Obey; he shall do no damage to his said Master, nor see to be done by Others without letting or giving Notice to his said Master, he shall not waste his said Master's goods, nor lend them unlawfully to any; he shall not Committ fornication nor Contract Matrimony within the said Term. At Cards, Dice, or any Other unlawfull Game he shall not play, Whereby his said Master may have Damage; with his Own Goods or the Goods of those during the said Term without Lycence from his said Master he shall neither buy nor sell. He shall not absent himself Day or Night from his Master's service without his leave, not haunt Alehouses or Playhouses, but in all things as a faithful apprentice he shall behave himself toward his said Master, and all during the said Term.[3]

After the term of the apprenticeship was up, the craftsman usually spent a number of years as a journeyman, working for others until he was in a position to open his own shop, and, as master, have apprentices and journeymen of his own.

Furniture-making establishments in urban centers were probably managed quite differently from those in the country, but both types of businesses were based on the apprenticeship system. In the urban centers the branches of the trade probably roughly corresponded to those represented by the English

[1] S. W. Wolsey and R. W. Luff, *Furniture in England—The Age of the Joiner* (New York, 1968), p. 14. The Turner's Company received a Charter of Incorporation in 1604, but as early as 1310 the Fellowship of Turners had been recognized by the grant of a code of ordinances. Likewise the joiners had been organized since the thirteenth century and were granted a charter in 1570. The upholders (upholsterers) began as dealers in second-hand goods, but by the end of the sixteenth century they were suppliers of domestic upholstery goods.

[2] Quoted in Ethel Hall Bjerkoe, *The Cabinetmakers of America* (New York, 1957), pp. 206–7.

[3] Quoted in Carl Bridenbaugh, *The Colonial Craftsman* (Chicago, 1971), pp. 130–31.

guilds and the later divisions of cabinetmaking and chairmaking. Such divisions in the craft can be documented from the earliest times; for instance, the 196 furniture-making craftsmen practicing in Boston from 1635 to 1725 included 134 joiners, 11 cabinetmakers, 16 turners (not including blockmakers), 9 cabinetmakers, 17 upholsterers, and 9 carvers.[4] In rural furniture-making shops the tendency toward specialization was less frequent.

A broad distinction in the craftsmanship of chairs can be drawn upon the basis of their construction. Two chairmaking traditions existed from the seventeenth century and continued throughout the handcraft period. In one, the chair was constructed of round pieces fitted into round holes. In the other, the chair was constructed of rectangular pieces with tenons fitted into rectangular holes, or mortises, that were fastened with wooden pegs. Turners, who produced a wide variety of turned work, including chairs, in their shops, are generally credited with making chairs in the first tradition. Joshua Eden (b. 1731) of Charleston, for instance, advertised in the *South Carolina Gazette* in 1767 that he did turning "in its several branches such as banisters, column bedposts, table frames . . . In the meantime he continues to make straw bottom chairs which he will sell very reasonable."[5]

Chairmakers. The distinction between turners and chairmakers is at best blurred. John DeWitt of New York City listed himself as a "turner" in the New York City Directory of 1794 and as a "chairmaker" in 1795. In 1798 in the *Mercantile Diary and Advertiser* he advertised as a "Windsor Chair Maker."[6] Windsor chairs are definitely part of the turned chair tradition, but "chairmakers" may also have been making chairs with framed mortise-and-tenon joints. In other words, chairmakers may have made chairs in either or both traditional manners described above.

[4] Benno M. Forman, "Urban Aspects of Massachusetts Furniture in the Late Seventeenth Century," *Country Cabinetwork and Simple City Furniture* (Charlottesville, Va., 1970), p. 4.—[5] Bjerkoe, p. 85.—[6] *Ibid.*, p. 79.

Joiners. In the seventeenth century joiners were the principal furniture makers producing wares requiring their special techniques of panel and frame construction, such as oak casepieces and fine interior woodwork like doors, window sash, and paneling. Wainscot chairs, which had paneled backs, were also made by joiners. Their turned ornament—legs and arm supports—may have been done by turners working in the same shop or have been supplied to joiners by an independent turning shop. Joiners were succeeded by cabinetmakers as makers of the most fashionable furniture in Boston at the end of the seventeenth century.[7] Despite the appearance of this new kind of furniture specialist, many woodworkers continued to call themselves "joiners" in the eighteenth century, and many of those who did—Thomas Affleck, Daniel Trotter, John Gillingham, and William Savery, for example—are known to have been producing chairs of the highest fashion.[8] Gilbert Ash (1717–85) of New York City advertised in the *New-York Mercury* of October and November 1759 that "The Shop-Joiner or Cabinet Business is still carried on at the same Place, where may be had all sorts of Work made in that Branch, Tables, Chairs, Desks, &."[9]

Cabinetmakers. The name cabinetmaker implies that these practitioners were responsible for cabinets, or casepieces, but English and American advertisements suggest that cabinetmakers supplied a general line of furniture—chairs and other seating furniture as well as casepieces. In the New York City newspapers of 1762 and 1763 John Brinner advertised himself as

> Cabinet and Chair Maker from London at the Sign of the Chair opposite Flatten Barrack Hill, in the Broad-Way, New York, where every article in the Cabinet, Chair-making, Carving and Gilding Business is enacted on the most reasonable Terms with the Utmost Neatness and Punctuality. He carves all Sorts of Architectural, Gothic, and Chinese Chimney-pieces, Glass and Picture Frames, Slab Frames, Girondels, Chandaliers,

[7] Forman, pp. 18–19.—[8] *Ibid.*, p. 20.—[9] Bjerkoe, p. 30.

> and all Kinds of Mouldings and Frontispieces, etc. etc., Desk and Book Cases, Library Book Cases, Writing and Reading Tables, Study Tables, China Shelves and Cases, Commode and Plain Chests of Drawers, Sofa Settees, Couch and Easy Chairs, Frames, all Kinds of Field Bedsteads, etc. etc. N. B. He also brought over from London six Artificers, well-skilled in the above branches.[10]

Carvers. Carving was a specialized branch of the cabinetmaking business. Carvers often maintained their own shops and took in work from several cabinetmakers. For instance, William Crisp advertised in the *Pennsylvania Chronicle* in 1769 that he "follows the business of Carving in all its branches, where Cabinet-Makers, and others, may have their business done with care and dispatch." Independent carvers were undoubtedly responsible for much of the carved work on the chairs discussed in this book. But Crisp also indicated, it should be noted, that he followed the business of cabinetmaking,[11] and thus he might have been responsible for both the making and the carving of some chairs.

Upholsterers. In the introductory chapters to his Winterthur catalogue, *American Furniture: The Federal Period,* Charles Montgomery stated that "the role of the upholsterer in America is one about which little is known. And the mystery will continue until upholsterers' accounts and records come to light."[12] The recent discovery by Brock Jobe of several volumes of the account books and letterbooks of the Boston upholsterer Thomas Fitch and his apprentice and successor, Samuel Grant, has led to a better understanding of the upholsterer's role in the Boston furniture trades between 1720 and 1740. Jobe writes, "During the eighteenth century the upholstery trade was deemed the most lucrative and prestigious craft profession."[13] The account books reveal not only that these Boston upholsterers made and sold bedding, bed curtains, and upholstered seating furniture, but also imported all types of textiles and dry goods for resale.

Knowledge of the ways in which furniture-making establishments were conducted in colonial America is limited by the scarcity of documentary evidence to shed light on shop practices. As yet, no surviving account or receipt book of an important seventeenth-century furniture-maker is known. Among the earliest documents known pertaining to an eighteenth-century chairmaker is the account book of John and Thomas Gaines of Ipswich, Massachusetts (father and brother of the famous Portsmouth chairmaker John Gaines) covering the years 1707–62 (now at the Winterthur Museum). Although Ipswich was a rural community, the account book reveals that even there the specialized trade of the turner was relied upon by other woodworking craftsmen; the cabinetmaker Francis Goodhue had Gaines turn table frames, "pillers," and bedposts for him.[14]

In the cities there was much greater specialization in the branches of the furniture trades, and the phenomenon of the craftsman-entrepreneur blossomed in the eighteenth century. Carl Bridenbaugh has described the repeated attempts of American craftsmen to raise themselves from the level of craftsman to that of merchant.[15] Even in the early eighteenth century master furniture makers in urban centers functioned more as businessmen who managed a shop operation than as craftsmen who put tools to wood. In the case of Thomas Fitch and Samuel Grant, the Boston upholsterers, the accounts reveal that Fitch operated an extensive mercantile trade, particularly in the distribution of English textiles, as well as directing an upholstery shop. This trend from craftsman to entrepreneur became even more evident after the American Revolution.

The advent of the furniture warehouse or the

[10] *Ibid.,* p. 50.—[11] *Ibid.,* p. 72.—[12] Charles F. Montgomery, *American Furniture: The Federal Period* (1788–1825) (New York, 1966), p. 15.—[13] Brock Jobe, "The Boston Furniture Industry 1720–1740," in *Boston Furniture of the Eighteenth Century* (Boston, 1974), p. 24.

[14] Helen Comstock, "An Ipswich Account Book 1707–1762," *Antiques* 65 (Sept. 1954): 188–92.—[15] Bridenbaugh, "The Craftsman as a Citizen," *The Colonial Craftsman,* pp. 155–81.

wareroom in the last years of the eighteenth century heralded new and complex arrangements in the American furniture-making trade. Cabinetmakers often referred to themselves by a new name: one advertised in the *Providence Gazette* of 1804 as "Thomas Howard, jun. Cabinet Manufacturer."[16] Among other things, the words "warehouse" and "manufacturer" imply larger operations, and the storage of great quantities of ready-made goods. With this expansion of the size and organization of shops came more complicated labor arrangements between management and workers. These are manifested by the price books that appeared at the end of the eighteenth century.

Price books were printed or manuscript lists of the prices for making furniture sought by journeymen, and agreed upon by masters.[17] The earliest known price book, in manuscript, is "Rule and Price of Joyners Work—Agreement of February 19, 1756," an agreement involving six cabinetmakers in Providence.[18]

In the last decade of the eighteenth century such manuscript price lists were superseded by printed ones, the earliest American printed price list being a Hartford list of 1792, a guide to retail prices. The printing of such lists may have been stimulated by the appearance of the first printed price book in the English-speaking world, *The Cabinet-Makers' London Book of Prices and Designs of Cabinet Work* of 1788. The first major American price book with the rates to be paid to journeymen, *The Philadelphia Cabinet and Chair-Makers' Book of Prices,* was published by the journeymen in 1794, with a second, enlarged edition of 1795 called *The Journeymen Cabinet and Chair-Makers Philadelphia Book of Prices.* When the journeymen demanded a raise in prices the following year, but were turned down by the masters, they took the unprecedented step of opening their own wareroom in Market Street. The result of this struggle between employers and employees was *The Cabinet-Makers' Philadelphia and London Book of Prices* (1796), which in effect showed that the journeymen had won their case, for the employers agreed that "whenever the necessaries of life, house-rent, &c. shall rise above what they are at present, the Employers agree to advance the precentum to what shall be agreed on: And in like manner, the Workmen do agree to reduce the prices in the same proportion as the said necessaries lower, which shall be agreed on by the Committee of both parties."[19] A similar management-labor battle took place in New York in 1802 and 1803.

The meaning of these documents and the implications for American furniture design have yet to be fully explained. The formation of the journeymen into societies and the formalization of their pay scales into published documents may indicate that in the Federal period a turning point was reached; the small individual craft shops of the seventeenth and eighteenth centuries were giving way to the large mass-production factories that emerged in the nineteenth century. The change had great significance for the individual craftsman. In the eighteenth century each adolescent who entered into an apprenticeship indenture had the opportunity someday to become a master in his own right after serving out his apprenticeship and the intermediate stage of journeymanship. With the advent of "cabinet manufactories," concentrating production in the hands of fewer masters, a division was drawn between labor and management, and the journeymen lost sight of the opportunity to become masters themselves.

Chairs were an ideal product for mass production, because their parts, turned on a lathe, could often be made up in advance and assembled later. Their actual assembly did not require the careful custom fitting necessary for case furniture. As early as the seventeenth century chairs were probably produced in large numbers in American cities. During the early eighteenth century an export trade in chairs de-

[16] Bjerkoe, p. 131.—[17] For information on price books this essay relies heavily upon the introduction to Montgomery, *American Furniture.*—[18] *Ibid.,* p. 20.

[19] *Ibid.,* p. 23.

veloped in Boston, and that city's dominance over all chairmaking in American cities during the first half of the century is illustrated by the advertisement of the Philadelphia chairmaker Plunkett Fleeson in the *Pennsylvania Gazette* of 1742: "Made and to be sold by Plunkett Fleeson, at the Easy Chair, in Chestnut-Street. Several sorts of good Chair-frames, black and red leather Chairs, finished cheaper than any made here, or imported from Boston. . . ."[20] Later in the century Philadelphia led in the exportation of windsor chairs. Rural windsor chairmakers also turned out large numbers of these wooden seated chairs, as the inventory of the Lisbon, Connecticut, craftsman Ebenezer Tracy indicates. Tracy had 6,400 "chair rounds" and 277 "chair bottoms" in his estate upon his death in 1803.[21]

Significant changes took place in the manufacture of chairs in the early nineteenth century, as can be illustrated by the history of Lambert Hitchcock and his chair manufactory. Ebenezer Tracy's inventory included the hand tools that he used in his work; fifteen years later, in 1818, Hitchcock set in operation his chair factory, using machinery driven by water-powered shafts. At first Hitchcock produced just chair parts. They were easier to ship, and in his small factory he did not have the space available to assemble and decorate chairs. The manufacture of chair parts proved to be so successful, however, that two or three years later he began to assemble and decorate chairs. By 1825 Hitchcock opened a new three-story brick factory of ten rooms with a large wheel house, turning shop, and drying kiln. He was now able to transport completed chairs to Hartford where many of the fifteen thousand chairs he made per year were shipped to distant points.

In addition to the utilization of water power, the production of goods principally for distant markets was the major difference in the manufacturing of goods in the new, industrialized era. Although in the eighteenth century American cabinetmakers had designed some of their furniture for export, by and large they were still in business to serve a local market. In the early nineteenth century, however, serving distant American and foreign markets became the norm.

By the mid-nineteenth century the business of cabinetmaking was in a state of flux, as Ernest Hagen's *Personal Experiences of an Old New York Cabinet Maker* reveals.[22] Hagen was a part of the wave of immigrants, particularly Germans, that came to America in the 1840's and 50's. He arrived in New York in 1844 and was apprenticed to a cabinetmaking firm the next year. With the arrival of great numbers of German immigrants in 1849–50, the Delancey Street neighborhood in which he lived was transformed; the old residents moved away "and a Colony of German mechanics took their place. There were cabinet makers shops, saw mills and marble mills everywhere." Much of the work was still done by hand. But, as Hagen reports, "the scroll sawing, of course was done at the nearest sawmill. The employers (boss Cabinet makers) having no machinery at all, all the moldings were bought at the molding mill and the turning done at turning mill." Most of the furniture was not made to order but was sold to furniture stores or exported. By 1858 Hagen was able to buy out his former employers and went into business with J. Mathew Meier. The beginnings were rough, but a decade or so later the business was going well. That fortunate state was not to persist, however, for then, Hagen states, a "great change came over the cabinet making trade of New York. The factory work, and especially the Western factory work drove everything else out of the market. All the smaller cabinet makers were simply wiped out. There are very few left now which make a very scanty living by repairing; and even the larger establishments have a

[20] Richard Randall, "Boston Chairs," *Old Time New England* 54 (July–Sept. 1936): 12.—[21] "Connecticut Cabinetmakers Part II: Checklist up to 1820," *The Connecticut Historical Society Bulletin* 33 (Jan. 1968): 25.

[22] The following excerpts from Hagen's account are quoted in Elizabeth A. Ingerman, "Personal experiences of an old New York cabinetmaker," *Antiques* 84 (Nov. 1963): 576–80.

hard time in competing with the Western concerns of Grand Rapids in Michigan and other out of town concerns." In 1870 New York, Massachusetts, and Pennsylvania were still the three ranking states in the furniture industry, but western centers, especially Cincinnati and St. Louis, were offering new competition.

The western factories, close to sources of raw materials and vast new markets, had been growing since the second quarter of the nineteenth century. By 1846 Cincinnati claimed to be the largest furniture manufacturing city in America. In 1850 Cincinnati had 136 establishments with 1,156 hands who produced furniture valued at $1,660,000. In that year sixty employees of John Broadfoot Smith "turned out 1,000 center tables, 1,200 sofas, and 2,500 parlour chairs." There the machines were run by steam, and finished furniture was shipped down the Mississippi River and throughout the Midwest. By 1890 there were 130 or more furniture-making establishments in the city, employing over 3,000 persons. Before the Civil War, Chicago also had well-equipped furniture factories and was shipping woodwork all over the prairie country; by 1870 her residents were proclaiming it the leading city in furniture making.[23] St. Louis, Grand Rapids, and Milwaukee were also important centers. Clearly one of the major effects of the exploitation of national (and in certain cases international) markets was the obliteration of the "regional styles" of furniture making that furniture historians have come to identify in the products of the handcraft shops of the seventeenth, eighteenth, and early nineteenth centuries.

The industrialization of the nineteenth century also brought with it not only water- and steam-powered production machinery, but also the utilization of new materials and innovative use of old materials. This is especially evident in the manufacture of chairs. The experiments range from the laminated and molded backs of the chairs patented by John Henry Belter of New York to the inventive use of bentwood by Michael Thonet on chairs that gained a very wide market in America as well as in Europe. The development of wire for the Atlantic cable allowed the creation of the "ice cream parlour chair," as well as the heavily upholstered chair with springs.

The voluminous production of nineteenth-century factories offered the American householder a wide range of choice in his furnishings. As *Harper's Bazar* reported in 1877, "There is certainly in modern furniture an immense variety to choose from—the picturesque medieval articles with their pointed arches and vertical lines, the magnificent Renaissance ones covered with carvings that take light and shade like bosses of metal work, the luxurious light and lustre of the articles of the Quatorze with their gilding and their inlay, and all the fantasticism of the styles of the Asiatic races."[24]

The rampant production of historical revival styles stirred a counter force in the nineteenth century, the Arts and Crafts Movement. Its chief spokesman in England was William Morris, poet, craftsman, and utopian socialist. Eschewing the supposed excesses of other historical revival styles and machine methods of production, he favored furniture based on medieval forms which was, like medieval furniture, strongly rectilinear and honest in its revelation of structure. The problem with Morris's point of view was that without reliance upon machine production such furniture could be made only in small quantities for the few, not for the masses. Late nineteenth-century architects, such as Frank Lloyd Wright, owed a debt to William Morris in the use of straightforward design and natural materials, but they nonetheless advocated the use of the machine. Among the best-known manufacturers of furniture of this kind is Gustav Stickley, whose Craftsman workshops were located in Eastwood, New York.

The recognition of and utilization of the machine and mass production became the hallmark of

[23] *The Industries of a Great City* (Chicago, 1912), p. 63.

[24] "Household Furniture: Modern Furniture," *Harper's Bazaar* (January 20, 1877).

twentieth-century furniture design. Following World War I furniture making began to enter a new phase. Undeniably, the Bauhaus, which began in Weimar in 1919, had an extraordinary influence on American design. Chairs by two Bauhaus architects, Marcel Breuer's Wassily chair and Cesca chair and Mies van der Rohe's cantilevered chair, made use of new material—bent tubular metal—to create stark, taut designs suitable for the new streamlined interiors. These and other outstanding chairs of the 1920's had such universal appeal that they are still produced today. During the 1930's many members of the Bauhaus left Germany, and those who came to America altered the course of American design. The thirties also saw the rise in America of the industrial designer and the founding of two important American companies, the Herman Miller Furniture Company and the Hans G. Knoll Furniture Company. In America after World War II, during the post-war boom, the mass production of a variety of new chair designs, using materials in new ways, truly came into its own. Outstanding among these innovations were the molded plywood creations and wire chairs of Charles Eames, produced by Herman Miller, the wire chairs of Harry Bertoia, produced by Knoll, and the plastic types introduced in the late 1950's. Although an appreciation for the handcrafting of wood, the traditional material from which seating furniture is made, has continued in the twentieth century, principally through the Scandinavian school of cabinetmaking, the inventive utilization of machine production from wood, metal, and plastic is the essence of the most outstanding twentieth-century seating furniture.

Short Title List

Am. Antiques	Butler, Joseph T. *American Antiques 1800–1900.* New York: Odyssey Press, 1965.
Aronson	Aronson, Joseph. *The Encyclopedia of Furniture.* New York: Crown Publishers, 1965.
Ayer Coll.	*American Antiques in New England, Collection of Fred Wellington Ayer.* New York: American Art Galleries, American Art Association, Inc., May 3–4, 1929.
BAFA	*Bulletin of the Association in Fine Arts at Yale University.*
Baltimore Furniture	*Baltimore Furniture: The Work of Baltimore and Annapolis Cabinetmakers from 1760 to 1810.* Baltimore: The Baltimore Museum of Art, 1947.
Barbour Coll.	*Frederick K. and Margaret R. Barbour's Furniture Collection.* Hartford, Connecticut: The Connecticut Historical Society, 1963.
Bigelow Coll.	*Colonial Furniture, the Superb Collection of Mr. Francis Hill Bigelow.* New York: Anderson Galleries, Jan. 17, 1924.
Bishop	Bishop, Robert. *Centuries and Styles of the American Chair 1640–1970.* New York: E. P. Dutton and Co., Inc., 1972.
Bissel	Bissel, Charles S. *Antique Furniture in Suffield Connecticut 1670–1835.* Hartford, Connecticut: Connecticut Historical Society and Suffield Historical Society, 1956.
Black Coll.	*Colonial Object Collection of John L. Black.* New York: American Art Galleries, American Art Association, Inc., January 9, 1926.
Boger	Boger, Louise Ade. *Complete Guide to Furniture Styles.* New York: Charles Scribner's Sons, 1959.
Burroughs	Burroughs, Paul H. *Southern Antiques.* Richmond: Garrett & Massie, Inc., 1931.
Burton	Burton, E. Milby. *Charleston Furniture, 1700–1825.* Charleston, South Carolina: The Charleston Museum, 1955.
Carpenter	Carpenter, Ralph E., Jr. *The Arts and Crafts of Newport Rhode Island 1640–1820.* Newport: The Preservation Society of Newport County, 1954.
Classical America	*Classical America 1815–1845.* Newark, New Jersey: The Newark Museum, 1963.
Colonial Antiques	*The American Heritage History of Colonial Antiques.* Marshall B. Davidson, ed. New York: The American Heritage Publishing Co., Inc., 1967.
Comstock	Comstock, Helen. *American Furniture: Seventeenth Eighteenth and Nineteenth Century Styles.* New York: Viking Press, 1962.
Connecticut Chairs	*Connecticut Chairs in the Collection of the Connecticut Historical Society.* Hartford, Connecticut, 1956.
Conn. Furn.	*Connecticut Furniture: Seventeenth and Eighteenth Centuries.* Loan Exhibition of Furniture, Wadsworth Atheneum, Hartford, Connecticut, Nov. 3–Dec. 17, 1967.
Cornelius	Cornelius, Charles Over. *Early American Furniture.* New York: Appleton-Century, 1926.
DAPC	Decorative Arts Photographic Collection. The H. F. duPont Winterthur Museum, Winterthur, Delaware.
Downs, *Am. Furn.*	Downs, Joseph. *American Furniture, Queen Anne and Chippendale Periods.* New York: The Macmillan Company, 1952.
Downs, *N.Y. State Furniture*	Downs, Joseph, and Ralston, Ruth. *A Loan Exhibition of New York State Furniture.* New York: The Metropolitan Museum of Art, 1934.

Fales, *Am. Painted Furn.* — Fales, Dean A., Jr., Cyril I. Nelson, gen. ed. *American Painted Furniture 1660–1880.* New York: E. P. Dutton and Company, Inc., 1972.

Fales, *Essex County Furn.* — Fales, Dean A., Jr. *Essex County Furniture: Documented Treasures from Local Collections, 1660–1860.* Salem, Massachusetts: The Essex Institute, 1965.

Flayderman Coll. — *Collection of the Late Philip Flayderman.* New York: American Art Association, Anderson Galleries, Inc., January 2–4, 1930.

Furn. by N.Y. Cabinetmakers — Miller, V. Isabelle. *Furniture by New York Cabinetmakers.* Museum of the City of New York, 1956.

Furn. of the New Haven Colony — Kane, Patricia E. *Furniture of the New Haven Colony: The Seventeenth Century Style.* New Haven: The New Haven Colony Historical Society, 1973.

Garvan Coll. — *The Collection of Francis P. Garvan.* New York: American Art Association, Anderson Galleries, Inc., January 8–10, 1931.

Girl Scouts Exhibition — *Loan Exhibition of Eighteenth and Nineteenth Century Furniture and Glass.* New York: American Art Galleries, 1929.

Goyne — Goyne, Nancy A. "American Windsor Chairs: A Style Survey," *Antiques* 95 (April 1969).

Greenlaw — Greenlaw, Barry A. *New England Furniture at Williamsburg.* Williamsburg, Virginia: The Colonial Williamsburg Foundation, 1974.

Harris — Harris, John. *Regency Furniture Designs 1803–1826.* London and Chicago: Alec Tiranti Ltd., 1961.

Hipkiss — Hipkiss, Edwin J. *Eighteenth-Century American Arts. The M. and M. Karolik Collection. . . .* Published for the Museum of Fine Arts, Boston, Massachusetts. Cambridge, Massachusetts: Harvard University Press, 1941.

Hornor — Hornor, William M., Jr. *Blue Book, Philadelphia Furniture William Penn to George Washington.* Philadelphia, 1935.

Hudnut Coll. — *Duncan Phyfe and Other Fine Early American Furniture and Decorations, Collection of Alexander M. Hudnut of Princeton, N. J.* New York: American Art Galleries, American Art Association, Inc., November 19, 1927.

Hummel — Hummel, Charles F. *With Hammer in Hand, The Dominy Craftsmen of East Hampton, New York.* Charlottesville: University Press of Virginia, 1968.

Iverson — Iverson, Marion Day. *The American Chair.* New York: Hastings House, 1957.

Kirk, *Am. Chairs* — Kirk, John T. *American Chairs: Queen Anne and Chippendale.* New York: Alfred A. Knopf, 1972.

Kirk, *Early Am. Furn.* — Kirk, John T. *Early American Furniture.* New York: Alfred A. Knopf, 1970.

L. G. Myers Coll. — *Collection of Early American and English Furniture . . . formed by Louis Guerineau Myers.* New York: American Art Association, Anderson Galleries, Inc., Feb. 24–26, 1921.

Litchfield Furn. — *Litchfield County Furniture, 1730–1850.* Litchfield, Conn.: The Litchfield Historical Society, 1969.

Lockwood — Lockwood, Luke V. *Colonial Furniture in America.* 2 vols., 3rd. ed. New York: Charles Scribner's Sons, 1926.

Lyon — Lyon, Irving W. *The Colonial Furniture of New England.* Boston and New York: Houghton Mifflin Company, 1924.

Macquoid & Edwards — Macquoid, Percy, and Edwards, Ralph. *Dictionary of English Furniture.* 3 vols. London: Country Life Ltd., 1924.

Margolis Coll. — *Early American Furniture Gathered by J. Margolis, Cabinetmaker. . . .* New York: Anderson Galleries, Nov. 12–15, 1924.

Maryland Furn. — *Maryland Queen Anne and Chippendale Furniture of the Eighteenth Century.* New York: October House, Inc., 1968.

McClelland — McClelland, Nancy V. *Duncan Phyfe and the English Regency, 1795–1830.* New York: W. R. Scott, Inc., 1939.

Miller — Miller, Edgar G., Jr. *American Antique Furniture.* 2 vols. Baltimore: Lord Baltimore Press, 1937.

MMA Guide — Metropolitan Museum of Art. *Guide to the Collections, American Wing.* New York: The Metropolitan Museum of Art, 1961.

Montgomery — Montgomery, Charles F. *American Furniture: The Federal Period (1788–1825).* New York: The Viking Press, Inc., 1966.

Moore — Moore, N. Hudson. *Old Furniture Book.* New York: F. A. Stokes, 1903.

Nagel — Nagel, Charles. *American Furniture, 1650–1850.* New York: Chanticleer Press, 1949.

N.Y. Furn. before 1840 — *New York Furniture before 1840 in the Collection of the Albany Institute of History and Art.* Albany, New York: Institute of History and Art, 1962.

Nutting, *Pilgrim Century* — Nutting, Wallace. *Furniture of the Pilgrim Century.* Framingham, Massachusetts: Old America Co., 1924.

Nutting, *Treasury* — Nutting, Wallace. *Furniture Treasury.* 3 vols. Framingham, Massachusetts: Old America Co., 1928–1933; reprinted New York: The Macmillan Company, 1948, 1954.

Nutting, *Windsor Handbook* — Nutting, Wallace. *A Windsor Handbook.* Saugus, Massachusetts: Wallace Nutting, Inc., Saugus, Massachusetts, 1917.

Offerman Coll. — *Illustrated Catalogue of Mr. T. Offerman's . . . Collections of Rare Early American and Colonial Furniture.* New York: American Art Association, American Art Galleries, December 8–12, 1922.

Ornamented Chair — *The Ornamented Chair: Its Development in American (1700–1890).* Zilla Rider Lea, ed. Vermont: Charles E. Tuttle Company, 1960.

Ott — Ott, Joseph K. *The John Brown House Loan Exhibition of Rhode Island Furniture.* Providence: The Rhode Island Historical Society, 1965.

Prown — Prown, Jules David. *John Singleton Copley.* 2 vols. Cambridge, Massachusetts: Harvard University Press, 1966.

Randall — Randall, Richard H., Jr. *American Furniture in the Museum of Fine Arts, Boston.* Boston, Massachusetts: Museum of Fine Arts, 1965.

Reifsnyder Coll. — *Colonial Furniture, the Superb Collection of the Late Howard Reifsnyder,* New York: American Art Association, Inc., American Art Galleries, April 24–27, 1929.

Rogers — Rogers, Meyric R. *American Interior Design.* New York: W. W. Norton & Company, Inc., 1947.

Sack, *Fine Points* — Sack, Albert. *Fine Points of Furniture: Early American.* New York: Crown Publishers, Inc., 1950.

Sack Coll., 1927 — *The Israel Sack Collection.* New York: American Art Association, Anderson Galleries, Inc., Nov. 11–12, 1927.

Sack Coll., 1957–72 — *American Antiques from Israel Sack Collection.* 3 vols. Washington, D.C.: Highland House Publishers, Inc., 1957–1972.

Schiffer — Schiffer, Herbert and Peter B. *Miniature Antique Furniture.* Wynnewood, Pennsylvania: Livingston Publishing Company, 1972.

Schmitz — Schmitz, Hermann. *The Encyclopaedia of Furniture.* New York: McBride and Company, 1926.

Seymour Coll. — *George Dudley Seymour's Furniture Collection in the Connecticut Historical Society.* Hartford, Connecticut: The Connecticut Historical Society, 1958.

Singleton — Singleton, Esther. *The Furniture of Our Forefathers.* 2 vols. New York: Doubleday, Page & Co., 2nd ed., 1906.

Ward-Jackson — Ward-Jackson, Peter. *English Furniture Designs of the Eighteenth Century.* London: H. M. Stationery Office, 1958.

Wenham — Wenham, Edward. *The Collector's Guide to Furniture Design (English and American).* New York: Collector's Press, Inc., 1928.

Notes on the Catalogue

Woods

The native American woods cited in the catalogue have been identified by microscopic analysis. The primary wood is usually listed first. Latin names for some of the common names given in the catalogue are:

Ash	black, *Fraxinus nigra* American white ash, *Fraxinus americana*
Beech	*Fagus Sylvatica*
Birch	*Betula*
Cedar	Atlantic white, *Chamaecyparis thyoides*
Cherry	*Prunus serotina*
Hickory	*Carya*
Maple	soft, either Red maple (*Acer rubrum*) or Silver maple (*acer saccharinum*) hard, sugar maple, *Acer Saccharum*
Oak	red, *Quercus rubra* white, *Quercus alba*
Pine	white, *Pinus strobus* yellow, *Pinus taeda*
Poplar	*Populus*
Red gum	*Liquidambar*
Sycamore	*Platanus occidentalis*
Tulip-Poplar	*Liriodendron tulipifera*
Walnut	American black, *Juglans nigra*

Dimensions

When John T. Kirk was Assistant Curator of the Garvan and Related Collections of American Art, he devised a measuring system that has been followed (where applicable) in this catalogue. The height (H.) is given first and is always measured at the center of the back. If some other point on the object exceeds that dimension, the measure is listed as BPH. (back post height), measured to the left. The seat height (SH.) is measured to the top edge of the framing member at the center of the seat. If the seat rail is covered with upholstery, the framing member is located with a pin or needle. If there is no framing member, the measurement is taken to the top of the upholstery. The measurements for width and depth are taken only on the seat rails unless the measurement is specified as overall (OW., OD.). Width (W.) is measured to the outside of the side seat rails immediately in front of the rear stiles. The maximum width (MW.) is the widest dimension measured to the outside of the side seat rails at right angles to the depth. Depth (D.) is measured from the back of the rear seat rail to the front of the front seat rail, at the center, beneath the rails. Where the carving interferes, the measurement is taken immediately to the left of the carving. "Left" and "right" refer to the vantage point of someone seated in the chair.

Bibliography

References under Bibliography include only those publications in which the individual object has appeared.

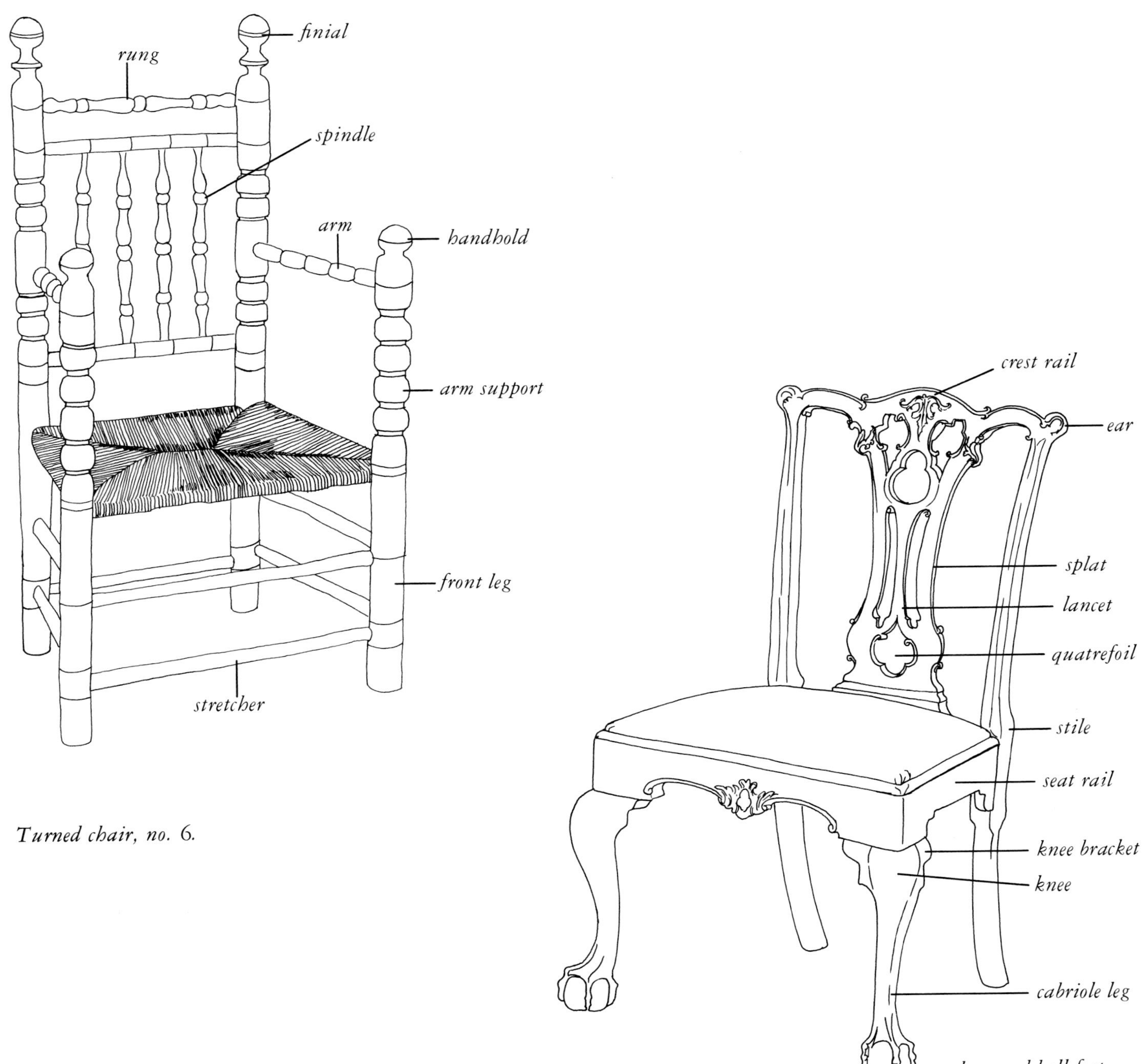

Turned chair, no. 6.

Chippendale style chair, no. 94.

Drawings by Steven Schnipper

THE CATALOGUE

Seventeenth-Century Chairs

THE EIGHT SEVENTEENTH-century chairs in this collection represent fairly well the range of seating furniture that has been preserved from the seventeenth-century American household. The forms are the wainscot chair (no. 1); the leather, or "Cromwellian," chair (no. 2); the "Carver," or turned type, chair (nos. 3–6); the chair-table (no. 7); and the slat-back chair (no. 8). With the exception of nos. 5 and 6, which may have been made in New York or New Jersey, these chairs, like most other surviving seventeenth-century furniture, were made in New England.

One of the earliest scholars of American furniture, Irving W. Lyon, suggested that the first New England households had few chairs, rarely more than two per household.[1] This thesis has often been repeated, but it is difficult to verify conclusively from the evidence of inventories, since chairs are usually listed as a group rather than enumerated singly. It is clear that at long tables chairs were supplemented by forms, or benches, as well as by joint stools.

[1] Lyon, p. 137.

1

1. Wainscot Chair

Connecticut, 1640–1660

Wainscot chairs were not found in every seventeenth-century household. Inventories refer to them less frequently than to other types of chairs, and they are more likely to be found in estates of the well-to-do. Probably fewer than two dozen examples survive today.

This wainscot chair is the official chair of Yale College presidents. Its association with Yale began with the Reverend Abraham Pierson, who in 1701 became Rector of the Collegiate School (later Yale University), then at Saybrook, Connecticut. According to family history, the Reverend Pierson acquired "one great wainscot chair," purportedly this one, from Widow Ward in 1672, when he was still living in Newark, New Jersey (1668–92), and brought it back to Connecticut with him in 1692.[1] The original owner, Deacon Lawrence Ward, was a turner, and he may have had some part in making the chair before he moved from Branford, Connecticut, to New Jersey. Wainscot chairs, which have framed construction, are generally believed to have been made by joiners rather than turners, but Ward may well have done the turned work for this particular chair. The superbly turned columnar legs reveal the influence of Renaissance designs on seventeenth-century American furniture. Similar turnings appear on a stool found in Guilford, Connecticut, now in the collection of the Wadsworth Atheneum.[2]

Description: The framed back contains two vertical fielded panels. The ends of the stiles project slightly above the top rail, and undercut arms slope from the stiles to the columnar arm supports. The board seat is supported on three sides by seat rails whose lower edges are beveled and cut into a double serpentine shape. The columnar-turned front legs are square in section where the seat rails and rectangular stretchers are mortised and tenoned into them. The rear legs are a continuation of the rectangular stiles.

Notes: The bottoms of the front feet and rear stiles are worn. Most of the chair has been repinned. The arms are tenoned through the stiles. The stiles were either bent backward above the seat or were made from wood with a natural curve. The seat is attached to the seat rails with roseheaded nails. Two small round holes at the top of the front face of each stile may indicate that the chair had a crest or finials at one time.

Wood: White oak.

Dimensions: H. 41¼ in. (104.8 cm), BPH. 43 in. (109.2 cm), SH. 17¾ in. (45.1 cm). Seat rails: W. 20$^{15}/_{16}$ in. (53.2 cm), MW. 23 in. (58.4 cm), D. 13⅞ in. (35.2 cm).

Exhibitions: Three Centuries of Connecticut Furniture, 1635–1935, Morgan Memorial, Hartford, Conn., June 15–Oct. 15, 1935, p. 14, no. 8; *Conn. Furn.,* p. 109, no. 188; *Furn. of the New Haven Colony,* pp. 58–59, pl. XXV.

Bibliography: "City of Elms," *Harper's New Monthly Magazine,* 17 (June 1858), p. 18 (illus. p. 2); Franklin Bowditch Dexter, *Biographical Sketches of the Graduates of Yale College* (New York, 1885), p. 64; Edwin Oviatt, *Beginnings of Yale, 1701–1726* (New Haven, 1916), pp. 210–19; Nutting, *Pilgrim Century,* no. 297; Nutting, *Treasury,* nos. 1788, 1789; Homer E. Keyes, "A Note on American Wainscot Chairs," *Antiques,* 17 (June 1930), p. 521, fig. 6; "Editor's Attic," *Antiques,* 55 (March 1934), p. 89; *American Collector,* 6 (Nov. 1937), (illus. p. 4); Bishop, p. 20, fig. 5; *Antiques,* 103 (May 1973), p. 960, pl. IV.

Provenance: Deacon Lawrence Ward (d. 1671), New Haven and Branford, Conn., and Newark, N.J.; Rector Abraham Pierson (1641–1707), Newark, N.J., and Greenwich and Killingworth, Conn.; Gift of the Reverend John E. Bray, Seymour, Conn., to Yale University, 1841.1.

[1] Edwin Oviatt, *Beginnings of Yale, 1701–1726* (New Haven, 1916), pp. 210–19.—[2] *Furn. of the New Haven Colony,* pp. 60–61, pl. XXVI.

2

2. Leather, or Cromwellian, Chair

New England, 1650–1690

The leather chair was introduced about 1650 according to most of the literature. However, an inventory of 1643 shows that John Atwood of Plymouth owned "Three leather chaires and 3 smaller leather chaires, £1.10."[1] Contemporary sources refer to these chairs as "leather chairs," but today they are popularly called "Cromwellian," based upon their association with the era of Oliver Cromwell, Lord Protector of the Commonwealth (1653–58). "Turkie work," "serge," and "leather" chairs are recorded, often in sets of six, in the estates of well-to-do New Englanders of the seventeenth and early eighteenth centuries. This example was undoubtedly made originally as a "leather chair," for pieces of leather were found under its old iron tacks when it was reupholstered. Oak and maple were generally used for such chairs; the oak provided a strong frame, and the maple could be beautifully turned. The similarity of the design and execution of many of them suggests that they were the product of a specialized shop system, like the later banister-back (nos. 35–38) and "Boston" chairs (no. 40). The Yale example is distinguished by the addition of a medial stretcher.

Description: The back panel, seat, and front faces of the stiles above the seat are upholstered in leather; an additional band of leather is applied to the outer edges of the seat rails. Double rows of brass tacks trim the upholstery. The front legs and lower side stretchers have pairs of double-ball turnings, while the front stretcher and medial stretcher have a central ring flanked by four ball turnings. The upper side stretchers and the rear stretcher are rectangular.

Notes: This chair appears to be very low to the ground because the front feet, which were probably ball turned, and the bases of the rear stiles are missing. The seat and the back have been reupholstered with old leather. On the inside faces of the stiles just above the seat are nail holes from a later rail which was removed before the recent upholstery was added. Traces of black and Spanish brown (with a purple cast) paint remain. The stretchers are pinned to the legs with squared oak pegs, as is the lower rail in the back panel.

Woods: Hard maple; upper and lower rails of back and seat rails, red oak.

Dimensions: H. 34⅞ in. (88.6 cm), SH. 17⅜ in. (44.1 cm). Seat rails: W. 18 in. (45.7 cm), MW. 18 in. (45.7 cm), D. 15³⁄₁₆ in. (38.6 cm).

Provenance: Found in Chester, N.H., by Roger Bacon, Exeter, N.H.; The Mabel Brady Garvan Collection, 1965.3.

---

[1] Lyon, p. 147.

3. Armchair

New England, 1690–1710

This armchair is of the type known as the "Carver" chair—a turned chair, usually with three spindles in the back. The name Carver became associated with this form during the nineteenth century because of the example in Pilgrim Hall, Plymouth, Massachusetts, named after the first governor of the colony, John Carver. "Brewster" chairs, named for William Brewster, another founder of Plymouth Colony, are similar but have spindles below the seat as well. This example exhibits the main attributes of the style in the spindles between the lower back rungs and the ogee-shaped turnings on the stiles. However, the thinness of its turned members suggests a date toward the end of the seventeenth century.

Description: The stiles are decorated with ogee-shaped turnings with flared tops; the back spindles have similar turnings combined with barrel-shaped forms. Knob finials at the tops of the stiles, modified mushroom handholds, and sausage-turned arms complete the vocabulary of turned ornament. The double side and front stretchers and

3

a single rear stretcher are plain rounds. The seat is flag or rush.

Notes: Traces of brown paint remain. The top front stretcher is a replacement. One hundred or more worm holes appear in the lower part of the back legs and some fifty in the front legs. The feet are worn. Faint grooves mark the placement of the rungs in the back, the arms, the seat rails, and the stretchers.

Woods: Hard maple; arms, rungs, spindles, and stretchers, hickory.

Dimensions: H. 37⅜ in. (94.3 cm), BPH. 41⅝ in. (105.7 cm), SH. 14⅜ in. (36.5 cm). Seat rails: W. 16⅛ in. (41.0 cm), MW. 22½ in. (57.2 cm), D. 16½ in. (41.9 cm).

Bibliography: "Living with Antiques," *Antiques,* 45 (April 1944), p. 191 (illus.); Kirk, *Early Am. Furn.,* fig. 163.

Provenance: Gift of C. Sanford Bull, Middlebury, Conn., 1952.50.1.

4. Side Chair

Coastal Connecticut between Branford and Saybrook, 1680–1710

A number of chairs from the New Haven Colony area—about eight—have attenuated ogee or vase turnings on the uprights and drumstick-shaped back spindles with ball ends like this example, which is believed to have been owned by the Gardiner family of Saybrook.[1] The scale of this chair without arms is surprisingly small compared with seventeenth-century armchairs.

Description: The vase-shaped turnings on the stiles are echoed in the three back spindles with ball ends. The finials are ball-and-reel forms. The seat is rush. The back rungs, front legs and stretchers are plain.

Notes: The chair has been refinished, but traces of black over green paint remain. The green paint does not cover the modern finishing nails that secure the joints; these nails were probably added to tighten the chair when it was refinished in the late nineteenth or early twentieth century. The absence of grooves to mark the placement of the lower back rung is exceptional.

Wood: American ash.

Dimensions: H. 30½ in. (77.5 cm), BPH. 34$^{11}/_{16}$ in. (88.1 cm), SH. 14⅜ in. (36.5 cm). Seat rails: W. 13½ in. (34.3 cm), MW. 17¼ in. (43.8 cm), D. 14 in. (35.6 cm).

Exhibitions: Conn. Furn., p. 114, no. 200; *Furn. of the New Haven Colony,* pp. 76–77, pl. XXXIV.

Provenance: Gardiner family, Saybrook, Conn.; William B. Goodwin, Hartford, Conn.; Fred W. Fuessenich, Litchfield, Conn.; The Mabel Brady Garvan Collection, 1963.6.

---

[1] *Furn. of the New Haven Colony,* pp. 70–77.

5. Side Chair

European (?), 1670–1710

The design of this side chair originated in the Lowlands, and not surprisingly the majority of such chairs found in America are from New Jersey and the Hudson River Valley, where the Dutch settled. Wood analysis on this example has raised some unresolved questions about its place of origin: some of the woods have been identified as European, but the lower right stretcher is of hickory, a wood believed to be native to America. A similar chair with ring-and-bulb feet is illustrated in Nutting.[1]

Description: The quadruple-ball turnings on the stiles are repeated in elongated form on the three back spindles. There are single-ball turnings on the lower stiles and pairs of double-ball turnings on the front legs. The form of the finials is a small ball resting atop a spire supported by a flattened ball. The two back rungs supporting the spindles have barrel-shaped turnings separated by small rings. The seat is splint or basswood. Rear and front stretchers are sausage turned; side stretchers are round; and there are remains of what may have been bulb feet.

Notes: Traces of reddish-brown paint remain. The top of the left finial is missing. Grooves mark the placement of the rungs, seat rails, and stretchers.

Woods: Right front leg, European or American cherry; left stile, European walnut; rear seat rail, European or American ash; lower right stretcher, hickory.

Dimensions: H. 30$^{11}/_{16}$ in. (77.9 cm), BPH. 34⅛ in. (86.7 cm), SH. 16⅜ in. (41.6 cm). Seat rails: W. 13 in. (33.0 cm), MW. 16½ in. (41.9 cm), D. 13⅜ in. (34.0 cm).

Bibliography: Nutting, *Treasury,* no. 2086; John T. Kirk, "Sources of Some American Regional Furniture, Part I," *Antiques,* 88 (Dec. 1965), p. 798, fig. 18.

Provenance: Charles W. Lyon, New York, N.Y.; Francis P. Garvan, New York, N.Y.; The Mabel Brady Garvan Collection, 1930.2291.

---

[1] *Treasury,* no. 2085.

4

5

6

6. Armchair

American, 1670–1700

This unusual chair, like no. 5, relates closely to the Lowlands tradition of elaborate turnery. Although it may have been made in a shop in New England, where Dutch and Flemish designs were transmitted via England, the possibility of its having originated in the Dutch settlements of the Hudson River Valley should not be ruled out. The robust quality of the design suggests a firm late seventeenth-century date.

Description: This armchair has pairs of vigorous double-ball turnings on the rear stiles and quadruple-ball-turned arm supports. The large finials are acorn shaped with reels below. The double-vase-and-ball form of the top rung is repeated in the four back spindles. Sausage-turned arms link the rear and front stiles, which are capped with ball-shaped handholds. The seat is rush. Below are seven round, turned stretchers, and slightly tapered feet.

Notes: The chair was cleaned and waxed in 1961, but traces of old red paint remain. The two front stretchers are probably replacements. Grooves mark the placement of the rungs, spindles, arms, seat rails, and stretchers, and are used as decorations.

Woods: Soft maple; front stretchers and seat rails, possibly American black ash.

Dimensions: H. 37½ in. (95.3 cm), BPH. 43 in. (109.2 cm), SH. 15 in. (38.1 cm). Seat rails: W. 16¾ in. (42.5 cm), MW. 20⅞ in. (53.0 cm), D. 15⅞ in. (40.3 cm).

Provenance: Irving W. Lyon, Hartford, Conn.; Charles W. Lyon, New York, N.Y.; Francis P. Garvan, New York, N.Y. (1929); The Mabel Brady Garvan Collection, 1930.2289.

7. Chair-Table

Massachusetts, 1680–1710

Few chair-tables can be positively identified in seventeenth-century inventories. Confusion arises from their cryptic wording: "one Chair Table 10s," for instance, could refer to the form illustrated here, or to one chair and a table. With its top lifted to form a chair, this example has a majestic, throne-like quality. Irving W. Lyon found it in Hingham, Massachusetts, and it may have been made in that area. The considerable restoration to the legs has probably altered the proportions, but the bottle-shaped balusters are unusual and the form is rare.

Description: The large, round table top with slightly rounded edge pivots on two cleats with serpentine ends attached to the rear of the arms. The arms are hollowed on the top edge and are supported on large bottle-shaped turnings at the tops of the legs. Beneath the seat is a drawer. The turning between the seat and the rectangular stretchers is a flattened ball. This form is repeated on the feet, but these are replacements.

Notes: The three boards of the top have shrinkage cracks. The drawer knob is replaced. The pegs on which the top pivots are probably not original. A crack in the center of the seat has been filled. The legs have been replaced from below the ball turning between the seat and stretchers. The stretchers appear to be old.

Woods: White pine top, seat, and drawer sides; legs, soft maple; stretchers and seat rails, white oak.

Dimensions: H. 29 in. (73.7 cm), SH. 16¾ in. (42.5 cm), SW. 22 11/16 in. (57.6 cm), SD. 21½ in. (54.6 cm), Diam. 50⅞ in. (129.2 cm).

Bibliography: Lyon, p. 197, figs. 94, 95.

Provenance: Found in Hingham, Mass., by Irving W. Lyon, Hartford, Conn.; Francis P. Garvan, New York, N.Y.; The Mabel Brady Garvan Collection, 1930.2467.

7

8. Armchair

New England, 1680–1700

Slat-back chairs have been popular in America from the seventeenth century to the present. This example may have been made close to the beginning of the tradition, judging from its robust forms: thick (2-inch) stiles with ogee turnings, rounded handholds, and slats of ample depth and thickness. Some of the earliest American slat-back chairs have slats with arched cut-outs at the ends and straight upper edges, and finials with flattened ball-, disc-, and knob-shaped turnings.[1] Here the gently arched slats have serpentine curves at the ends and the finials are ball-and-reel shaped—features persisting in the eighteenth century and suggesting that this example was made toward the end of the seventeenth.

Description: The three slats have curved upper edges ending in gentle serpentine curves. The stiles have ogee turnings and flattened ball-and-reel finials. The arm supports are ogee turned, and the flattened arms have cut-out ends; the handholds are ball shaped. The seat is rush. The ends of the front stretchers are modified vase shapes, but the rear and the side stretchers are plain round forms.

Notes: Traces of red paint. The top slat and lower front stretcher are held in place with wooden pegs. Grooves mark the placement of the slats, seat rails, arms and stretchers.

Woods: Poplar (*Populus*); stretchers and slats, ash.

Dimensions: H. 39⅛ in. (99.4 cm), BPH. 43 1/16 in. (109.4 cm), SH. 16 in. (40.6 cm). Seat rails: W. 15¾ in.

8

(40.0 cm), MW. 21 5/16 in. (54.9 cm), D. 16 3/16 in. (41.1 cm).

Provenance: The Museum of the Rhode Island School of Design, Providence, R.I.; Roger Bacon, Exeter, N.H. (1960); Israel Sack, Inc., New York, N.Y.; The Mabel Brady Garvan Collection, 1963.13.

[1] Comstock, no. 33.

9a

9b

9

Slat-Back Chairs

The New England Type

SLAT-BACK CHAIRS were made in America from the middle of the seventeenth century. They remained in fashion until the close of the century and have been made continuously to the present time. Thus for the furniture scholar they are difficult to regionalize and date. The form has innumerable variations, but eight chairs in this collection share a number of distinctive features and may be characterized as a New England type. The deep top slat of these chairs has a gently curved upper edge in contrast with the lower slats, whose ends taper where they join the stiles. The ball-and-reel finials repeat on a smaller scale the finials found on seventeenth-century chairs (no. 8). The turnings on the stiles and front legs are usually ball forms, sometimes flattened, surrounded by soft hollows. The turnings of the stretchers vary, but rounded forms such as those on the stretchers of a high chair (no. 10) and an armchair (no. 11) in this collection are found frequently.

9. Side Chair

New England, 1700–1725

The dark, mellow surface, softly undulating outlines, and tall, delicate back reflecting the William and Mary style set this slat-back chair apart as a fine, early example of the form. A date around 1700 has traditionally been assigned in the literature to these chairs with curved slats, softly outlined ball turnings, ball-and-double-reel finials, and sausage-turned stretchers. They were made in many localities and are difficult to regionalize.[1] In addition to the chairs in the following entries, closely related examples are at the Museum of Fine Arts, Boston, the Connecticut Historical Society, and in the Bybee Collection.[2]

Description: The five slightly concave slats are curved on the upper edges. The stiles and front legs have softly outlined ball turnings and the finials are balls supported on a double reel. Below the flag seat are sausage-turned front and side stretchers, and one plain rear stretcher that shows signs of wear.

Inscription: Carved on back of second slat from top: SB.

Notes: Old red paint is found under brown paint decorated with yellow lines. The lower front stretcher and possibly the top and third slats are replacements; these two slats are of a different wood and do not fit loosely in their mortises as the other slats do. If the top slat is indeed a replacement, the restorer has accurately duplicated the gently curved upper edge found on the top slats of chairs of this type. The placement of the stretchers and seat rails (but not of the slats) is marked by grooves.

Woods: Soft maple; side and rear seat rails, side and rear stretchers, three slats, ash.

Dimensions: H. 43 9/16 in. (110.6 cm), BPH. 46 3/8 in. (117.8 cm), SH. 18 in. (45.7 cm). Seat rails: W. 13 3/16 in. (33.5 cm), MW. 18 3/8 in. (46.7 cm), D. 13 1/4 in. (33.7 cm).

Bibliography: *Offerman Coll.,* no. 128; Nutting, *Pilgrim Century,* p. 342 (illus. p. 333, fig. 408); Nutting, *Treasury,* no. 1875; Sack, *Fine Points,* p. 11.

Provenance: Theodore Offerman, New York, N.Y.; Francis P. Garvan, New York, N.Y.; The Mabel Brady Garvan Collection, 1930.2290.

[1] Randall, pp. 160–61, no. 123.—[2] See *George Dudley Seymour's Furniture Collection in the Connecticut Historical Society,* p. 75, and *Antiques,* 92 (Dec. 1967), p. 836.

10

10. High Chair

New England, 1700–1725

This child's high chair with straddled front legs is exceptional because of its unusual cone-shaped arm supports. The softly outlined ball turnings on the stiles and front legs, the ball-and-double-reel finials, and the arched contours of the top slat contrasting with the more serpentine shape of the lower slats are the key features that relate it to no. 9. Here, however, the sausage turnings are found only at the center of the front stretchers, and the less rounded form of the ball turnings diminishes the three-dimensional quality observed in the preceding chair.

Description: Ball-and-double-reel finials, ball turnings outlined by soft hollows, and cone-shaped arm supports complete the vocabulary of turned ornament. The slats are similar to those on no. 9. A board is fastened to the seat rails for a seat. The rectangular arms have thickened ends for handholds.

Notes: Traces of red paint are found under later layers of blue, green, and buff colored paint. The foot rest is missing. The board seat, added prior to the last two coats of paint, probably replaced a rush seat. The top slat is pinned from the back with square wooden pegs. The arms are pinned from the side into the stiles and arm supports.

Woods: Birch; slats, seat rails, stretchers, ash.

Dimensions: H. 37 9/16 in. (95.4 cm), BPH. 39 13/16 in. (101.1 cm), SH. 19 3/8 in. (49.2 cm). Seat rails: W. 11 3/16 in. (28.4 cm), MW. 13 9/16 in. (34.4 cm), D. 11 1/4 in. (28.6 cm).

Provenance: Frank McCarthy, Longmeadow, Mass.; Francis P. Garvan, New York, N.Y.; The Mabel Brady Garvan Collection, 1930.2297.

11. Armchair

New England, 1725–1750

This chair shares with the two preceding ones the typical elements of the New England slat-back chair, with slight variations in the execution of those details. The ball turnings here are not as full, and the line describing them is less fluid than in nos. 9 and 10; the reel turnings on the finials are not as thin, and the discs are less clearly articulated; the profiles of the sausage turnings on the front stretchers have lost their gentle curves. These changes suggest that this example warrants a slightly later date.

Description: A curved top slat and three angular slats link stiles with ball-and-double-reel finials. Resting on the vase-shaped arm supports are rectangular arms which end in a block-like form with scrolled handholds. Below the rush or flag seat, the legs and feet are ball turned. The two front stretchers have sausage turnings at the center, and the side and rear stretchers are plain.

Notes: Traces of paint suggest the chair was first red, then green, and then black. The top of the upper slat has been cracked, and the slat itself has been repinned from the back. Approximately one inch of each of the front feet is replaced. Grooves mark the placement of the top slat, stretchers, and seat rails. Arms are pinned from the sides into the stiles and arm supports.

Woods: Poplar (*Populus*); slats, arms, and stretchers, black ash.

Dimensions: H. 43⁹⁄₁₆ in. (110.6 cm), BPH. 46⅝ in. (118.4 cm), SH. 16½ in. (41.9 cm). Seat rails: W. 16⅜ in. (41.0 cm), MW. 21 in. (53.3 cm), D. 16⅛ in. (41.0 cm).

Provenance: Irving W. Lyon, Hartford, Conn.; Francis P. Garvan, New York, N.Y.; The Mabel Brady Garvan Collection, 1930.2477.

11

12

12. Roundabout Chair

New England, 1750–1775

"Round-backed" chairs can be found in New England inventories as early as 1705, when Israel Chauncey's estate was assessed in Stratford, Connecticut. They were made by urban craftsmen up to the time of the Revolution and continued to be produced by rural chairmakers into the nineteenth century.[1] From his research in eighteenth-century manuscripts Irving W. Lyon concluded that "they are recorded under quite a variety of names of which the following are the principal, namely: 'round chair,' 'three-cornered chair,' 'triangular chair,' 'roundabout chair,' 'half-round chair.' But of these and similar designations, the one most frequently met is 'roundabout chair.' "[2] On this example the turnings on the stiles are quite far removed from their original ball form but are still outlined with gentle curves. The bowed seat rails, an unusual feature, add to this chair's squat, rotund appearance.

Description: Below a semi-circular arm rail with applied, block-like crest are two curved slats. The tops of the stiles supporting the arm rail end in ogee turnings. Below the flag seat stiles have flattened ball turnings with gently curved outlines. The four stretchers have oval ends.

Notes: Red, tan, and brown are under the present black paint. Cut nails were used to secure the stretchers to the legs prior to the coat of black paint. The crest rail is attached to the arm rail with three dowels which come through the top. Under the crest the ends of the arm rails are lapped and secured by the turned end of the rear stile. Approximately twenty-five worm holes appear in the stretchers.

Woods: Hard maple; slats and stretchers, ash.

Dimensions: H. 28 1/2 in. (72.4 cm), SH. 16 3/16 in. (41.1 cm). Seat rails: W. 23 3/16 in. (58.9 cm), D. 23 5/8 in. (60.0 cm).

Provenance: Henry H. Taylor, Bridgeport, Conn.; Francis P. Garvan, New York, N.Y.; The Mabel Brady Garvan Collection, 1930.2453.

---

[1] Hummel, p. 253.—[2] Lyon, p. 168.

13

13. Roundabout Chair

Connecticut or Western Massachusetts, about 1760

According to family tradition, this chair was used by the Reverend John Strickland, Jr., of Hadley, Massachusetts, while he attended Yale College, from which he graduated in 1761. The elements vary only slightly from those on the preceding example, but the outlines of the ball turnings on the arm supports just above the seat and on the front leg are more angular. The ball itself is ridged.

Description: The chair is similar to no. 12. Here the decorative turning is confined to the front leg and arm supports. The seat is basswood, the stretchers are plain, and the crest is thinner than that of no. 12.

Notes: The black paint covers red paint. Nail holes on the underside of the center of the arm rail indicate the crest was once upholstered. The black paint does not cover the back of the crest or the underside of the arm rail below the crest. The right end of the crest is cracked and repaired with a hand-wrought nail. The front leg is secured to the seat rails with a square wooden peg driven in on the right side of the block. The joints of the stiles and stretchers are secured with modern nails. Grooves mark the placement of the slats, seat rails, and stretchers.

Woods: Soft maple; arm rail, birch; slats, seat rails, stretchers, ash.

Dimensions: H. 29 13/16 in. (75.7 cm), SH. 17 1/16 in. (43.3 cm). Seat rails: W. 24 1/8 in. (61.3 cm), D. 24 1/4 in. (61.6 cm).

Provenance: The Reverend John Strickland, Jr., Hadley, Mass.; Gift of Albert D. Morgan, Socorro, N. Mex., 1966.119.

14. Child's Rocking Chair

New England, 1750–1775

When rocking chairs became popular late in the eighteenth century many older chairs were fitted with rockers, but apparently this child's chair is not such a conversion—the chair and rockers have identical layers of paint and seem to have been made as a unit. The ball form outlined by soft hollows on the first chair in this series (no. 9) is now compressed to a ring form on the stiles and front legs of this chair. The soft

14

15. Armchair

New England, 1775–1800

The date assigned to this chair, evidently the latest representative of the common New England slat-back chair in the collection, is conjectural, since no evidence other than stylistic is available. It is based upon the assumption that changes were wrought in the vocabulary of ornament between nos. 9 and 15 by successive generations of craftsmen reworking the initial idea. Here the transformation of the turnings from a ball outlined by soft hollows to a ring or disc similarly framed has been carried furthest. On the finials the ball has also become flatter and more disc-like, although the double-reel form at the base of the finial remains.

Description: The four curved slats are supported between stiles with ring turnings outlined by soft hollows, and flattened ball-and-double-reel finials. The serpentine arms with scrolled handholds are supported on elongated,

hollows remain, however, as do the arched slats and ball-and-double-reel finials found on the earlier example.

Description: Two curved slats fill the back. The stiles are ornamented with a single ring turning outlined by soft curves and with ball-and-double-reel finials. Similar turnings appear on the front legs, which end in mushroom handholds. The arms, connecting the tops of the front legs and stiles, are disc-and-sausage turned. The seat is rush; below are four plain turned stretchers and rockers with serpentine curved front ends.

Notes: Traces of green and brown paint appear under the black paint. Tacks are driven into the top of each finial. The top slat is pinned from the back with square wooden pegs. The rockers are pinned to the stiles with wooden pegs. Three tack holes and circular outlines appear on the top of each arm, one tack hole at the rear end of each stretcher, and one on the front legs where the seat rails join.

Woods: Soft maple; rockers, white oak.

Dimensions: H. 22 9/16 in. (57.3 cm), BPH. 25 1/16 in. (63.7 cm), SH. 9 1/4 in. (23.5 cm). Seat rails: W. 10 9/16 in. (26.8 cm), MW. 13 7/16 in. (34.1 cm), D. 10 3/16 in. (25.9 cm).

Provenance: Henry H. Taylor, Bridgeport, Conn.; Francis P. Garvan, New York, N.Y.; The Mabel Brady Garvan Collection, 1930.2302.

15

vase-shaped arm supports. Below the rush seat, the turnings of the stiles are repeated on the front legs. Double-vase-and-ring-turned front stretchers contrast with the plain turned stretchers of the sides and rear.

Notes: The chair was refinished in 1964, but traces of black paint remain. The top slat is repinned from the back, but may have been pinned that way originally. The bottom edges of the lower two slats have been broken off; originally they would have been as deep as the second slat from the top, as the grooves below them on the stiles indicate. The top side and top front stretchers are repinned to the stiles. Grooves mark the placement of the slats, arms, seat rails, and stretchers.

Woods: Soft maple; slats, front and side stretchers, ash.

Dimensions: H. 44¼ in. (112.4 cm), BPH. 46⅝ in. (118.4 cm), SH. 16¾ in. (42.5 cm). Seat rails: W. 15 5/16 in. (38.9 cm), MW. 21¾ in. (55.2 cm), D. 15 1/16 in. (38.3 cm).

Bibliography: Miller, I, p. 117, fig. 27.

Provenance: Henry V. Weil, New York, N.Y.; Francis P. Garvan, New York, N.Y.; The Mabel Brady Garvan Collection, 1930.2609.

Coastal Connecticut and Long Island

INNUMERABLE VARIATIONS of the slat-back chair were probably made in coastal Connecticut and Long Island, but as yet few examples have been positively identified as types peculiar to the region. With the exception of Charles F. Hummel's classic study of the Dominy family of craftsmen from East Hampton, Long Island, *With Hammer in Hand* (1968), the other specialized studies of the furniture of this region, *Connecticut Furniture: Seventeenth and Eighteenth Centuries* (1967); *Furniture of the New Haven Colony: The Seventeenth-Century Style* (1973);[1] and *New London County Furniture* (1974),[2] have not rigorously probed the question of what kinds of slat-back chairs were manufactured there. Two variations of the type in this collection (nos. 16 and 17) have been associated with that area, and one of them is attributed to Nathaniel Dominy V of East Hampton.

[1] Both exhibition catalogues; see Short Title List.—[2] Minor Myers, Jr., and Edgar de N. Mayhew, *New London County Furniture* (New London, 1974).

16. Armchair

Connecticut, 1800–1825

Connecticut is suggested as the place of origin for this chair because of its similarity to another example that, according to Nutting, is of Connecticut origin,[1] and because only one of the two front stretchers is embellished—a practice of Connecticut chairmakers.[2] The corners of the old rush seat are painted a reddish-brown color, leaving a cross-shaped pattern at the center. An unusual feature of the chair is the use of oak for the stretchers and arm supports.

Description: The four curved slats are held between stiles with very thin ring turnings and flattened ball-and-single-reel finials. The short arms with scrolled handholds rest on elongated vase-shaped arm supports which pierce the side seat rails and are attached to swellings in the upper side stretchers. Below the rush seat the front legs have thin ring turnings similar to those on the rear leg stiles. The upper front stretcher is double-vase-and-reel turned, and the four lower stretchers are plain, slightly enlarged at the center.

Notes: Old black paint is found under old red paint. The rush seat has traces of both colors, suggesting the seat has been in place for a considerable time. Two thin boards are sandwiched in the rush between the front seat rail and the center of the seat. Holes in the base of the stiles and front legs indicate that the chair was fitted with casters at one time. Square wooden pegs driven in from the back secure the top slat. The arms are pegged from the sides into the tops of the arm supports and stiles. Grooves mark the placement of the slats, seat rails, and stretchers.

Woods: Soft maple; arm supports, seat rails, and stretchers, white oak; boards in seat, white pine.

Dimensions: H. 37 in. (94.0 cm), BPH. 39 11/16 in. (100.8 cm), SH. 14½ in. (36.8 cm). Seat rails: W. 15 13/16 in. (40.2

16

17

cm), MW. 21 13/16 in. (55.4 cm), D. 15¼ in. (38.7 cm).

Exhibitions: Conn. Furn., p. 112, no. 196.

Provenance: John Tynan, Middletown, Conn.; Henry H. Taylor, Bridgeport, Conn.; Francis P. Garvan, New York, N.Y.; The Mabel Brady Garvan Collection, 1930.2423.

[1] *Treasury,* no. 1885.—[2] *Conn. Furn.,* fig. 196.

17. Rocking Chair

Long Island, 1800–1825
Possibly by Nathaniel Dominy V (1770–1852)

Of a similar documented armchair made in 1809 in East Hampton, Long Island, by Nathaniel Dominy V, Charles Hummel wrote: "At first glance this type of chair would appear to be early eighteenth century, but the urn-shaped finials atop the rear posts, oval block and spindle side stretchers, curved arched slats, and arm rests with a small tenon joining them to the post are all signs of late eighteenth- and early nineteenth-century chair design."[1] The similarity of the slats on this chair to another rocking chair attributed to Dominy adds strength to the supposition that this chair may also have been made by him.[2]

Description: The four slats are arched on the bottom and top edges and are held between stiles with thin ring turnings flanked by bevels. The finials on the stiles are a flattened urn shape on a single reel. The short, sloping arms with scrolled handholds are supported on vase-shaped arm supports that pierce the side stretchers and fit into a block on the side seat rails. The rockers fasten to mortises in the bottom of the stiles and front legs. The front stretcher is a double-vase-and-ring form and the rear stretcher is plain.

Notes: Traces of red paint remain even though the chair has been refinished. The bottom slat is cracked on the right side. The top two slats are held in place with wooden pegs driven from the back. The arms are pegged into the tops of the arm supports only. Grooves mark the placement of the slats, seat rails, and stretchers.

Wood: Soft maple.

Dimensions: H. 39 in. (99.1 cm), BPH. 41⅜ in. (105.1 cm), SH. 14⅝ in. (37.2 cm). Seat rails: W. 17⅛ in. (43.5 cm), MW. 23¼ in. (59.1 cm), D. 16½ in. (41.9 cm).

Bibliography: "Annapolis Windows," *Antiques,* 17 (May 1930), p. 428 (illus.).

Provenance: Francis P. Garvan, New York, N.Y.; The Mabel Brady Garvan Collection, 1930.2621.

[1] Hummel, pp. 248–49.—[2] *Ibid.,* fig. 183.

Philadelphia and New Jersey

SLAT-BACK CHAIRS made in Philadelphia and the Delaware River Valley exhibit certain regional characteristics that set them apart from their New England counterparts, such as slats arched on both the top and bottom edges, pointed bulb finials, plain tapered stiles, ball-and-double-vase-turned front stretchers, and ball-and-reel feet. The date for the introduction of the style into Philadelphia is difficult to determine. A portrait of Johannes Kelpius, painted about 1705, shows him sitting in a chair with arched slats.[1] At mid-century many chairmakers in Philadelphia were making chairs answering this general description, such as the "6 five Slat Chairs with turned frunts" bought by William Parker in 1747.[2]

[1] Craig A. Gilborn, *American Furniture, 1660–1725* (London, 1970), p. 20.—[2] Hornor, p. 293.

18. Armchair

Delaware River Valley, 1720–1760

With its high slats, thick stiles, and the full, round profiles of the turnings, this chair is probably a fairly early example in the tradition of Delaware River Valley slat-back chairs. Although it is impossible to say with certainty whether the chair was made in Philadelphia or its hinterlands, the reversed "F" cut into the right rear stile may be the mark of the maker. The old, woven braid seat is a most unusual feature.

Description: The four slats are arched on the upper and lower edges. The plain, tapered stiles end in acorn-shaped finials. The turned arms rest on vase-and-cone-shaped arm supports. The seat is woven from braided flag, below which are ball-and-vase-turned front stretchers, and plain side and rear stretchers. The front feet are ball-and-reel forms and the rear feet are tapered.

Inscription: Carved in right rear stile below seat rail: "ꟻ".

Notes: Traces of red paint remain. The top slat is held in place with square wooden pegs driven from the back. Metal sockets in the bottoms of the feet indicate the chair once had casters. Grooves mark the placement of slats, seat rails, and stretchers. There are more than one hundred worm holes, mostly concentrated in the lower portion of the chair.

Wood: Soft maple.

Dimensions: H. 39 9/16 in. (100.5 cm), BPH. 41 1/4 in. (104.8 cm), SH. 16 3/8 in. (41.6 cm). Seat rails: W. 14 9/16 in. (37.0 cm), MW. 18 in. (45.7 cm), D. 14 in. (35.6 cm).

Provenance: C. M. Van Houten, Hackensack, N.J.; Francis P. Garvan, New York, N.Y.; The Mabel Brady Garvan Collection, 1930.2042.

18

19. Side Chair

Delaware River Valley, 1780–1810

The tall, narrow proportions and the delicacy of the turned parts give this chair a sprightly appearance not evident in the preceding example. The turner who made it was surely a master craftsman, for considerable skill is exhibited in the way the design is sharpened by incised lines, the rear stiles are subtly tapered, and the front stretcher is turned with bold forms. Similar chairs are often attributed to Maskell Ware, who worked in Roadstown, Cumberland County, New Jersey, from about 1790 to 1846, but they were undoubtedly made by a number of chairmakers in the Delaware Valley. The curly maple and flag seat are typical features.

Description: The five graduated slats are arched on their upper and lower edges. The plain stiles end in pointed ball finials. Below the old flag seat are ball-turned front legs with flattened ball-and-reel feet. The front stretcher is double-ball-and-disc turned, and the side and rear stretchers are plain.

Inscription: Paper label attached to underside of seat reads: "Property of George B. Brown."

Notes: The varnish or shellac finish is slightly abraded and crazed. The right stile is repaired at the seat rails with a metal brace. The top slat is pinned from the back with square wooden pegs. The top of the bottom slat is re-

19

19a 19b

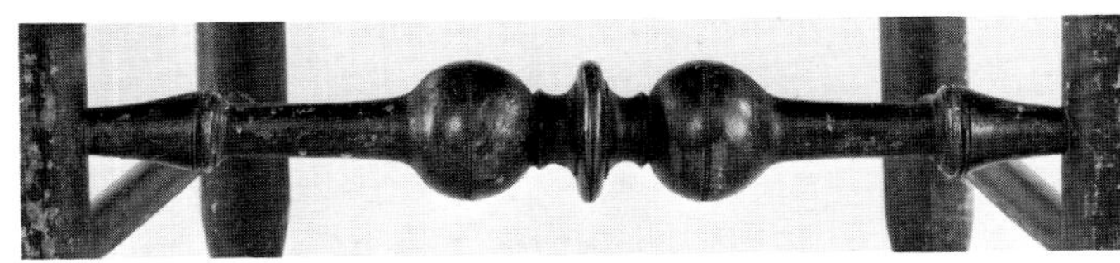

19c

placed. Grooves mark the placement of the slats, seat rails, and stretchers.

Wood: Soft maple.

Dimensions: H. 43 15/16 in. (111.6 cm), BPH. 45 in. (114.3 cm), SH. 16 7/8 in. (42.9 cm). Seat rails: W. 13 3/4 in. (34.9 cm), MW. 17 7/8 in. (45.4 cm), D. 13 11/16 in. (34.8 cm).

Provenance: John Walton, New York, N.Y.; The Mabel Brady Garvan Collection, 1963.7.

20. Armchair

Middle Atlantic States, 1830–1850

This chair represents the continuation of the Delaware River Valley chairmaking tradition into the nineteenth century. The design retains the slats arched on the top and bottom edges, the tapered stiles, and the flattened, undercut arms found on eighteenth-century Delaware Valley chairs. The turnings, however, are not characteristic of the eighteenth century; the ring turnings on the front stretcher, in particular, recall the motifs of nineteenth-century Hitchcock chairs.

20

Description: The four graduated, arched slats are held between tapered stiles with ovoid finials. The flattened, serpentine arms are undercut in the manner found on Pennsylvania chairs and rest atop the double-barrel–turned arm supports. Below the rush seat the stiles, legs, and stretchers are plain, except for the front stretcher, which has a barrel turning at the center flanked by three ring turnings on either side.

Notes: The seat frame and supporting rails are replacements. The chair has been refinished.

Wood: Maple.

Dimensions: H. 42 1/8 in. (107.0 cm), BPH. 43 in. (109.2 cm), SH. 17 1/2 in. (44.5 cm). Seat rails: W. 18 7/8 in. (48.0 cm), MW. 23 3/4 in. (60.4 cm), D. 18 1/4 in. (46.0 cm).

Provenance: Francis P. Garvan, New York, N.Y.; The Mabel Brady Garvan Collection, 1930.2616.

21. Side Chair

New Jersey, 1800–1820

Slat-back chairs from the northern part of New Jersey developed regional characteristics different from those of the Delaware River Valley. A large number of chairs found in Bergen County, New Jersey, share with this example a combination of distinctive features: compressed ring turnings on the stiles and front legs, urn-shaped finials, thin double-vase-and-ring stretchers, bulb front feet and tapered rear feet. Thirty-four such chairs have been found within a ten-mile radius of Ridgewood, New Jersey, and a related child's chair was once owned by the Demarest family of Bergen County.[1] The Yale chair differs from these Bergen County examples only in that the slats are not notched in the center. Of the details cited, it is the urn shape of the finials and the similarity of the stretchers to those on chairs made between 1800 and 1825, by the Dominy craftsmen of East Hampton, Long Island—which suggest a post–1800 date.[2] Three related side chairs inscribed "HZ" are

21

22

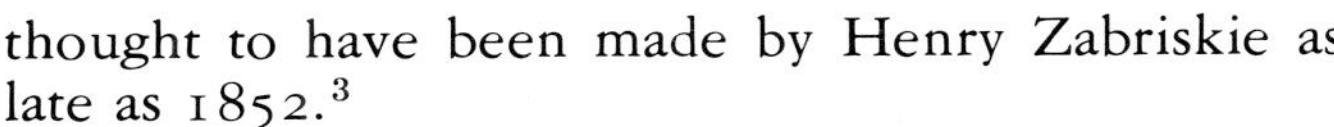

thought to have been made by Henry Zabriskie as late as 1852.[3]

Description: The three slightly curved slats are held between ring-turned stiles with urn-shaped finials. The ring turnings are repeated on the front legs, which end in bulb-like feet. Below the flag or rush seat are two double-vase–and–ring front stretchers and plain side and rear stretchers.

Notes: Traces of red paint are found under brown paint. The top slat is pinned with square wooden pegs from the back. Grooves mark the placement of the slats, seat rails, and stretchers.

Woods: Soft maple; stretchers and slats, hickory.

Dimensions: H. 33⅛ in. (84.1 cm), BPH. 36⅜ in. (92.4 cm), SH. 16³⁄₁₆ in. (41.1 cm). Seat rails: W. 14⅛ in. (35.9 cm), MW. 17¹⁄₁₆ in. (43.3 cm), D. 13⅝ in. (34.6 cm).

Provenance: Jacob Margolis, New York, N.Y. (probably sale, Anderson Galleries, April 11–12, 1924); Francis P. Garvan, New York, N.Y.; The Mabel Brady Garvan Collection, 1930.2179a.

---

[1] See Wilson Lynes, "Slat-back Chairs of New England and the Middle-Atlantic States," *Antiques,* 25 (March 1934), p. 104. The chair from the Demarest family is illustrated by Margaret E. White, "Some Early Furniture Makers of New Jersey," *Antiques,* 74 (Oct. 1958), p. 323.—[2] Hummel, p. 249.—[3] Lynes, p. 104.

22. Armchair

Hudson River Valley, 1725–1775

The attribution of this chair to the Hudson River Valley is based upon its similarity to one found near Tarrytown and now at the Philipsburg Manor, where it is considered a Hudson River Valley chair.[1] The use of the multiple ball turnings, such as those on the arm supports, is related to the Lowlands tradition of elaborate turnery, as represented by no. 5, and strengthens the case for an origin in the New York area.

Description: Ball turnings articulated by deeply incised lines appear on the rear stiles. The stiles end in ovoid and double-reel finials and support five slats with gently arched upper edges—the lower four of which are peaked. The edges of the curved arms with scrolled handholds are faceted. The arms are supported by an unusual quadruple-ball–and–pear-shaped turning at the top of the front legs. Below the seat are ball turnings, somewhat fatter than those on the rear stiles. The two front stretchers are sausage turned and the side and rear stretchers are plain.

Notes: A modern finish was removed in 1964, but traces

of black paint remain. The front posts were repaired at the junction with the seat in 1961. The partial bulb feet are worn. The top slat has been repinned from the back. There are more than two hundred worm holes in the lower portion of the rear stiles and front legs. The arms are pinned from the side to the stiles and arm supports. Grooves in the stiles mark the placement of the slats, stretchers, and seat rails. The stretchers are replacements. The seat rails are round.

Woods: Soft maple; seat rails and stretchers, hickory.

Dimensions: H. 44⅛ in. (112.1 cm), BPH. 47⅛ in. (119.7 cm), SH. 15¼ in. (38.7 cm). Seat rails: W. 18⁵⁄₁₆ in. (46.5 cm), MW. 23 in. (58.4 cm), D. 17¹¹⁄₁₆ in. (45.4 cm).

Bibliography: Miller, Vol. I, p. 117, fig. 28; Aronson, 1st ed., fig. 231.

Provenance: Henry V. Weil, New York, N.Y.; Francis P. Garvan, New York, N.Y.; The Mabel Brady Garvan Collection, 1930.2611.

[1] *Antiques,* 97 (June 1970), p. 867.

Other Variations

BECAUSE slat-back chairs were made over such a long period of time, and because they were a common form of seating, produced by chairmakers in every city and hamlet in America, most of the examples that have survived cannot be identified as distinct regional types. For the most part furniture scholars have yet to turn their attention to the study of these chairs. The examples which follow in this section will probably ultimately be proved to belong to larger groups of slat-back chairs, but for the present they must be regarded as individual expressions.

23. Side Chair

American, 1700–1750

The vigorous outlines and exaggerated bowed-out form of the slats of this example are so unusual that it has even been suggested that the chair was made in Europe, although microscopic analysis of the wood supports an American origin.[1] The use of the double-arched top slat is reminiscent of chairs made in the Delaware River Valley, but that feature alone is too slim a basis for assigning a place of origin.

Description: The four slats are deeply bowed. The top edge of the upper slat is double-serpentine shaped and the lower slats have single serpentine curves which return to

23

small angular peaks before the slats join the stiles. The turnings are elaborate and unusual: on the stiles and front legs are double reels with a disc between them; the finials have a flattened ball with an elongated vase form topped by the same reel-and-disc turning found on the stiles. The chair has a rush seat and plain stretchers.

Notes: Black paint was applied over red paint. The left top of the upper slat and the top of the second slat from the bottom have been restored. The flag or rush seat is a replacement. Each of the four slats is held in place with wooden pegs driven from the front through to the back. Grooves mark the placement of the seat rails, stretchers, and slats. The top grooves on the stiles indicate the placement of the tenons mortised into the stiles, rather than the placement of the upper edge of the slat (the usual practice).

Wood: American white ash.

Dimensions: H. 43½ in. (110.5 cm), BPH. 47⅜ in. (120.4 cm), SH. 16½ in. (41.9 cm). Seat rails: W. 13⅞ in. (35.3 cm), MW. 17⅞ in. (45.4 cm), D. 13⅝ in. (34.7 cm).

Bibliography: Kirk, *Early Am. Furn.*, fig. 186.

Provenance: Francis P. Garvan, New York, N.Y.; Mabel Brady Garvan (1937); The Mabel Brady Garvan Collection, 1950.714.

[1] Kirk, *Early Am. Furn.*, fig. 186.

24. Side Chair

American, 1725–1750

The contrasting curves of the turnings give this chair its unusual character, but neither its early history nor documented counterparts aid in the identification of its maker or place of origin. The contours of the sausage-turned stretchers, the tall, narrow back, and the urn-shaped finials with rounded caps all suggest a date of about 1725. The latter two features relate this chair to William and Mary style cane-back chairs. The visual squeeze of the ring turnings on both the front and rear stiles makes a striking contrast to gentle contours found on the New England slat-back chairs, where ball turnings are outlined with soft hollows (see nos. 9–15).

Description: The unusual ring turnings seem to compress the wood on the stiles and front legs. The finials have the conventional form of an urn supporting a flattened ball. Four gently arched slats are in the back, and below the rush seat are sausage-turned front and side stretchers and plain rear stretchers.

Notes: Traces of red paint remain. The top slat is pierced at the center with two holes. The lower front stretcher is a replacement; 1⅞ inches was added to the base of the rear legs and 3⅞ inches to the base of the front legs. The top slat is held in place with wooden pegs. Grooves mark the placement of the slats, seat rails, and stretchers.

Wood: American white ash.

Dimensions: H. 39⅝ in. (100.6 cm), BPH. 43⅝ in. (110.8 cm), SH. 16⅜ in. (41.6 cm). Seat rails: W. 13⅜ in. (34.0 cm), MW. 19$\frac{5}{16}$ in. (49.1 cm), D. 12¾ in. (32.4 cm).

Bibliography: Kirk, *Early Am. Furn.*, fig. 188.

Provenance: Gift of C. Sanford Bull, Middlebury, Conn., 1953.50.2.

25. Armchair

American, 1750–1800

Lemon-shaped or ovoid finials were an alternative to the ball-and-urn and ball-and-reel finials found on the preceding slat-back chairs. This motif in America goes back to the seventeenth century, in finials seen on chairs from the Norwich, Connecticut, area, for example.[1] A chair similar to no. 25 is owned by the Wadsworth Atheneum.[2]

Description: The turnings on the stiles and front legs are rings defined by sharply incised lines. The lemon-shaped finials are separated from the stiles by a double-reel form. The five graduated slats are gently arched, and the serpentine arms with scrolled handholds are supported on vase-and-reel–shaped arm supports. Below the rush seat the two front stretchers are sausage turned, the side and rear stretchers are plain, and the front feet have rings below modified cone forms.

Notes: Traces of black and green paint remain. There are about one to two hundred worm holes, found on all parts of the chair with the exception of the stretchers. The front stretchers are replacements.

Woods: Soft maple; slats, seat rails, and stretchers, hickory.

Dimensions: H. 43¼ in. (109.9 cm), BPH. 48$\frac{1}{16}$ in. (122.1 cm), SH. 18⅛ in. (46.0 cm). Seat rails: W. 18⅛ in. (46.0 cm), MW. 23$\frac{15}{16}$ in. (60.8 cm), D. 18 in. (45.7 cm).

Provenance: Gift of C. Sanford Bull, Middlebury, Conn., 1953.50.6.

[1] See Nutting, *Treasury*, no. 1887; Minor Myers, Jr., and Edgar de N. Mayhew, *New London County Furniture 1640–1840*, New London, Conn.: Lyman Allyn Museum, 1974, no. 3.—[2] Nutting, *Treasury*, no. 1852.

24

25

26

26. Side Chair

American, 1780–1820

Slat-back chairs are often very anonymous, like this example, whose turnings, plain except for the ovoid finials on reels, offer few clues to its origin. In its restrained use of ornament, it shares qualities with no. 33, a Shaker rocking chair.

Description: The lemon-shaped finials are separated from the stiles by a single-reel turning, unlike the double reel of no. 25. Otherwise the turning of the stiles, front legs, and stretchers is plain. The chair has three arched slats and a rush seat.

Notes: The chair has been refinished, but traces of old red and green paint remain. The top slat is held in place with square wooden pegs. One wooden peg secures the right side of the bottom stretcher. Worm channels appear on both the left side stretchers. Faint grooves mark the placement of the slats, seat rails, and stretchers.

Woods: Soft maple; seat rails and stretchers, white ash.

Dimensions: H. 35 1/16 in. (89.1 cm), BPH. 39 1/2 in. (100.3 cm), SH. 16 1/8 in. (41.0 cm). Seat rails: W. 14 3/16 in. (36.0 cm), MW. 17 7/8 in. (45.4 cm), D. 16 1/16 in. (40.8 cm).

Provenance: Irving W. Lyon, Hartford, Conn.; Francis P. Garvan, New York, N.Y.; The Mabel Brady Garvan Collection, 1930.2449b.

27. Armchair

American, 1800–1825

The transformation of the finial from a double-reel–and–ball form to a double-reel–and–disc form is one of the stylistic features that aid in dating slat-back chairs. On this basis a nineteenth-century date has been assigned to this chair, whose turnings lack the vigor of those on eighteenth-century chairs.

27

Description: The ring turnings on the stiles and front legs are reminiscent of those on no. 25. Double-reel-and-flattened-disc finials, mushroom-shaped handholds, and ogee turnings on the arm supports complete the vocabulary of turned ornament. The four slats have gently curved upper edges. Turned arms are fitted between the arm supports and stiles. Below the basswood seat the stretchers are plain with the exception of those at the front, which have a small ball turning in the center.

Notes: The chair has been refinished, but traces of red paint remain. Grooves mark the placement of the slats, arms, seat rails, and stretchers.

Woods: Soft maple; arms, side and back seat rails, and stretchers, ash.

Dimensions: H. 44 in. (111.8 cm), BPH. 46³⁄₁₆ in. (117.3 cm), SH. 17¹³⁄₁₆ in. (45.3 cm). Seat rails: W. 17⅛ in. (43.5 cm), MW. 21 in. (53.3 cm), D. 16¹¹⁄₁₆ in. (42.4 cm).

Provenance: Henry H. Taylor, Bridgeport, Conn.; Francis P. Garvan, New York, N.Y.; The Mabel Brady Garvan Collection, 1930.2296.

28. Child's Armchair

American, 1775–1800

A related example with mushroom handholds is illustrated by Nutting.[1] The wear visible on the front faces of the stiles of this chair, a common occurrence on children's chairs, may have been caused by its being dragged about.

Description: Unlike most turned chairs, where the motif on the stiles is repeated on the legs, this child's armchair has incised lines on the rear stiles and ring turnings outlined by sharply incised lines on the front legs. The ball finials are separated from the posts with a double reel. The placement of the three arched slats is marked on the stiles with grooves. Turned arms are fitted between the stiles and arm supports with ball handholds. Below the rush seat the side and rear stretchers are plain and the front stretcher has cone-shaped ends and a faint ring turning at the center.

Notes: The chair has been refinished, but traces of black paint remain. The faces of the front stiles are quite flat. About seventy-five worm holes are found throughout the chair. The top slat is secured with wooden pegs driven from the back. Grooves mark the placement of the slats, arms, seat rails, and stretchers and are also used for decoration.

28

Wood: Soft maple.

Dimensions: H. $27\frac{13}{16}$ in. (70.6 cm), BPH. $30\frac{9}{16}$ in. (90.5 cm), SH. $10\frac{1}{16}$ in. (25.6 cm). Seat rails: W. $12\frac{1}{8}$ in. (30.8 cm), MW. $14\frac{7}{8}$ in. (37.8 cm), D. $11\frac{5}{8}$ in. (29.5 cm).

Provenance: Charles W. Lyon, New York, N.Y.; Francis P. Garvan, New York, N.Y. (1925); The Mabel Brady Garvan Collection, 1930.2046.

[1] *Pilgrim Century,* no. 369.

29. Wheel Chair

American, 1750–1800

Wheel chairs, probably made for invalids, are unusual in American furniture. A chair with wheels on the stiles and similarly turned balusters and finials was formerly in the collection of B. A. Behrend.[1] This chair has very plain turned ornament except for the profiles of the finials, which recall those on no. 23.

29

Description: Four oak wheels are fitted into the squared ends of the stiles and front legs. Between the plain tapered stiles are four curved slats. The ogee-shaped finials have small knobs. Flat arms are fitted between the stiles and ogee-turned arm supports with ball handholds. The seven stretchers are plain.

Notes: The old black paint is decorated with yellow lines. The top two slats are secured with square wooden pegs driven from the back—the upper pair come through to the front. The lower stretchers are held in place with square wooden pegs, as are the front seat rail and arms. Faint grooves mark the placement of the slats, arms, seat rails, and stretchers.

Woods: Soft maple; stretchers, slats, side and back seat rails, ash; arms and wheels, white oak.

Dimensions: H. $37\frac{5}{16}$ in. (94.8 cm), BPH. $40\frac{3}{4}$ in. (103.5 cm), SH. $17\frac{3}{8}$ in. (44.1 cm). Seat rails: W. $18\frac{5}{16}$ in. (46.5 cm), MW. $21\frac{5}{16}$ in. (54.1 cm), D. $17\frac{5}{8}$ in. (44.8 cm).

Provenance: Henry H. Taylor, Bridgeport, Conn.; Francis P. Garvan, New York, N.Y.; The Mabel Brady Garvan Collection, 1930.2432.

[1] Nutting, *Treasury,* no. 1854.

30. Child's Armchair

American, 1800–1825

The date assigned to this chair is a quarter-century later than that of the preceding example. The chairs appear to be related in their basic use of elements—an elongated arm support, arms fitted between the front and rear legs, and plain stiles—but here the turnings of the arm supports reveal a lack of concern for academic forms that suggests a late date.

Description: The profiles of the finials are similar to those on no. 29. The three arched slats are held between round stiles. The arms, seat rails, and stretchers have plain round turnings. Indented cylindrical turnings decorate the arm supports, which end in flattened-ball handholds.

Notes: Orange and red paint is found under the grayish-brown paint. The basswood or rush seat was replaced by boards prior to the addition of the orange and red paint. The top slat is secured by wooden pegs driven from the front and coming through to the back. All the joints of the seat rails, stretchers, and arms are secured with square wooden pegs. The placement of the slats, arms, seat rails, and stretchers is marked by faint grooves.

Woods: Soft maple; arms, seat rails, and stretchers, hickory.

30

Dimensions: H. 23⅜ in. (59.4 cm), BPH. 26⅛ in. (66.4 cm), SH. 8¾ in. (22.2 cm). Seat rails: W. 11⅛ in. (28.3 cm), MW. 13¼ in. (33.7 cm), D. 11⁷⁄₁₆ in. (29.1 cm).

Provenance: Frank McCarthy, Longmeadow, Mass.; Francis P. Garvan, New York, N.Y.; The Mabel Brady Garvan Collection, 1930.2301.

31. High Chair

Possibly Virginia, 1710–1760

Despite its somewhat awkward turnings, this child's chair displays the qualities of strength and individuality that give fine primitive objects their appeal. A southern origin is suggested on the basis of provenance. The seat, woven of thin wooden strips, is most unusual.

Description: Two angular slats are set between raked and tapered baluster-turned stiles with small double-reel and ovoid finials. The rake is repeated on the baluster-turned front legs, whose vase-shaped tops support the turned arms. The seat is woven.

Notes: The chair was cleaned and painted black in 1961, but traces of green paint remain. Pieces have broken off the finials and top slat. The top slat is pinned from the front and back with square wooden pegs. The arms are pinned to arm supports, but not to the stiles. The front faces of the front feet are very worn. Narrow grooves mark the placement of the slats, stretchers, seat rails, and arms and are used as decoration.

31

32

Woods: Soft maple; stretchers, ash.

Dimensions: H. 31 in. (78.7 cm), BPH. 34¼ in. (87.0 cm), SH. 19 in. (48.3 cm). Seat rails: W. 10 in. (25.4 cm), MW. 11⅛ in. (28.3 cm), D. 10⁷⁄₁₆ in. (26.5 cm).

Bibliography: Schiffer, p. 87, fig. 76.

Provenance: Kate Doggett Boggs, Fredericksburg, Va.; Henry H. Taylor, Bridgeport, Conn.; Francis P. Garvan, New York, N.Y.; The Mabel Brady Garvan Collection, 1930.2450.

32. Rocking Chair

American, 1810–1830

This child's rocker demonstrates both the persistence of the slat-back form into the nineteenth century and the incorporation of elements of higher style furniture. The idea of flattening the front faces of the stiles was introduced on fancy painted furniture of the second decade of the century.

Description: The slats are supported between round stiles, tapered on the front faces above the joint with the arms. The front legs taper to support the arms and are decorated with three pairs of ring turnings. The round arms have bulbous handholds. The seat is rush. The four stretchers are round, and the rockers are screwed to the sides of the legs.

Notes: Red paint is under the old black paint decorated with yellow lines. The left rocker is restored. Wire nails are used to secure the joints of the seat rails and stiles. Square-headed, perhaps early machine-made, nails were used to secure the arms to the arm supports and the top slat to the stiles.

Woods: Maple; rockers, white oak.

Dimensions: H. 17¼ in. (43.8 cm), BPH. 18 in. (45.7 cm), SH. 6¾ in. (17.1 cm). Seat rails: W. 8⅞ in. (22.5 cm), MW. 10⅞ in. (27.6 cm), D. 8⅜ in. (21.3 cm).

Provenance: Francis P. Garvan, New York, N.Y.; The Mabel Brady Garvan Collection, 1931.1211.

33. Shaker Rocking Chair

Mt. Lebanon, New York, about 1875

Chairmaking was a major industry of the Shakers, and the slat-back chair was one of the chief forms they produced. This rocking chair was made at Mt. Lebanon, New York, where from the mid-nineteenth century the industry was skillfully managed by Brother Robert Wagan. The first Mt. Lebanon chair catalogue was issued in 1874; it lists the price of a No. 3 rocker with arms as $3.50.[1] Under the "Directions for Ordering Chairs" the catalogue notes that the chairs could be ordered "white," that is, "the natural color of the wood," which seems to have been the case with this example.[2]

Description: The plain, tapered stiles and legs of this rocking chair are decorated with acorn-shaped finials and vase-shaped arm supports. The arm supports appear to pierce the flat arms, the top surfaces of which have round, domed discs. Above the seat, woven of red and yellow cotton strips, are three slightly arched slats, and below are plain, round stretchers. The rockers with curved front ends fit into slots in the bottom of the legs.

Inscription: Label on inside of left rocker reads: "SHAKER'S / N° 3 / TRADE MARK / MT. LEBANON, N. Y."

Notes: The chair apparently was never painted. The woven tape seat may not be original. The rockers are nailed to the base of the stiles from the inside with small nails. Small nails are driven into the rear of the stiles to secure the rear seat rail. Nails driven from the inside secure the seat rails and stiles. Small nails driven from the back also secure the joint of the slats and stiles. The joints

33

of the arms and rear stiles are held secure with small nails driven from the front.

Woods: Stiles and stretchers, birch; slats, arms, and rockers, soft maple.

Dimensions: H. 31¼ in. (79.4 cm), BPH. 34¼ in. (87.0 cm), SH. 13½ in. (34.3 cm). Seat rails: W. 14⅝ in. (37.2 cm), MW. 18¼ in. (46.3 cm), D. 23½ in. (59.7 cm).

Provenance: Gift of Mrs. A. Duer Irving, Wilmington, Del., 1971.23.

[1] *An Illustrated Catalogue and Price List of the Shakers' Chairs* (1874?; reprinted Newton, Mass.: Emporium Publications, 1971), p. 16.—[2] *Ibid.*, inside front cover.

Chairs for Export

ON THE OCCASION of the marriage of his daughter, Judith, in 1720, Samuel Sewall ordered from England "A Duzzen of good black Walnut Chairs, fine Cane, with a Couch. A Duzzen of Cane Chairs of a different figure, and a great Chair, for a Chamber: all black Walnut."[1] The manufacture of cane chairs was a specialized industry in London, beginning in 1664 and continuing into the eighteenth century.[2] Cane chairs apparently supplanted the fashionable Turkey-work chairs because they offered the advantages of "Durableness, Lightness, and Cleanness from Dust, Worms and Moths which inseparably attend Turkey-work, Serge, and other Stuff-Chairs and Couches. . . ."[3] In the late seventeenth century a quarter of a million ("2,000 dozen") cane chairs were exported yearly.[4] Many of these found their way to America.

Some American chairmakers attempted to compete with London's specialized cane chair industry, but the majority seem to have turned to other ways of ornamenting their chairs. Boston developed a chairmaking industry of its own and exported chairs of the types seen in this section—banister-backs and leather chairs—to the other colonies. The date the Boston chair industry was established is difficult to determine, but it may have begun with the export of leather chairs of the Cromwellian type in the seventeenth century. The account book of Francis Browne who captained a sloop between New Haven and Boston shows that in 1711 sets of black chairs, perhaps of the type illustrated by nos. 35–38, were imported from Boston to New Haven.[5] Evidence has recently been published indicating that between 1728 and 1740 the Boston upholsterer Samuel Grant delivered 755 chairs to three different Boston merchants, some of which were undoubtedly for export.[6] That the Boston chair trade was still flourishing in 1742 has often been documented by the advertisement placed in the *Pennsylvania Gazette* in September 1742 by the Philadelphia chairmaker Plunkett Fleeson, which states, "Made and to be sold by Plunkett Fleeson, at the Easy Chair, in Chestnut-Street. Several Sorts of good Chair-frames, black and red leather Chairs, finished cheaper than any made here, or imported from Boston. . . ."[7] Clearly, Boston dominated the chair exporting trade among the American colonies during the first half of the eighteenth century.

---

[1] M. Halsey Thomas, ed., *The Diary of Samuel Sewall 1674–1729*, 2 vols. (New York: Farrar, Straus and Giroux, 1973), II, p. 954.—[2] R. W. Symonds, "English Cane Chairs—Part I," *Connoisseur* 127 (March 1951), p. 11.—[3] *Ibid.*, p. 13. Symonds quotes a petition from the cane chairmakers to Parliament.—[4] *Ibid.*, p. 14.—[5] The Account Book of Captain Francis Browne of the Sloop *Speedwell*, 1706–1716, Beinecke Rare Book and Manuscript Library, Yale University, not paged. The six black chairs at four shillings each were purchased by John Bradly [*sic*].—[6] Brock Jobe, "The Boston Furniture Industry 1720–1740," *Boston Furniture of the Eighteenth Century* (Boston, 1974), p. 33.—[7] Richard H. Randall, Jr., "Boston Chairs," *Old-Time New England*, 54, no. 1 (July–Sept. 1963), p. 12.

34. Side Chair

England, about 1700

The Reverend James Pierpont is purported to have been the original owner of this chair.[1] A Harvard graduate (class of 1681), Pierpont came to New Haven in 1684 and ultimately became pastor of the First Church. With his colleagues, the Reverend Samuel Andrew of Milford and the Reverend Samuel Russell, he was instrumental in founding Yale College.[2] Pierpont apparently ordered his chairs from England (microanalysis indicates that the wood in this side chair is English beech; beech, stained dark, was used for a somewhat less expensive variety of cane chair than that made of black walnut). The date Pier-

34

pont purchased his chair is not known. The first reference to caned chairs in Boston inventories is in 1688/89,[3] and cane chairs appear in the inventories after 1693 with increasing frequency;[4] the first reference to them in New Haven inventories, however, does not occur until about ten years later.[5] A related chair is illustrated by Nutting.[6]

Description: The caned back panel is set between columnar-turned stiles which support a pierced crest with carved volutes. The rush seat was once caned. Below it the rear stiles have pairs of tubular turnings. The front legs have elongated ogee turnings to support the front corners of the seat, as well as small ogee turnings and ogee-and-ball front feet. The front stretcher is carved in a pattern echoing the crest rail, and the side, medial, and rear stretchers are variations on the ogee or double-vase form.

Notes: A large piece of the right scroll on the crest rail has been replaced. The cane in the back panel is damaged. The caning holes in the seat rails are visible beneath the rush.

Wood: Beech.

Dimensions: H. 50¼ in. (127.6 cm), SH. 19 in. (48.2 cm). Seat rails: W. 13¾ in. (35.0 cm), MW. 17⅛ in. (43.5 cm), D. 15⅛ in. (38.5 cm).

Bibliography: Edwin Oviatt, *Beginnings of Yale 1701–1726* (New Haven, 1916), p. 133, pl. XX.

Provenance: Said to have been the property of the Reverend James Pierpont (d. 1714) and reported to have been in the 1742 Yale Library. Library Transfer, 1969.52.2.

[1] Oviatt states that the chair then in the Yale Library lobby had been owned by Pierpont. Since there is no inventory of Pierpont's personal estate filed in the New Haven Probate Court, it cannot be determined whether he did indeed own cane chairs.—[2] John Langdon Sibley, *Biographical Sketches of Graduates of Harvard University* (Cambridge, 1885), Vol. 3, p. 226.—[3] Lyon, p. 153.—[4] Benno M. Forman, "Urban Aspects of Massachusetts Furniture in the Seventeenth Century," *Country Cabinetwork and Simple City Furniture* (Charlottesville, Virginia, 1970), p. 22.—[5] *Furn. of the New Haven Colony,* p. 8.—[6] *Treasury,* no. 1977.

35. Side Chair

Eastern Massachusetts, 1690–1720

The item "6 slitt back Chairs carv[d] tops flagg bottoms" valued at £1 10s in the 1738 inventory of Sampson Mason "Glasyer" of Boston offers a good contemporary description of a chair like that illustrated here.[1] In his research of early inventories, Irving W. Lyon failed to find a consistent terminology applied to these chairs; any of their physical features were used to describe them. Today they are usually called banister-back chairs. The banisters were turned on a lathe in the same pattern as the stiles and are often referred to as "split." Actual "splitting" would

35

have been difficult, if not impossible, and it is more likely that the banisters were made from two pieces of wood fastened together so that they could be readily separated after turning. The English adopted the style from the Continent in the 1680's, and in American shops in Boston and the larger towns of eastern Massachusetts manufacture of these chairs may have begun during the last decade of the seventeenth century. In the literature on American furniture their beginnings are traditionally given a date of around 1700.

Description: This black-painted chair, grained with red lines, has four columnar-turned banisters which echo the shape of the flanking stiles. The stiles end in urn-and-ball finials, and support between them a carved and pierced crest of C-scrolls and foliage. The front corners of the rush seat are supported by ogee and double-reel turnings. A smaller ogee turning separates the rest of the front leg, which ends in a Spanish foot. The front stretcher is ball-and-ring turned, the side stretchers are double balls, and the rear stretcher is a double baluster.

Inscriptions: The ends of the left side stretcher and stile are marked "I", and the ends of the right side stretcher and stile are marked "II".

Notes: The crest rail is held in place with square wooden pegs driven from the back. There are worm channels on the underside of the front stretcher, particularly concentrated on the ball turnings.

Woods: Soft maple; seat rails, birch; stretchers and banisters, ash.

Dimensions: H. 47 15/16 in. (121.8 cm), SH. 19 in. (48.3 cm). Seat rails: W. 14 1/16 in. (35.7 cm), MW. 18 1/2 in. (47.0 cm), D. 12 1/8 in. (33.3 cm).

Bibliography: Lyon, p. 165, fig. 75; "American Rooms," *Handbook of the Gallery of Fine Art* (Associates in Fine Arts at Yale University), 5 (1931), p. 44 (illus.); Nagel, p. 19, pl. 1; Meyric R. Rogers, "The Mabel Brady Garvan Collection of Furniture," *Yale Alumni Magazine,* 25 (Jan. 1962), p. 7 (illus.); Kirk, *Early Am. Furn.,* p. 48.

Provenance: Charles W. Lyon, New York, N.Y.; Francis P. Garvan, New York, N.Y. (1929); The Mabel Brady Garvan Collection, 1930.2295c.

[1] Lyon, p. 166.

36. Side Chair

Eastern Massachusetts, 1690–1720

The strong central axis of early banister-back chairs like this one (emphasized here by the large ball-and-disc-turned front stretchers) is not characteristic of slat-back chairs made at approximately the same time (see no. 9). Slat-back chairs grew out of an old tradition, but banister-back chairs were the expression of a fashionable style introduced from the Continent to England and then to America. This chair is closely related to no. 35, but it has a more finely drawn crest rail, slightly better placement of the banisters, bolder turnings on the upper front legs, and a more clearly articulated foot.

Description: In general this chair is like no. 35. Among the noticeable differences is the shape of the turning at the top of the front leg. The ogee shape is capped by a flattened ball and cone.

Notes: The black paint is old. The right side stretcher is cracked, and there are about twenty-five worm holes in various parts of the chair. The crest rail is secured from the back with square wooden pegs. The blocks at the front corners of the seat are cut from the ends of the front seat rail.

Woods: Poplar (*Populus*) or aspen; banisters, lower rail, seat rails, and stretchers, ash.

Dimensions: H. 48⅝ in. (123.5 cm), SH. 18⅝ in. (47.3 cm). Seat rails: W. 13⅞ in. (35.2 cm), MW. 17$^{13}/_{16}$ in. (45.2 cm), D. 13¾ in. (34.9 cm).

35a 36a 37a

36 37

Bibliography: Sack Coll., 1927, p. 139, no. 285; "Gallery Notes," *BAFA,* 3 (Dec. 1928), p. 34 (illus.); Kirk, *Early Am. Furn.,* fig. 34.

Provenance: Fitzwilliam Waters family, Salem, Mass.; Sack Coll. (1927); Francis P. Garvan, New York, N.Y.; The Mabel Brady Garvan Collection, 1930.2523.

37. Side Chair

Eastern Massachusetts, 1690–1720

The illustration of this banister-back chair without a rush seat reveals the construction of the seat frame: there are small blocks at the front corners of the seat into which the front legs and the pared ends of the flat seat rails are fitted.

Description: The turnings show slight variations from nos. 35 and 36. Here the ball turnings on the front stretcher are compressed and a double-reel-and-cone form caps the ogee turning at the top of the front leg.

Notes: The black paint is old. The right banister is a restoration, and about fifty worm holes are found throughout the chair. The crest rail is secured from the back with square wooden pegs which come through to the front. The left side stretcher is nailed to the stile and pinned from the back.

Woods: Soft maple; back and side seat rails and right side stretcher, hickory.

Dimensions: H. 47⅞ in. (121.6 cm), SH. 18¹⁄₁₆ in. (45.9 cm). Seat rails: W. 13¼ in. (33.7 cm), MW. 17¼ in. (43.8 cm), D. 13³⁄₁₆ in. (33.5 cm).

Bibliography: Sack Coll., 1927, p. 139, no. 285; "Gallery Notes," *BAFA*, 3 (Dec. 1928), p. 34 (illus.); Kirk, *Early Am. Furn.*, fig. 33.

Provenance: Fitzwilliam Waters family, Salem, Mass.; Sack Coll. (1927); Francis P. Garvan, New York, N.Y.; The Mabel Brady Garvan Collection, 1930.2160.

38. Side Chair

Eastern Massachusetts, 1690–1720

Many details of this chair are similar to those of no. 37, but there is a curious disjuncture between the accomplished level of the upper part here and the less sophisticated level of the lower. The tops of the front legs are square blocks instead of turned supports. The rectangular side and rear stretchers and the turned rather than carved front feet also make this example much less elegant. All this suggests the chair was made by a less skillful craftsman, or was perhaps a cheaper model.

Description: The front stretcher is a double-baluster form, the side and rear stretchers are rectangular, and the front feet are bulb shaped.

Notes: The chair has been refinished, but traces of old black paint remain. Patches and nail holes appear on the stiles, just below the seat. Four inches of the back inside section of the right side stretcher have been restored. The side and rear stretchers are pinned to the stiles, as are the crest and lower rail of the back.

Woods: Soft maple; seat rails, red oak.

Dimensions: H. 47⅞ in. (121.6 cm), SH. 17¼ in. (43.8 cm). Seat rails: W. 14 in. (35.6 cm), MW. 17⁵⁄₁₆ in. (44.0 cm), D. 14 in. (35.6 cm).

Bibliography: Kirk, *Early Am. Furn.*, fig. 35.

Provenance: Charles W. Lyon, New York, N.Y.; Francis P. Garvan, New York, N.Y.; The Mabel Brady Garvan Collection, 1930.2136a.

38

39. Side Chair

Eastern Massachusetts, 1700–1725

Determining the place of manufacture of early eighteenth-century leather chairs is a complex problem which has not yet been successfully solved. Widely dispersed provenances suggest that chairs of this type may have been made by shops producing chairs for export. This chair, for example, was owned for many generations by a family in Windsor, Connecticut; Richard Randall, however, has pointed to related chairs frequently found in New Hampshire

39

known as the "Piscataqua type."[1] The distinctive feature of this example is the double-ogee-turned stretcher. Related examples can be found at Winterthur, in the Blagojevich Collection,[2] and elsewhere.[3] The chamfered top rail on this one might lead to speculation that the crest is missing; that does not appear to be the case, but a similar chair with carved crest rail is in the Wadsworth Atheneum.[4]

Description: The back panel, between columnar-turned stiles with urn-and-ball finials, and the seat are upholstered in leather. Two pairs of ogee turnings are found on the front legs, which end in bulb feet. The side and rear stretchers are rectangular and the front stretcher is made up of a pair of elongated ogee turnings flanking a pair of small ogee turnings.

Notes: The front feet and bottom of the rear stiles are replacements. The top rail, lower back rail, and the rear stretcher are pinned to the stiles from the back. The lower side stretchers, but not the upper ones, are pinned to the legs. The front stretcher is pinned to the front legs from the front. The chair was reupholstered and painted black in 1962.

Woods: Soft maple; frame for upholstered back, seat rails, and rectangular stretchers, red oak.

Dimensions: H. 43⅛ in. (109.5 cm), BPH. 47 in. (119.4 cm), SH. 19³⁄₁₆ in. (48.7 cm). Seat rails: W. 14⁷⁄₁₆ in. (36.7 cm), MW. 17¼ in. (43.8 cm), D. 14⁹⁄₁₆ in. (37.0 cm).

Bibliography: Lyon, p. 156, fig. 69.

Provenance: Found in Windsor, Conn., by Edwin Simons, Hartford, Conn.; Irving W. Lyon, Hartford, Conn.; Francis P. Garvan, New York, N.Y.; The Mabel Brady Garvan Collection, 1930.2520.

[1] Randall, "Boston Chairs," *Old Time New England,* 54, no. 1 (July–Sept. 1963), p. 17.—[2] See *Antiques,* 83 (Feb. 1963), p. 187.—[3] Lockwood, II, p. 29, fig. 460; *Sack Coll.,* 1957–72, no. 239.—[4] Nutting, *Treasury,* no. 1969.

40. Side Chair

Eastern Massachusetts, probably Boston, 1720–1740

The term "Boston" chair usually brings to mind a chair of this type. Having the back panel and stiles follow the contour of the sitter's back is a dramatic departure from the preceding chairs, where the stiles angle backward above the seat. This innovation reflects the predominance of serpentine curves in mid-eighteenth-century furniture design, and for this rea-

40

son these chairs traditionally have been given slightly later dates than their angular-backed counterparts. In fact, newly published information on the Boston furniture industry between 1720 and 1740 indicates that in 1724 the Boston upholsterer Thomas Fitch began to sell crooked-back leather chairs without carving—"crooked-back" being interpreted as the serpentine shape found here.[1] Chairs of this type may have been made for the next two decades. Other examples have variations not found on the chair at Yale, such as so-called Spanish feet in front.[2]

Description: The serpentine stiles of this chair support a back panel upholstered in leather. The edges of the stiles are beaded above the leather seat and join a curved crest with indented corners. The front legs have pairs of ogee turnings, and the front stretcher is ball-and-ring turned. The side and rear stretchers are rectangular.

Notes: The chair has been refinished, but traces of red paint remain. The diced leather of the back panel and band edging the seat appear to be old. The chair has sustained considerable repair, and the Roman numerals found at the joints of its individual members may have been put there when the chair was taken apart for repair. The rear seat rail and front stretcher are replacements. The left front leg was cracked and repaired where the stretcher joins it. The left front foot is a replacement. There are about two or three hundred worm holes throughout the chair, mostly concentrated in the stretchers.

Woods: Soft maple; front and side seat rails, red oak.

Dimensions: H. 42 13/16 in. (108.7 cm), SH. 17 1/2 in. (44.4 cm). Seat rails: W. 14 3/8 in. (36.5 cm), MW. 17 1/4 in. (43.8 cm), D. 14 1/2 in. (36.8 cm).

Provenance: Luke V. Lockwood, Greenwich, Conn.; Francis P. Garvan, New York, N.Y.; The Mabel Brady Garvan Collection, 1930.2658.

[1] Brock Jobe, "The Boston Furniture Industry 1720–1740," *Boston Furniture of the Eighteenth Century* (Boston, 1974), p. 40.—[2] For related examples see Lockwood, II, figs. 484 and 485; Comstock, fig. 28.

The Rural Turner

Reflections of Urban Taste

RURAL TURNERS were guided in their work by urban models. Academic turnings and carved ornaments were given individual interpretations by the provincial craftsmen who produced the following banister-back chairs. A basic distinction can be made within this group: on some chairs the rear stiles and front legs retain square portions and the stiles are angled backward above the seat like the urban models (see nos. 41, 49–52); on others (nos. 42–48), the stiles and legs are completely round and the stiles are vertical like those of slat-back chairs. Some of these chairs are identifiable as regional types: nos. 41–45 are believed to have been made in Connecticut workshops, and nos. 47, 49, and 50 in New Hampshire. However, the origin of the others is as yet unknown. Like slat-back chairs, banister-back chairs are difficult to date. It is generally assumed that the style was accepted somewhat later in rural areas and continued to be produced over a longer period of time.

41. Side Chair

Connecticut, 1710–1750

41

The flat sides of the banisters usually face forward on banister-back chairs, but on this and some other Connecticut examples they are reversed, creating the highly decorative surface associated with much of the furniture of this region. A related chair with "MM" scratched on the back was found in the area of Fairfield, Connecticut.[1]

Description: The columnar-turned stiles of this chair rake backward above the seat like those of its urban counterparts (nos. 34–38). The banisters, whose round sides face frontward, repeat the pattern of the stiles. Between the urn-and-ball finials is a crest with an arched central section whose beveled edges meet in a point and whose sides are flanked by two small ears. Below the rush seat the legs have pairs of ogee turnings and elongated bulb feet. The front stretcher is double-ball turned and double-vase forms are used at the sides and rear.

Notes: New paint partially covers older paint and gilt stripes on the ring turnings of the legs, stretchers, banisters and stiles and a floral, or anthemion, motif at the top of the front legs and on the block portions of the rear stiles. The left banister has been cracked and repaired. The crest rail is secured from the back with square wooden pegs. The left end of the lower rail in the back is repaired at the rear with three wooden pegs.

Woods: Soft maple; seat rails, bottom rail on back, and stretchers, ash.

Dimensions: H. 45 9/16 in. (115.7 cm), BPH. 46 3/8 in. (117.8 cm), SH. 17 in. (43.2 cm). Seat rails: W. 13 5/8 in. (34.6 cm), MW. 18 3/4 in. (47.6 cm), D. 13 7/16 in. (34.1 cm).

Bibliography: Kirk, *Early Am. Furn.*, fig. 10.

Provenance: Irving W. Lyon, Hartford, Conn.; Mrs. John P. Penney, Pittsburgh, Pa.; Francis P. Garvan, New York, N.Y.; The Mabel Brady Garvan Collection, 1930.2421.

[1] *Conn. Furn.*, p. 123, fig. 219.

42. Armchair

Coastal Connecticut, 1725–1775

This armchair can be compared to a group of finely ornamented coastal Connecticut banister-back chairs found from Guilford to Fairfield, especially in peculiarities of turning, such as the unusual straight-sided cylindrical section on the rear stile below the crest rail and above the ball turning.[1] The examples at Guilford and Stratford also share other special features with this example: squat ogee turnings on the front legs; flattened sides on the vase-shaped arm supports; and a small ring on the stiles just above the seat. Of the chairs in this group the Yale example is exceptional, however, in having three heart cut-outs on its crest.

Description: The crest rail with three-part scalloped top is pierced with three hearts. The stiles have lemon-shaped finials and cylinder, ball, and elongated vase turnings, which are repeated in the three banisters. In the fashion of many Connecticut chairs, separate arm braces appear below the arms. The front legs have pairs of ogee turnings and end in elongated vase-shaped arm supports. Below the rush seat the side and rear stretchers are plain and the front stretchers are turned in a thin, double-vase form.

42

Inscription: The initials "A.P." are carved into the top of the right handhold.

Notes: The backs of both finials had been broken before green paint was applied over the black. The bottom parts of the scrolls are missing from the handholds. The arms are pinned to the arm supports and stiles. The crest rail and lower back rail are pinned to the stiles from the front with square wooden pegs. The arm braces are pinned to the stiles with square wooden pegs. At some points thick layers of paint obliterate the thin grooves used to mark the placement of the members.

Wood: Hard maple.

Dimensions: H. 43⅝ in. (110.8 cm), BPH. 44¾ in. (113.7 cm), SH. 15¼ in. (38.7 cm). Seat rails: W. 15⅝ in. (39.7 cm), MW. 23⅝ in. (60.0 cm), D. 15⅞ in. (40.3 cm).

Provenance: Warren W. Creamer, Waldeboro, Me.; Henry H. Taylor, Bridgeport, Conn.; Francis P. Garvan, New York, N.Y.; The Mabel Brady Garvan Collection, 1930.2294.

[1] *Conn. Furn.*, nos. 210–12. Another armchair whose crest rail has a heart cut-out is owned by the Stratford Historical Society. Two others are at the Dorothy Whitfield Historic Society, Guilford.

43. Side Chair

Connecticut, 1710–1750

A number of banister-back chairs like the one illustrated, which delightfully echo their more sophisticated counterparts from eastern Massachusetts (nos. 35–38), have been found in the Wethersfield-Avon area of Connecticut.[1] The interplay of round and straight shapes in the legs and stretchers, and the way in which the vertical, molded slats move the eye to an arched crest rail flanked by well-proportioned finials are visually effective. A related chair with similar finials, ball-and-baluster turnings, and crest rail (but with a solid splat) is in the collection of John T. Kirk.

Description: The four banisters do not repeat the double-ball-and-vase turnings of the stiles but were molded with a plane. The stiles are capped with urn-and-ball finials and between them is an arched crest with three carved rosettes and two slanted, pierced openings. The double-ball turnings of the stiles are repeated in pairs on the front legs, and the elongated ball feet are divided from the legs by a reel turning. The front stretchers are sausage turned and the side and rear stretchers are plain.

Inscription: The front of the crest rail is stamped with the initials "DF".

Notes: The chair was refinished and tinted with colored wax in 1961. The bottoms of both rear stiles are worm damaged. The crest rail is secured with square wooden

43

43a

44

44a

pegs driven from the back. The placement of the crest rail, seat rails, and stretchers is not marked by grooves. The top front stretcher is a replacement.

Woods: Soft maple; banisters, white pine.

Dimensions: H. 48 1/16 in. (122.1 cm), SH. 17 3/8 in. (44.1 cm). Seat rails: W. 13 15/16 in. (35.4 cm), MW. 19 1/16 in. (48.4 cm), D. 13 1/4 in. (33.2 cm).

Provenance: Charles W. Lyon, New York, N.Y.; Francis P. Garvan, New York, N.Y.; The Mabel Brady Garvan Collection, 1930.2304.

[1] *Conn. Furn.*, nos. 214–16.

44. Armchair

Connecticut, 1710–1750

The proliferation of elaborate turnery and the whimsical carving on this banister-back armchair and on similar chairs leaves little doubt about the delight rural Connecticut taste found in fanciful ornament. The striking similarity of the finials and double-ball turnings on this and on no. 43 suggests that they probably originated in the same area. Here the C-scrolls in the pierced crest rail imitate even more closely the designs of eastern Massachusetts chairs. A similar chair is owned by the Henry Ford Museum.

Description: The urn-and-ball finials and double-ball-turned stiles and legs of this chair have much in common with the preceding example. The four banisters are turned, echoing the shape of the stiles, and the crest is cut out in a rosette and C-scroll form. The arms end in scrolled handholds above vase-shaped arm supports. The front stretchers are elongated vase forms flanking a ball and rings. The side and rear stretchers are plain.

Notes: The chair has been refinished, but traces of red paint remain. The side of the crest rail is repaired. The feet are replacements. The arms, crest, and lower rail are pinned to the stiles. The placement of crest rail, seat rails and stretchers is not marked by grooves.

Woods: Soft maple; side and rear stretchers, ash.

Dimensions: H. 48⅞ in. (124.1 cm), SH. 16½ in. (41.9 cm). Seat rails: W. 16⅝ in. (42.2 cm), MW. 22¹¹⁄₁₆ in. (57.6 cm), D. 16 in. (40.6 cm).

Bibliography: Miller, I, p. 127, fig. 46; Aronson (1st ed.), fig. 227; Rogers, p. 31, fig. 8.

Provenance: Henry V. Weil, New York, N.Y.; Francis P. Garvan, New York, N.Y.; The Mabel Brady Garvan Collection, 1934.405.

45. Armchair

Connecticut, 1725–1775

The similarity of this banister-back armchair to one from the Churchill House at Newington, Connecticut, and its ownership by Irving Lyon, who collected Connecticut furniture, suggest Connecticut as the place of origin.[1] The turned rear feet are an unusual feature.

45

Description: The double-arched and scalloped crest rail is held between round vase-and-reel-turned stiles with urn-shaped finials. The serpentine arms have a pronounced sag and are supported on vase-turned arm supports. Below the flag seat are flattened-ball-turned front legs, two vase-and-ring-turned front stretchers, and plain side and rear stretchers.

Notes: The chair was refinished in 1964. The feet are worn. The crest rail is pinned to the stiles from the back. The arms are pinned to the stiles and the arm supports. Faint grooves mark the placement of the crest rail, lower back rail, seat rails, and stretchers.

Woods: Poplar (*Populus*); seat rails and front stretchers, ash; lower rung of back, poplar.

Dimensions: H. 44⅜ in. (112.7 cm), BPH. 45¾ in. (116.2 cm), SH. 16⅞ in. (42.9 cm). Seat rails: W. 15½ in. (39.4 cm), MW. 22½ in. (57.1 cm), D. 14⅝ in. (37.1 cm).

Provenance: Irving W. Lyon, Hartford, Conn.; Francis P. Garvan, New York, N.Y.; The Mabel Brady Garvan Collection, 1930.2663.

---

[1] *Seymour Coll.*, p. 72.

46. High Chair

New England, 1725–1750

The fine proportions and the unusual interplay of turned and shaped elements in this banister-back high chair contribute to an outstanding example of the form. The ball turnings outlined by soft hollows on the front legs are reminiscent of the turnings on the New England type slat-back chairs (nos. 9–15). The split banisters do not repeat the turnings of the stiles, but rather incorporate various silhouettes found throughout the chair. A closely related example has been published and is said to have come from Connecticut.[1]

Description: The legs are raked for greater stability. The rear stiles are round below the rush seat. Above the seat the stiles are turned in a barrel shape where the arms join, with a cone and flattened ball above, and urn-and-disc finials. There are three banisters between the crest with a double scalloped top and the double serpentine bottom rail. The square arms with rounded edges end in scrolled handholds and rest on ogee-shaped arm supports. The ball turnings on the front legs are outlined by soft hollows. The front stretchers are double balusters with ball turnings, and the side and rear stretchers are plain.

46

Notes: The front feet and bases of the rear stiles are replacements. The crest rail is pinned to the stiles with square wooden pegs. Faint grooves mark the placement of the arms, seat rails, and stretchers.

Woods: Soft maple; seat rails and stretchers, ash.

Dimensions: H. 33⅜ in. (84.8 cm), BPH. 35⅛ in. (89.2 cm), SH. 20⅜ in. (51.8 cm). Seat rails: W. 10¼ in. (26.0 cm), MW. 13¹⁄₁₆ in. (33.2 cm), D. 10½ in. (26.7 cm).

Bibliography: Nutting, *Pilgrim Century,* p. 366 (illus. p. 378, no. 471); Nutting, *Treasury,* no. 2499; Iverson, p. 42, fig. 32; Kirk, *Early Am. Furn.,* fig. 38.

Provenance: Hazen House, Haverhill, Mass.; Wallace Nutting, Framingham, Mass. (sale New York, Wanamaker's, 1918); Francis P. Garvan, New York, N.Y.; The Mabel Brady Garvan Collection, 1931.1219.

[1] *Sack Coll.,* 1957–72, no. 1067.

47. Armchair

Portsmouth area, New Hampshire, 1725–1775

Numerous chairs with distinctive "fish-tail" or "staghorn" crest rails have been found in the area of Portsmouth, New Hampshire, and northern Massachusetts. This singular feature is related to the ornamentation of chairs attributed to the Gaines family who worked in that locale.[1] Flamboyantly outlined splats of Gaines family chairs recall the jagged profile of this crest rail. The characteristic shape of the crest rail is not the only feature which identifies this as a New Hampshire chair: the straight line under the ball turning on the stile and arm support appears on other New Hampshire chairs.[2]

Description: The semi-circular cut-out at the center of this crest rail and the comma-shaped cut-outs on either side emphasize the bird-like projections at the top of the crest. Below the crest are five elongated vase-and-ball-turned banisters that repeat the turnings of the stiles. The stiles end in reel-and-ball finials and are plain below the seat. The serpentine arms with scrolled handholds are supported on vase-and-ball-turned arm supports at the top of the ball-turned front legs. The double-vase-turned front stretchers with a double ball at the center contrast with the plain side and rear stretchers.

Notes: The crest rail is cracked, and the front feet are worn. The arms are pinned to the stiles and the arm supports. The crest rail is pinned with square wooden pegs from the back.

Woods: Soft maple; crest rail, bottom rail, seat rails, and stretchers, ash.

Dimensions: H. 42⅛ in. (107.0 cm), BPH. 46⅛ in. (117.2 cm), SH. 15½ in. (39.4 cm). Seat rails: W. 17⅛ in. (43.5 cm), MW. 21¾ in. (55.2 cm), D. 16⅞ in. (42.9 cm).

Bibliography: Kirk, *Early Am. Furn.,* fig. 168.

Provenance: Henry H. Taylor, Bridgeport, Conn.; Francis P. Garvan, New York, N.Y.; The Mabel Brady Garvan Collection, 1930.2256a.

[1] Randall, no. 132.—[2] *The Decorative Arts of New Hampshire 1725–1825* (Manchester, New Hampshire: The Currier Gallery of Art, 1964), fig. 4; chairs with similar turnings are in the collection of the New Hampshire Historical Society (acc. nos. 1956.273, 1966.30.14, and 1965.505).

47

48

49

48. Armchair

New England, 1720–1750

With its bold finials and fan-carved crest rail, this chair is a fine example of rural chairmaking. A few chairs with fan-carved crest rails have been attributed to Connecticut and Massachusetts, but most apparently originated in New Hampshire. An example now at the Shelburne Museum has a New Hampshire family history.[1] The thickness of the turned parts supports the relatively early date assigned to the chair. The unusual constricting ring turnings on the front legs resemble the turnings on a slat-back chair in this collection (no. 24).

Description: The fan-carved crest rail of this black-painted armchair sits between double-reel finials. The round stiles are ornamented with elongated vase-, ball-, and reel-shaped turnings whose profiles are repeated in the four banisters. Arms with scrolled handholds slope from the stiles to the vase-shaped arm supports. Pairs of ring turnings compress the roundness of the front legs. The large double-baluster-turned front stretchers contrast with the plain stretchers at the sides and rear.

Notes: The side of the top right stretcher is badly damaged by worms and there are approximately one hundred worm holes in the other stretchers. The arms are pinned to the tops of the arm supports, and the two rails in the back are pinned to the stiles. The top of the left rear stile is cracked. The joints of the crest rail and stiles are reinforced with hand-wrought nails driven from the back. Faint grooves mark the placement of the crest rail and lower rail in the back, seat rails, and stretchers.

Woods: Maple; stretchers and seat rails, ash.

Dimensions: H. 43½ in. (110.5 cm); BPH. 44¼ in. (112.4 cm); SH. 15½ in. (39.4 cm). Seat rails: W. 16½ in. (41.9 cm), MW. 21½ in. (54.6 cm), D. 15⅞ in. (40.4 cm).

Provenance: Gift of Mrs. Paul H. Moore, New York, N.Y., 1971.15.1.

---

[1] *Antiques,* 71 (May 1957), p. 442 (illus.).

49. Armchair

New Hampshire or Northern Massachusetts, 1750–1775

The square stiles that angle backward above the seat, the vase-and-ball-turned stretchers, and the chamfered arms with drooping handholds on this chair reveal this rural craftsman's awareness of urban models. The thinness of the turned parts in comparison with no. 48 suggests a somewhat later date. This is particularly true of the finials, where the double-reel-and-ball form has been transformed to a flattened ball or disc.

Description: The fan-carved crest rail is supported between stiles that angle backward above the seat and are square below. The stiles are turned in a reel and elongated vase pattern, and end in a double-reel and flattened-ball finial. The four banisters echo the shape of the stiles. The arms slope and turn outward from the stiles, ending in scrolled handholds above vase-shaped arm supports. The square blocks of the front legs are punctuated below the seat by a pair of double-reel and ball-shaped turnings and a pair of ogee-shaped turnings. The two double-vase-and-ring front stretchers are set off by the plain stretchers at the rear and sides.

Notes: This chair has recently been cleaned and repainted black and has been given a new seat. A crack in the left banister was repaired in 1960. The crest rail and lower back rail are pinned to the stiles from the back with square wooden pegs. The arms are pinned to the tops of the arm supports. Faint grooves mark the placement of the crest and lower back rail.

Woods: Soft maple; seat rails and stretchers, ash.

Dimensions: H. 46⅜ in. (117.8 cm), SH. 16$^{11}/_{16}$ in. (42.4 cm). Seat rails: W. 16 in. (40.6 cm), MW. 22$^{11}/_{16}$ in. (57.6 cm), D. 15$^{1}/_{16}$ in. (38.3 cm).

Bibliography: Antiques, 16 (Dec. 1929), p. 467.

Provenance: Fred W. Fuessenich, Torrington, Conn.; Henry H. Taylor, Bridgeport, Conn.; Francis P. Garvan, New York, N.Y.; The Mabel Brady Garvan Collection, 1930.2269.

50. Armchair

Possibly New Hampshire, 1750–1775

50

With its crisply turned front stretchers and block-and-ogee-turned stiles and legs, this chair, like no. 49, recalls more academic banister-back chairs. On the other hand, the profusion of ornament—six banisters instead of the usual four, molded corners of the uprights, an elaborate bottom rail, and turned rear legs—reveals its rural origin.

Description: The turning of the rear stiles below the seat and the six banisters are unusual features. The rear stiles end in urn-and-ball finials. The top edge of the crest rail is cut to form a double scroll at the center. The serpentine arms have scrolled handholds and rest on vase-shaped arm supports. The front legs have pairs of ogee turnings and bulb-shaped feet. The double vase-and-reel-turned front stretchers complement the bulbous side and rear stretchers.

Notes: The old (but not original) black paint was removed and the chair was repainted in 1961, although traces of green paint remain. The top front stretcher is restored. Square wooden pegs driven from the back secure the crest rail and lower back rail. The arms are pinned to the arm supports and rear stiles with square wooden pegs.

Woods: Soft maple; seat rails, side and rear stretchers, ash.

Dimensions: H. 45 in. (114.3 cm), BPH. 46½ in. (118.1 cm), SH. 17⅜ in. (44.1 cm). Seat rails: W. 16⅛ in. (41.0

cm), MW. $19\frac{1}{4}$ in. (48.9 cm), D. $15\frac{3}{4}$ in. (40.0 cm).

Bibliography: Kirk, *Early Am. Furn.*, fig. 11.

Provenance: Jacob Margolis, New York, N.Y. (probably sale New York, Anderson Galleries, April 3–4, 1925); Francis P. Garvan, New York, N.Y.; The Mabel Brady Garvan Collection, 1930.2202.

51. Side Chair

New England, 1750–1775

With its squared stiles and single front stretcher, this rural banister-back chair adheres to the academic tradition. However, the three widely spaced banisters do not follow the usual practice of repeating the pattern of the stiles.

Description: The crest rail has a scalloped top edge, complemented by a serpentine lower rail, a variation found on other banister-back chairs in this collection. The square stiles end in ball-and-reel finials and have an elongated vase-shaped turning, which is repeated (though not exactly) in the three banisters. The seat rails of the rush seat fit into the square blocks at the tops of the front legs, below which are ridged, bulbous turnings. The front stretcher has a double-vase form and the side and rear stretchers are plain.

Notes: The chair has been refinished, but traces of dark brown paint remain. The crest and lower back rail are pinned to the stiles with square wooden pegs. Scored lines mark the placement of the crest, lower back rail, seat rails, and stretchers.

Woods: Soft maple; seat rails, side and rear stretchers, ash.

Dimensions: H. $43\frac{9}{16}$ in. (110.6 cm), BPH. $44\frac{1}{2}$ in. (113.0 cm), SH. $16\frac{5}{8}$ in. (42.2 cm). Seat rails: W. $14\frac{3}{16}$ in.

51

52

(36.0 cm), MW. 18 in. (45.7 cm), D. 13⅝ in. (34.6 cm).

Provenance: Henry H. Taylor, Bridgeport, Conn.; Francis P. Garvan, New York, N.Y.; The Mabel Brady Garvan Collection, 1930.2417b.

52. Side Chair

Possibly Connecticut Valley, 1750–1775

The unusual double-serpentine crest rail of this country chair caps both stiles and banisters in the manner of caned-back chairs of the early eighteenth century; its serpentine shape reflects mid-eighteenth-century styles, however. Many similar chairs have been found in the Connecticut Valley. The use of oak for the banisters is most unusual.

Description: The crest rail with its double-serpentine top edge rests on elongated vase-and-ball-turned stiles and banisters. The square front legs have pairs of ogee turnings and ball feet. The ball flanked by rings at the center of the front stretcher is an unusual motif. The side and rear stretchers are plain, and the inner edges of the rear feet are chamfered.

Notes: The chair has been refinished, but traces of old red paint remain. The crest rail has been repinned to the tops of the stiles.

Woods: Soft maple; banisters, red oak.

Dimensions: H. 40½ in. (102.9 cm), SH. 16$^{5}/_{16}$ in. (41.4 cm). Seat rails: W. 13⅜ in. (34.0 cm), MW. 17⅜ in. (44.1 cm), D. 12$^{15}/_{16}$ in. (32.9 cm).

Provenance: Henry V. Weil, New York, N.Y.; Francis P. Garvan, New York, N.Y.; The Mabel Brady Garvan Collection, 1930.2556a.

Queen Anne Style

Early Expressions

SCHOLARS of English furniture generally concede that during the reign of Queen Anne (1702–14) a new style of walnut chair, featuring curved uprights, a broad splat and cabriole legs, was introduced to England from Holland. In America chairs following this fashion are generally said to be in the Queen Anne style, although there is as yet little proof that any American chairmaker's shop ever produced one before that monarch's death in 1714. Early scholars arrived at no consensus as to when chairs in this style began to be made. Lockwood suggested a date as early as 1710,[1] Nutting 1720,[2] and more modern scholars such as Downs[3] and Randall[4] have proposed a date of 1730. Although in the third decade of the eighteenth century such leading members of Boston society as Judith Sewall (see introduction to *Chairs for Export*) were still purchasing cane chairs, by 1730 taste must have been shifting to the newer styles.

In fact, just as this book was going to press new information was published on the Boston furniture industry that substantiates what recent scholars had supposed, at least as regards Boston. Brock Jobe's article, "The Boston Furniture Industry 1720–1740,"[5] sets forth important new evidence to document the beginnings of the Queen Anne style in that city. From the account books and letterbooks of the Boston upholsterers Thomas Fitch and Samuel Grant it becomes apparent that the Queen Anne style was introduced during the late 1720's. On October 14, 1729, a red cheyney upholstered chair with a "New fashion round seat" was sold by Grant.[6] Although William M. Hornor, Jr.'s *Blue Book Philadelphia Furniture* (1935) treats the same era in Philadelphia, unfortunately no similar body of documentary evidence has been found to offer equal insight into the rise of the style there.

Since the publication in 1952 of Joseph Downs's catalogue of the Winterthur Collection, *American Furniture: Queen Anne and Chippendale Periods,* in which he set forth the theory that furniture could be assigned a regional origin based upon the peculiarities of design and construction, scholars have consistently attempted to identify furniture regionally.[7] The dozen examples of Queen Anne style chairs in this catalogue come from New England to Philadelphia. Among connoisseurs of American furniture, chairs in this style have been prized as the ultimate expression in wood of the furniture maker's craft. More than any others of the early period these chairs rely upon line, form, and the abstract play of solids and voids to create their visual effect.

[1] *Colonial Furniture in America,* II, p. 57, fig. 494.—[2] *Treasury,* no. 2115.—[3] *Am. Furn.,* nos. 107, 112.—[4] No. 133.—[5] In *Boston Furniture of the Eighteenth Century* (Boston, 1974).—[6] *Ibid.,* p. 42.—[7] pp. XXIV–XXVII.

53. Side Chair

Boston area, 1730–1760

This side chair is representative of the classic New England Queen Anne style chair; its serpentine-shaped stiles flattened on the front faces, elongated vase splat, compass seat, and cabriole front legs braced by turned-and-block stretchers are characteristic. The account book of the Boston upholsterer

Samuel Grant reveals that in 1730 he sold a couch frame with "horseshoe feet"—which Brock Jobe presumes to be "a cabriole leg, perhaps with a notch near the bottom of the back of the leg resembling the indentation just above a horse's hoof."[1] Four years later Grant first produced chairs with compass-shaped seats, like that on this example.[2] Both references offer sound evidence for dating the introduction of chairs of this type to the early 1730's. Typical of Massachusetts workmanship is the construction of the seat frame, with the front and side seat rails mortised and tenoned into the tops of the legs. Numbered "I" of a set, it is believed to have been made in the Boston area for the Reverend Edward Holyoke, president of Harvard College (1737–69).

Description: The bowed stiles with flattened front faces join the round-shouldered crest above a vase-shaped splat. The front corners of the compass-shaped seat house the tops of cabriole front legs that end in pad feet. The rear legs are chamfered between the rear seat rail and the rear stretcher. The rear and medial stretchers have bulbous centers and ends; the medial stretcher fits into blocks on the turned side stretchers.

Inscriptions: The top of the front seat rail is marked with a crescent-shaped "I", and the slip seat frame is marked with three crescent-shaped "I"s.

Notes: The triangular front corner blocks are replacements. The side stretchers end at the front in rectangular tenons and are fitted into mortises in the front legs. Each joint of the seat rails and legs is secured with a single wooden peg. The side stretchers are pinned to the rear legs. The knee brackets are fastened with roseheaded nails which are missing on the left side. The eighteenth-century English crewelwork upholstery illustrated has recently been replaced by a reproduction of mid-eighteenth-century rose moreen in a stamped pattern (Scalamandré, 1945–1).

Woods: American black walnut; slip seat, soft maple.

Dimensions: H. 39 11/16 in. (100.8 cm), SH. 16 7/8 in. (42.9 cm). Seat rails: W. 15 in. (38.1 cm), MW. 20 13/16 in. (52.9 cm), D. 16 7/8 in. (42.9 cm).

Bibliography: *Sack Coll.,* 1927, p. 107, no. 236; "Annapolis Windows," *Antiques,* 17 (May 1930), p. 429 (illus.); Miller, I, p. 129, fig. 50, and p. 139, fig. 71; Meyric R. Rogers, "Garvan Furniture at Yale," *Connoisseur Year Book* 1960, p. 55, fig. 3; Meyric R. Rogers, "The Mabel Brady Garvan Collection of Furniture," *Yale Alumni Magazine,* 25 (Jan. 1962), p. 7 (illus.); Comstock, fig. 157; Boger, p. 381; *Colonial Antiques,* p. 135, fig. 163; Kirk, *Early Am. Furn.,* fig. 107; Kirk, *Am. Chairs,* p. 98, fig. 101; Brock Jobe, "The Boston Furniture Industry 1720–1740," *Boston Furniture of the Eighteenth Century* (Boston, 1974), p. 46, no. 34.

Provenance: According to tradition, owned by the Reverend Edward Holyoke, Cambridge, Mass.; descended in the Abbot family, Groton, Mass., until 1911; Israel Sack, New York, N.Y.; Francis P. Garvan, New York, N.Y. (1927); The Mabel Brady Garvan Collection, 1930.2626e.

[1] Jobe (see Bibliography), p. 42.—[2] *Ibid.,* p. 47.

54. Side Chair

New England, 1730–1760

In this side chair a square seat frame is substituted for the compass seat, a variation often encountered on fine Queen Anne chairs from New England. Of a similar chair Richard Randall has said: "Localization of such chairs is virtually impossible as they were made in all parts of New England and must be localized by history or by the type of wood. Connecticut examples were in the family of Gov. Fitch [*Connecticut Chairs,* pp. 34, 35]; a Rhode Island one was shown in the Newport exhibition [Carpenter, no. 19]";[1] and Randall himself illustrates an example from Boston.[2] Lack of data hinders the establishment of a place of origin for this chair. However, the use of walnut rather than cherry suggests Massachusetts or Rhode Island rather than Connecticut, as walnut was the fashionable furniture wood in this era in most urban centers.

Description: The elements of this chair are similar to those of the preceding example, with the exceptions of a square seat frame with a scalloped front rail and the absence of a cushion under the pad feet.

Inscriptions: The number "IIII" appears on the top of the front seat ledge; the front of the slip seat frame is marked "III".

Notes: The back seat rail may be a replacement. The knee bracket on the left side has been replaced. The knee brackets originally were secured with roseheaded nails, one of which remains. The side seat rails and stretchers are pinned to the rear stiles. The top of the left stile is pinned to the crest rail to secure the wood, which is split at that point. The splat shoe is nailed to the rear seat rail. The upholstery is modern yellow woolen twill.

Woods: American black walnut; slip seat frame, soft maple.

53

54

55

Dimensions: H. 38 3/4 in. (98.4 cm), SH. 16 13/16 in. (42.7 cm). Seat rails: W. 14 3/4 in. (37.5 cm), MW. 18 3/4 in. (47.6 cm), D. 16 3/8 in. (41.6 cm).

Bibliography: Kirk, *Am. Chairs,* p. 96, fig. 97.

Provenance: E. F. Sanderson, Moor's End, Nantucket, Mass. (sale New York, B. Altman & Co., Oct. 1928); Francis P. Garvan, New York, N.Y.; The Mabel Brady Garvan Collection, 1930.2078.

[1] Randall, no. 135.—[2] *Ibid.,* no. 139.

55. Roundabout Chair

Massachusetts, 1740–1760

A number of details of this chair are related to those of other roundabout chairs also believed to have originated in Massachusetts. The serpentine ends of the crest rail terminating in small scrolls, the peak in the arm rail between the handhold and crest, the very full flattened ball shape at the top of the columnar turning, and the splats with sharply incut necks are found on other illustrated examples.[1] This chair is unusual in that it has square legs and rectangular crossed stretchers.

Description: The semi-circular arm rail and its crest with serpentine ends are supported by three columnar-turned arm supports. The vase-shaped splats have sharply incut necks. The square legs are braced by rectangular crossed stretchers.

Inscriptions: Beginning with the rear side of the left leg, the stile and seat rails are marked with the chiselled figures "I, II, III, V". The right side of the front leg is marked "V".

Notes: The crest rail is attached to the arm rail with roseheaded nails. The seat rails are fastened to the front leg with single wooden pegs, while the other three legs and the seat rails are fastened with double wooden pegs. The left arm has been repaired. Supports for a chamber pot have been removed. Nail holes on the insides of the seat rails probably indicate that the right rear seat ledge is a replacement. The two sections of the arm rail are butted together at the center and pinned to the arm supports from the back. The brackets on the front leg are held in place with nails and glue. The modern upholstery illustrated has been replaced by a reproduction of blue-green eighteenth-century wool damask (F. Schumacher, Peyton Randolph Damask).

Woods: American black walnut; slip seat frame, white pine.

Dimensions: H. 30 9/16 in. (77.6 cm), SH. 14 7/8 in. (37.8 cm). Seat rails: W. 18 7/8 in. (47.9 cm), D. 18 13/16 in. (47.8 cm).

Provenance: Charles R. Morson, New York, N.Y.; Francis P. Garvan, New York, N.Y. (1925); The Mabel Brady Garvan Collection, 1930.2559.

---

[1] See *Antiques,* 74 (July 1958), back cover; *Sack Coll.,* 1957–72, II, no. 766. An example with cabriole front leg and deep skirts, but very similar back, is in the collection of Mr. and Mrs. Charles Garvin.

56. Side Chair

Rhode Island, 1740–1760

Many features of this chair are typical of Rhode Island Queen Anne style side chairs. The carved shell, although more hesitantly executed than most, is a motif that appears on furniture attributed to the Goddard and Townsend families of Newport. Tubular-turned rear legs, a common feature of early eighteenth-century English chairs, are found with some frequency in America on Rhode Island chairs, and occasionally on Massachusetts chairs.[1] The slightly curved splat that follows the form of the sitter's back has a sharply incut neck and prominent lobes near the base. These distinctive features appear on chairs owned by the Bull family of Newport.[2] The "6 chares colt feet" which Obadiah Brown bought from the Providence cabinetmaker William Barker in 1762 perhaps offer a clue to a contemporary name for pad feet such as appear on this chair.[3]

Description: The stiles of this Rhode Island chair follow a pattern different from those of its New England counterparts (nos. 53 and 54): a tubular turning replaces the chamfering below the seat; above the seat the stiles are straight before curving in toward the splat, sweeping out as they join the crest rail with its carved central shell. The narrow waist of the vase-shaped splat follows the curves of the stiles. The neck of the splat is sharply incut. The front corners of the compass-shaped seat house the tops of the cabriole front legs, which terminate in pad feet. The stretchers are like those of nos. 53 and 54.

Inscriptions: Both the front seat rail and the slip seat frame are marked "XI".

Notes: The chair has been refinished. The rear corner blocks are new and the triangular front corner blocks with horizontal grain have been reattached. Both side knee brackets are restored. The front knee brackets are held in

56

56a

place with small sprigs. The crest rail is pinned to the stiles. The joint of the right stile and crest rail is repaired. The base of the shell carving is slightly cracked. The front of each of the side stretchers ends in a rectangular tenon which fits into mortises in the front leg, where it is pinned from the side. The side stretchers are pinned to the rear stiles. The seat rails are pinned to the legs with square wooden pegs. The modern silk damask illustrated has recently been replaced by a reproduction of mid-eighteenth-century yellow moreen (Scalamandré, 1946–3).

Woods: American black walnut; front corner blocks, white pine; sides and rear of slip seat frame, birch; front of slip seat frame, maple.

Dimensions: H. 39¼ in. (99.7 cm), SH. 17¼ in. (43.8 cm). Seat rails: W. 15½ in. (39.4 cm), MW. 20¾ in. (52.7 cm), D. 17⅞ in. (45.4 cm).

Bibliography: Kirk, *Am. Chairs,* p. 133, fig. 169.

Provenance: Charles R. Morson, New York, N.Y.; Francis P. Garvan, New York, N.Y. (1929); The Mabel Brady Garvan Collection, 1930.2712.

[1] Brock Jobe, "The Boston Furniture Industry 1720–1740," *Boston Furniture of the Eighteenth Century* (Boston, 1974), p. 44, no. 32.—[2] Carpenter, figs. 6, 12.—[3] Joseph K. Ott, "Recent Discoveries Among Rhode Island Cabinetmakers and Their Work," *Rhode Island History,* 28, 1 (Winter 1969), p. 17.

57. Side Chair

Connecticut, 1740–1760

Connecticut craftsmen often developed a freedom of expression not known in America's urban centers, which were more directly in touch with high-style European furniture. A number of features of this chair, which has evidently been owned in Connecticut since the eighteenth century, reveal its rural origin: the cabriole legs are somewhat stiff; the curve of the stiles does not reverse as it reaches the crest rail; the outline of the splat is broad at the top and narrow at the base; and the knee brackets are placed over the faces of the deep seat rails rather than in their usual position between the leg and seat. Other Connecticut chairs constructed in this way are known.[1] The solid slip seat used here has also been found on another Connecticut chair.[2] The character of this rural chair, especially its use of a single rear stretcher, is reminiscent of country chairs found in northern England.

Description: The stiles of this Connecticut chair are like those of its New England counterparts (nos. 53 and 54), although the curve does not reverse as it reaches the crest rail. The seat rails are deeper than usual and the knee brackets are fastened to their faces rather than to their lower edges.

Inscription: A paper label, with writing in ink (removed from the chair and now in the collection's files) reads: "This chair I bought of / Mr. H. C. Wales, East Hartford / Conn. in 1877. It had be / longed to Miss Patty Flagg / who died 60 or 70 years ago / very old. and the chair had / belonged to her grandfather / This supposed to be about / 135 years old. / Irving W. Lyon / Nov. 1880."

Notes: The crest is cracked above the splat. The corner blocks and splat shoe are replacements. The pins fastening the side seat rails with the rear stiles are also new. The crest rail is not pinned to the stiles. About thirty worm holes are visible in the front seat rail. The striped upholstery illustrated has been replaced by a reproduction of a mid-eighteenth-century yellow moreen (Scalamandré, 1946–3).

Woods: Cherry; slip seat, soft maple.

Dimensions: H. 40 in. (101.6 cm), SH. 16¾ in. (42.5 cm). Seat rails: W. 14⅞ in. (37.8 cm), MW. 19¹¹⁄₁₆ in. (50.0 cm), D. 15⅞ in. (40.3 cm).

Bibliography: Kirk, *Am. Chairs,* p. 144, fig. 190.

Provenance: Descended to Miss Patty Flagg; H. C. Wales, East Hartford, Conn.; Irving W. Lyon, Hartford, Conn. (1877); Irving P. Lyon, New York, N.Y.; Francis P. Garvan, New York, N.Y.; The Mabel Brady Garvan Collection, 1930.2416.

[1] *Sack Coll.,* 1952–72, II, no. 1246; *Conn. Furn.,* no. 227.—[2] *Barbour Coll.,* p. 16.

58. Side Chair

Wethersfield, Connecticut, 1740–1760

Ezekiel Porter (1707–75) of Wethersfield originally owned this chair, which displays many characteristics of Connecticut workmanship, such as the attenuated back, slender splat with ringed neck, and pointed knee brackets. A similar chair from the Wilcox family of Westbrook also shares an occasional Connecticut structural feature—seat rails tenoned through the stiles.[1] The construction of the compass seat is atypical of New England craftsmanship (see no. 53). Here, the front and side seat rails are mortised and tenoned and the tops of the front legs are turned to round

57

58

tenons which fit into the underside of the front seat rail. A molding is then applied around the top edge of the seat frame. This method of construction, plus the chamfered rear legs and seat rails tenoned through the stiles, are characteristics of Philadelphia workmanship, suggesting that the maker of this chair may have trained there. The original seat cover is eighteenth-century needlework in a flamestitch pattern on canvas. A mate to this chair is owned by the Museum of Fine Arts, Boston.[2]

Description: The chair's unusually thin stiles and splat create voids that are larger than those on nos. 53–57. The cabriole front legs are fitted into the underside of the compass-shaped seat, whose slip seat frame is upholstered with its original flamestitch needlework. The rear legs are chamfered below the seat, particularly on the inside faces near the floor.

Inscriptions: The initials "AP" are cut into the top surface of the front seat rail. The chair also has a number of craftsman's marks: the rear seat rail, the right side rail, and the right knee bracket are marked with an "X"; the right front knee bracket and the front seat rail near it are marked "↓"; the left front knee bracket and the seat rail near it are marked "XI"; and finally on the left rear knee bracket and on the adjacent left seat rail the numeral "XIX" appears.

Notes: The side seat rails and rear brackets are tenoned through the stiles. The front and side seat rails are fastened with mortises and tenons. The two wooden pegs in these joints may be replacements. The front legs are fitted into this frame with a round mortise and tenon. All the brackets are secured with large roseheaded nails. The molding applied to the top of the seat frame is fastened with wooden pegs; the rear and side seat rails are fastened to the stiles with two wooden pegs. The right knee is cracked at the junction with the seat rail. The original needlework seat cover is attached to a modern backing.

Woods: Cherry; slip seat frame, soft maple and pine of the *taeda* group.

Dimensions: H. 40 11/16 in. (103.3 cm), SH. 17 1/16 in. (43.3 cm). Seat rails: W. 15 1/4 in. (38.7 cm), MW. 19 7/8 in. (50.5 cm), D. 17 7/16 in. (44.3 cm).

Bibliography: Lockwood, II, p. 58, fig. 495; Nutting,

Treasury, no. 2126; *Sack Coll.,* 1957–72, no. 198 (illus.); Randall, pp. 173–74 (illus. p. 175, fig. 136); John T. Kirk, "The Distinctive Character of Connecticut Furniture," *Antiques,* 92 (Oct. 1967), p. 527, fig. 6; Kirk, *Early Am. Furn.,* fig. 108; Kirk, *Am. Chairs,* p. 142, fig. 186.

Provenance: Ezekiel Porter (1707–75), Wethersfield, Conn.; Mrs. Gertrude Camp, Whitemarsh, Pa.; Israel Sack, Inc., New York, N.Y.; Charles L. Bybee, Houston, Tex.; Israel Sack, Inc., New York, N.Y.; The Mabel Brady Garvan Collection, 1963.10.

[1] *Conn. Chairs,* pp. 38–39.—[2] Randall, no. 136.

59

59. Roundabout Chair

Probably Connecticut, about 1760–1780

The roundabout chair form was introduced in the William and Mary period and was adapted to different stylistic modes as the eighteenth century progressed. A Connecticut origin is proposed for this example on the basis of its provenance: Dr. Irving Lyon purchased it from one of his Hartford patients, and many of the pieces he acquired in this way probably originated locally. Furthermore, the use of cherry, the simple outlines of the slightly hollowed vase-shaped splats, and the bulbous arm supports are in accord with Connecticut practice.

Description: The semi-circular arm rail and its serpentine-ended crest are supported on three vase-shaped arm supports. The two vase-shaped splats have languid outlines and are slightly hollowed. The square legs are braced by rectangular crossed stretchers.

Inscription: A paper label with writing in ink (now removed from the chair and placed in the collection's files) reads: "No. 403. / A old Corner / chair. got from / one of my patients / . . . the summer of 1880. / thoroughly repaired / and done over at Robbins Bros / and presented to my daugh / ter Mamie E. Lyon with / the wish that she always / keep it as a gift from / her father Irving W. Lyon / Nov 1880."

Notes: The crest rail is attached to the arm rail with roseheaded nails. The front arm supports come through the arm rail, whose two sections are lapped at the center. The mortise-and-tenon joints of the legs and seat rails are fastened with two square wooden pegs. The front leg is cracked at the top. Two seat ledges are replacements. The slip seat frame was originally covered with leather. The upholstery is a modern damask-weave textile.

60

Pl. 3—*Banister-back armchair, New England, 1720–1750 (no. 48).*

Pl. 4—*Queen Anne side chair, Philadelphia, about 1750 (no. 62).*

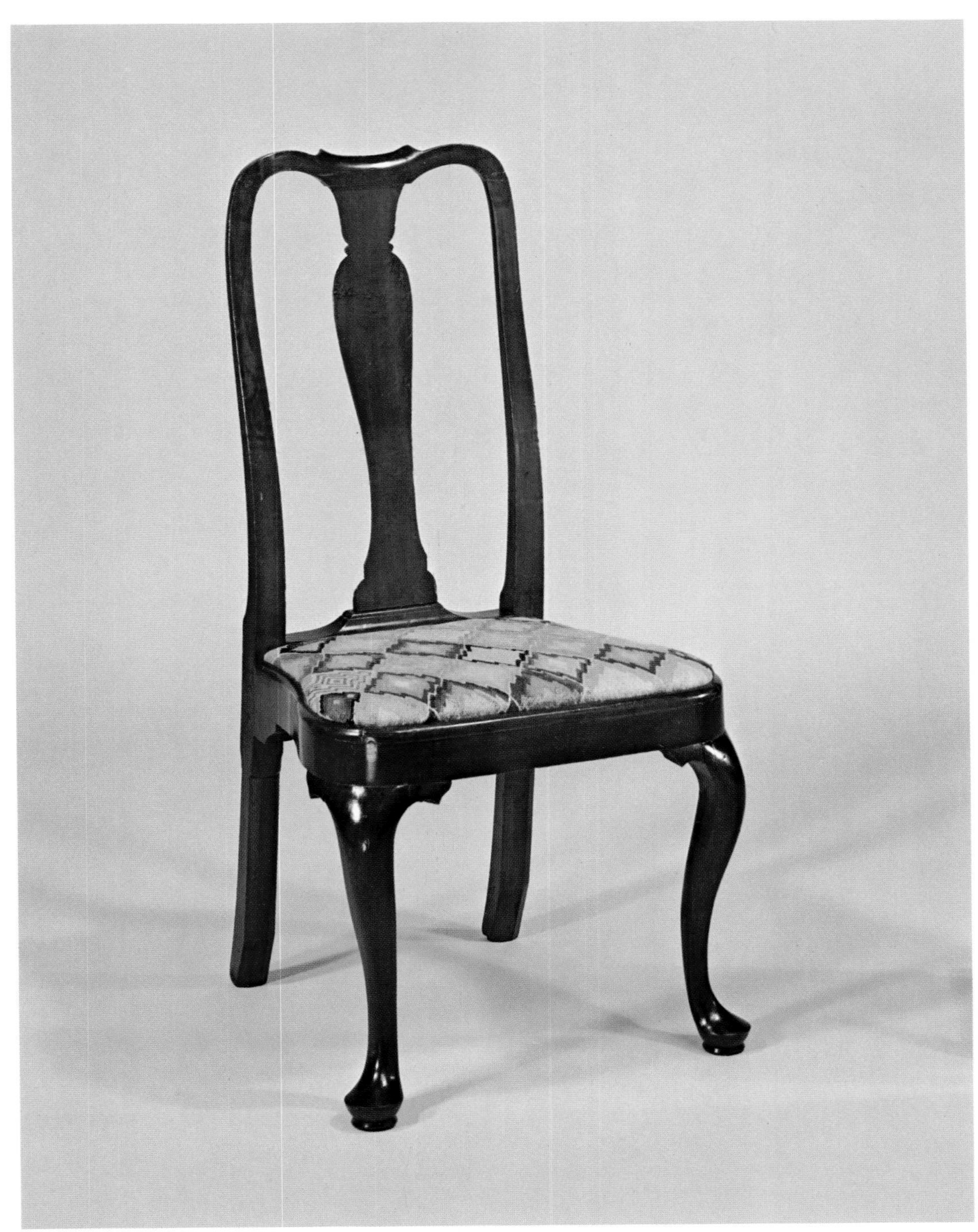

Pl. 5—*Queen Anne side chair, Wethersfield, Connecticut (no. 58).*

Pl. 6—*Queen Anne slipper chair, Philadelphia, 1750–1770 (no. 66).*

Woods: American black cherry; seat ledge, pine of the *taeda* group; slip seat frame, white pine.

Dimensions: H. 30 5/16 in. (77.0 cm), SH. 15 7/8 in. (40.3 cm). Seat rails: W. 17 7/8 in. (45.4 cm), D. 17 7/8 in. (45.4 cm).

Provenance: Irving W. Lyon, Hartford, Conn.; Mrs. John P. Penney (Mamie E. Lyon), Pittsburgh, Pa.; Francis P. Garvan, New York, N.Y.; The Mabel Brady Garvan Collection, 1930.2419.

60. Roundabout Chair

Albany area, New York, 1740–1760

The robust appearance of this chair—with thick scrolled crest rail, rounded knees, and deep, pointed shod feet—is characteristic of mid-eighteenth-century New York furniture. Cherry was often favored there and was used to make side chairs with similar feet.[1] Roundabout chairs of this type in the Queen Anne style are often attributed to the Albany area. One at Winterthur shares with this example the comparatively rare feature of a quadrant-shaped seat.[2] Related examples have also been published.[3]

Description: The unusual quadrant-shaped seat of this roundabout chair is supported by three cabriole legs ending in pointed shod feet, and a turned rear leg. The arm rail, with deep crest with serpentine ends, rests on three columnar turnings. Small, fussy serpentine curves outline the neck and bases of the vase-shaped splats.

Notes: The seat frame is made without corner blocks. The knee brackets are of double thickness and are attached with roseheaded nails. The tip of the front foot has been restored. The ends of the arm rail are constructed in such a way that the boards overlap about five inches at the back of the crest rail and only about 3/8 of an inch at the front. The crest rail is attached to the arm rail with glue; the turned end of the center arm support pierces the arm rail and fits into the crest. The seat ledges are attached with roseheaded nails, and the bases of the splats are attached to the rear seat rails with small sprigs. The upholstery is an early eighteenth-century blue silk damask, probably French.

Woods: Cherry; seat ledges, white pine.

Dimensions: H. 33 7/16 in. (84.9 cm), SH. 16 1/4 in. (41.3 cm; measured on left side of curved front rail). Seat rails: W. 32 in. (81.3 cm), D. 20 1/2 in. (52.0 cm).

Provenance: Jacob Margolis, New York, N.Y. (sale New York, Anderson Galleries, April 9–10, 1926, p. 23, no. 102); Francis P. Garvan, New York, N.Y.; The Mabel Brady Garvan Collection, 1930.2040.

---

[1] Downs, *Am. Furn.*, fig. 108.—[2] *Ibid.*, fig. 62.—[3] See *Antiques*, 11 (June 1927), cover; 64 (Dec. 1953), p. 474, fig. 2; 70 (Nov. 1956), p. 400; 75 (April 1959), p. 329.

61. Side Chair

New York, about 1745–1755

This side chair is one of a set of six which are the only American chairs known whose splats are pierced to form a cypher with the initials of their owners. The initials are thought to be those of Robert and Margaret (Beekman) Livingston, who were married in 1742. (Robert Livingston was to become a justice of the New York Supreme Court and a member of the Stamp Act Congress of 1765.) The chair has features typical of mid-eighteenth-century New York furniture: a wide horseshoe-shaped seat; large claw-and-ball feet; squared-off rear feet. The beautifully interlaced cypher corresponds to the finely engraved initials so popular on New York silver. The other chairs from the set are in the collections of The Museum of the City of New York, The Metropolitan Museum of Art, The Art Institute of Chicago, Bayou Bend (Museum of Fine Arts, Houston), and Winterthur.

Description: The splat is pierced to form a monogram of the letters R, M, and L. Between the two rounded arches of the crest rail is a seven-lobed shell with undulating outline. The outline of the upper stiles is similar to that of no. 56, but below the seat the stiles are quite different. The wood on no. 61 is pared to form thin rear legs with squared-off feet. The cabriole legs terminate in claw-and-ball feet. The tops of the legs are housed in the front corners of the compass-shaped seat.

Notes: The open front corner braces are dovetailed and nailed with roseheaded nails into the seat frame. Each of the corners of the slip seat frame has triangular braces. The corner blocks and right knee blocks are new. A 1- by 1/2-inch strip is replaced on the inner edge of the seat rail on the right side. Both rear leg brackets are new. The left stile is repaired at the foot. The front right leg was broken at the junction with the seat rails, and its inner corner is a replacement. The left knee blocks are attached with four hand-wrought nails. The pierced section of the splat is cracked and repaired at the rear; the crest rail was cracked and repaired at the junction with the splat and left stile. The upholstery is a reproduction silk damask.

61

61a

Woods: Mahogany; front corner braces and slip seat frame, white oak; blocks on slip seat frame, white pine; rear seat rail, beech.

Dimensions: H. 41 13/16 in. (106.2 cm), SH. 17 in. (43.2 cm). Seat rails: W. 18 1/8 in. (46.0 cm), MW. 22 5/16 in. (56.7 cm), D. 19 1/2 in. (49.5 cm).

Bibliography: Meyric R. Rogers, "Garvan Furniture at Yale," *The Connoisseur Year Book* 1960, p. 55, no. 4; Kirk, *Am. Chairs,* p. 112, fig. 127.

Provenance: Robert R. and Margaret B. Livingston, New York, N.Y.; Roger Bacon, Exeter, N.H.; John S. Walton, New York, N.Y.; The Mabel Brady Garvan Collection, 1952.20.2.

62. Side Chair

Philadelphia, about 1750

The S-curve—"the wavy line" celebrated by William Hogarth as the line of beauty—is basic to the Queen Anne style. On this chair (made about 1750 in Philadelphia, where at that time America's most sophisticated seating furniture was being made), the serpentine line of the crest rail, the stiles framing the intricately outlined splat, the compass-shaped seat, and the cabriole legs echo each other, as do the

62

62b

62c

volutes. Some of the curves conform to the human body, and their repetition unites the various parts. Walnut, which was both strong and easily carved with scallop shells and volutes—favorite decorative devices of the time—was the fashionable wood. Sometimes it was highly figured, as in the splat of this chair. Like other fine Philadelphia Queen Anne style chairs, this example has very small claw-and-ball feet.

Description: The bowed stiles continue their vertical course for a short distance above the seat and then become serpentine. The vase-shaped splat, with projecting cusps and lobes where the stiles curve in, has a sharply incut neck and is capped by a pair of sinuous volutes and a shell on the crest. The compass-shaped seat is supported at the front corners with cabriole legs ending in claw-and-ball feet. The knees of the legs are carved with shells and pendant husks.

Inscription: The numeral "IIII" is marked on the top of the front seat rail.

Notes: The chair has been refinished, and the slip seat frame is new. The front of the crest rail is cracked beneath the shell. The side seat rails are tenoned through the rear stiles. The rear and side seat rails are pinned to the rear stiles with two square wooden pegs, and the crest rail is pinned to the stiles. The front and side seat rails are mortised and tenoned together. The front legs are fitted into this frame with a round mortise and tenon. A molding is applied around the top edge of the seat frame. The upholstery is a reproduction silk damask.

Wood: American black walnut.

Dimensions: H. 42 in. (106.7 cm), SH. 16¾ in. (42.5 cm). Seat rails: W. 20¼ in. (51.4 cm), MW. 20¾ in. (52.7 cm), D. 16½ in. (41.9 cm).

Provenance: Gift of Mr. and Mrs. David Stockwell, Wilmington, Del., 1971.122.

63. Roundabout Chair

Philadelphia, 1740–1760

Roundabout chairs were often made to hold chamber pots, and in that case their seat rails were especially deep, as on this example. The trifid feet, the cusps on the vase-shaped splats, and the well-knuckled handholds of this chair point to an origin in the Philadelphia area.

Description: The cusps on the splats of this roundabout chair are related to those on no. 62, but the necks are not as sharply incut. The splats fill the space between the seat and the semi-circular arm rail, which rests on three elongated vase-shaped arm supports. The ends of the arm rail form scrolls as they taper off into knuckled handholds. The lower edges of the extraordinarily deep seat rails are scalloped. The four cabriole legs end in trifid feet.

63

Notes: The tulip ledges to hold the board for the chamber pot are attached with roseheaded nails. Later seat ledges are attached to the rear seat rails with cut nails. Holes in the knee brackets suggest that they were attached to the legs with roseheaded nails. The knee brackets have been glued and renailed with wire nails. The two sections of the arm rail are butted at the center. Two holes on either side of the center arm support indicate that the crest rail may have been nailed to the arm rail at one time. The splat shoes are nailed to the seat rails. The modern *gros-point* needlework illustrated has been replaced by a reproduction of mid-eighteenth-century wool damask (F. Schumacher, Peyton Randolph Damask).

Woods: American black walnut; slip seat frame, pine of the *taeda* group; seat ledges, tulip.

Dimensions: H. 32¾ in. (83.2 cm), SH. 17⅛ in. (43.5 cm). Seat rails: W. 19¹⁄₁₆ in. (48.4 cm), D. 19¹⁄₁₆ in. (48.4 cm).

Bibliography: Reifsnyder Coll., p. 123, no. 485.

Provenance: Howard Reifsnyder, Philadelphia, Pa.; Francis P. Garvan, New York, N.Y. (1929); The Mabel Brady Garvan Collection, 1930.2409.

64. Armchair

Pennsylvania, 1740–1760

A Pennsylvania origin for this chair is indicated by the pointed shoulders of the splat, concave faces of the arms and arm supports, cushioned pad feet, and stump rear legs. Examples with similar splats appear in Nutting and Downs and have often been attributed to William Savery.[1] It is unusual for chairs of this type to have the side rails tenoned through the stiles as in this example.

Description: The bowed stiles of this side chair are oval below the seat and have a flattened face with beaded edge above. The center of the round-shouldered crest rail is yoked. The voids on either side of the top of the splat are rounded shapes formed in part by the splat's pointed shoulders. The curvilinear arms, attached at mid-point on the stiles, are braced in front by ridged, C-shaped arm supports. The front edge of the square seat frame is ornamented with a double-serpentine curve. The cabriole front legs end in pad feet.

Inscriptions: The insides of the side seat rails are each marked "IIII"; the ledge on the front seat rail is marked "III".

Notes: The side seat rails are tenoned through the stiles. The seat frame is made without corner blocks, and the crest rail is not pinned to the stiles. The tenons from the stiles are visible on the inner edge at the junction with the crest rail. The arm supports are secured from inside the seat rails with nails. Large wooden pegs or dowels (two on the right side) are visible on the outside of the base of the arm supports. The tops of the arm supports are pinned to the arms with wooden pegs. The knee brackets are attached with roseheaded nails. A large dowel is visible on the rear of the stiles where the arms join, perhaps to cover

64

65

a screw fastening them together. The upholstery is an eighteenth-century yellow plain woven silk, probably French.

Woods: American black walnut; slip seat frame, pine of the *taeda* group.

Dimensions: H. 40 1/16 in. (101.8 cm), SH. 17 7/16 in. (44.3 cm). Seat rails: W. 17 3/4 in. (45.1 cm), MW. 22 1/4 in. (56.5 cm), D. 16 1/2 in. (41.9 cm).

Bibliography: Kirk, *Am. Chairs,* p. 69, fig. 47.

Provenance: Francis D. Brinton, West Chester, Pa.; Francis P. Garvan, New York, N.Y. (1929); The Mabel Brady Garvan Collection, 1930.2077a.

---

[1] See *Treasury,* nos. 2124 and 2199, and Downs, *Am. Furn.,* fig. 33.

65. Side Chair

Pennsylvania, 1740–1760

Except for scale, this side chair is nearly identical with the preceding armchair; it has the narrower back and the splat with shallower base usual in a side chair. Surely the two were made in the same shop (and perhaps were even part of the same set), since the style of numbering is similar and the type is rare. Few Pennsylvania chairs have pad feet, yoke crests, or vase-shaped splats of such simple outline.

Description: See no. 64.

Inscriptions: The inside of the front seat rail is marked "II", and the slip seat frame is marked "I".

Notes: The bottom of the left rear leg has been repaired with wooden pegs, and the bottom of the right rear leg is a replacement. The upholstery is an eighteenth-century yellow plain woven silk, probably French.

Woods: American black walnut; slip seat frame, cherry.

Dimensions: H. 38 3/4 in. (98.4 cm), SH. 17 1/2 in. (44.4 cm). Seat rails: W. 14 5/8 in. (37.1 cm), MW. 19 1/8 in. (48.6 cm), D. 15 3/8 in. (39.1 cm).

Bibliography: Kirk, *Early Am. Furn.,* fig. 3.

Provenance: Francis D. Brinton, West Chester, Pa.; Francis P. Garvan, New York, N.Y. (1929); The Mabel Brady Garvan Collection, 1930.2077c.

Later Expressions

OCCASIONALLY IN NEW ENGLAND, but more typically in Philadelphia, chairs of the type pictured in this section are found. Their square seat frames and serpentine-shaped crest rails with flared ears depart from the curvilinear outlines and self-contained design of earlier Queen Anne forms. Because those two elements moved toward the conception of rococo chairs, chairs of this type are generally assigned a somewhat later date.

66. Slipper Chair

Philadelphia, 1750–1770

In 1928 William M. Hornor, Jr., attributed this slipper chair to William Savery on the basis of its close relationship to an example with a Savery label now at Winterthur.[1] However, other than the fact that both chairs have cut-outs on their crests and trifid front feet, their features bear little comparison. The inclination to attribute this example to Savery may also have been strengthened by the lambrequin motif on the knee, found on a Savery family lowboy.[2] In general, a comparison of this example with other documented Savery chairs offers little basis for the Savery attribution.[3] This chair easily surpasses the documented chairs in the skillfulness of its execution. The documented Savery chairs have crest rails and splats with languid outlines and stiles with flat faces, and thus lack the animation found in the details of this example. The subtlety with which the maker has molded and shaped the stiles—they have a beaded edge which diminishes as it reaches the cresting

66

rail—can be matched by few chairs of the period. A closely related example is illustrated by Nutting,[4] and an example without the cut-out appears in Hornor.[5]

Description: The bowed stiles are oval below the seat; above it their faces are molded and have a beaded edge which narrows as the stile approaches the crest rail. The beaded edge continues around the ear of the crest and joins with that outlining the serpentine-shaped crest. An oblong cut-out with circular ends provides a handhold at the center of the crest. Prominent scrolls at the top of the splat contrast with its narrow waist and serpentine base. The square seat is supported by short cabriole legs with a lambrequin motif carved on the knee. The legs terminate in trifid feet.

Inscription: The top of the ledge on the front seat rail is marked "X".

Notes: The joints of the front legs and seat frame have been repaired. The slip seat frame is a replacement. The side seat rails are tenoned through the stiles. The splat shoe is attached with small sprigs. The left side knee bracket has been replaced; the remaining knee brackets are attached with roseheaded nails. The heavy horizontal-grain, open-corner braces (attached with cut nails) are old but not original. The left rear corner block has been reattached. The damask textile illustrated has been replaced by a reproduction of a mid-eighteenth-century rose moreen with a stamped pattern (Scalamandré, 1945–1).

Woods: American black walnut; corner blocks, tulip.

Dimensions: H. 36¼ in. (92.1 cm), SH. 13¾ in. (34.9 cm). Seat rails: W. 16⅞ in. (42.9 cm), MW. 21 in. (53.3 cm), D. 17 5/16 in. (44.0 cm).

Bibliography: William M. Hornor, Jr., "William Savery Chairmaker and Joiner," *The Pennsylvania Museum Bulletin,* XXIII, 118 (Feb. 1928), pp. 14–20, fig. 8; *Reifsnyder Coll.,* p. 85, no. 361; Kirk, *Am. Chairs,* p. 77, fig. 63.

Provenance: Howard Reifsnyder, Philadelphia, Pa.; Francis P. Garvan, New York, N.Y. (1929); The Mabel Brady Garvan Collection, 1930.2406.

[1] See Hornor, "William Savery Chairmaker and Joiner" (see Bibliography above). The chair at Winterthur is in Downs, *Am. Furn.,* no. 39.—[2] *The Pennsylvania Museum Bulletin,* 20 (Jan. 1925), p. 62.—[3] See Hornor, pl. 314; Comstock, no. 176; *Sack Coll.,* 1957–72, II, no. 1077.—[4] *Treasury,* no. 2173.—[5] Pl. 318.

67. Side Chair

Philadelphia, 1750–1770

Rarely is such a fine splat found on a Philadelphia transitional chair; the bold lines of the carved volutes and beading define the upper half, while the lower part is more playfully outlined by two lively curves. A chair with a similar splat, without beading, has been illustrated.[1] In writing about a chair of this type at Winterthur, Joseph Downs cited a drawing of April 1766 sketched by the Philadelphia joiners Jonathan Shoemaker and Samuel Mickle.[2] This document offers an approximate date for the Yale chair.

Description: The bowed stiles on this chair, unlike those on no. 66, are not molded. The beaded edge continues onto the ear of the crest rail, which is modeled with two flaring grooves. A beaded edge outlines the two serpentine curves flanking the shell at the center of the crest. On the shoulders of the splat are carved volutes with beading carried halfway down the splat. The square seat is supported at the front corners with cabriole legs ending in trifid feet.

Inscription: The top of the ledge on the front seat and the slip seat frame rail are marked "V".

Notes: The corner blocks are new. The side seat rails have been repinned to the stiles. The side seat rails are tenoned through the stiles. The splat shoe is attached with square wooden pegs. The knee brackets are attached with roseheaded nails. An unusual 3/8-inch facing of soft wood on the inside of the rear seat rail appears to be original. The upholstery illustrated has been replaced by a reproduction of a mid-eighteenth-century rose moreen with a stamped pattern (Scalamandré, 1945–1).

Woods: American black walnut; slip seat frame, pine of the *taeda* group; facing on inside rear seat rail, southeastern American white cedar.

Dimensions: H. 40 7/16 in. (102.7 cm), SH. 17 1/16 in. (43.3 cm). Seat rails: W. 16 1/2 in. (41.9 cm), MW. 21 5/8 in. (54.9 cm), D. 16 15/16 in. (43.0 cm).

Bibliography: Nutting, *Treasury,* no. 2214; Meyric R. Rogers, "Garvan Furniture at Yale," *The Connoisseur Year Book* 1960, p. 59, fig. 11.

Provenance: E. F. Sanderson, Moor's End, Nantucket, Mass. (sale New York, B. Altman & Co., 1928); Francis P. Garvan, New York, N.Y.; The Mabel Brady Garvan Collection, 1930.2491.

[1] *Sack Coll.,* 1957–72, II, no. 924.—[2] Downs, *Am. Furn.,* no. 121.

68. Armchair

Philadelphia, 1750–1770

This armchair—with its beautifully shaped serpentine arms and gentle play of curved lines between the crest and splat—fully commands the space in which it stands. The prominent scrolled shoulders and cusps at mid-point on the splat are similar to those on no. 63, a roundabout chair. The two chairs also share an undulating curve on the lower edge of the seat rails, and a trifid foot formed by two concave hollows with rounded tops. Here the similarities end, however, for no. 63 is stolid and boxy, in contrast to this example, which has an impressive presence.

Description: An exceptional feature of this chair is the curvilinear arm whose knuckled handhold is clearly delineated by the scrolled end. In other respects the outlines of the stiles and crest rail are similar to those of no. 67, but

67

68

they lack the clarity achieved through the use of beaded edges. The seat rails are slightly deeper than normal and the one in front is cut with an elongated serpentine curve. The cabriole front legs end in trifid feet; the rear legs are oval.

Notes: The corner blocks are new. The side seat rails are tenoned through the stiles. The right front leg has been repaired at the junction with the seat. Square nail holes and shadows on the inner faces of the seat rails indicate that the chair was fitted with supports for a chamber pot at one time. The inlays on the left rear stile and on the underside of the seat rail suggest the leg was broken and that the iron brace used to repair it was subsequently removed. The arm supports are fastened to the side seat rails from the inside with old screws. Large round dowels or pegs appear on the backs of the stiles at the junction with the arms, which are pinned to the arm supports from the outside with square wooden pegs. The knee brackets are attached with nails and glue. The joints of the seat rails and the stiles are pinned only at the back. The damask-weave upholstery illustrated has been replaced by a blue rayon, cotton, and linen fabric (Brunschwig & Fils, 14150.00/25).

Woods: American black walnut; slip seat frame, pine of the *taeda* group.

Dimensions: H. 40⅛ in. (101.9 cm), SH. 16¹³⁄₁₆ in. (42.7 cm). Seat rails: W. 18¹⁄₁₆ in. (45.9 cm), MW. 23⅛ in. (58.7 cm), D: 17⅝ in. (44.8 cm).

Bibliography: Nutting, *Treasury,* no. 2213; Kirk, *Am. Chairs,* p. 75, fig. 60.

Provenance: E. F. Sanderson, Moor's End, Nantucket, Mass. (sale New York, B. Altman & Co., 1928); Francis P. Garvan, New York, N.Y.; The Mabel Brady Garvan Collection, 1930.2545.

69

69. Side Chair

Philadelphia, 1750–1770

Additional serpentine curves enliven the outline of the splat of this chair, producing a rhythm similar to that found on the splats of some of the best Philadelphia Queen Anne style chairs (such as no. 62).[1] Here the neck of the vase is described by serpentine curves and there is an extra serpentine curve above the cusp.

Description: The parts of this chair exhibit a tautness of line and paring away of materials not found in nos. 66–68. The shells at the tops of the slim cabriole legs are flanked by small scrolls on the knee brackets. A pendant shell appears at the front of the square seat frame. The cusps and scrolls outlining the splat very nearly duplicate those on no. 62. The edges of the stiles and crest rail are bordered with an incised line. At the center of the crest rail is a ruffled shell with pendant, asymmetrical foliage.

Inscriptions: The ledge on the front seat rail is marked "VII", and the slip seat frame is marked "VI".

Notes: The side seat rails are tenoned through the stiles. The seat frame is made without corner blocks. The mortise-and-tenon joints of the front legs and seat rails, and also those of the side seat rails and rear stiles, are fastened with single wooden pegs. The rear seat rail is fastened to the stiles with two wooden pegs. Each knee bracket is held in place with two roseheaded nails. The shell on the front seat rail is applied. The splat shoe is held in place with small nails. The upholstery is a modern French silk damask.

Woods: American black walnut; slip seat frame, pine of the *taeda* group.

Dimensions: H. 39⅞ in. (101.3 cm), SH. 16¹⁵⁄₁₆ in. (43.0 cm). Seat rails: W. 16⁷⁄₁₆ in. (41.8 cm), MW. 21¼ in. (54.0 cm), D. 17½ in. (44.4 cm).

Bibliography: Bondome, "What Chairs for the Dining Room," *Antiques,* 13 (June 1928), p. 500, fig. 5; *Reifsnyder Coll.,* p. 200, no. 640; Rogers, p. 54, fig. 29; Kirk, *Early Am. Furn.,* fig. 140; Kirk, *Am. Chairs,* p. 76, fig. 61.

Provenance: Howard Reifsnyder, Philadelphia, Pa.; Francis P. Garvan, New York, N.Y.; The Mabel Brady Garvan Collection, 1930.2635.

[1] See Hornor, pl. 79, 82, 83; Kirk, *Am. Chairs,* fig. 56.

70. Side Chair

Philadelphia, 1750–1770

"Eagles foot & shell on the knee" was the way in which seven chairs in the inventory of the Boston upholsterer Theodore Wheelwright were described in 1750.[1] The description might also have been applied to the Philadelphia chair illustrated here. Whereas in England the claw-and-ball foot appeared on furniture as early as the second decade of the eighteenth century, in America this feature was probably introduced later, and it is generally thought to be characteristic of the mid-century rococo style. Hornor quotes a reference of 1745 to "an *old* Pillar & *Claw* Mahogy Table," and states that claw-and-ball feet were "several times referred to in 1748 as more or less of a novelty."[2] A chair not unlike the one illustrated here was sold by the cabinetmaker John Elliott to Charles Norris between 1755 and 1756.[3] The contoured splat, boldly scrolled ears, and well-articulated feet contribute significantly to the superior quality of this mid-eighteenth-century Philadelphia chair.

Description: A feature this chair shares with no. 69 is the use of small scrolls flanking the shells on the knees. Here the motif is also repeated at the center of the crest rail. The curve of the cabriole legs with their claw-and-ball feet is similarly reminiscent of the other chair. An incised line silhouettes the stiles and the large, flaring ears. The splat is contoured in a long serpentine shape.

70

Inscriptions: The top of the front seat ledge is marked "I", and the slip seat frame is marked "IIII".

Notes: The side seat rails are tenoned through the stiles. The front corner blocks are two pieces of wood with vertical grain. The rear corner blocks are new. The seat rails and legs are fastened with two square wooden pegs (with the exception of the joint of the left side seat rail and rear stile, which has only one peg). Each knee bracket is attached with two roseheaded nails and glue. The splat shoe is nailed to the rear seat rail. The modern silk damask illustrated has been replaced by a blue-green wool velvet (Brunschwig & Fils, 3648.00/7).

Woods: American black walnut; slip seat frame, pine of the *taeda* group; fronts of corner blocks, Atlantic white cedar; rear parts of corner blocks, pine of the *taeda* group.

Dimensions: H. 40½ in. (102.9 cm), SH. 17⅜ in. (44.1 cm). Seat rails: W. 16¹⁄₁₆ in. (40.8 cm), MW. 20⅝ in. (52.4 cm), D. (to the left to avoid dip in skirt) 15¹³⁄₁₆ in. (40.2 cm).

Bibliography: Meyric R. Rogers, "The Mabel Brady Garvan Collection of Furniture," *Yale Alumni Magazine,* 25 (Jan. 1962), p. 8 (illus.); Kirk, *Am. Chairs,* fig. 64.

Provenance: E. Platt, Wallingford, Pa.; Francis P. Garvan, New York, N.Y. (1929); The Mabel Brady Garvan Collection, 1930.2411a.

[1] Lyon, p. 161.—[2] Hornor, pp. 38–39.—[3] *Ibid.*, p. 133, pl. 68.

71. Side Chair

Philadelphia, 1750–1770

This chair is reputed to have been owned by George Washington, and is identical with an example at Mount Vernon.[1] Stylistically it is similar to Philadelphia chairs. Washington is known to have purchased furniture in Philadelphia when he lived there, and he continued to do so after he retired to Mount Vernon. In one instance he wrote Colonel Clement Biddle of Philadelphia: "I will thank you to pay Samuel Powel, Esq. for a chair which he was so good as to produce for me as a pattern."[2] Apparently Washington was planning to have the Powel chair copied by Virginia craftsmen. The chair illustrated here belongs to a group of Philadelphia chairs on which relaxed lines are used to describe the crest rail and splat. Various examples of this type can be found in the literature.[3]

71

Description: The fluid serpentine curves outlining the splat and crest rail lack the tautness and sharp contrasts of those on nos. 66–70. The trifid feet on the cabriole legs are formed by three raised tongues somewhat in the manner of the foot on no. 69.

Inscription: The front rail of the slip seat frame is marked "MIC".

Notes: The toes of the left foot were restored in 1961, and the rear corner blocks are replaced. The side seat rails are tenoned through the stiles. The quarter-round front corner blocks consist of two pieces of wood with vertical grain. The crest rail is pinned to the stiles with square wooden pegs. The knee brackets are attached with roseheaded nails (the original nails are missing from the side knee brackets). The splat shoe is attached with small sprigs. The modern silk damask upholstery illustrated has been replaced by a reproduction of mid-eighteenth-century yellow moreen (Scalamandré, 1946–3).

Woods: American black walnut; corner blocks, Atlantic white cedar and pine of the *taeda* group; slip seat frame, pine of the *taeda* group.

Dimensions: H. 37⅝ in. (95.6 cm), SH. 16⅝ in. (42.2 cm). Seat rails: W. 14⅞ in. (37.8 cm), MW. 19¾ in. (50.2 cm), D. 16 in. (40.6 cm).

Bibliography: Kirk, *Early Am. Furn.*, fig. 141.

Provenance: Henkel's, Philadelphia, Pa.; Francis P. Garvan, New York, N.Y.; The Mabel Brady Garvan Collection, 1930.2414.

[1] Iverson, p. 202, fig. 157.—[2] Hornor, p. 206.—[3] *Sack Coll.*, 1957–72, II, no. 1075; Hornor, pl. 240, 313; Nutting, *Treasury*, no. 2201.

72. Side Chair

Philadelphia area, or possibly New Jersey, 1775–1800

The maker of this chair appears to have been fascinated with arcs, using them to outline the splat, ears, and crest rail. The graceful flow of those partial circles into one another contrasts with the boldly rippling surface of the curly maple. A chair illustrated by Miller has a splat and crest rail of similar silhouette, but it has cabriole front legs with shells carved on the knees, suggesting that it is of Philadelphia origin[1]—as this one may be too. However, curly maple is a wood not commonly associated with urban workshops and may indicate the chair originated in a more rural locale, perhaps even in New Jersey.

Description: The solid splat of this curly maple side chair, one of a set of five, at Yale, is outlined by three opposed arcs connected by small beads. Circular shapes are repeated on the ears of the double-serpentine crest rail. Square front legs support the seat; the four stretchers are rectangular.

Inscription: Four crescent-shaped gouge marks appear on the rear seat rail.

Notes: The quarter-round rear corner blocks are of one piece of wood with vertical grain. The front corner blocks are replacements. Single square wooden pegs fasten the rear seat rail to the rear stiles. The inner corners of the front legs are chamfered, and a slight chamfer appears on the inner corners of the rear legs. The upholstery is early nineteenth-century horsehair.

Woods: Soft maple; rear corner blocks, mahogany.

Dimensions: H. 38½ in. (97.8 cm), SH. 16⅞ in. (42.9 cm). Seat rails: W. 17 11/16 in. (44.9 cm), MW. 21¾ in. (55.2 cm), D. 18 in. (45.7 cm).

Bibliography: Kirk, *Early Am. Furn.*, fig. 171.

Provenance: Jacob Margolis, New York, N.Y.; Francis P. Garvan, New York, N.Y.; The Mabel Brady Garvan Collection, 1930.2407d.

[1] Miller, I, no. 91.

72

Vernacular Expressions

COMBINING AS THEY DO the block-and-turned legs and double-ball stretchers of earlier forms with the serpentine stiles and vase-shaped splats of the Queen Anne style, chairs of the type represented in this section have often been described as transitional. Taking their inspiration for the design of the back from that of the standard New England Queen Anne chair (nos. 53–54), they were probably introduced at the same time, but were a cheaper alternative. They were more economical to produce than their black walnut counterparts, since they were made of maple, stained or painted, and bottomed with rush. Another basic difference is that the front legs of the walnut chairs are framed into the seat rails, whereas the front legs of these rest on blocks at the front corners of the seat frame in a stilt-like manner.

Assigning accurate regional origins to these chairs, which appear to have been manufactured throughout New England, is difficult. Some individual interpretations exist, such as the chairs made by the Gaines family of Massachusetts and New Hampshire. Traditionally the dating of these chairs has corresponded with that of the standard New England chair, but more recently the suggestion has been made that they were manufactured until the end of the eighteenth century.[1] As yet, evidence to verify their period of production has not been forthcoming. No. 85 suggests that the model was updated as stylistic traditions changed. In New England this chair filled the need for economical seating and may be compared in this sense with the Delaware River Valley slat-back chairs that seem to have served the same purpose in the Philadelphia area (nos. 18–20). By the second half of the eighteenth century, the versatile windsor chair probably eclipsed this form in popularity.

[1] Barry A. Greenlaw, *New England Furniture at Williamsburg* (Charlottesville, 1974), p. 51, no. 41.

73. Side Chair

New England, 1730–1750

Certain details make this chair a somewhat unusual example of the type. The lower turnings on the legs are a ball form rather than an ogee. The ball turnings on the front stretcher are slightly elongated and the splat is somewhat broader than usual.

Description: The bowed stiles have beaded edges above the rush seat. The beading continues on the two arcs of the crest rail that flank the yoked center, which is bordered by beveled ridges. The splat is vase-shaped. The front corners of the seat are supported by a reel-and-pear-shaped turning. Ball turnings appear between the blocks above the Spanish front feet. The double-ball-and-ring-turned front stretcher is complemented by rectangular stretchers at the sides, and a bulbous rear stretcher.

Notes: The recent black paint covers yellow, red, and buff paint. Tack holes in the underside of the rush and in the seat rails indicate that the seat was once upholstered over the rush. The side stretchers are pinned to the legs, and the lower rail of the back is pinned to the stiles. Square wooden pins secure the crest rail to the stiles and splat.

Woods: Soft maple; front seat rail, beech; rear and side seat rails, ash.

Dimensions: H. 41 in. (104.1 cm), SH. 17 13/16 in. (45.2 cm). Seat rails: W. 13 5/8 in. (34.6 cm), MW. 18 3/4 in. (47.6 cm), D. 13 7/8 in. (35.2 cm).

Provenance: Frank McCarthy, Longmeadow, Mass.; Francis P. Garvan, New York, N.Y.; The Mabel Brady Garvan Collection, 1930.2422b.

73

74. Armchair

New England, 1730–1750

This armchair and its accompanying side chair, no. 75, were both in the collection of Irving W. Lyon, Hartford, Connecticut. The side chair, in particular, is similar to a chair from the collection of H. W. Erving, which Nutting called Connecticut.[1] With their Connecticut provenances, these chairs may prove in the future to be the nucleus of a Connecticut regional type, but at present they are designated simply as hailing from New England.

Description: In basic form this armchair is essentially like no. 73, but the details—particularly of the turnings—differ. The serpentine arms thrust outward beyond the elongated, vase-shaped arm supports, and end in scrolled handholds. The two pairs of turnings alternating with blocks on the front legs repeat the same form, which is an ogee shape sitting on a ridged ring. The double-ball-and-ring front stretcher has much smaller tapered ends than those on the preceding chair. The side stretchers are a double-ball form within the ring, and the rear stretcher is a double-vase form.

Notes: The chair has been refinished, but traces of red paint remain. The front feet and bottoms of the stiles have been replaced. The bottom of the central ring on the front stretcher is missing. Wooden pegs secure the arms to the stiles and arm supports. The crest rail is pegged to the stiles. Scored lines mark the placement of the stretchers, seat rails, arms, and lower back rails.

Wood: Soft maple.

Dimensions: H. 41 15/16 in. (106.5 cm), SH. 17 in. (43.2 cm). Seat rails: W. 15 1/4 in. (38.7 cm), MW. 21 1/2 in. (54.6 cm), D. 14 7/8 in. (37.8 cm).

Provenance: Irving W. Lyon, Hartford, Conn.; Francis P. Garvan, New York, N.Y.; The Mabel Brady Garvan Collection, 1930.2029a.

---

[1] Nutting, *Treasury,* no. 2100.

74

75. Side Chair

New England, 1730–1750

This side chair is a companion to no. 74, but the line describing the termination of the lower ogee turnings on its front legs is not as crisply articulated as that on the armchair. Furthermore, the turnings on the right

75

76

77

front leg of the side chair are not identical with those on its left. Such variations in execution of handmade parts is to be expected.

Description: The turning at the top of the front legs is an ogee whose profile tapers to form a pear-like shape. The side stretchers are paired, and the upper ones are thin, with an elongated double-vase-and-reel turning at the center.

Notes: Traces of old green paint appear under later stain and varnish. Square wooden pegs were used to secure the lower back rail and crest rail to the stiles. Scored lines mark the placement of the stretchers. About fifteen worm holes are visible along the legs and stretchers.

Woods: Soft maple; side and rear stretchers, hickory.

Dimensions: H. 40½ in. (102.9 cm), SH. 17¼ in. (43.8 cm). Seat rails: W. 13⅞ in. (35.2 cm), MW. 18¼ in. (46.4 cm), D. 13¹⁵⁄₁₆ in. (35.4 cm).

Provenance: Irving W. Lyon, Hartford, Conn.; Francis P. Garvan, New York, N.Y.; The Mabel Brady Garvan Collection, 1930.2029b.

76. Side Chair

New England, 1730–1750

The practice of streamlining features and the use of cherry wood are often associated with Connecticut craftsmen, but these factors alone are not sufficient to assign a place of origin. Upon the basis of its slender splat, this chair was previously thought to have come from Connecticut. Further, microanalysis of the wood has now revealed it to be cherry, not maple, as formerly assumed.[1] However, the attribution of origin must remain general. The unusual flattened ball turnings may ultimately prove to be the clue to the chair's specific regional origin.

Description: The shoulder on the splat of this chair is rounder than that on no. 75 and the line of the serpentine curve that defines the waist is more exaggerated. The ogee turnings on the legs are heavy toward the bottom, and the ball turnings on the stretchers have been transformed into flattened discs.

Notes: The chair has been refinished, but traces of red paint remain. Scored lines mark the placement of the stretchers, seat rails, and lower back rail. The crest rail is pegged to the stiles.

Wood: Cherry.

Dimensions: H. 40 15/16 in. (104.0 cm), SH. 18 1/16 in. (45.9 cm). Seat rails: W. 13 13/16 in. (35.1 cm), MW. 18¼ in. (46.4 cm), D. 14 1/16 in (35.7 cm).

Exhibitions: Conn. Furn., p. 125, no. 226.

Bibliography: Homer E. Keyes, "A Study in Differences," *Antiques*, 22 (July 1932), pp. 6–7, figs. 1–6; "Living With Antiques," *Antiques*, 45 (April 1944), p. 191 (illus.).

Provenance: Gift of C. Sanford Bull, Middlebury, Conn., 1953.50.8.

[1] *Conn. Furn.*, p. 125, no. 226.

77. Armchair

New England, 1730–1750

The style of the arm of this chair (and of no. 74) echoes earlier American banister-back and leather chairs, and European caned chairs.[1] There are many variations in the literature of such vase-splat armchairs with concave arms whose upper surfaces are modeled to form a ridge flanked by soft hollows ending in scrolled handholds with volutes.[2] Invariably the arms rest on vase-shaped arm supports, many more beautifully articulated than those found here. These chairs are ascribed to many areas of New England. This one is unusual in that the seat was designed to be upholstered in leather, not wrapped with rush.

Description: Although carved volutes flank the handholds, the overall form of the arms lacks the sweep and movement of those on no. 74. Here, as on no. 76, the ogee turnings are heavier toward the bottom than those on the first chairs in this series.

Notes: Traces of old red paint can be found on the surface. The left upper corner of the splat and the bottoms of the stiles are replacements. The crest rail may have been shortened. The seat recently has been reupholstered in brown leather. Scored lines mark the placement of the stretchers and lower rail in the back. The side stretchers are pegged to the legs; the crest rail is pegged to the stiles.

Wood: Soft maple.

Dimensions: H. 40¼ in. (102.2 cm), SH. 17 in. (43.2 cm). Seat rails: W. 17 15/16 in. (45.6 cm), MW. 22¼ in. (56.5 cm), D. 17⅜ in. (44.1 cm).

Provenance: Frank McCarthy, Longmeadow, Mass.; Francis P. Garvan, New York, N.Y.; The Mabel Brady Garvan Collection, 1930.2426.

[1] Nutting, *Treasury*, nos. 1979 and 1982.—[2] Downs, *Am. Furn.*, no. 23; Greenlaw, nos. 43 and 44; *Conn. Furn.*, no. 225; Bishop, nos. 73 and 76; *Sack Coll.*, 1957–72, I, no. 375; Nutting, *Treasury*, no. 2103.

78

78. Roundabout Chair

New England, 1730–1750

The attractive grained decoration on this roundabout chair covers the cut nails used to reattach the splat shoes and bands around the seat rails, and was therefore probably added sometime in the nineteenth century. Previously the chair had been painted a reddish brown. Similar ring-and-vase-turned stretchers appear on a set of chairs found in Amesbury, Massachusetts, and now in the collection of Mary Allis, and on examples illustrated by Nutting and Bishop.[1]

Description: The semi-circular arm rail with its attached, serpentine-ended crest rests on three elongated vase-shaped arm supports. Two vase-shaped splats fill the space between the basswood seat and the arm rail. The ogee-turned legs end in Spanish feet with the exception of the rear leg, which has a bulb-shaped foot. A pair of stretchers with double elongated-vase turnings is at each side. The ogee turnings of the legs rest on scotia moldings rather than on the ridged rings found on the preceding chairs, nos. 74–77.

Notes: Old reddish-brown paint is under the cream and brown graining (the latter was probably added in the nineteenth century). The center of the arm rail was reglued in 1961. The front Spanish foot has been split and repaired with two round wooden pegs. The bands applied to the outside of the rear seat rails and the splat shoes are attached with cut nails. Square wooden pegs were used to fasten the outside arm supports to the semi-circular arm rail. The braces at the tops of the splats are fastened with roseheaded nails; four such nails are used to attach the crest rail to the semi-circular arm rail, which is made of two pieces butted at the center arm support.

Wood: Soft maple.

Dimensions: H. 30⅜ in. (77.2 cm), SH. 15 15/16 in. (40.5 cm). Seat rails: W. 16⅝ in. (42.2 cm), D. 17 in. (43.2 cm).

Provenance: Jacob Margolis, New York, N.Y. (sale New York, Anderson Galleries, April 3–4, 1925); Francis P. Garvan, New York, N.Y.; The Mabel Brady Garvan Collection, 1930.2434.

[1] *Treasury,* nos. 2092 and 2101; Bishop, no. 79.

79. Side Chair

New England, 1730–1750

There is one group of vase-splat chairs with block-and-turned legs whose general elements were executed in the individualistic manner seen in this chair.[1] The edges of the front legs are chamfered; the tops of the round pad feet end with a collar; and the ends of the stretchers have a minimal amount of taper; the centers of the side and rear stretchers are ridged and grooved; the high-shouldered splat has a flared neck. A chair from Hampton Falls, New Hampshire, with similar details on the legs and stretchers perhaps offers a clue to the place of origin.[2]

Description: The absence of beading on the stiles and carving on the crest rail enhances the graceful, curvilinear back. Chamfered corners appear on the blocks of the front legs, which are also decorated with pairs of ogee turnings resting on ovolo moldings. The front legs terminate in pad feet with ring-like collars. The ball-and-ring-turned front stretcher is complemented at the sides by bulbous turnings with a central groove and tapered ends. The rear stretcher does not have the additional turnings at the ends.

Notes: Red paint covers old black and yellow paint. The front of the right foot has been restored. The seat is a replacement. The crest rail is pinned to the stiles with wooden pegs.

Woods: Maple; front seat rail, birch.

Dimensions: H. 40⅛ in. (101.9 cm), SH. 16⅝ in. (42.2 cm). Seat rails: W. 13⅞ in. (35.2 cm), MW. 18⅛ in. (46.0 cm), D. 14 in. (35.6 cm).

Provenance: R. S. Somerville, New York, N.Y.; Francis P. Garvan, New York, N.Y. (1929); The Mabel Brady Garvan Collection, 1930.2446.

[1] For other chairs with these details see *Antiques,* 92 (Dec. 1967), p. 833; Nutting, *Treasury,* nos. 2109 and 2110; *Sack Coll.,* 1957–72, I, no.

79

251 (see also Kirk, *Early Am. Furn.*, fig. 112) and I, no. 482; and chairs owned by Bob Spencer, Essex, Connecticut; Historic Deerfield; and the Cape Ann Scientific, Literary and Historical Association, Gloucester.—[2] *Sack Coll.*, 1957–72, III, no. 1372.

80. Roundabout Chair

New England, 1730–1750

With its slim, columnar-turned arm supports, curvilinear splats, and four boldly turned front stretchers, this is an exceptionally dynamic chair. The stretchers, pad feet, ogee turnings on the legs, and neatly chamfered edges of the front legs are reminiscent of no. 79, and despite the differences (noted in the description), this chair belongs in the same general group. The diamond-shaped seat, shorter from front to back than from side to side, is unusual. Related roundabout chairs at Winterthur and in a private collection have been published,[1] and an unpublished example is at the Cape Ann Scientific, Literary and Historical Association.

80

Description: Many details are similar to those on no. 79. However, the ogee turnings rest on a scotia molding and the serpentine neck of the splat has a rounder shoulder.

Notes: The black paint covers red; the white paint on the seat is probably not original. The splats were once outlined with gold decoration. The right splat shoe has been repaired. The ends of the semi-circular arm rail are lapped in the center. The tops of the arm supports are pinned to the arm rail. The splat shoes are attached with cut nails.

Woods: Hard maple; soft maple; birch.

Dimensions: H. 30¼ in. (76.8 cm), SH. 16⅛ in. (41.0 cm). Seat rails: W. 17 in. (43.2 cm), D. 17³⁄₁₆ in. (43.7 cm).

Provenance: Charles R. Morson, New York, N.Y.; Francis P. Garvan, New York, N.Y. (1928); The Mabel Brady Garvan Collection, 1930.2292.

[1] Lockwood, II, fig. 518; *Antiques*, 66 (Nov. 1954), p. 378; for the example at Winterthur see Bishop, no. 116.

81. Side Chair

New England, 1775–1800

A quarter-century may separate this chair from no. 79. In that period many of the elements which contributed to the vitality of the earlier chair were stripped away. Yet enough of the details remain—the chamfered edges of the blocks, turned pad feet with collars, central ridges on the side stretchers—to suggest they belong to the same general school.

Description: The chamfered edges of the front legs, turned pad feet, and turned stretchers with central groove recall details on nos. 79 and 80. The serpentine-shaped crest rail ends in flared ears.

Notes: The chair has been refinished, but traces of red and black paint remain. The crest rail is pinned to the stiles and splat; the tops of the front legs are pinned to the front seat rail. Scored lines on the rear stiles mark the placement of the side and rear stretchers. Nail holes on the undersides of the seat rails indicate that the rush seat was once covered by upholstery.

Wood: Soft maple.

Dimensions: H. 39¹⁵⁄₁₆ in. (101.4 cm), SH. 17⅛ in. (43.5 cm). Seat rails: W. 13⅝ in. (34.6 cm), MW. 18³⁄₁₆ in. (46.2

81

cm), D. 13⅝ in. (34.6 cm).

Bibliography: Miller, I. pp. 143–44 (illus. p. 145, no. 82).

Provenance: Jacob Margolis, New York, N.Y.; Francis P. Garvan, New York, N.Y. (1923); The Mabel Brady Garvan Collection, 1930.2615a.

82. Side Chair

New Jersey, 1730–1750

Although chairs like this are generally thought of as a New England type, the unusual square front legs and extra-large front stretcher may be New Jersey attributes. When this chair was acquired by the Yale University Art Gallery in 1930 its place of origin was described as New Jersey. In recent years its inclusion in two exhibitions of New Jersey furniture has continued that tradition.

Description: The square front legs terminating in Spanish feet and having an ogee turning at the top are the unique features. The ball-and-ring-turned front stretcher is unusually large and contrasts with the thin double-vase-turned stretchers and rectangular lower stretchers at the sides.

Notes: Crazed varnish appears over the old reddish-brown finish.

Woods: American black cherry; seat rails, hickory; stretchers, soft maple.

Dimensions: H. 40¹³⁄₁₆ in. (103.7 cm), SH. 17¹⁵⁄₁₆ in. (45.6 cm). Seat rails: W. 15¹⁄₁₆ in. (38.3 cm), MW. 20⅜ in. (51.8 cm), D. 15 in. (38.1 cm).

Exhibitions: Early Furniture Made in New Jersey 1690–1870, October 10, 1958–January 11, 1959, The Newark Museum, Newark, New Jersey; *From Lenape Territory to Royal Province: New Jersey 1600–1750*, April 30–September 12, 1971, The New Jersey State Museum, Trenton, p. 61, no. 170.

Provenance: Henry H. Taylor, Bridgeport, Conn.; Francis P. Garvan, New York, N.Y.; The Mabel Brady Garvan Collection, 1930.2258a.

82

83. Side Chair

New England, 1750–1775

The elements of the design of this chair have been transformed since their first vigorous expression, seen on nos. 73–80. The turnings on the front legs no longer rest on a flange with an architectural profile, and the double-vase front stretcher has lost the boldness of the earlier ball-turned forms. This chair has been given a slightly later date than those assigned to nos. 73–80.

Description: The bowed stiles lack the graceful sweep of those on no. 82. An awkward break appears just below the seat and on the inner faces of the stiles near the floor. The outlines of the ogee turnings are similar to those on the preceding chairs, but here the architectural form of the moldings beneath the turning is reduced to a flat disc. The front turning is a double baluster with a reel. The side stretchers have bulbous centers ornamented with a double groove, and the rear stretcher is plain.

Notes: The brown paint appears to be old and the flag seat is painted yellow. The crest rail is pinned to the stiles with square wooden pegs.

Woods: Stiles, sycamore; left front legs, soft maple; rear stretcher, hard maple; seat rails, ash.

Dimensions: H. 39⅝ in. (100.6 cm), SH. 17¼ in. (43.8 cm). Seat rails: W. 15 1/16 in. (38.3 cm), MW. 19⅞ in. (50.5 cm), D. 14⅛ in. (35.9 cm).

Provenance: Henry H. Taylor, Bridgeport, Conn.; Francis P. Garvan, New York, N.Y.; The Mabel Brady Garvan Collection, 1930.2303.

84. Side Chair

Connecticut, about 1800

The similarity of this chair, one of a set of six, to other Connecticut Valley models, points to Connecticut as the probable place of origin. A crest rail with the central scallop rolled backward, sharply angled grooved ears, a deep bottom rail, a baluster-turned front stretcher, swelled side stretchers, and bottle-shaped turnings at the tops of the front legs are features also found on a chair once belonging to Gideon Granger of Suffield, Connecticut.[1] A daybed also from Suffield has a nearly identical splat.[2] The chair's original owner was a Connecticut man, the Reverend David Dudley Field (1781–1867), born in East Guilford and graduated from Yale College; he served as a minister in Haddam, Connecticut, from 1804 to 1818 before moving to Stockbridge, Massachusetts (1819–37). Paint originally covered the surface of the chair and concealed the differences now apparent in the various woods—the cherry splat, maple stiles, and birch front legs.

Description: The scalloped crest rail and grooved ears of this side chair crown a splat with an atypical outline. The reversed serpentine curve and angular break in the shoulder give the splat the effect of having a collar. The ogee turnings at the tops of the front legs have been transformed from ogee forms to bottle-like ones. The turnings between the blocks on the legs are barrel-like. The shape at the top of the leg is echoed in the front stretcher; the side and rear stretchers are bulbous, having very small tapered ends.

Notes: Traces of old red paint remain even though the late-nineteenth or twentieth-century varnish was removed in 1966. Small repairs have been made to the bases of the rear stiles. The corners of the stiles are chamfered between the seat rails and the upper side stretchers. The center toe of the right front foot has been replaced. Small patches appear on the edges of the upper stiles. The crest rail and lower back rail are pinned to the stiles. A few scored lines mark the placement of the stretchers.

Woods: Soft maple; front legs and stiles, birch; splat, cherry; side and rear seat rails, ash.

Dimensions: H. 40⅝ in. (103.2 cm), SH. 18⅛ in. (46.0 cm). Seat rails: W. 14 3/16 in. (36.0 cm), MW. 19½ in. (49.3 cm), D. 14 in. (35.6 cm).

Provenance: The Reverend David Dudley Field (1781–1867) (Haddam, Conn., 1804–1818, and Stockbridge, Mass., 1819–1837); Descended to Mrs. David Brewer Karrick, Washington, D.C.; Gift of Mrs. David Brewer Karrick, 1966.47b.

---

[1] Bissell, p. 69, pl. 12.—[2] *Ibid.*, p. 71, pl. 14.

85. Side Chair

New England, 1775–1800

As the eighteenth century progressed, rush-seat chairs with block-and-turned legs were updated to reflect high style trends, such as the pierced splat of this example. Here too the vigor of the turnings has not diminished appreciably. Chairs of this general

83

84

85

type can be found throughout New England, but precise localization is difficult to establish. A related example is illustrated by Nutting,[1] and a virtually identical chair is in the Lyman Allyn Museum, New London, Connecticut.

Description: The double peak and the tapered ears give the crest of this chair a scalloped outline. The splat, pierced with four finger-like cut-outs and a heart, has a sharply incut neck. The profiles of the turnings are very full on the ogees of the legs, the double-ball stretchers and the double-vase side stretchers.

Notes: The crest rail is pinned to the stiles. Scored lines on the insides of the legs mark the placement of the stretchers. The chair was refinished in 1962, but traces of old red paint remain. Some worm damage appears on the legs. The flag seat is old.

Wood: Soft maple.

Dimensions: H. 39⅞ in. (101.3 cm), SH. 17¹¹⁄₁₆ in. (44.9 cm). Seat rails: W. 14 in. (35.6 cm), MW. 17⅜ in. (44.1 cm), D. 14¼ in. (36.2 cm).

Bibliography: Kirk, *Early Am. Furn.*, fig. 115.

Provenance: Henry V. Weil, New York, N.Y.; Francis P. Garvan, New York, N.Y.; The Mabel Brady Garvan Collection, 1930.2428.

[1] *Treasury*, no. 2097.

86. Roundabout Chair

Possibly Connecticut, 1750–1775

A closely related roundabout chair, said to come from Litchfield, Connecticut, suggests the possible place of origin for this example.[1] A chair with similar feet was also owned in a Connecticut collection.[2] Sycamore was not commonly used by American craftsmen, but is found with some frequency on Connecticut furniture. The sweep of the scrolled crest rail, the thinness of the legs and arm supports, and the absence of slats or splats contribute to the chair's sparse appearance.

Description: Three attenuated, vase-shaped turnings support the semi-circular arm rail and its attached crest with scrolled ends. The seat is basswood. The legs have ogee turnings sitting on straight-sided discs reminiscent of those on no. 81. The bottoms of the square legs are scooped away to form small pad feet. The front stretchers are double-vase turned. The rear stretchers, two on each side, have bulbous centers ornamented with a double groove.

Notes: The chair has been refinished, but traces of red paint remain. The wrought-iron ties, though old, are not original. The tops of the arm supports are pinned to the arm rail from the back with square wooden pegs (the center pin is new). The ends of the arm rail are lapped at the center, and the top part of the joint has been cracked and repaired. The crest rail is held in place with roseheaded nails, only one of which remains.

Woods: Arm and crest rail, sycamore; seat rails, white oak; legs and stretchers, soft maple.

Dimensions: H. 31¼ in. (79.4 cm), SH. 17³⁄₁₆ in. (43.7 cm). Seat rails: W. 16¹⁵⁄₁₆ in. (43.0 cm), D. 16½ in. (41.9 cm).

Provenance: John Tynan, Middletown, Conn.; Francis P. Garvan, New York, N.Y.; The Mabel Brady Garvan Collection, 1930.2433.

[1] *Antiques*, 97 (March 1970), p. 295.—[2] Nutting, *Treasury*, no. 1839.

86

87. Side Chair

Probably Branford, Connecticut, 1740–1760

This chair is different from all the preceding examples in this section in one essential respect: the rear legs are not sawn, bowed stiles; they are instead turned, round posts. This difference between chairs that had square and partially turned rear stiles and chairs on which the rear stiles were completely turned is also to be noted among rural banister-back chairs in this catalogue. This chair is said to have been originally at the Rose House in North Branford, Connecticut (the interior paneling of which is now at the Yale University Art Gallery). Other chairs with ogee-and-vase-turned posts and the peculiar taper just below the finial are ascribable to the area east of New Haven. A counterpart and another example closely related except for its banister-back are at the Dorothy Whitfield Historic Society, Guilford, Connecticut.

Description: The rear posts have an ogee and elongated-vase shape between the lower back rail and crest, and end in modified urn-shaped finials. The tall center section of the crest has a double scalloped top edge and heart-shaped cut-out. The splat is a vase form. The seat is basswood. Two pairs of narrow rings decorate the front legs. The unusually thin front stretchers are so badly worn that the vase shapes, separated by a cylindrical turning, are barely perceptible.

Notes: Brown paint covers black. Faint grooves mark the placement of the crest, lower back rail, seat rails, and stretchers. The crest rail is secured with square wooden pegs driven from the front through to the back. About a dozen worm holes can be found, mostly in the legs and stretchers. Wire nails were added to hold the front stretchers in place.

Woods: Soft maple; splat, tulip; crest rail, seat rails, and stretchers, hickory.

Dimensions: H. 39¾ in. (101.0 cm), BPH. 41⅛ in.

87

(104.5 cm), SH. 15⅜ in. (39.1 cm). Seat rails: W. 13¾ in. (34.9 cm), MW. 17⅜ in. (44.1 cm), D. 13⅛ in. (33.3 cm).

Bibliography: Conn. Furn., no. 222.

Provenance: Rose House, North Branford, Conn.; Descended to Mrs. William Woodcock Goodbody, Branford, Conn.; Gift of Mrs. William Woodcock Goodbody, 1950.694.

88. Side Chair

Hudson River Valley, Long Island, or Connecticut, 1790–1830

Between the years 1790 and 1830 Nathaniel Dominy V of East Hampton, Long Island, made chairs similar to this example, which he sold for eight shillings apiece in sets of six or nine.[1] In the first decade of the nineteenth century, chairmaker James Chestney's advertisement in the *Albany Gazette* was illustrated by a woodcut of a similar chair.[2] This evidence reveals that in certain instances American craftsmen perpetuated elements of early eighteenth-century furniture design into the nineteenth. The chairs themselves, which are usually painted black or reddish-brown, have been called "Hudson River Valley" chairs, but shops in New Jersey, Long Island, Connecticut, and Rhode Island undoubtedly manufactured them as well. The date at which the style was introduced is difficult to determine: it has been suggested recently that in Connecticut they were called "York" chairs and were being made there by the Durand family in Milford as early as 1762.[3] It is not known whether they were generally called by this name throughout Connecticut. How the York chairs differed from fiddle-back chairs—the name given them by the Dominys—is as yet unclear.

Description: Cone shapes, on top of the ball-and-taper-turned posts, fit into the ends of the yoke-shaped crest rail. The splat is vase shaped. The front corners of the rush seat are supported by an ogee-and-reel turning atop a tapering, bat-like leg terminating in pad-and-disc feet. The extremely rounded forms of the double-ball-and-ring-turned front stretchers contrast with the plain side and rear stretchers.

Notes: Recent black paint covers old red paint. Faint grooves mark the placement of the stretchers and seat rails.

Woods: Stiles, soft maple; splat, tulip; seat rails, side and rear stretchers, hickory; front stretcher, birch.

Dimensions: H. 39$^{15}/_{16}$ in. (101.4 cm), SH. 17 in. (43.2 cm). Seat rails: W. 15$^{1}/_{16}$ in. (38.3 cm), MW. 18⅞ in. (47.9 cm), D. 14⅝ in. (37.1 cm).

Bibliography: Reifsnyder Coll., p. 68, no. 297; Kirk, *Early Am. Furn.,* fig. 109.

Provenance: Howard Reifsnyder, Philadelphia, Pa.; Francis P. Garvan, New York, N.Y. (1929); The Mabel Brady Garvan Collection, 1930.2185.

---

[1] Hummel, p. 254.—[2] Norman S. Rice. *New York Furniture Before 1840* (Albany: Albany Institute of History and Art, 1962), p. 38.—[3] Benno M. Forman, "The Crown and York Chairs of Coastal Connecticut and the Work of the Durands of Milford," *Antiques,* 105 (May 1974), p. 1148.

88

89

89. Side Chair

Probably Rhode Island, 1790–1830

Certain features of this chair—otherwise generally similar to no. 88—suggest a Rhode Island origin: the reel-and-ball turning at the top of the stile, the foot constructed with a more horizontal slope and without an intermediary ring between the sloped section and the pad, and the circular cut-outs on the ends of the crest rail. A related example found in that state near the Connecticut border[1] and more elegant walnut Rhode Island chairs also possess circular cut-outs.[2]

Description: This chair differs from no. 88 in the execution of a number of details. The ends of the yoke crest rail here are cut out. The neck of the splat is described by straight rather than serpentine lines. The turning of the post is an elongated vase on an ogee form. An ogee-and-cone turning is used at the top of the somewhat heavier tapered leg. The ball forms on the stretcher are not as round, nor are the ends as bulbous as those on the preceding chair.

Notes: The brown paint is old. The upper left stretcher is a replacement. Faint grooves mark the placement of the stretchers, seat rails, and lower back rail. The tops of the front legs are pinned to the front corners of the seat with square wooden pegs. The crest rail is pinned to the stiles.

Woods: Soft maple; splat, tulip.

Dimensions: H. 40⅜ in. (102.6 cm), SH. 17⁹⁄₁₆ in. (44.6 cm). Seat rails: W. 13½ in. (34.3 cm), MW. 19 in. (48.3 cm), D. 14 in. (35.6 cm).

Bibliography: Flayderman Coll., p. 29, no. 137.

Provenance: Philip Flayderman, Boston, Mass.; Francis P. Garvan, New York, N.Y. (1930); The Mabel Brady Garvan Collection, 1930.2425a.

[1] Huyler Held, "Long Island Dutch Splat Backs," *Antiques,* 30 (Oct. 1936), p. 168, fig. 4.—[2] Carpenter, fig. 18.

Pl. 7—*Rococo period side chair, Philadelphia, 1760–1780 (no. 112).*

Pl. 8—*Rococo period armchair, East Windsor, Connecticut, about 1780. Possibly by Eliphalet Chapin (no. 119).*

Pl. 9—*Easy chair, Philadelphia, 1755–1775 (no. 214).*

Pl. 10—*Upholstered armchair, Massachusetts, 1760–1785 (no. 208).*

The Rococo Period

Patterns from Chippendale

IN THE 1730's a new style, the rococo, began to gain currency in England. In place of the generous curves and majestic ornament of the baroque style, it substituted refined foliage and flowers, often arranged asymmetrically and intermixed with ruffled shells. The ambiance was one of fragile delicacy. The date at which this new vogue began to filter to America is not easily determined. In his discussion of this era in the *Blue Book Philadelphia Furniture,* William M. Hornor begins with this memorable sentence: "The Golden Age of Philadelphia furniture-making occurred during the brilliant Chippendale period in America—roughly speaking from 1745 to 1789."[1] Hornor thus suggests that the first American furniture forms in the Chippendale style appeared approximately a decade prior to the publication in London of the first edition (1754) of Thomas Chippendale's most unusual book, *The Gentleman and Cabinet-Maker's Director* (see Fig. 1). Other scholars have decided upon dates of 1750[2] or 1755[3] for the introduction of the style to America, but as yet its inception in America has not been thoroughly documented.

What is clear is that this publication of Chippendale had a profound influence in disseminating the English rococo style in the American colonies, at least in Philadelphia. Although two cabinetmakers from other areas are known to have owned copies of Chippendale's designs (and they were probably not unique), it is only in Philadelphia that furniture was produced that faithfully renders the elegant engravings of those pages.[4] As the Massachusetts examples in this section (nos. 95, 97–98) suggest, chairs produced in northern shops were vaguer renderings of

Fig. 1—*Plate XIII, Thomas Chippendale,* The Gentleman & Cabinet-Maker's Director, *1762. Yale University Art Gallery.*

the mode. The provocative question of why cabinetmakers in Philadelphia chose to imitate Chippendale's patterns closely and furniture makers in New England and elsewhere did not has yet to be explored.

[1] Hornor, p. 72.—[2] Bishop, p. 121.—[3] Comstock, pp. 115–134.—[4] Nathaniel Gould, a cabinetmaker of Salem, Massachusetts, owned a copy when he died in 1808 (*Antiques,* 97 [Jan. 1970], p. 52), as did the Williamsburg, Virginia, cabinetmaker Edmund Dickinson, when he died in 1778 (*Antiques,* 100 [July 1971], p. 52).

90. Armchair

Philadelphia, 1760–1780

The opening framed by ruffled carving on the crest rail relates this armchair and the three succeeding side chairs to designs in Plates XIII and XIV of Chippendale's *Director* (1762). Chairs of this type have often been attributed to Benjamin Randolph of Philadelphia on the basis of labeled examples in the Karolik Collection at the Museum of Fine Arts, Boston;[1] however, the authenticity of that label has been questioned. The present whereabouts of another labeled example is not known, leaving the Randolph attribution somewhat in doubt.[2] The large number of chairs of this type that survive, with slight differences among them in construction and carving, suggests that they may have been a popular form made in more than one Philadelphia shop. A particularly fine feature of this example is the carving on the top surface of the arms and the richly carved knees, similar to that on the chair in the Karolik Collection and to another illustrated example.[3] A related armchair at Winterthur lacks the carving on the arms.[4] An example with Marlborough style legs decorated with fretwork is owned by the Henry Ford Museum.[5] Another armchair with opposed C-scrolls on the skirt has been advertised.[6]

90a

Description: The details of the carved, ruffled frame at the juncture of the serpentine crest and pierced splat suggest the subtle qualities of this chair. Leaf carving outlines the top edge of the crest and the outer edges of the serpentine-shaped arms, which end in knuckled handholds. The square seat frame is supported at the front corners by cabriole legs with leaf-carved knees. The legs terminate in claw-and-ball feet.

Inscription: The figure "II" is marked on the inside of the rear seat rail and on the slip seat frame.

Notes: The side seat rails are tenoned through the stiles and wedged. The front and rear corner blocks are quarter-round with vertical grain; those at the front are of two pieces. A thin piece of wood fits between the rear corner block and rear seat rail. The latter is secured to the stiles with two squared wooden pegs. The side and front seat rails are pinned to the legs with single wooden pegs. The top of the left arm support has been broken and repaired. The arm supports are screwed to the side seat rails from the inside, and the arms are pinned to the rear stiles from the back. The knee brackets are screwed to the seat rails with modern screws.

Woods: Mahogany; slip seat frame and right rear corner block, pine of the *taeda* group; front and left rear corner blocks, Atlantic white cedar.

Dimensions: H. 37¾ in. (95.9 cm), SH. 15¼ in. (38.7 cm). Seat rails: W. 19½ in. (49.5 cm), MW. 23⁷⁄₁₆ in. (59.5 cm), D. 19⅝ in. (49.9 cm).

Bibliography: Collection of Louis Guerineau Myers (1921), no. 679; "Gallery Notes," *BAFA* 3 (Dec. 1928), p. 35

90

(illus.); "American and British Art, XVIII Century," *Handbook of the Gallery of Fine Arts* (Associates in Fine Arts at Yale University), 5 (1931), p. 45 (illus.); Kirk, *Am. Chairs,* p. 86, fig. 82.

Provenance: Louis Guerineau Myers, New York, N.Y.; Francis P. Garvan, New York, N.Y. (1921); The Mabel Brady Garvan Collection, 1930.2103.

[1] Hipkiss, no. 89.—[2] *Antiques,* 47 (Jan. 1943), inside front cover.—[3] *Sack Coll.,* 1957–72, II, no. 774.—[4] Downs, *Am. Furn.,* no. 50.—[5] Comstock, no. 248.—[6] *Antiques,* 97 (March 1970), inside front cover.

91. Side Chair

Philadelphia, 1760–1780

This beautiful Philadelphia side chair, with gracefully intertwined streamers on the front seat rail, is the richest variant among the American chairs based on Plates XIII and XIV in Chippendale's designs. Compared with its three counterparts in this collection, nos. 90, 92, 93, the carving on the knees is flatter and the arrangement looser. A set of eight chairs like this one is at Winterthur.[1]

91

91a

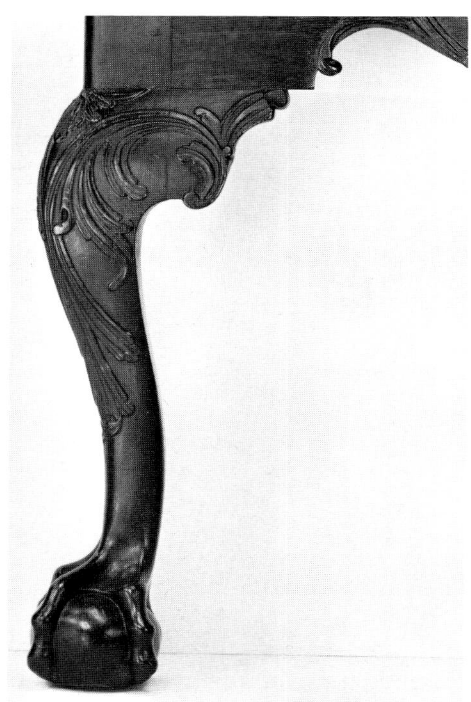

91b

Description: In many details this chair appears to be identical with no. 90, but the slight variations may indicate the hand of a different carver, perhaps one working for another shop. Here the bead on the splat is flatter; the molding of the splat shoe is an ogee; the carving on the knee brackets is more linear; a rosette is used on the knee; and the webbing of the claw-and-ball feet is deeper.

Inscriptions: The number "III" is marked on the top edge of the front seat ledge, and "II" appears on the slip seat frame.

Notes: The side seat rails are tenoned through the stiles and wedged. The front halves of the vertically grained front corner blocks remain. The inner section of the rear seat rail is 3/16 inch thick. The left rear stile has been broken and repaired at the seat rail. The rear seat rail is pinned to the stiles with two square wooden pegs. Two square wooden pegs are also used to secure the joint of the right side seat rail and rear stile. Single wooden pegs are used to secure the joints of the front and side seat rails with the front legs, and the left side seat rail with the rear stile. The side and right front knee brackets are restored. The left front knee bracket is held in place with two roseheaded nails. The ribs on the left of the splat are restored.

Woods: Mahogany; rear seat rail, red gum; front corner blocks, Atlantic white cedar; slip seat frame, pine of the *taeda* group.

Dimensions: H. 39 3/16 in. (99.5 cm), SH. 17 3/16 in. (43.7 cm). Side rails: W. 16 15/16 in. (43.0 cm), MW. 22 7/8 in. (58.1 cm), D. 17 1/4 in. (43.8 cm).

Bibliography: "Outstanding Examples from the Mabel Brady Garvan Collection," *BAFA,* 8 (Feb. 1938), p. 44 (illus.); Meyric R. Rogers, "Garvan Furniture at Yale," *The Connoisseur Year Book* 1960, p. 58, no. 9; Kirk, *Am. Chairs,* p. 86, fig. 81.

Provenance: One of a group of chairs acquired from the Misses Biddle, Philadelphia, Pa., Charles R. Morson, New York, N.Y., and Charles W. Lyon, New York, N.Y., by Francis P. Garvan, New York, N.Y.; The Mabel Brady Garvan Collection, 1930.2104.

[1] Downs, *Am. Furn.,* no. 133.

92. Side Chair

Philadelphia, 1760–1780

The more irregular outline of the ruffled carving surrounding the pierced opening on the crest and the more frequent repetition of the punching on the leaf carving bordering the crest rail gives this chair greater animation than the preceding example, no. 91. Another chair of the type whose knees also feature carved rosettes has been illustrated.[1]

Description: The carving around the circular piercing has a more irregular outline than that on nos. 90 and 91 and the ribs of the leaves of the crest are cut with small chips. The carving on the knees is much richer here—especially in such details as the ends of some of the leaves, which twist back upon themselves to create a lively effect.

Inscriptions: The top of the ledge on the front seat rail is marked "V" and also "I". The slip seat frame is marked "I".

Notes: The side seat rails are tenoned through the stiles. One original corner block remains at the front and is quarter-round, of two pieces with vertical grain. A 1/4-inch mahogany facing is found on the rear seat rail. The knee brackets of the right front leg and the side knee bracket of

92

92a

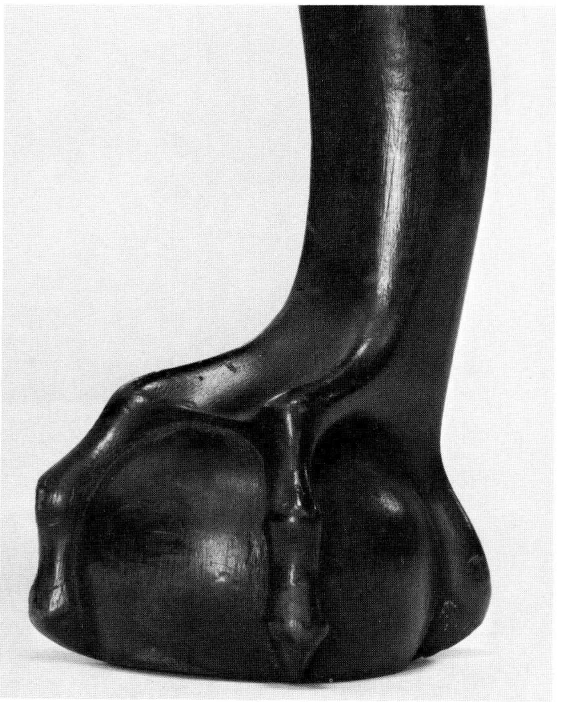

92b

the left leg are restored. The original knee bracket is attached with glue. The joints of the front legs and seat rails are secured with a single wooden peg; those of the rear stiles and seat frame are secured with two wooden pegs. A ¼-inch addition has been made to the bases of the rear stiles. Nail holes at the center of the inside faces of the rear and front seat rails suggest that a center brace may have been present at one time. A ½-inch piece has been added to the left side of the crest rail where it joins the splat. Breaks and small repairs appear in the splat. The upholstery is a modern silk damask.

Woods: Mahogany; rear seat rail, tulip; corner blocks, Atlantic white cedar; seat frame, pine of the *taeda* group.

Dimensions: H. 38¾ in. (98.4 cm), SH. 17⅜ in. (44.1 cm). Seat rails: W. 16⅝ in. (42.2 cm), MW. 21⅛ in. (53.7 cm), D. 17⅛ in. (43.5 cm).

Provenance: One of a group of chairs acquired from the Misses Biddle, Philadelphia, Pa., Charles R. Morson, New York, N.Y., and Charles W. Lyon, New York, N.Y., by Francis P. Garvan, New York, N.Y.; The Mabel Brady Garvan Collection, 1930.2102b.

---

[1] *Sack Coll.,* 1957–72, II, no. 1082.

92c

93. Side Chair

Philadelphia, 1760–1780

This chair, the last in the series of Philadelphia chairs which began with no. 90, is separated from its fellows by the degree of assurance with which the carving is handled. Its unusual features are the straight lower edges of the seat rails and the use of a knee bracket lipped to fit over the lower edge of the seat rails. Also at variance with customary practice is the absence of through tenons on the side seat rails.

Description: This chair is similar to nos. 90–92 but the carving on the knees is deeper and an elongated C-scroll outlines the edges of the leg and knee bracket.

Inscriptions: The top of the front seat ledge is marked "111", and the seat frame "1111".

Notes: The right C-scroll and ruffle on the splat are restored. The joint of the right stile and seat frame has been repaired. The side and front seat rails are cracked above the left front leg. Both the front and the left side knee brackets have been restored. The right side knee bracket, the original, is lipped to fit over the lower edge of the seat rail. The corner blocks are replacements. A ¾-inch piece of wood has been added to the top of the right front leg where it joins the side seat rail. The ends of the rear seat rail are cut to a bracket shape. The upholstery is an eighteenth-century French silk damask.

Woods: Mahogany; seat frame, pine of the *taeda* group.

Dimensions: H. 38⅛ in. (96.8 cm), SH. 17⅜ in. (44.1 cm). Seat rails: W. 17¾ in. (45.1 cm), MW. 22⅞ in. (58.1 cm), D. 18 in. (45.7 cm).

Bibliography: Nutting, *Treasury,* no. 2159; Kirk, *Am. Chairs,* p. 85, fig. 80.

Provenance: One of a group of chairs acquired from the Misses Biddle, Philadelphia, Pa., Charles R. Morson, New York, N.Y., and Charles W. Lyon, New York, N.Y., by Francis P. Garvan, New York, N.Y.; The Mabel Brady Garvan Collection, 1930.2101b.

93

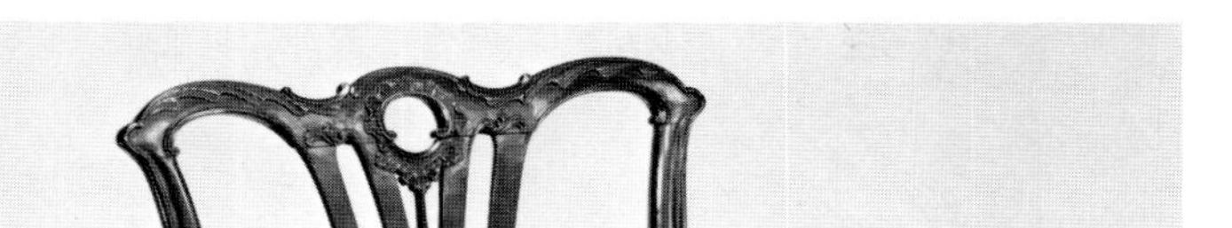

94. Side Chair

Philadelphia, 1760–1780

The design of this chair is greatly restrained, with the rococo motifs of the skirt and crest combined with an English love for Gothic ornament. The quatrefoils, cusps, and lancets of the splat are all borrowed from Gothic tracery. On the basis of a labeled example in the Taradash Collection, the Yale chair as well as a number of similar chairs (such as examples at the Museum of Fine Arts, Boston, the Philadelphia Museum, and Winterthur) have been attributed to the Philadelphia joiner James Gillingham.[1] However, the design, derived from Plate XIII of the 1754 and 1755 editions of Chippendale's *Director,* and Plate X (Fig. 2) of the 1762 edition, was widely used by many other Philadelphia chairmakers—as the numerous interpretations in Hornor indicate.[2] Like the labeled Taradash example, the chair at Yale has plain knees, although the front seat rail and the crest rail are more elaborately carved.

Description: The splat and crest rail are pierced with four variations of the quatrefoil shape. A foliated pendant decorates the center of the crest, and small areas of leaf carving appear on the ears. The center of the front seat rail is decorated with a small cartouche-like piece of carving

Fig. 2—*Plate X, Thomas Chippendale,* The Gentleman & Cabinet-Maker's Director, *1762. Yale University Art Gallery.*

flanked by two C-scrolls. The cabriole front legs have plain knees and terminate in claw-and-ball feet.

Inscription: The rear seat rail and the slip seat frame are marked "II".

Notes: The side seat rails are tenoned through the stiles and wedged. The front corner blocks are a two-piece quarter-round form with vertical grain; the rear corner blocks are of a single quarter-round piece with vertical grain. The side seat rails are secured to the rear stiles with two square wooden pegs. Single wooden pegs secure the joints of the side seat rails with the front legs. Each knee bracket is held in place with two nails. The upholstery is a modern yellow silk damask in an eighteenth-century *chinoiserie* pattern.

Woods: Mahogany; corner blocks, Atlantic white cedar; seat frame, pine of the *taeda* group.

Dimensions: H. 38½ in. (97.8 cm), SH. 17¼ in. (43.8 cm). Seat rails: W. 16¾ in. (42.5 cm), MW. 21½ in. (54.6 cm), D. 17$\frac{1}{16}$ in. (43.3 cm).

Provenance: John L. Black, Washington, D.C. (sale New York, American Art Galleries, American Art Association, Inc., Jan. 2–9, 1926); Francis P. Garvan, New York, N.Y.; The Mabel Brady Garvan Collection, 1930.2498.

---

[1] "Tables and Chairs from the Collection of Mr. and Mrs. Mitchell Taradash," *Antiques,* 49 (June 1946), p. 359. For the examples cited see Downs, *Am. Furn.,* no. 139; Hipkiss, no. 88; and Comstock, no. 268.—[2] Pl. 342–49.

94a

95. Side Chair

Probably Boston, about 1765

95

Joseph Sherburne, a wealthy Boston merchant, was painted by John Singleton Copley about 1768 or 1770; he is shown seated in a chair with an identical back.[1] Reminiscent of a design in Plate XVI of Chippendale's *Director* (1762), this Massachusetts interpretation of the English rococo reveals a less exact imitation of the idiom than its Philadelphia counterparts. Like many Massachusetts chairs of the second half of the eighteenth century, for instance, this example retains the use of stretchers. A closely related example is illustrated by Lockwood.[2] Among the other known chairs with this splat design are a pair with straight front legs and one example with square rear legs, no stretchers, and cabriole legs ending in hairy paw feet.[3] Two other examples, one with straight front legs,[4] and the other with hairy paw feet and asymmetrical carving on the knees like that of no. 97, have foliated leaf carving suspended from the elongated C-scrolls on the sides of the splat.[5] This idea for the treatment of the edges of the splat also appears to be derived from the *Director* (Plate XIIII, left; Plate XI, right; Plate X, right).

Description: The volute-shaped ends of the crest rail, elongated C-scrolls on the outer edges of the splat, prominent lobes on the knee brackets, and soft contours of the medial stretcher are all distinctive features of this chair. The understructure is braced by turned block-and-spindle stretchers.

Inscriptions: The numerals "IIII" and two slanted lines appear on the top of the front seat ledge; "II" is marked on the slip seat frame.

Notes: The corner blocks are replacements. Each of the knee brackets is held in place with three roseheaded nails and glue. A new ½-inch thick piece of wood has been added to the inside of the rear seat rail. Unexplained nail holes appear on the undersides of the side seat rails. The modern *gros-point* needlework illustrated has been replaced by an eighteenth-century green silk damask, probably Italian.

Woods: Mahogany; slip-seat frame, soft maple.

Dimensions: H. 37 in. (94.0 cm), SH. 16⅞ in. (42.9 cm). Seat rails: W. 16 11/16 in. (42.4 cm), MW. 20½ in. (52.1 cm), D. 18 1/16 in. (45.9 cm).

Bibliography: Hudnut Coll., no. 71; Wenham, p. 28, no. 70; Kirk, *Am. Chairs,* p. 108, fig. 120.

Provenance: Alexander M. Hudnut, New York, N.Y., and Princeton, N.J.; Francis P. Garvan, New York, N.Y.; The Mabel Brady Garvan Collection, 1930.2562.

[1] Prown, I, p. 218.—[2] Lockwood, fig. 552.—[3] *Sack Coll.,* 1957–72, I, no. 673, and III, no. 1391.—[4] Nutting, *Treasury,* no. 2249.—[5] *Antiques,* 56 (Nov. 1949), p. 338.

96

96. Side Chair

Philadelphia, 1760–1780

Among the most exotic of all Chippendale chair designs were the "Ribband Back Chairs."[1] Although known American chairs do not compare with the delicacy of the English designs, the intertwining bands (shirred to look like ribbon) at the center of the splat of this chair may have been inspired by the illustrations in Chippendale. Appropriately enough, the "ribbon" here is accompanied by tassels on the crest, another element borrowed from the English source. This chair and others like it have sometimes been assigned to Pennsylvania or Maryland. A carved shell was probably once present on the skirt of this example, as may be seen on its counterpart in the Brooklyn Museum.[2] Related examples are at Winterthur,[3] and have been illustrated by Hornor and others.[4]

Description: Fluted stiles support a crest with carved cords and tassels and an asymmetrical central shell. The center of the splat is carved to resemble ribbon, and the base and splat shoe are richly carved with rosettes. The cabriole front legs have carved knees and terminate in rather small claw-and-ball feet.

Inscription: The number "20" is written in ink on the inside of the rear seat rail; the slip seat frame is marked "XX".

Notes: The side seat rails are tenoned through the stiles and wedged. The front corner blocks are a two-piece quarter-round form with vertical grain, and the rear corner blocks are missing. Each joint of the seat rails and legs is secured with two squared wooden pegs. Each knee bracket is held in place with three nails. The feet are worn at the bottom. The back of the crest rail at the junction with the splat has been repaired. The shell is missing from the center of the front seat rail. The upholstery is a modern silk damask.

Woods: Mahogany; front corner blocks, mahogany; slip seat frame, tulip.

Dimensions: H. 40 in. (101.6 cm), SH. 16 13/16 in. (42.7 cm). Seat rails: W. 16 9/16 in. (42.1 cm), MW. 21 5/8 in. (54.9 cm), D. 17 7/16 in. (44.3 cm).

Provenance: Louis Richmond, Freehold, N.J.; Francis P. Garvan, New York, N.Y.; The Mabel Brady Garvan Collection, 1930.2501.

[1] *Director,* pl. XV.—[2] Comstock, no. 266.—[3] Downs, *Am. Furn.,* nos. 38 and 119.—[4] Pl. 351; *Antiques,* 70 (Nov. 1956), p. 397.

97. Armchair

Probably Boston, 1765–1785

In the early nineteenth century Abraham Bishop recorded what he thought was an accurate history for the set of ten side and two arm chairs to which this chair belongs. According to Bishop, the chairs were brought from England in 1727 by William Burnett, Governor of Massachusetts, upon whose death in 1729 they passed to Governor Jonathan Belcher (1681/82–1757) and later to his heirs.[1] In actuality the chairs were probably made after Belcher's death in 1757 and were manufactured in America, not in England as Bishop suggested. The secondary woods—soft maple and birch—strongly indicate an American origin. More importantly, however, the chairs belong to a group of seating furniture which seems to have originated in Massachusetts. This group includes an armchair at Winterthur,[2] an armchair with bird's-head handholds said to have been owned by Elias Hasket Derby,[3] a side chair also ascribed to Derby family ownership,[4] and settees in the Metropolitan Museum of Art (acc. no. 30.170.59) and Winterthur;[5] there is also a card table in a private collection.[6] A theory has recently been proposed that the armchair at Winterthur, which uses beech exclusively as the secondary wood, is the English model from which the American examples took their inspiration.[7] All these examples have in common slender, wiry front legs with strongly retracted side claws and

97

C-scroll carving on the knees. The chair at Winterthur has hairy paw feet which link the group to chairs whose counterparts are known to have similarly carved legs and feet, such as nos. 95 and 102 in this catalogue. The elaborately carved backs of the Yale chairs cannot be directly related to the designs of Chippendale, but the shirred, interlaced bands in the splat seem to convey something of the feeling of ribbon. These designs are among the most ambitious attempted by Massachusetts chairmakers in the third quarter of the eighteenth century.

Description: The leaf-and-ruffle-carved crest rail of this armchair rests above a splat outlined at the top with two scrolls with leaf carving and decorated at the center with plain and shirred interlaced bands. The stiles are stop-fluted at the base. The serpentine arms with hollowed elbow rests are attached midway along the stiles. The handholds form tight scrolls ending at the sides in small knobs and are decorated on their upper surfaces with leaf carving. The latter is repeated at the base of the arm supports. The seat frame, upholstered over the rails, is supported at the front corners with cabriole legs terminating in claw-and-ball feet with very thin talons. The knees are richly carved with C-scrolls and asymmetrical foliage.

Inscription: A brass plaque on the underside of the rear seat rail reads: "One of a dining-room set brought from England in 1727 by W.m Burnett, Governor of Massachusetts under George II, and used by him in the / Old Province house in Boston. On his death 1729 the set passed to Gov. Belcher and later 1757 to his heirs. Bought at auction by / Paschal N. Smith his widow brought it to New Haven and later sold it to Abram Bishop Jr. Mr. Bishop gave this chair to B. Silliman in 1828 who bequeathed it 1864 to Mrs. J. D. Dana; another armchair he presented to Sereno Dwight and the remainder of the set (ten chairs / without arms and table) to Yale College; they are now 1904 in the Library. This history is from Mr. Bishop's memorandum copied by B. Silliman 1844."

Notes: The long cross braces in each corner of the seat frame and the triangular blocks at the rear are attached to the seat rails with roundheaded nails. The white pine quarter-round blocks at the front corners are possibly not original. The splat is housed in the rear seat rail which passes behind the shoe. An additional brace has been added inside the rear seat rail. The bottom edges of the seat rails were restored, and the shafts of old brass tacks were removed in preparation for new upholstery in 1969. The old finish is quite dark. The upholstery is reproduction horsehair.

Woods: Mahogany; cross braces and seat frame, soft maple; rear corner blocks, birch.

Dimensions: H. 37 7/16 in. (95.1 cm), SH. 16 7/16 in. (41.8 cm). Seat rails: W. 18 3/4 in. (47.6 cm), MW. 24 3/4 in. (62.9 cm), D. 19 9/16 in. (49.7 cm).

Bibliography: Lyon, pp. 171–72; Singleton, I, pp. 274 and 278; Kirk, *Am. Chairs,* p. 109, fig. 123; Mary Ellen Hayward Yehia, "Ornamental Carving on Boston Furniture of the Chippendale Style," *Boston Furniture of the Eighteenth Century* (Boston, 1974), p. 203, no. 141.

Provenance: One of two armchairs from a set of twelve chairs whose recorded, but inaccurate, history states they were owned by the Royal Governor William Burnett, upon whose death in 1729 they passed to his successor, Jonathan Belcher (d. Boston 1757) and subsequently to his heirs. The chairs were bought at auction by Paschal N. Smith, who brought them to New Haven where they were sold at auction by Mrs. Smith to Mrs. Ingersoll, wife of the

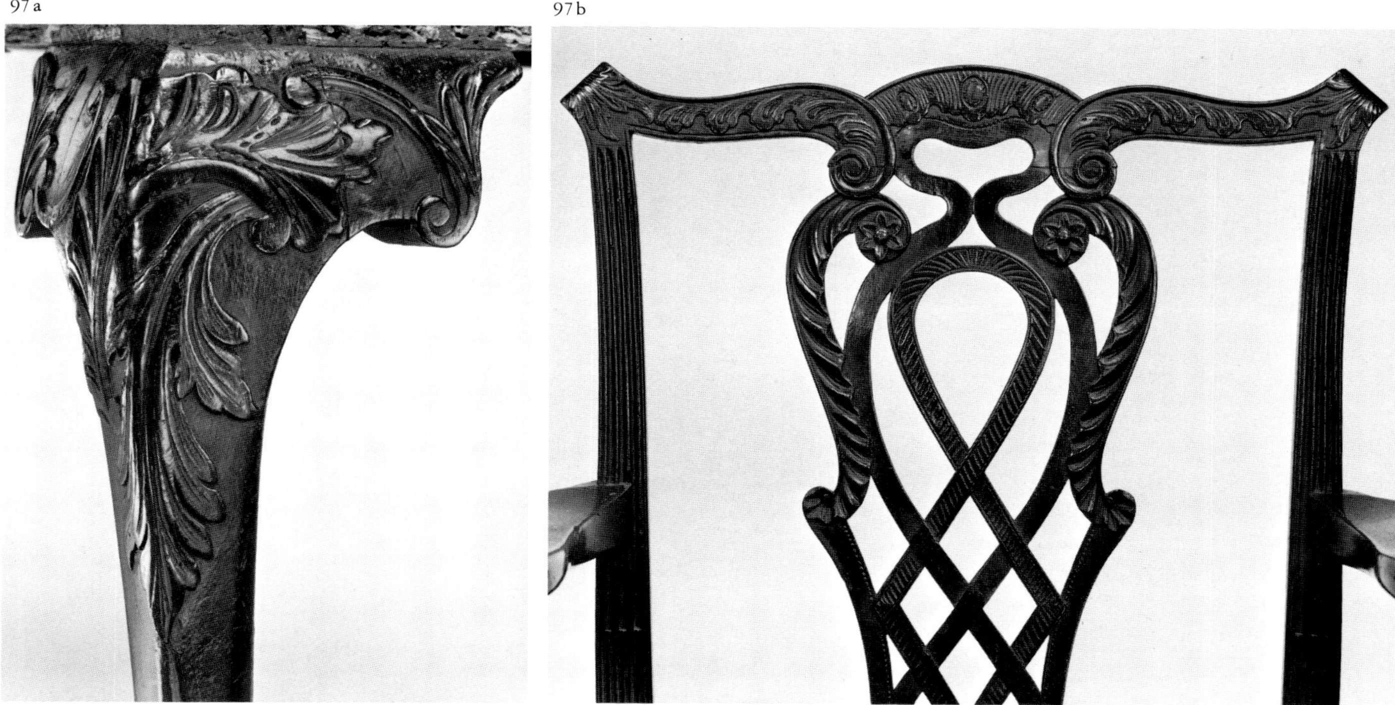

97 a 97 b

Lieutenant Governor. On July 27, 1819, Abraham Bishop purchased the armchairs from Mrs. Ingersoll. In 1828 he gave one armchair to Sereno E. Dwight and the other to Benjamin Silliman. The chair not illustrated may have passed from Sereno E. Dwight to the Rev. Ellsworth Daggett. In 1885 it was owned by Mrs. C. E. Daggett, and it eventually rejoined the set. Upon his death in 1864 Benjamin Silliman's armchair (illustrated) passed to his daughter, Henrietta Silliman Dana (Mrs. James Dwight Dana), and from her to Maria Trumbull Dana, who presented it to the Sterling Memorial Library of Yale University in 1955. The armchair has been transferred from the Sterling Memorial Library to the Yale University Art Gallery, 1967.26.

[1] Singleton, I, p. 278 (illus. opp. p. 274); see also the brass plaque on the chair itself.—[2] Downs, *Am. Furn.*, no. 55.—[3] *Antiques*, 97 (June 1970), inside front cover.—[4] *Antiques*, 99 (June 1971), p. 760.—[5] Downs, *Am. Furn.*, no. 270.—[6] Mary Ellen Hayward Yehia, "OrnamentalCarving on Boston Furniture of the Chippendale Style," *Boston Furniture of the Eighteenth Century* (Boston, 1974), p. 201.—[7] *Ibid.*, pp. 204–05.

98. Side Chair

Boston, 1765–1785

See comments, no. 97.

Description: See no. 97.

Inscription: Written in pencil on top of left front corner block: "P. O. Schwab / uph / 1891" (see no. 97).

Notes: The triangular, horizontally grained corner blocks are attached with glue and nails. Four open cross braces are nailed to the seat rails. The corner blocks and cross braces have been reattached. The splat passes behind the shoe and is housed in the rear seat rail. The upholstery is reproduction horsehair.

Woods: Mahogany; three corner braces and seat rails, soft maple; left front corner brace, American black ash; corner blocks, white pine.

Dimensions: H. 37⅝ in. (95.6 cm), SH. 16⁷⁄₁₆ in. (41.8 cm). Seat rails: W. 17¹⁵⁄₁₆ in. (45.6 cm), MW. 22⅜ in. (56.8 cm), D. 18¾ in. (47.6 cm).

Bibliography: Singleton, I (illus. opp. p. 274); Lyon, fig. 78, pp. 171–72.

Provenance: One of the ten side chairs from a set of twelve chairs traditionally, but inaccurately, said to have been owned by the Royal Governor, William Burnett, passing on his death in 1729 to his successor, Jonathan Belcher (d. Boston, 1757) and subsequently to his heirs. The chairs were bought at auction by Paschal N. Smith, who brought them to New Haven where they were sold at auction by Mrs. Smith to Abraham Bishop. On April 28, 1829, the Prudential Committee of Yale College requested that President Jeremiah Day thank Abraham Bishop (1763–1844) for his gift of the ten chairs for use in the College Library. The chairs have been transferred from the Sterling Memorial Library to the Yale University Art Gallery, 1967.28.1.

98

Diamond-Patterned Splats

THE PAGES of Thomas Chippendale's *Director* do not contain a design for a chair with a diamond-patterned splat, but the shape was not unknown to the English rococo. In the 1762 edition of the *Director* the motif can be found on the leg of one of the Chinese chairs in Plate XXVIII and on one of the designs for a bracket for a marble slab in Plate CLXII. English chairmakers found the motif appropriate for the design of chair backs, as did their American counterparts. From Pennsylvania to Massachusetts, chairs with diamond-patterned splats appealed to colonial customers.

99. Side Chair

Philadelphia, 1760–1780

The direct source for the design of this chair back has not been identified, but it may have been commonly available, since makers in Philadelphia and Massachusetts created chairs with a diamond and figure-eight interlaced splat below a tassel, drapery swag, and semi-circular opening.[1] The richly carved knees, well modeled claw-and-ball feet whose side talons are essentially vertical, the rounded rear legs, and large flaring ears identify this chair as a Philadelphia example of the form, other examples of which are known.[2] The design is very ambitious and the scrolled center of the crest rail with its ruffled edge is similar to chairs attributed to James Gillingham of Philadelphia.[3]

Description: The unusual splat has a diamond shape interwoven with a figure-eight at the center flanked by elongated S-scrolls at the edges. Suspended from the lower loop of the figure-eight is a tassel; another tassel is suspended from the fringed swag of drapery at the top of the splat. Above a semi-circular opening, the center of the crest rail scrolls backward, its top edge laced with a ruffled motif. The prominent grooved ears have scrolled ends and a string of interrupted bead carving at the center. The molded stiles become oval in cross section below the square seat frame. The lower edge of the front seat rail has the unusual feature of a straight line flanked by a pair of serpentine curves. The cabriole front legs have leaf-carved knee brackets and knees, and terminate in claw-and-ball feet.

Inscriptions: "NI" is written in pencil on the inside of the rear seat rail. The top of the front seat ledge is marked "I".

Notes: The side seat rails are tenoned through the stiles. The corner blocks are replacements. The junction of the right stile and seat rails has been repaired. The joints of the seat frames are secured with a single square wooden peg, with the exception of those at the front. Each knee bracket is attached with two roseheaded nails, some of which are missing. The upholstery is a modern silk damask.

Woods: Mahogany; slip seat frame, pine of the *taeda* group.

Dimensions: H. 37 1/4 in. (94.6 cm), SH. 16 11/16 in. (42.4 cm). Seat rails: W. 17 3/8 in. (44.1 cm), MW. 21 9/16 in. (54.8 cm), D. 17 7/16 in. (44.3 cm).

Bibliography: Kirk, *Am. Chairs,* fig. 75.

Provenance: Collings and Collings, New York, N.Y.; Francis P. Garvan, New York, N.Y.; The Mabel Brady Garvan Collection, 1930.2105a.

[1] For the Massachusetts interpretation, see *Sack Coll.,* 1957–72, I, nos. 499 and 568; Downs, *Am. Furn.,* no. 151; Nutting, *Treasury,* no. 2196; Singleton, II, p. 429; *Antiques,* 18 (Sept. 1930), p. 264; *Antiques,* 56 (Nov. 1949), p. 338.—[2] Hornor, pl. 337 and 339; *Antiques,* 53 (April 1948), inside front cover.—[3] Hipkiss, no. 88; Downs, *Am. Furn.,* nos. 41 and 140.

99a

99 99b

100. Side Chair

Massachusetts, 1765–1785

This chair represents the Massachusetts interpretation of the interlaced diamond and figure-eight splat design, and can be compared with the preceding Philadelphia chair, no. 99. The seat upholstered over the rails, the knees with low relief carving and sharply ridged profile, the claw-and-ball feet with swept-back side talons, and the rectangular rear legs are all indications of Massachusetts workmanship. The lunette and foliated pendant on the crest rail are more unusual on Massachusetts chairs of this type, which usually have a drapery swag with semi-circular opening like their Philadelphia counterparts.[1] A particularly elaborate version owned by the Metropolitan Museum of Art in New York is illustrated by Lockwood.[2]

Description: A carved foliated lunette fills the scallop at the center of the crest rail and from it is suspended a three-lobed pendant of leaf carving. In the manner of Massachusetts chairs, the beaded edges of the grooved ears sweep down the lower edge of the crest rail onto the top of the splat. The high-shouldered, vase-shaped splat is pierced at the center with interlaced loops and a diamond form. A small tassel appears on the void above the upper loop. The flat-faced stiles are squared off below the seat to form slightly flared rear feet. The square seat frame, upholstered over the rails, is supported in front by cabriole legs with carved knees and claw-and-ball feet.

Notes: The triangular, horizontally grained corner blocks are attached with glue and nails. The splat passes behind the splat shoe and is housed in the rear seat rail. The joints of the rear and side seat rails with the stiles are secured with two square wooden pegs. Each knee bracket is held in

100

101

place with two nails and glue. The modern silk damask upholstery illustrated has been replaced by a reproduction of a mid-eighteenth-century rose moreen with a stamped pattern (Scalamandré, 1945–1).

Woods: Mahogany; front and side seat rails, soft maple; corner blocks, white pine.

Dimensions: H. 37 7/16 in. (94.1 cm), SH. 17 1/8 in. (43.5 cm). Seat rails: W. 16 7/16 in. (41.8 cm), MW. 21 5/16 in. (54.1 cm), D. 17 5/16 in. (44.0 cm).

Bibliography: Kirk, *Am. Chairs,* fig. 116.

Provenance: Paul N. and Olive L. Dann, New Haven, Conn.; Bequest of Olive L. Dann, 1962.31.1.

---

[1] *Sack Coll.,* 1957–72, I, nos. 499 and 568; Downs, *Am. Furn.* no. 151; Nutting, *Treasury,* no. 2196; Singleton, II, p. 429; *Antiques,* 18 (Sept. 1930), p. 264; *Antiques,* 56 (Nov. 1949), p. 338; Kirk, *Am. Chairs,* figs. 117 and 118.—[2] Fig. 550.

101. Side Chair

Middle Atlantic Colonies, 1755–1775

The interlacing of a figure-eight with a diamond was favored by craftsmen throughout the American colonies. In the catalogue of a 1968 exhibition of Maryland furniture, a chair from this set was said to have come from the Annapolis area, but this regional attribution is difficult to establish.[1] Many of the stylistic and structural features—such as the nicely knuckled claw-and-ball feet, the side seat rails tenoned through the stiles, the chamfered rear legs, and the white cedar and *taeda* pine used as secondary woods—are common features of Philadelphia chairs. The inverted shell on the knee is unusual, but a high chest with a similar shell is said to have descended in the family of Joshua Bunn of Philadelphia.[2] This chair is not so urbane as most examples attributed to Philadelphia, however, and a shop in Philadelphia, or in the surrounding areas—Delaware, Maryland, Pennsylvania, or New Jersey—may have been its place of manufacture. Other examples from this set are now at Colonial Williamsburg.

Description: The splat consists of a figure-eight intertwined with a diamond whose lateral points end in carved volutes. The vase shoulders, base, and neck are pierced with lancets. Grooved ears decorate the ends of the double-serpentine crest rail with a pierced shell at the center. The flat-faced stiles have chamfered edges below the square seat frame supported at the front corners with cabriole legs. Carved inverted shells are found on the knees.

Inscription: The numeral "I" appears on the inside of the rear seat rail and on the seat frame.

Notes: The side seat rails are tenoned through the stiles. The front corner blocks are vertically grained quarter-round blocks made up of three pieces. The triangular rear corner blocks with horizontal grain are attached with glue and nails. Two square wooden pegs are used to secure each joint of the seat rails and legs. The right knee brackets are replacements, and the left knee brackets are glued only. The crest rail is pinned to the top of the stiles with square wooden pegs. The upholstery is a mid-eighteenth-century light blue silk damask, possibly English.

Woods: American black walnut; front corner blocks, Atlantic white cedar; rear corner blocks, tulip; slip seat frame, pine of the *taeda* group.

Dimensions: H. 37 9/16 in. (95.4 cm), SH. 17 in. (43.2 cm). Seat rails: W. 16 in. (40.6 cm), MW. 19 5/8 in. (49.9 cm), D. 17 7/8 in. (45.4 cm).

Bibliography: Hudnut Coll., p. 56, no. 76; Wenham, pl. 21, no. 49; Nutting, *Treasury,* no. 2233; Miller, I, p. 158 (illus. p. 159, no. 138).

Provenance: Alexander M. Hudnut, New York, N.Y., and Princeton, N.J.; Francis P. Garvan, New York, N.Y. (1927); The Mabel Brady Garvan Collection, 1930.2479.

1. *Maryland Furn.,* fig. 6.—2. *Reifsnyder Coll.,* p. 156, no. 548 (illus.).

102

102. Side Chair

New York, 1755–1765

The provenance of this chair is obscure at best, but it has long been assumed that it was part of the set which came from Johnson Hall—built in 1764 by Sir William Johnson (1715–1770), Superintendant of Indian Affairs in New York—near Johnstown, New York. In a discussion of another chair from the set, now at Winterthur, Downs cites an entry of November 6, 1760, in the Martin Van Bergen account books: "To Wm Johnson to freight 6 chairs £0.6.0" from Manhattan.[1] This chair may not have been among the six in question, but the entry indi-

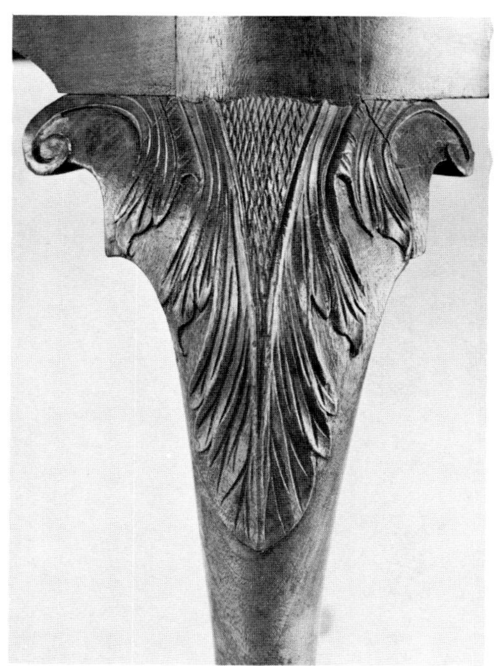

102a

102b

cates that on occasion Johnson purchased goods in Manhattan, where this finely executed chair may have been made. The chairs are often ascribed to Gilbert Ash, based upon the similarity of their splats to the one on a chair from the Van Rensselaer estate whose seat frame is inscribed in pencil "Made by Gilbert Ash in Wall St. warranted sold April 2, 1756 III in set."[2] The diamond and scrolled splat was a favorite of New York chairmakers.[3] Other chairs from the set are at Bayou Bend and in the collection of Stanley Stone.[4]

Description: The depression between the two halves of the double-serpentine crest rail is filled with a diapered lunette whose upper edge has ruffle carving. Serpentine grooves in each half of the crest rail are extensions of the voids formed by the scrolls of the splat. A diamond shape links those scrolls at the center; below the diamond the splat is pierced with two lancet shapes. The tops of the flat-faced stiles are decorated with leafy pendants trailing down from the shells on the ends of the crest rail. Below the seat the stiles are shaped to form square rear feet. The compass-shaped seat has a double-serpentine curve at the front and is supported by cabriole legs terminating in claw-and-ball feet. The leaf carving on the knees begins from volutes on the knee brackets and is filled at the center with a wedge of diapering.

Inscriptions: The front seat rail is marked "IX" and the slip seat frame is marked "VI".

Notes: The front corner blocks are a quarter-round of two pieces with vertical grain; the rear corner blocks are a quarter-round of one piece with vertical grain. Two wooden pegs secure the joints of the side seat rails and brackets and the rear stiles. The rear seat rail is pinned to the stiles with single wooden pegs. The knee brackets are attached with glue only. An intermediary piece of wood is used between the knee brackets and the blocks. The joint of the crest rail and splat has been repaired. The chair was refinished in 1962, but the original webbing and primary covering remains on the slip seat. The horsehair and needlework upholstery illustrated has been replaced with an early eighteenth-century blue silk damask, probably French.

Woods: Mahogany; corner blocks, white pine; slip seat frame, red oak.

Dimensions: H. 39⅜ in. (100.0 cm), SH. 17 in. (43.2 cm). Seat rails: W. 16¹⁄₁₆ in. (40.8 cm), MW. 21⁹⁄₁₆ in. (54.8 cm), D. 18⁹⁄₁₆ in. (47.1 cm).

Exhibitions: Furn. by N.Y. Cabinetmakers, p. 32, no. 39.

Bibliography: "Gallery Notes," *BAFA,* 3 (Dec. 1928), p. 33 (illus.); Meyric R. Rogers, "The Mabel Brady Garvan Collection of Furniture," *Yale Alumni Magazine,* 25 (Jan. 1962), p. 9 (illus.); Kirk, *Am. Chairs,* p. 120, fig. 143.

Provenance: Sir William Johnson (1715–1770), Johnstown, New York; Harry Arons, Ansonia, Conn.; Francis P. Garvan, New York, N.Y. (1924); The Mabel Brady Garvan Collection, 1930.2114.

[1] Downs, no. 149.—[2] Homer Eaton Keyes, "A Clue to New York Furniture," *Antiques,* 21 (March 1932), p. 122.—[3] For more simplified chairs see Comstock, no. 260; *Sack Coll.,* 1957–72, II, no. 937; Lockwood, II, figs. 544 and 546; Singleton, I, p. 309, and II, p. 427.—[4] *Antiques,* 69 (May 1956), p. 439.

Gothic-Patterned Splats

THE ENGLISH have always been enamoured of the Gothic style. Gothic motifs played a major role in the English interpretation of the rococo style proper as well as in its American counterpart. The fusion of Gothic elements such as cusps, crochets, pointed arches, and quatrefoils with other rococo motifs was a particularly English interpretation of the rococo taste. In architecture the Gothic style had persisted in England since medieval times and in the eighteenth century increasingly it was used for domestic buildings, perhaps the best known expression being Horace Walpole's Strawberry Hill, which he began to remodel in 1747. Along with the Chinese influence, the Gothic apparently was considered an appropriate addition to the English rococo style because of its inherently exotic qualities. A design for a chair back in Plate XVI (top middle) of Chippendale's *Director* (1762) shows a montage of elements derived from Gothic architecture. Fairly faithful renderings of this motif, combined with individual embellishments, can be found on chairs made throughout the American colonies. On the Philadelphia and Connecticut chairs from the various Yale collections illustrated in this catalogue, nos. 103–110, the patterns of the Gothic chair backs closely follow the English design. On the Massachusetts chair (no. 111) the Gothic lancets are a freer adaptation of the mode.

103. Side Chair

Philadelphia, 1770–1780
Probably by Thomas Tufft (working about 1770–87)

The attribution of this Philadelphia chair to Thomas Tufft (who worked in Philadelphia *ca.* 1770–87) appears warranted on the basis of a combination of distinctive features in its design and execution: the peculiar small ears of the cresting rail, the narrow Gothic splat with open trefoil and two pierced daggers at its base, and the fluted stiles. Although the carving is richer on the crest rail and skirt, this unusual combination of features is found in Tufft's labeled chair at Winterthur, which also has fluted stiles.[1] Another chair with similar splat and ears but plain stiles is cited by Hornor as having been made by Tufft for the Logan family.[2]

Description: The design from Plate XVI of Chippendale's *Director* (1762) is elaborated upon by the beaded outline of the crest rail and volutes with leaf-carved ends on the ears. A small finial of leaf carving rests on the pinnacle of the pointed arch. The stiles are fluted above the square seat and below it are oval in cross section. The carving on the knees of the cabriole legs has a rosette at the center and a C-scroll, beginning on the knee bracket and outlining the leg, which is similar to the treatment of no. 93.

Inscriptions: The signature "Joseph" [?] appears on the

rear seat rail. The top of the front seat ledge is marked "VI", and the slip seat frame is marked "VI"; the inside of each seat rail is marked "IIII".

Notes: The side seat rails are tenoned through the stiles. The junction of the right stile and seat rail has been repaired. Traces of glue indicate that rear corner blocks were present at one time. Each mortise-and-tenon joint of the seat frame is secured with two square wooden pegs, with the exception of the front legs and the front seat rail. The knee brackets are attached with glue. The upholstery is part silk brocatelle, possibly eighteenth-century.

Woods: Mahogany; seat frame, pine of the *taeda* group.

Dimensions: H. 38½ in. (97.8 cm), SH. 16⁹⁄₁₆ in. (42.1 cm). Seat rails: W. 17⅜ in. (44.1 cm), MW. 21½ in. (54.6 cm), D. 17⁵⁄₁₆ in. (44.0 cm).

Bibliography: Nutting, *Treasury,* no. 2224; *Hudnut Coll.,* p. 52, no. 72; *Antiques,* 13 (Jan. 1928), p. 11 (illus.); *Antiques,* 13 (Feb. 1928), p. 89 (illus.); "Outstanding Examples from the Mabel Brady Garvan Collections," *BAFA,* 8 (Feb. 1938), p. 45 (illus.).

Provenance: Alexander M. Hudnut, New York, N.Y., and Princeton, N.J.; Francis P. Garvan, New York, N.Y.; The Mabel Brady Garvan Collection, 1930.2242b.

[1] Downs, *Am. Furn.,* no. 134.—[2] Pl. 272.

104. Side Chair

Philadelphia, 1760–1780

This chair rivals the preceding example in quality. Here the knees and the feet are more massive and richly carved. Punchwork around the leaf carving of the knees is unusual on Philadelphia chairs (though also present on no. 129). The use of it on the knee brackets and the fact that the spray of carving on the bracket flows from the top rather than from the base is not customary.

Description: In contrast to no. 103, the top edge of the crest rail is not decorated with a bead. The carving at the center—flanked by streamers of small petaled flowers—is richer, but the three flutes instead of four on the stiles are somewhat more coarsely delineated. The carving on the cabriole legs is in lower relief.

Inscriptions: The top of the front seat ledge is marked "II" and the slip seat frame is marked "VI"; the inside of the rear seat rail is marked "II".

Notes: The side seat rails are tenoned through the stiles. The quarter-round front corner blocks are made up of two

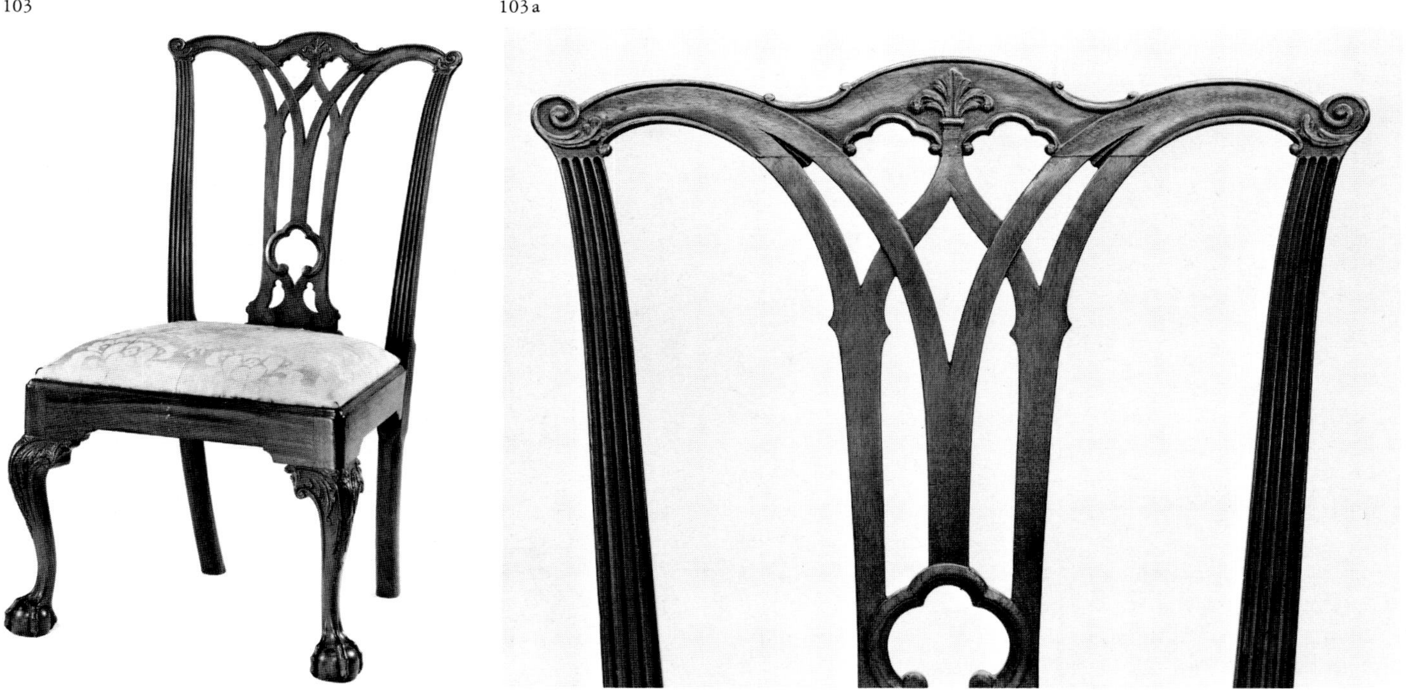

103 103a

104

104a

pieces with vertical grain. The corner blocks may not be original. A 1-inch piece has been added beneath the splat shoe. Single square wooden pegs secure the side seat rails and front legs. Two square wooden pegs secure the joints of the rear seat rail and stiles. The knee brackets are attached with glue. A ½-inch piece has been added to the back of the crest rail where it joins the splat. The top corners of the splat are cracked. The rear seat rail repeats the shape of the front seat rail. The upholstery is part silk brocatelle, possibly eighteenth-century.

Woods: Mahogany; seat frame, pine of the *taeda* group.

Dimensions: H. 38⅜ in. (97.5 cm), SH. 16 13/16 in. (42.7 cm). Seat rails: W. 17 5/16 in. (44.0 cm), MW. 22¼ in. (56.5 cm), D. 17 7/16 in. (44.3 cm).

Bibliography: Miller, I, p. 148 (illus. p. 147, no. 95); Kirk, *Am. Chairs,* p. 91, fig. 89.

Provenance: Frances Wolfe Carey, Haddonfield, N.J.; Francis P. Garvan, New York, N.Y.; The Mabel Brady Garvan Collection, 1930.2518.

104b

105

105a

105. Armchair

Philadelphia, 1760–1780

Armchairs, or "elbow" chairs as they were called, were not always made to accompany sets of chairs. Hornor points out that they were generally more expensive than side chairs. Benjamin Randolph, in one case, charged thirty-five shillings for a side chair, and seventy for an armchair.[1] To accommodate the arms, the width of the back usually had to be expanded so that the arms could be attached to the center of the stiles, but in some instances side chairs were made into armchairs at a great reduction of cost by avoiding that change and attaching the arms to the outside of the stiles. The proportions of this chair have been altered and the space between the stiles and splat is much greater than on no. 104. Its basic outline is similar to that of nos. 103 and 104, but the absence of carving makes it appear much simpler. A related example has been illustrated.[2]

Description: The outline of the crest rail is like that on no. 104, minus the carving. Serpentine arms are attached to the front faces of the flat stiles and end in scrolled handholds. The cabriole legs have plain knees and claw-and-ball feet.

Notes: The side seat rails are tenoned through the stiles. The front halves of the front corner blocks are quarter-round with vertical grain. The rear halves of the front corner blocks are replacements. The rear corner blocks are new. The junction of the seat frame and right stile is damaged. The right side knee bracket is restored. Nail holes on the inside of the seat rails indicate that a board for a chamber pot was present at one time. Each joint of the seat rails and legs is secured with two square wooden pegs. The arm supports are screwed to the side seat rails. Four inches have been restored on the inside face of the right rear stile near the floor. The knee brackets are attached with glue only. The upholstery is a modern striped material.

Woods: Mahogany; corner blocks, tulip and eastern white cedar; slip seat frame, pine of the *taeda* group.

Dimensions: H. 38¼ in. (97.2 cm), SH. 17 1/16 in. (43.3 cm). Seat rails: W. 19 1/16 in. (48.4 cm), MW. 22½ in. (57.1 cm), D. 18 3/16 in. (46.2 cm).

Bibliography: Nutting, *Treasury,* nos. 2206, 4995.

Provenance: E. F. Sanderson, Moor's End, Nantucket, Mass.; Francis P. Garvan, New York, N.Y. (1928); The Mabel Brady Garvan Collection, 1930.2530.

[1] Hornor, p. 215.—[2] *Sack Coll.,* 1957–72, II, no. 260.

106. Side Chair

Philadelphia, 1760–1780

106

A variation on the interlaced Gothic splat is found on this chair, in which C-scrolls ending in small curls flank the pointed arch and give the splat much wider proportions. Hornor illustrates a straight-legged chair with a similar back—for which he claims there is documentation proving that it was made by Samuel Walton.[1] The details of the foliated carving at the top of the pointed arch, the beveled edges of the outer ribs of the splat, and the small curls on the Yale chair bear close comparison with that example.

Description: A bead of three opposing C-scrolls outlines the center of the crest rail, whose ears end in small curls of leaf carving. A piece of leaf carving rests on top of the pointed arch. Flanking the arch, the points and edges on the ribs are accentuated with bevels ending in small curls. Here the crest rail is not as richly carved as on nos. 103 and 104, nor does the quatrefoil have volutes at the base as on those chairs. The stiles are molded above the seat and are oval below. The cabriole front legs have plain knees and claw-and-ball feet.

Inscription: The number "1111" is marked on the inside of the rear seat rail.

Notes: The seat was at one time upholstered over the rails. The top molding of the front seat rail has been restored, and holes on the outer faces of the side seat rails have been repaired. The slip seat frame is a replacement. The knee brackets are attached with nails and glue. The side seat rails are tenoned through the stiles. The quarter-round front corner blocks are made up of two pieces of wood with vertical grain; the rear corner blocks are quarter-round, made of one piece of wood with vertical grain. The joints of the rear seat rails and stiles are secured with square wooden pegs. The upholstery is a modern yellow silk damask in an eighteenth-century *chinoiserie* pattern.

Woods: Mahogany; corner blocks, pine of the *taeda* group.

Dimensions: H. 38 7/16 in. (97.6 cm), SH. 17 in. (43.2 cm). Seat rails: W. 17 3/16 in. (43.7 cm), MW. 20⅞ in. (53.0 cm), D. 17 3/16 in. (43.7 cm).

Provenance: John Black, Washington, D.C. (sale New York, American Art Galleries, American Art Association, Inc., Jan. 2–9, 1926); Francis P. Garvan, New York, N.Y.; The Mabel Brady Garvan Collection, 1930.2499e.

[1] Hornor, pl. 274, p. 188.

107

107. Side Chair

Philadelphia, 1760–1780

When they are not cut straight across, the front seat rails on Philadelphia side chairs usually have C-scrolls, but few examples have reverse curves. Related examples without this feature have appeared in the literature, one of which is supposed to have been owned by Stephen Girard.[1]

Description: The outer edges of the flat stiles and crest rail are decorated with a small bead and small scrolls, and the outer edges of the splat have a treatment similar to that on no. 106, but the integration of the crest rail and the splat is not as complete. The lower edge of the front seat rail is a double-serpentine shape. The cabriole front legs have plain knees and claw-and-ball feet.

Notes: The side seat rails are tenoned through the stiles. The front corner blocks are quarter-round in shape, made up of two pieces of wood with vertical grain. The quarter-round rear corner blocks are made of one piece of wood with vertical grain. The corner blocks have been reattached. The original webbing, primary covering, and stuffing remain on the slip seat, but the outer covering is new. The right side knee bracket and the left front and the side knee brackets are restored. A 9/16-inch strip at the bottom of the rear seat rail is restored. Two insets of wood on the rear stiles and screw holes on the side seat rails suggest that arms were added at one time. Indicative of the vicissitudes this chair must have suffered are the unexplained nail holes in the rear and front seat rails, patches on the stiles, and the slightly different color of the crest rail. Each joint of the legs and seat rails is secured with a single wooden peg. The upholstery is a modern *gros-point* needlework.

Woods: Mahogany; corner blocks, pine of the *taeda* group and Atlantic white cedar; seat frame, pine of the *taeda* group.

Dimensions: H. 37 7/8 in. (96.2 cm), SH. 16 15/16 in. (43.0 cm). Seat rails: W. 16 1/2 in. (41.9 cm), MW. 21 1/4 in. (54.0 cm), D. 16 3/16 in. (41.1 cm).

Bibliography: Margolis Coll., p. 13, no. 81 (illus.).

Provenance: The Boardman Collection, Hartford, Conn.; Jacob Margolis, New York, N.Y.; Francis P. Garvan, New York, N.Y.; The Mabel Brady Garvan Collection, 1930.2060.

[1] *Sack Coll.,* 1957–72, II, no. 1084, and III, p. 673, P3275. Esther Singleton illustrates the chair said to have been Girard's, II, p. 414.

108. Side Chair

Philadelphia, 1760–1780
Benjamin Randolph (active 1760–1782)

This modest, broadly proportioned side chair is a rare documented example of the work of the Philadelphia cabinetmaker and carver Benjamin Randolph, to whom more elaborate rococo furniture—in particular the six "sample" chairs passed down by his descendants—have been attributed. Six walnut chairs exhibited at the New Jersey State Museum in 1930 also bear his label. An undocumented mate to this chair is at Winterthur.[1] The liveliness and precision of the outline reveal the hand of a master craftsman who used fine bead to outline the stiles and crest. The tracery of the splat is crisply articulated, and opposed C-scrolls border its upper part, which has a broader configuration than is usually found on more elaborate Philadelphia chairs.[2]

Description: The narrow, vertical proportions of the Gothic splat on no. 107 are broadened by the opposing C-scroll outlines of the upper part of this splat. The flat stiles and crest rail are outlined here with a series of beads ending in small scrolls. Below the square seat frame, the stiles are square and raked backward. The front legs are square and have molded front corners. Thin, rectangular stretchers brace the understructure.

Inscription: A printed paper label (torn on right side) on inside of rear seat rail reads: "ALL SORTS of . . . / CABINET / AND / CHAIRWORK / MADE and SOLD . . . / BENJ^{N} RAND . . . / At the Sign of the *Golden* . . . / in *Chestnut-Street,* PHILADEL . . ." A partially torn label on the inside of the right side seat rail reads: "219 N. Sharp / Fine Furniture Mantels and Artistic Decorations / 27838 H. L. / repairing 1 mah chair."

Notes: The front left corner block is quarter-round, made of two pieces of wood with vertical grain. The seat frame was made without rear corner blocks. No wooden pegs were used in constructing the seat frame. The center stretcher is dovetailed to the side stretchers. The slip seat frame and right front corner block are replacements. The right side stretcher has been repaired. The upholstery is a light gold reproduction silk damask.

108

108a

Woods: Mahogany; corner block, Atlantic white cedar.

Dimensions: H. 37 in. (94.0 cm), SH. $16\frac{7}{16}$ in. (41.8 cm). Seat rails: W. $18\frac{15}{16}$ in. (48.1 cm), MW. $22\frac{5}{8}$ in. (57.5 cm), D. $19\frac{9}{16}$ in. (49.7 cm).

Bibliography: Nutting, *Treasury,* no. 2285; Fiske Kimball, "The Sources of the Philadelphia Chippendale. A Chair with the Label of Benjamin Randolph," *The Pennsylvania Museum Bulletin,* 23 (Dec. 1927–Jan. 1928), pp. 15–19, fig. D; Samuel W. Woodhouse, Jr., "More about Benjamin Randolph," *Antiques,* 17 (Jan. 1930), p. 24, fig. 5; *Picture Book of Philadelphia Chippendale Furniture,* The Pennsylvania Museum of Art (1931), fig. 13; Kirk, *Am. Chairs,* p. 93, figs. 92 and 92a.

Provenance: Howard Sill; Francis P. Garvan, New York, N.Y.; The Mabel Brady Garvan Collection, 1930.2495.

---

[1] Downs, *Am. Furn.,* no. 142.—[2] Downs, *Am. Furn.,* nos. 129 and 130.

109. Side Chair

Connecticut, 1770–1790
Possibly by Eliphalet Chapin (1741–1807)

The patterns of the back splat of this Connecticut chair and that of a Philadelphia chair labeled by Ben-

109

110

jamin Randolph (no. 108) have a great deal in common. The similarity of the design and the use of through tenons in the Philadelphia manner have in the past suggested an attribution to Eliphalet Chapin (1741–1807), a Connecticut native who is known to have served his apprenticeship in Philadelphia before returning to Connecticut in 1771.[1] However, as objects of art there is no comparison between the two chairs. By eliminating the bead around the edges of the stiles and crest rail, and the small cusps on the splat, the Connecticut craftsman has lost much of the clarity and brilliance of the design.

Description: The outline of the back closely parallels that of the preceding Philadelphia example, no. 108, but the line, unbroken by a bead and small scrolls, is awkward in comparison. The treatment of the base is also similar, although the proportions are narrower.

Inscriptions: The number "VIII" is marked on the inside of the rear seat rail and "V" is marked on the slip seat.

Notes: The side seat rails are tenoned through the stiles. Each through tenon has two small wedges. The front corner blocks are triangular with vertical grain and are nailed in place. Rear corner blocks were not used. The rear and side seat rails and side and rear stretchers are fastened to the rear stiles with single wooden pegs. The right stretcher is repaired at the junction with the medial stretcher. The center stretcher has a blind dovetail. The original webbing, primary covering, and stuffing remain on the slip seat, although the top covering is new. The chair was refinished in 1961. The upholstery is a modern silk damask.

Woods: Cherry; corner blocks and slip seat frame, white pine.

Dimensions: H. 39⅜ in. (100.6 cm), SH. 16¾ in. (42.5 cm). Seat rails: W. 16$\frac{7}{16}$ in. (41.8 cm), MW. 20⅞ in. (53.0 cm), D. 17⅜ in. (44.1 cm).

Exhibitions: Conn. Furn., p. 135, no. 243.

Bibliography: Kirk, *Am. Chairs,* p. 149, fig. 200.

Provenance: Irving W. Lyon, Hartford, Conn.; Mrs. John P. Penney (Mamie P. Lyon), Pittsburgh, Pa.; Francis P. Garvan, New York, N.Y.; The Mabel Brady Garvan Collection, 1930.2565.

---

[1] *Conn. Furn.*, no. 243.

110. Side Chair

Connecticut, 1775–1790

Although this chair is similar to no. 109, the sweep of line of the Gothic arches into the crest rail creates a more unified and animated design. This chair follows Philadelphia practices closely in the choice of design and the use of through tenons. However, the advisability of basing an attribution to Eliphalet Chapin on this evidence is called into question by a very similar chair in the Connecticut Historical Society that descended in the family of the Hartford cabinetmaker George Belden.

Description: This chair is very similar to no. 109, but the edges of the medial ribs are continued on the crest rail and two small lancets appear below the quatrefoil.

Inscription: The number "IIII" is marked on the inside of the rear seat rail and on the slip seat frame.

Notes: The side seat rails are tenoned through the stiles. Each through tenon has two small oak wedges. The front and rear corner blocks are triangular, made up of two pieces of wood with vertical grain. The rear seat rail is fastened to the rear stiles with two square wooden pegs. The side seat rails and side stretchers are fastened to the front and rear legs with single wooden pegs. The bottom edge of the back of the crest rail that overlaps the top of the splat has been replaced with a piece of mahogany. Pieces of wood have been set into the back of each stile and overlap onto the back of the crest rail, suggesting that the crest was broken off at one time. The original webbing, primary covering, and stuffing remain on the slip seat, under the modern silk damask upholstery.

Woods: Cherry; corner blocks and slip seat frame, white pine.

Dimensions: H. 38 in. (96.5 cm), SH. 16⅛ in. (41.0 cm). Seat rails: W. 16⅜ in. (41.6 cm), MW. 20⅝ in. (52.4 cm), D. 16 7/16 in. (41.8 cm).

Provenance: Irving W. Lyon, Hartford, Conn.; Mrs. John P. Penney (Mamie P. Lyon), Pittsburgh, Pa.; Francis P. Garvan, New York, N.Y.; The Mabel Brady Garvan Collection, 1930.2566.

111. Side Chair

Boston, about 1780

The sparse ornamentation and light, straight lines mark this as a Massachusetts chair. The swept-back talons on the feet are lean and elegant. The lancets and cusps on the Gothic splat provide the effect of tracery. This chair was one of a set of six used by the family of James Swan (1754–1830) in Boston and Dorchester. Others are owned by the Museum of Fine Arts, Boston,[1] a Swan heir, and Winterthur.[2] Two others have been illustrated.[3]

Description: The splat of this chair is composed of two rows of radiating pointed arches, with a finial of leaf carving on the top central one. The interior edges of the pointed arches are decorated with cusps and small scrolls. Above the splat the top edge of the crest is outlined with opposing C-scrolls. Leaf carving appears at the lower edge of the outer pair. The stiles have molded faces above the seat and are square below. The cabriole front legs have plain, slightly ridged knees, and claw-and-ball feet with backward sweeping side talons.

Inscriptions: The number "II" is marked on the top edge of the front seat rail; "I" is marked on the slip seat frame.

Notes: The splat shoe is only 8½ inches wide, and does not extend the full width of the rear seat rail to touch the

111

111a

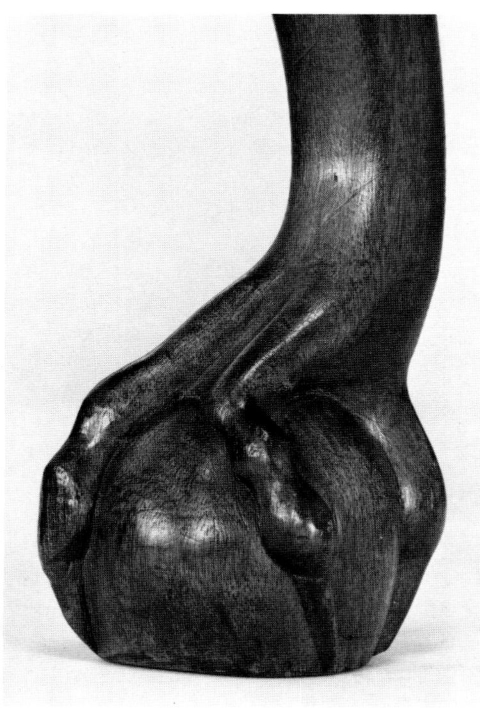

111b

stiles. The crest rail is pinned to the stiles. Two wooden pegs were used to secure each joint of the seat rails and legs. Single wooden pegs were used to secure the joints of the side brackets on the rear legs and stiles. The triangular blocks, possibly original, are held in place with glue and nails. Each knee bracket is held in place with two roseheaded nails and glue. The upholstery is a modern green satin-weave silk.

Woods: Mahogany; corner blocks, white pine; slip seat frame, soft maple.

Dimensions: H. 38³⁄₁₆ in. (97.0 cm), SH. 16⅞ in. (42.9 cm). Seat rails: W. 18¹⁄₁₆ in. (45.9 cm), MW. 22¹¹⁄₁₆ in. (57.6 cm), D. 18⅞ in. (47.9 cm).

Bibliography: Kirk, *Am. Chairs,* p. 109, fig. 122.

Provenance: James Swan, Boston and Dorchester, Mass.; descended to Mary W. Bartol, John W. Bartol, and Abigail W. Clark; Museum of Fine Arts, Boston, Mass.; The Mabel Brady Garvan Collection, 1963.18.2.

---

[1] Randall, no. 155 (illus.).—[2] Downs, *Am. Furn.,* no. 155.—[3] *Sack Coll.,* 1957–72, II, no. 879, and III, no. 1393 (the latter has straight legs).

Interlaced – Scroll Splats

IN THE MID-EIGHTEENTH century chairs with interlaced-scroll splats were a favorite in most American cabinetmaking centers. Their design cannot be directly linked to the plates in Thomas Chippendale's *Director.* In general they represent a less exuberant interpretation of the rococo mode, with their very substantial strapwork rarely encrusted with delicate rococo carving. For their visual effect they rely upon line more than on surface ornament.

112. Side Chair

Philadelphia, 1760–1780

Of the many variations of Philadelphia chairs with interlaced-scroll splats, this one stands out among the best. The outline of the splat—two scrolls that curve down from the crest and meet two scrolls that curve up from the base with double crossed straps in the center—appears on a wide range of chairs, but few capture the free-flowing, three-dimensional effect of this splat, which is also framed by fluted stiles. The most elaborate chairs in the group have tassels suspended between the double crossed straps and have rich carving on the crest rail.[1] The ornament on the Yale chair may not be as rich, but its restrained and harmonized use of decoration is difficult to surpass.

Description: The splat, consisting of scrolls and interlaced straps, provides the center of interest. Fluted stiles and a double-serpentine crest rail with a central carved shell frame the splat. The shell is repeated on the front seat rail. The cabriole front legs have carved knees set within scrolls and claw-and-ball feet; the rear legs are oval in cross section.

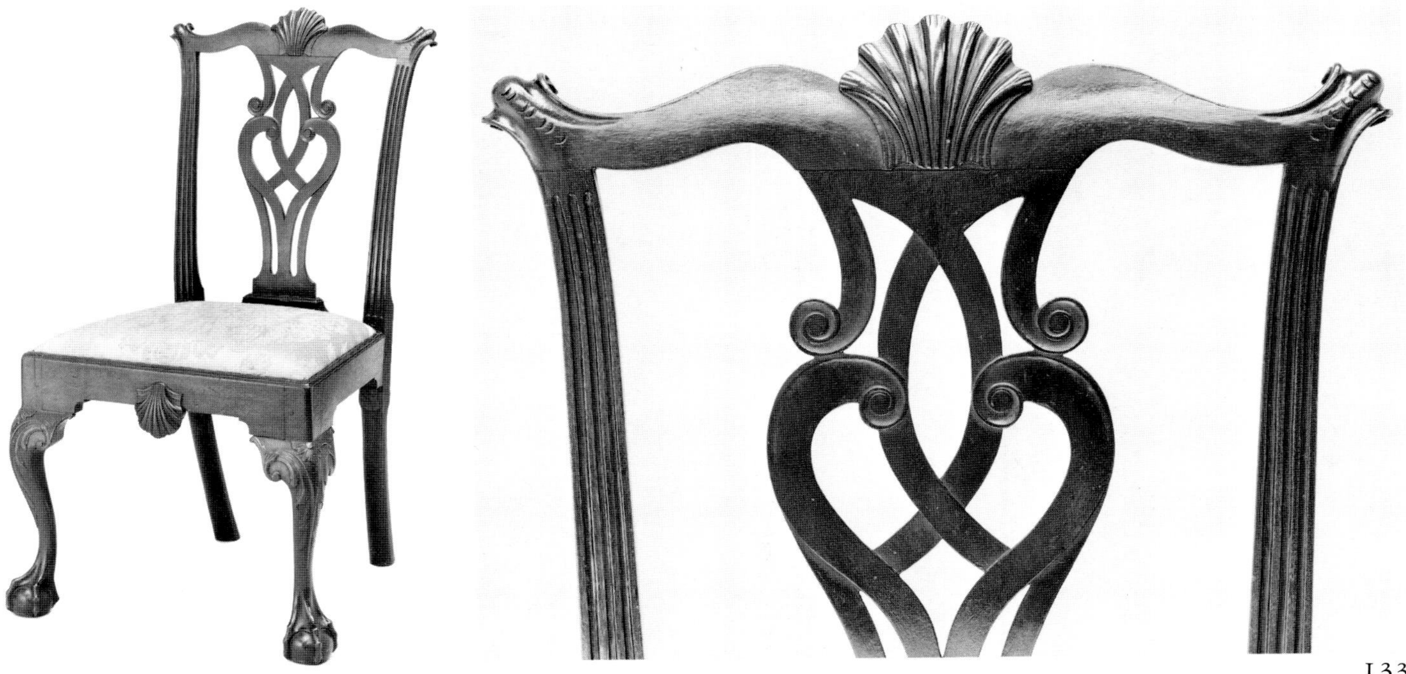

112 112a

Inscription: The top of the ledge on the front seat rail is marked "VIII".

Notes: The corner blocks are replacements, and the knee brackets on the right leg have been restored. The side seat rails are tenoned through the stiles. Nail holes on the inside of the seat rails may indicate that seat ledges were present at one time. Each mortise-and-tenon joint of the seat frame is secured with a single wooden peg. The knee brackets on the left front leg are glued, and the carved shell on the front seat rail is applied. The upholstery is a modern silk damask.

Woods: Mahogany; slip seat frame, tulip.

Dimensions: H. 39¾ in. (101.0 cm), SH. 17⁷⁄₁₆ in. (44.3 cm). Seat rails: W. 16⅞ in. (42.9 cm), MW. 21³⁄₁₆ in. (53.8 cm), D. 16⅞ in. (42.9 cm; measured to the left of shell.)

Bibliography: Edward Warwick, "The Source of an American Chippendale Chair," *Antiques,* 15 (March 1929), p. 215, fig. 7 (owner incorrectly listed as the Pennsylvania Museum, where the chair was then exhibited); *Antiques,* 98 (Sept. 1970), p. 428, fig. 1; Kirk, *Early Am. Furn.,* figs. 46 and 113; Kirk, *Am. Chairs,* p. 80, fig. 69.

Provenance: William W. Smith, Hartford, Conn.; Charles W. Lyon, New York, N.Y.; Francis P. Garvan, New York, N.Y.; The Mabel Brady Garvan Collection, 1930.2502.

[1] See Hipkiss, nos. 85 and 86.

113. Side Chair

Philadelphia, 1765–1780
Possibly by Thomas Affleck (active 1763–1795)

This richly ornamented chair is virtually identical with an example reputedly made for Levi Hollingsworth by Thomas Affleck (active 1763–95) about 1770.[1] It is one of a small group of scroll-back chairs decorated with fluted stiles, shells on the ears, a shell with pendant leafage at the center of the crest rail, branches of leaf carving between the central shell and ears, and leaf carving on the lower scrolls in the

113 113a

splat.[2] A closely related group of chairs has a pierced opening below the central shell from which the branches of leaf carving for the splat begin.[3] The basic form of the chair is not very different from the other examples in this series, but it is more richly embellished. Only the scroll-back chairs with tassels on their crests[4] or in the backs[5] are more ornate examples of the type.

Description: Leaf carving, tightly spiraled volutes, and rosettes embellish the scrolled splat of this chair. Fluted stiles support a crest rail enriched with carved shells on the ears and in the center. The central shell is flanked by branches of foliated carving. A symmetrical shell is applied to the center of the front seat rail. The cabriole front legs have leaf-carved knees and brackets.

Inscription: The number "II" is marked on the top of the ledge inside the front seat rail.

Notes: The side seat rails are tenoned through the stiles and wedged. The front corner blocks are quarter-round, made of two pieces of wood with vertical grain; the rear corner blocks are missing. Each joint of the seat rails and legs is secured with two square wooden pegs. The splat shoe is nailed to the top of the rear seat rail. Both the front and the right side knee brackets are restored. The left side knee bracket is held in place with two roseheaded nails. The slip seat frame is a replacement. The upholstery is a modern silk damask.

Woods: Mahogany; front corner blocks, Atlantic white cedar.

Dimensions: H. 39 5/16 in. (99.9 cm), SH. 16 11/16 in. (42.4 cm). Seat rails: W. 15 7/16 in. (39.2 cm), MW. 21 1/4 in. (54.0 cm), D. 16 in. (40.6 cm).

Provenance: William W. Smith, Hartford, Conn.; Charles W. Lyon, New York, N.Y.; Francis P. Garvan, New York, N.Y.; The Mabel Brady Garvan Collection, 1930.2117.

---

[1] Hornor, p. 217, pl. 220.—[2] Downs, *Am. Furn.,* no. 127; Hipkiss, no. 83; Hornor, pl. 221.—[3] See *Sack Coll.,* 1957–72, III, no. 1400; Hipkiss, no. 84; Kirk, *Am. Chairs,* fig. 70; Nutting, *Treasury,* no. 2183.—[4] See Downs, *Am. Furn.,* no. 37; Nutting, *Treasury,* no. 2181; Kirk, *Am. Chairs,* fig. 67; *Sack Coll.,* 1957–72, I, nos. 32 and 576; Hornor, pl. 154.—[5] See Kirk, *Am. Chairs,* fig. 73; Comstock, no. 263; Hipkiss, nos. 85 and 86; Downs, *Am. Furn.,* no. 125.

114. Side Chair

Philadelphia, 1760–1780

114

Philadelphia chairs often have asymmetrical shells carved on the crest (see nos. 115 and 116), but the ruffled and pierced carving on the seat rail here is a comparatively rare feature. A table attributed to Thomas Affleck is similarly decorated.[1] Identical carving on the knees and shell of the crest appear on a chair at Winterthur,[2] and a related example is illustrated in Hornor.[3]

Description: The basic design is similar to no. 112, but many of the details are different. A pair of scrolls with volutes curves downward from the crest. The straps rising from the deeper base of the splat are not in relief as they cross the outer straps, nor do they end in carved volutes. The edges of the stiles and crest rail are beaded. An asymmetrical shell motif is carved in the center of the crest rail, and an asymmetrical piece of ruffled and pierced carving is found on the front seat rail. The top of the splat shoe is also carved.

Inscriptions: The slip seat frame is marked "V", and the top of the ledge on the front seat rail is marked "IIII".

Notes: The side seat rails are tenoned through the stiles. The front corner blocks are quarter-round, made up of two pieces of wood with vertical grain; the rear corner blocks are also quarter-round, made of one piece of wood with vertical grain and a rectangular block in the corners beneath the splat shoe. Each mortise-and-tenon joint of the seat frame is secured with two wooden pegs. The splat shoe is fastened to the rear seat rail with small sprigs. The shell on the front seat rail is applied, and the knee brackets are attached with nails and glue. The upholstery is an eighteenth-century hand-woven linen.

Woods: Mahogany; corner blocks and slip seat frame, Atlantic white cedar.

Dimensions: H. $40\frac{11}{16}$ in. (103.4 cm), SH. $17\frac{7}{16}$ in. (44.3 cm). Seat rails: W. $15\frac{15}{16}$ in. (40.5 cm), MW. $21\frac{3}{8}$ in. (54.3 cm), D. $16\frac{5}{8}$ in. (42.2 cm).

Bibliography: Kirk, *Am. Chairs*, p. 79, fig. 68.

Provenance: Charles R. Morson, New York, N.Y.; Francis P. Garvan, New York, N.Y. (1929); The Mabel Brady Garvan Collection, 1930.2058.

---

[1] Hornor, pp. 137, 218, pl. 131.—[2] Downs, *Am. Furn.*, no. 126.—[3] Pl. 232.

115. Side Chair

Philadelphia, 1760–1780

One significant difference in the splat design of this chair and of no. 114 as compared with the first chair in the series (no. 112) is that a single pair of carved volutes is used in the splat. The chair is yet another variation of the Philadelphia scroll-back chair, but exact counterparts do not appear in the literature.

Description: This chair is very similar to no. 114, but the carving is not as rich. The splat shoe and knees are plain. The shell on the front seat rail is symmetrical.

Inscriptions: The top of the ledge on the inside of the front seat rail is marked "IIII" and the slip seat frame is marked "V".

Notes: The side seat rails are tenoned through the stiles. The corner blocks are like those on no. 114. The tenon at the joint of the right stile and crest rail has been broken

115 115a

116

116a

and skillfully mended. Each mortise-and-tenon joint of the seat frame is secured with two wooden pegs. The shell is applied to the front seat rail. The knee brackets are attached with nails and glue. The upholstery is a modern silk damask.

Woods: Mahogany; corner blocks, Atlantic white cedar; slip seat frame, red gum.

Dimensions: H. 40 5/16 in. (102.4 cm), SH. 17 3/8 in. (44.1 cm). Seat rails: W. 16 9/16 in. (42.1 cm), MW. 21 9/16 in. (54.8 cm), D. 16 7/8 in. (42.9 cm).

Bibliography: Kirk, *Early Am. Furn.*, fig. 155.

Provenance: Francis D. Brinton, West Chester, Pa.; Francis P. Garvan, New York, N.Y. (1928); The Mabel Brady Garvan Collection, 1930.2086b.

116. Side Chair

Philadelphia, 1760–1780

The side seat rails on Philadelphia chairs are usually tenoned through the stiles, but here that stronger (optional) form of construction, which cost the customer sixpence extra, was omitted.[1]

Description: The volutes on the splat are somewhat tighter and the ears do not flare as much on this example as they do on no. 115.

Inscription: The seat frame and the top of the ledge on the inside of the front seat rail are marked "III".

Notes: The corner blocks are like those on nos. 114 and 115, but they lack the rectangular block beneath the splat shoe. The crest rail has an applied strip behind the splat. The mortise-and-tenon joints of the side seat rails with the rear stiles are secured with two square wooden pegs. A small piece was added to the crest rail where it joins the splat. The left rear corner block was replaced many years ago. The knee brackets are attached with nails. The shell is applied to the front seat rail. The upholstery is a modern yellow silk damask in an eighteenth-century *chinoiserie* pattern.

Woods: Mahogany; corner blocks, Atlantic white cedar; slip seat frame, tulip.

Dimensions: H. 40 7/16 in. (102.7 cm), SH. 17 7/16 in. (44.3 cm). Seat rails: W. 16 1/16 in. (40.8 cm), MW. 21 1/4 in. (54.0 cm), D. 16 15/16 in. (43.0 cm).

Bibliography: Margolis Coll., p. 114, no. 579 (illus.); Kirk, *Early Am. Furn.,* p. 151, fig. 154.

Provenance: Jacob Margolis, New York, N.Y.; Francis P. Garvan, New York, N.Y.; The Mabel Brady Garvan Collection, 1930.2497a.

[1] Hornor, p. 207.

117. Side Chairs (pair)

East Windsor, Connecticut, 1781
Eliphalet Chapin (1741–1807)

In his pioneer book on American furniture, Dr. Irving W. Lyon states: "The writer is familiar with a set of Chippendale chairs with ball and claw feet made by Eliphalet Chapin of South Windsor, Connecticut, as late as the year 1781. The price paid for them at the time was £1 apiece."[1] His son, Irving P. Lyon, reported that when his father purchased the chairs in 1877 he saw the original bill from Chapin to Alexander King, the first owner. The bill is now lost, and Lyon's statement in his book plus the inscription copied by someone from Lyon's notebook onto one of the slip seat frames of these chairs are the basis for the attribution to Eliphalet Chapin. Chapin (1741–1807) was apparently trained as a cabinetmaker in Enfield, Connecticut, spent about four years of apprenticeship in Philadelphia and then returned to East Windsor, where he opened a shop in 1771 which he presumably continued to run until his death in 1807.[2] The influence of his Philadelphia training is evident in the design of this chair, which bears a close relationship to no. 112. In the details of construction—through tenons, stump rear legs, and quarter-round, two-piece corner blocks—Chapin also followed Philadelphia practice. However, in its total conception the chair is not a duplicate of the Philadelphia example. The wood is cherry rather than black walnut. The absence of carving on the knees, the abstraction of the shell, and the continuation of the lines of the strapwork splat from the crest rail through the lower scroll streamline the design in a way not manifested on the Philadelphia counterpart.

Description: The double pair of scrolls on the splat of this chair is like that on no. 112. In general the surface

117a

ornamentation is less rich. The stiles are flat and the center of the seat rail and the knees are plain.

Inscriptions: A note written in pencil on the underside of the slip seat frame of 1930.2516b reads: "The two. . . were part of a set. . . 1781 by Eph. . . Chapin. of South Windsor. . . .their original price in 17. . .was $5. . .Lyon work book." Also in pencil: "They were made for Alexander King in 1781 when he was married. . .him to [daughter] Miss Har[ie]t King, South Windsor, Conn. . . .Oct 31 1877 by Dr. I. W. Lyon." The slip seat and seat frame of 1930.2516a are marked "IIII"; those of 1930.2516b are marked "III".

Notes: The side seat rails are tenoned through the stiles and wedged. The rear seat rails are pinned to the stiles with two wooden pegs.The front corner blocks are quarter-round, made of two pieces of wood with vertical grain and held in place with glue and nails. The quarter-round rear corner blocks are of one piece. The left rear and right front corner blocks on "a" are renailed. The inner face of the rear seat rail is masked with a 3/8-inch pine facing. Each

knee bracket is held in place with three nails and glue. The crest rail on "b" has been repaired. The original webbing, primary covering, and stuffing remain on both slip seats, which were upholstered originally in leather. The modern upholstery is brown leather.

Woods: Cherry; corner blocks and slip seat frame, white pine.

Dimensions: H. 38 9/16 in. (97.9 cm), SH. 16 1/8 in. (40.9 cm). Seat rails: W. 15 11/16 in. (39.8 cm), MW. 20 1/2 in. (52.1 cm), D. 16 11/16 in. (42.4 cm).

Bibliography: "More Evidence for Eliphalet," *Antiques*, 31 (Jan. 1937), p. 11, fig. 7; Emily M. Davis, "Eliphalet Chapin," *Antiques*, 35 (April 1939) p. 172, fig. 2; *Conn. Furn.*, p. 131, no. 236 (illus. p. 130); Kirk, *Am. Chairs*, p. 146, fig. 193.

Provenance: Alexander King, East Windsor, Conn. (1781); descended to Harriet King, South Windsor, Conn.; Irving W. Lyon, Hartford, Conn. (1877); Charles W. Lyon, New York, N.Y.; Francis P. Garvan, New York, N.Y. (1929); The Mabel Brady Garvan Collection, 1930.2516 a and b.

---

[1] Lyon, p. 171.—[2] Phyllis Kihn, ed., "Connecticut Cabinetmakers," *The Connecticut Historical Society Bulletin,* XXXII, 4 (Oct. 1967), pp. 113–14.

118. Side Chair

East Windsor, Connecticut, about 1780
Possibly by Eliphalet Chapin (1741–1807)

Except for such minor differences as the smaller base of the shell on the crest and the carving of the scrolled volutes in the splat, which sharpens the linear quality of the design, this example is a virtual duplicate of no. 117, and is also attributed to Eliphalet Chapin.

Description: This chair is very similar to no. 117, but the carved volutes in the splat create a livelier visual effect.

Inscription: The insides of the rear seat rail and slip seat frame are marked "V".

Notes: The construction of the seat rails and blocks on this chair is like that of no. 117. The nails are missing from the rear corner blocks. The original webbing and primary covering remain on the slip seat. The knee brackets were glued on originally, but now are nailed. The rear seat rail is pinned to the stiles with two wooden pegs. The upholstery is an early eighteenth-century blue silk damask, probably French.

Woods: Cherry; corner blocks, white pine; seat frame, white oak.

Dimensions: H. 38 3/8 in. (97.5 cm), SH. 16 3/8 in. (41.6 cm). Seat rails: W. 16 1/2 in. (41.9 cm), MW. 20 1/2 in. (52.1 cm), D. 16 5/8 in. (42.2 cm).

Exhibitions: Conn. Furn., p. 131, no. 237 (illus.).

Bibliography: Nutting, *Treasury*, no. 2192; Kirk, *Early Am. Furn.*, p. 123, fig. 114; Kirk, *Am. Chairs*, p. 146, fig. 194.

Provenance: Harry Arons, Ansonia, Conn.; Francis P. Garvan, New York, N.Y. (1924); The Mabel Brady Garvan Collection, 1930.2561.

118

118a

119. Armchair

East Windsor, Connecticut, about 1780
Possibly by Eliphalet Chapin (1741–1807)

This close variant of no. 118 is also attributed to Eliphalet Chapin, even though in some respects it does not exhibit the same sureness of hand. The legs are nearly identical to those on the preceding side chairs, but the knuckles on the claws are not as well articulated. The shell, which has only eight lobes, lacks the fullness of the nine-lobed shells on nos. 117 and 118. The ears do not flare as boldly as those on no. 118, nor do the scrolls in the splat—executed without incised lines—capture the feeling of three-dimensional strapwork. The arms, with their unusually successful outward thrust and knuckled handholds, bring the eye down the reverse curve of the arm supports into the seat rails just above the front legs, providing both a visual and structural unity. A related armchair is owned by Mr. and Mrs. Frank Chapman.[1]

Description: This armchair is essentially like nos. 117 and 118, but with the addition of arms. Those arms follow the general outline of Philadelphia chairs with their serpentine shape and scrolled handholds.

Inscription: The number "I" is marked on the back rail of the slip seat frame.

Notes: The construction of the corner blocks and side seat rails is like that of nos. 117 and 118. Breaks in the right side of the splat have been repaired. The junction of the right stile and seat frame has been repaired from the side with two wooden pegs. The right front knee and foot are scarred. The corner blocks have been reattached. The original webbing and primary covering remain on the slip seat. The rear seat rail is pinned to the stiles with two wooden pegs, and the splat shoe is nailed to the rear seat rail. The top of the right arm support has been broken and repaired. The arm supports are screwed to the side seat rails. The knee brackets are held in place with nails and

119

120

Fig. 3—*Drawing of a chair owned by the Stevenson family of Albany, New York, and probably by the maker of no. 120.*

glue. The upholstery is an early eighteenth-century blue silk damask, probably French.

Woods: Cherry; corner blocks and slip seat frame, white pine.

Dimensions: H. 40⁵⁄₁₆ in. (102.4 cm), SH. 16¼ in. (41.3 cm). Seat rails: W. 17⅞ in. (45.4 cm), D. 18¼ in. (46.4 cm).

Bibliography: Kirk, *Am. Chairs*, p. 147, fig. 195.

Provenance: Harry Arons, Ansonia, Conn.; Francis P. Garvan, New York, N.Y. (1924); Mabel Brady Garvan, New York, N.Y. (1937); The Mabel Brady Garvan Collection, 1965.21.

[1] *Conn. Furn.*, p. 133, no. 238 (illus.).

120. Roundabout Chair

New York, 1760–1780

The handsomely formed claws with their pronounced knuckles and straight rear talon are typical of New York carving, as is the stringy leaf carving on the front cabriole leg. This chair has a close counterpart in a chair with a history of ownership in the Stevenson family of Albany.[1] Like the Stevenson chair, this example once served as a commode chair. Fresh looking saw marks along the lower edges of the seat rails and nail holes in the seat rails (probably from the board to support the chamber pot) suggest that the deep skirts of a commode chair have been cut from the seat rails. Such an alteration would have necessitated the addition of knee brackets; in this case the knee brackets are new.

Description: The semi-circular arm rail and crest of this roundabout chair are supported on three elongated vase-shaped arm supports with ogee-shaped ends. Two splats with double pairs of scrolls fill the spaces of the back. Four cabriole legs terminating in claw-and-ball feet support the seat. The front leg has leaf carving on the knee.

Notes: The slip seat frame and knee brackets have been replaced. Numerous repairs have been made in the arm rail. The deep lower edge of the seat rails and supports for a chamber pot have been removed. The end of the C-scroll on the right side of the left splat has been replaced. The mortise-and-tenon joints of the front leg and seat rail are secured with wooden pegs. The upholstery is a modern silk damask.

Woods: Mahogany; inner facing right rear seat rail, white pine; right rear seat ledge, tulip.

Dimensions: H. 30 13/16 in. (78.3 cm), SH. 16 in. (40.6 cm). Seat rails: W. 18 5/8 in. (47.3 cm), D. 18 13/16 in. (47.8 cm).

Bibliography: Miller, I, pp. 252–54 (illus. p. 253, no. 431); Kirk, *Early Am. Furn.*, p. 172, fig. 175.

Provenance: Mrs. Franklin Bartlett, New York, N.Y. (probably sale New York, American Art Association, American Art Galleries, Jan. 10–15, 1921); Francis P. Garvan, New York, N.Y.; The Mabel Brady Garvan Collection, 1930.2695.

[1] Singleton, I, p. 294 (illus.) (fig. 3, facing page); see also *Antiques*, 66 (Oct. 1954), p. 248, for a more recent illustration of the chair.

121. Side Chair

New York, 1765–1785

The source for the splat of this chair—in which one pair of scrolls is suspended from the crest rail and another comes up from the base of the splat and loops over on itself—is Plate 9 of Robert Manwaring's *The Cabinet and Chair-Maker's Real Friend and Companion* (1765). This scrolled-splat design was not so popular as some others, but can be found on chairs made in Philadelphia,[1] Newport,[2] Massachusetts,[3] and on other New York chairs.[4]

Description: The double-loop pattern of the scrollwork on the splat of this chair is tighter than that of the preceding examples. The crest rail with grooved ears is carved at the center with leafage flanked by two rosettes. The square seat frame is supported at the front corners by cabriole legs with coarsely carved knees. The carving on the knee brackets is an amorphous rosette form.

Inscriptions: The top edge of the front seat rail is marked "VI", and the slip seat frame is marked "IIIIII".

Notes: The rear brackets are pinned to the stiles. The left front corner block is quarter-round in shape, made of one piece of wood with vertical grain. The right rear corner block is similar, with an additional rectangular block under the splat shoe. Two square wooden pegs appear at the joints of the side seat rails and front legs, and of the side seat rails and rear legs. The left rear leg has been broken and repaired about 4 inches below the seat. The right volute and right side of the scrolled section of the splat have been restored. The knee brackets are attached with glue only. The rear half of the right front knee bracket has been restored. The upholstery is a modern green silk.

Woods: Mahogany; right rear corner block, red gum; left front corner block, mahogany; rectangular rear corner block under splat shoe, red gum; rear seat rail and seat frame, red gum.

Dimensions: H. 39 5/16 in. (99.9 cm), SH. 17 3/4 in. (45.1 cm). Seat rails: W. 17 7/8 in. (45.4 cm), MW. 22 1/4 in. (56.5 cm), D. 18 9/16 in. (47.1 cm).

Bibliography: *Garvan Coll.*, p. 236, no. 365; *Sack Coll.*, 1957–72, I, no. 307; Kirk, *Am. Chairs*, p. 122, fig. 147.

Provenance: Francis P. Garvan, New York, N.Y.; Israel Sack, Inc., New York, N.Y.; The Mabel Brady Garvan Collection, 1963.11a.

[1] *Sack Coll.*, 1957–72, no. 667; II, nos. 1253, 667; and III, p. 672, P2864; Kirk, *Am. Chairs*, fig. 78.—[2] *Sack Coll.*, 1957–72, III, p. 746, P3380; Ott, no. 12; Kirk, *Am. Chairs*, fig. 182.—[3] *Sack Coll.*, 1957–72, II, no. 942.—[4] Kirk, *Am. Chairs*, figs. 146, 148.

121

122. Side Chair

Providence, Rhode Island, 1760–1780

A few chairs with stiles which sweep into rounded crest rails and splats of dynamic strapwork can be found in the designs published in 1745 by De La Cour, a French engraver who worked in England between 1741 and 1747.[1] The design is unusual in America, but chairs with backs reminiscent of the published design turn up in Rhode Island. One set of chairs related to this example was handed down in the family of General James of Providence.[2] Another pair, with their original needlework seats, and claw-and-ball feet, descended in the Bangs family of Newport (now at Winterthur).[3] "Providn" is found on the slip seat of this chair and also on the slip seat of a similar chair in the collection of Mr. and Mrs. Bayard Ewing. A slipper chair similar to this example has also been published.[4]

Description: The flat-faced stiles curve in to meet the crest rail where two halves give the effect of interlacing to form the top of the splat. The lower part of the splat is pierced with one wedge-shaped and two elongated voids. The compass seat is supported at the front corners with cabriole legs terminating in pad feet. Block and spindle stretchers brace the legs.

Inscriptions: Written in ink on the slip seat frame: "Providn". The number "III" is marked on the top of the front seat rail.

122a

122

Notes: The joints of the slip seat are secured with large pins. The seat frame is made without corner blocks. The front corner blocks are new. The crest rail is pinned to the stiles. Two square wooden pegs are used to fasten the side seat rails to the rear stiles; single wooden pegs are used to secure the joints of the rear seat rail and stiles and the side and front seat rails with the front legs. The splat shoe is nailed to the rear seat rail. The side stretchers are pinned to the front and rear legs. The knee brackets are held in place with wire nails and glue. The original webbing, primary covering, and stuffing remain on the slip seat. The modern upholstery illustrated has been replaced by a reproduction red silk damask.

Woods: American black walnut; slip seat frame, soft maple.

Dimensions: H. 36 15/16 in. (93.8 cm), SH. 17 in. (43.2 cm). Seat rails: W. 15 in. (38.1 cm), MW. 19 7/8 in. (50.5 cm), D. 16 7/16 in. (41.8 cm).

Bibliography: Nutting, *Treasury,* no. 2177.

Provenance: Gift of C. Sanford Bull, Middlebury, Conn., 1953.50.4.

[1] Ward-Jackson, p. 34, fig. 19.—[2] Carpenter, p. 40, fig. 14.—[3] Acc. No. G59.83.1.,.2.—[4] *Sack Coll.*, 1957–72, II, no. 928.

123. Side Chair

Massachusetts(?), 1760–1780

According to Irving W. Lyon's label, this chair was owned by William Pitkin, Governor of Connecticut from 1765 to 1769. It has many features of eastern Massachusetts chairs,[1] and in fact a comparable example has a Charlestown, Massachusetts, history of ownership.[2] The ears with central groove, the raised crescent of the crest rail, the simple knee brackets scooped out on the lower edge, the block and spindle stretchers, and the ridged knees are all features associated with chairs made in Massachusetts.

Description: The two serpentine-shaped halves of the crest rail of this chair are linked by a pierced semi-circle. The line of the crest rail continues into the double scrolls of the splat. The flat-faced stiles are square below the seat, where block and spindle stretchers brace the legs. The cabriole front legs have sharp, ridged knees and terminate in pad feet.

Inscription: An ink inscription on a torn paper label (now removed from the chair to gallery files) reads: "Gov W^{m}. . ./ Chair - s. . ./ my Catalo. . ./ Page 45. No. . ./ I W Lyo. . ."

Notes: The front corner blocks are triangular in shape with horizontal grain and are attached with roseheaded nails and glue. The crest rail is pinned to the stiles. The rear seat rail is pinned to the stiles with single wooden pegs. The side seat rails are pinned to the stiles with double wooden pegs. The side stretchers are pinned to the rear stiles. The splat shoe is nailed to the rear seat rail. Each knee bracket is held secure with two nails. A new 1-inch-deep piece has been added to the inside of the rear seat rail. The rear corner blocks are new. The left stile has been cracked and repaired above the seat. The upholstery is a modern silk damask.

Woods: American black walnut; seat rails, soft maple; corner blocks, white pine.

Dimensions: H. 38 9/16 in. (97.9 cm), SH. 17 1/8 in. (43.5 cm). Seat rails: W. 15 3/4 in. (40.0 cm), MW. 20 in. (50.8 cm), D. 16 7/8 in. (42.9 cm).

Provenance: William Pitkin (1694–1769), Hartford, Conn.; Irving W. Lyon, Hartford, Conn.; Mrs. John P. Penney (Mamie P. Lyon), Pittsburgh, Pa.; Francis P. Garvan, New York, N.Y.; The Mabel Brady Garvan Collection, 1930.2415.

[1] The probate papers on file for William Pitkin at the Connecticut State Library, Hartford, do not contain an inventory of his personal estate.—[2] Randall, no. 143.

123

124. Side Chair

Massachusetts, 1760–1780

The classic Massachusetts scroll-back chair is different in conception than its Philadelphia counterpart (nos. 112–116). The scrolls in the upper part of the splat are visually extended from the crest rail by the bead on the lower edge of the ear and by the pair of tapering indentations under the central ornament. From those indentations the strapwork of the second pair of scrolls also begins. This placement of those scrolls, beginning at the crest and then curving in toward the center of the chair, is unlike the Philadelphia type. The next four entries (nos. 125–128) illustrate some of the variations made in Massachusetts. A set of four chairs very nearly identical to the Yale chair (including the unusual bulbous turning on the medial stretcher) has been illustrated.[1] Another chair supposedly lent to George Washington in 1775 for his use at Cambridge, Massachusetts, by the Hon. William Greenleaf of Boston also shares with this example a carved shell on the crest, volutes, and carved knees.[2] Most examples have fewer carved details than those exhibited on this chair.

Description: A shell with a pierced opening below spans the two halves of the crest rail, on which tapering indentations begin to define the individual straps of the splat. Two pairs of scrolls end in carved volutes, and below them a heart-shaped opening is flanked by two elongated voids. Flat leaf carving, heightened by incised lines and punchwork, spills from the corners of the square seat frame over the knees of the cabriole legs. The claw-and-ball feet have swept-back side talons.

Inscription: Written in pencil on the underside of the

124a

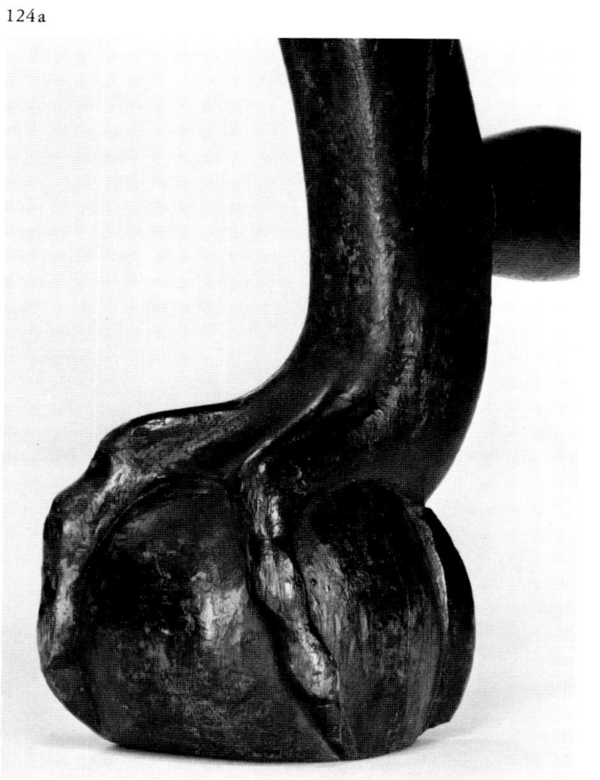

124b

124

slip seat frame: "C. D. Barnitz 1890/ 2010 St. Paul St Balt." The same inscription (in one line) is written in pencil on the inside of the slip seat frame. The number "IIII" is marked on the top of the ledge of the front seat rail, and "I" is marked on the slip seat frame.

Notes: The front corner blocks are like those on no. 123. Each joint of the legs and seat rails is held secure with a single wooden peg. The side stretchers are pinned to the rear stiles. Each knee bracket is held in place with glue and two nails. The left leg is cracked just above the point where it joins the stretcher. The splat shoe is pinned to the rear seat rail. The upholstery is old black horsehair.

Woods: Mahogany; corner blocks, white pine; slip seat frame, soft maple.

Dimensions: H. 37½ in. (95.3 cm), SH. 16⁷⁄₁₆ in. (41.8 cm). Seat rails: W. 15⅞ in. (40.3 cm), MW. 20 in. (50.8 cm), D. 17⁵⁄₁₆ in. (44.0 cm).

Bibliography: Kirk, *Early Am. Furn.*, figs. 45, 47; Kirk, *Am. Chairs*, p. 101, fig. 106.

Provenance: Barton Brothers, Centreville, Md.; Francis P. Garvan, New York, N. Y.; The Mabel Brady Garvan Collection, 1930.2127a.

---

[1] *Sack Coll.* 1957–72, II, no. 911.—[2] *Sack Coll.* 1957–72, I, no. 605.

125. Side Chair

Possibly Boston, 1760–1780

Seats upholstered over the rails, like this one, are found more frequently on Massachusetts chairs made during this period than on chairs made elsewhere in America. The dates offered in the literature for Mas-

125

sachusetts scroll-back chairs vary enormously. If these chairs have pad feet, as they often do, Nutting was inclined to date them as early as 1740.[1] If they were more elaborately carved, he chose a date range of 1760–75.[2] More recent authors tend to choose the date 1760 for their introduction.[3] The inscription on this chair suggests it was owned in Boston and may possibly have originated there.

Description: This chair, similar to no. 124, has a pair of rosettes rather than volutes carved in its splat. The seat is upholstered over the rails. The carving on the knees is in higher relief than on no. 124, and the claw-and-ball feet are badly worn.

Inscription: A torn paper label on the rear seat rail reads: "...rty of/ WIS HOWEL.../ ATTY./ BOSTO..."

Notes: The splat passes behind the shoe and is housed in the rear seat rail. The splat shoe is nailed to the rear seat rail. The rear and side seat rails are pinned to the stiles with a single square wooden peg. The side stretchers are pinned to the stiles and the knee brackets are held in place with glue and nails. The corner blocks are new. The upholstery is a modern silk damask.

Woods: Mahogany; slip seat frame, soft maple.

Dimensions: H. 37 7/16 in. (95.1 cm), SH. 16 1/4 in. (41.3 cm). Seat rails: W. 15 3/4 in. (40.0 cm), MW. 20 3/8 in. (51.8 cm), D. 17 1/4 in. (43.8 cm).

Bibliography: *Ayer Coll.*, p. 110, no. 436; Kirk, *Am. Chairs*, p. 102, fig. 108.

Provenance: Fred Wellington Ayer, Bangor, Me.; Francis P. Garvan, New York, N.Y.; The Mabel Brady Garvan Collection, 1930.2738.

[1] *Treasury*, no. 2169.—[2] *Ibid.*, no. 2226.—[3] Randall, no. 143; Greenlaw, no. 54.

126. Side Chair

Boston, 1760–1780

The pendant of leaf carving surrounded by punchwork on this Massachusetts scroll-back chair is a popular variation from the shell ornament found on the crest of nos. 124 and 125. An example in the Museum of Fine Arts, Boston, ascribed to the Boston area has a splat on which both pairs of volutes are carved.[1] A chair at Winterthur has volutes treated like the Yale chair, but the knees are carved rather than plain.[2] Two other examples illustrated have similar crest ornaments, but do not have stretchers.[3]

126

Description: A pendant of foliated carving flanked by C-scrolls replaces the shell on the crest rail. The knees are plain.

Inscriptions: Written in black on the underside of the rear seat rail: "Dr. Packard 951 Park Ave". The number "IIII" is marked on the top of the ledge on the front seat rail; the slip seat frame is marked "III".

Notes: The seat frame is made without corner blocks. Each joint of the seat rails and legs is secured with a single wooden peg. The side stretchers are pinned to the rear stiles. The knee brackets are attached with new nails and glue. The upholstery is an eighteenth-century silk damask.

Woods: Mahogany; slip seat frame, soft maple.

Dimensions: H. 37 1/2 in. (95.2 cm), SH. 16 7/16 in. (41.8 cm). Seat rails: W. 15 11/16 in. (39.8 cm), MW. 21 in. (53.3 cm), D. 17 7/16 in. (44.3 cm).

Bibliography: Kirk, *Am. Chairs*, p. 101, fig. 107.

Provenance: Henry H. Taylor, Bridgeport, Conn.; Francis P. Garvan, New York, N.Y.; The Mabel Brady Garvan Collection, 1930.2478b.

[1] Randall, no. 146.—[2] Downs, *Am. Furn.*, no. 152.—[3] *Sack Coll.* 1957–72, II, no. 875; Nutting, *Treasury*, no. 2226.

127. Side Chair

Massachusetts, 1760–1780

The center of the crest rail is uncarved on this Massachusetts scroll-back chair, and the compass seat is also an unusual feature. Here the medial stretcher terminates in square blocks rather than tapered ends, a detail found on both examples of the form at Winterthur,[1] and on chairs at the Bayou Bend Collection[2] and at the Henry Ford Museum.[3]

Description: The seat is compass shaped, instead of square, on this typical Massachusetts scroll-back chair. The knees on the cabriole legs are rounded, not ridged as on the preceding chairs of this type, nos. 124–126.

Inscription: The number "I" is marked on the top of the front seat rail and on the slip seat frame.

Notes: The seat frame is made without corner blocks. The side stretchers are pinned to the rear stiles. Each joint of the seat rails and legs is secured with a single wooden peg. Each knee bracket is held in place with three old nails and glue. The upholstery is nineteenth-century needlework.

Woods: Mahogany; slip seat frame, soft maple.

Dimensions: H. 37¾ in. (95.9 cm), SH. 16⅞ in. (42.9 cm). Seat rails: W. 16¼ in. (41.3 cm), MW. 21⅝ in. (54.9 cm), D. 18 in. (45.7 cm).

Bibliography: Kirk, *Am. Chairs*, p. 99, fig. 103.

Provenance: Henry V. Weil, New York, N.Y.; Francis P. Garvan, New York, N.Y. (1923); The Mabel Brady Garvan Collection, 1930.2116.

[1] Downs, *Am. Furn.*, nos. 56 and 152.—[2] Comstock, no. 258.—[3] *Sack Coll.*, 1957–72, I, no. 605.

128. Side Chair

Massachusetts, 1760–1780

Among the most streamlined and graceful of the Massachusetts scroll-back chairs is this example,

127

128

128a

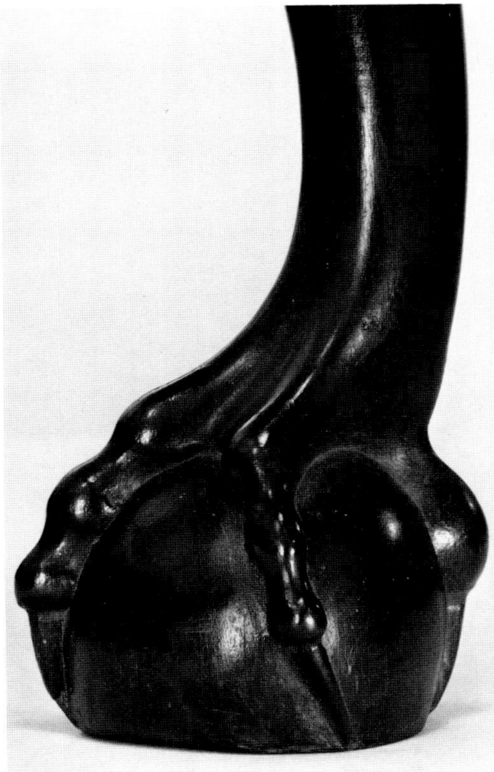

which is unified by the curvilinear form of the seat and the vitality of the front legs. The beauty of the slender ankles is matched by the bold backward sweep of the side talons. Squared rear feet are more characteristic of English, Rhode Island, and New York chairs, but they occasionally appear on examples made in Massachusetts, such as a chair in the Museum of Fine Arts, Boston,[1] and one at Winterthur.[2]

Description: The compass-shaped seat is supported at the front by cabriole legs terminating in beautifully carved claw-and-ball feet with swept-back side talons. The flat-faced stiles continue below the seat to form rear legs with feet squared off in the English manner.

Inscriptions: The number "VI" is marked on the top of the front seat rail and "I" appears on the slip seat frame.

Notes: Triangular, horizontally grained corner blocks are attached with glue and nails. The crest rail is pinned to the tops of the stiles. The splat shoe is nailed to the rear seat rail. Single wooden pegs secure the joints of the seat rails with the legs. Each of the knee brackets and the brackets on the rear legs are held in place with two roseheaded nails. The upholstery is eighteenth-century blue silk damask, probably French.

Woods: Mahogany; corner blocks, white pine; slip seat frame, soft maple.

Dimensions: H. 38 in. (96.5 cm), SH. 17 1/16 in. (43.3 cm). Seat rails: W. 15 11/16 in. (39.9 cm), MW. 21 3/16 in. (53.8 cm), D. 17 5/8 in. (44.8 cm).

Bibliography: Kirk, *Am. Chairs*, p. 100, fig. 104.

Provenance: R. S. Somerville, New York, N.Y.; Francis P. Garvan, New York, N.Y.; The Mabel Brady Garvan Collection, 1930.2563.

[1] Randall, no. 149.—[2] Downs, *Am. Furn.*, no. 154.

Other Types of Pierced Splat

THE FASHION of chair backs with pierced splats has been related heretofore (nos. 90–128) to designs published by Thomas Chippendale or by Robert Manwaring. The mode was widely accepted and had many interpretations in the mid-eighteenth century, and in the preceding chairs the designs of the backs have fallen into recognizable groups of patterns. The last four mid-eighteenth-century chairs with pierced splats (nos. 129–132), cannot be related in this way to other chairs in the collection. These four come from widely dispersed areas (Pennsylvania to Connecticut) and three of them (nos. 130–132) share a more simplified arrangement of the pierced decoration.

129. Armchair

Philadelphia, 1760–1780

The sculptural quality of the arms and arm supports, the carved volutes on the crest rail, and the depth of the seat rails relate this armchair to the more massive examples made in Philadelphia before the mid-eighteenth century, rather than to the lighter rococo-style chairs of the 1760's and 1770's. An identical chair is owned by the Henry Ford Museum[1] and the unusual splat, more elaborately carved, appears on a chair at Winterthur,[2] and on a number of chairs illustrated by Hornor.[3] An example in the Karolik Collection (Museum of Fine Arts, Boston) has virtually identical carving on the crest rail and knees.[4] Restored feet are a serious defect in any chair and greatly reduce its market value. In this case their skillful replacement, which almost defies detection, makes the chair a fine study object for the student—as does the inconsistency of the severely plain splat and the rich carving of the crest rail, arms, arm supports, and knees.

Description: The beaded edges of the stiles and crest rail outline the large flared ears and the volutes flanking the center of the splat. A shell with pendant leaves and rosettes decorates the center of the crest rail. The pierced splat is

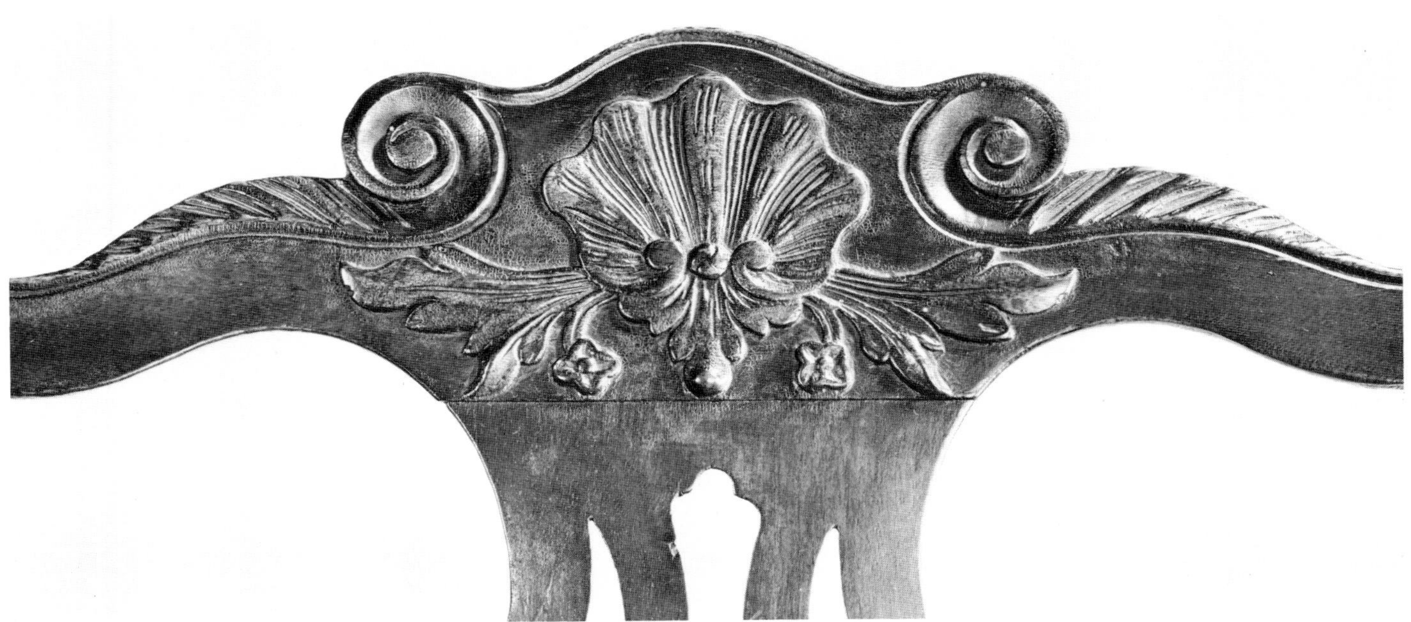

129 a

129

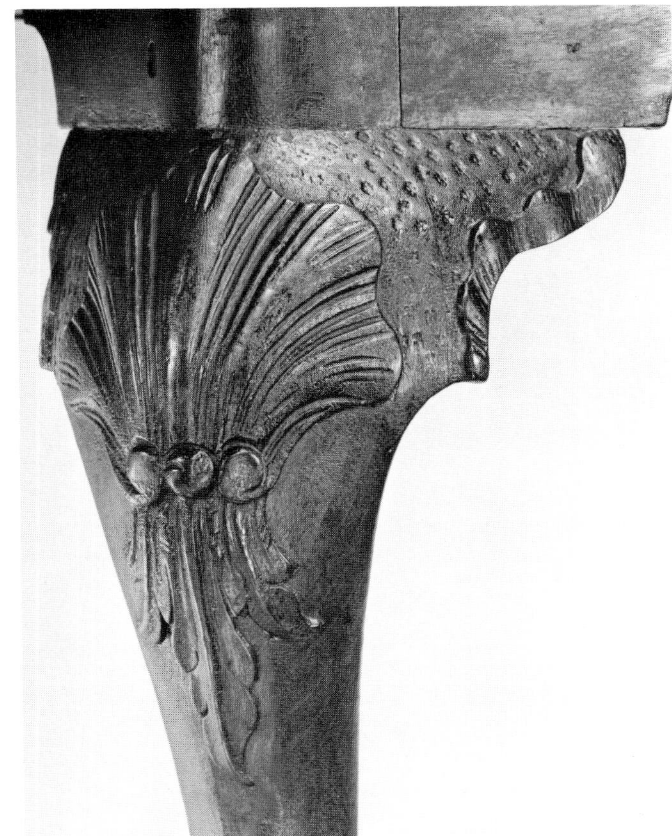

129 b

plain except for the carved rosettes at its neck. The serpentine arms have scrolled handholds and C-shaped, ridged arm supports. The rounded front corners of the seat frame are supported by cabriole legs with shell carving on the knees.

Notes: Holes on the inside of the rear seat rail indicate that a seat ledge is missing. Small repairs have been made to the splat. On the back of the crest rail there are holes from a Victorian crest, which was present when the chair was sold at the Black sale and was later removed. The chair may at one time have been converted to a rocking chair, since the front and rear feet were cut off; the lower half of the claw-and-ball feet and ten inches of the rear stiles are new. The arms and side seat rails have been tenoned through the stiles. The seat frame is made without corner blocks. The mortise-and-tenon joints of the seat frame are pinned with large square wooden pegs—one at the front, two on each side of the front, and two on each side at the back. The nail holes at the center of the front seat rail suggest that an applied shell was present at one time. The upholstery is a modern yellow silk damask in an eighteenth-century *chinoiserie* pattern.

Woods: American black walnut; slip seat frame, pine of the *taeda* group.

Dimensions: H. 43 in. (109.2 cm), SH. 17 in. (43.2 cm). Seat rails: W. 17⅞ in. (45.4 cm), MW. 22⅜ in. (56.8 cm), D. 17½ in. (44.5 cm).

Bibliography: Black Coll., p. 35, no. 122; Kirk, *Am. Chairs,* p. 78, fig. 66.

Provenance: John L. Black, Washington, D.C.; Francis P. Garvan, New York, N.Y. (1926); The Mabel Brady Garvan Collection, 1930.2500.

[1] Comstock, fig. 244.—[2] Downs, *Am. Furn.,* no. 124.—[3] Pl. 325–28.—[4] Hipkiss, no. 78.

130. Side Chair

Philadelphia, 1760–1780

When writing about a similar chair at Winterthur, Downs noted that collectors had designated chairs of this type as hailing from Chester County, to distinguish their slightly coarser detail from more urbane Philadelphia workmanship. Downs himself decided that the chair in the Winterthur Collection was probably a product of the Baltimore and Annapolis school of chairmaking.[1] However, the similarity of the large ears and of the shell-and-tassel carving on the crest with examples whose Philadelphia origin is not questioned raises doubts about Downs's attribution. An upholstery label on the slip seat frame of this chair also indicates it was in Philadelphia in the early twentieth century. Another example has been illustrated which descended in the Morton family of Philadelphia;[2] an armchair is owned by the Art Institute of Chicago;[3] and other side chairs are known.[4]

Description: Suspended along the crest rail from the large, tightly scrolled ears are tassels that flank the shell at the center. The splat has five elongated voids and leaf-carved edges. The stiles are fluted. The striated surface of the shell carving covers both the center of the leaf carving on the knees and the rounded front corners of the seat frame. An inverted shell ornaments the front seat rail. The front legs terminate in undersized claw-and-ball feet and the ends of the rear stiles are slightly bulbous.

Inscriptions: Two upholstery labels are attached to the webbing of the slip seat. The first reads: "OFFICIAL STATEMENT / MATERIALS USED IN FILLING / STERILIZED AND DISINFECTED / Hair Previously used / Weirich & Schnetzler / 4001 Sansom Street / PHILADELPHIA, PA. / THIS ARTICLE IS MADE IN COMPLIANCE / WITH THE ACT OF ASSEMBLY OF PENN / SYLVANIA, APPROVED ON THE 14TH DAY / OF JUNE A.D. 1923. / PERMIT NUMBER 95." The second reads: "Commonwealth of Pennsylvania / DEPARTMENT OF LABOR AND INDUSTRY / HARRISBURG / REGISTRY NO. / 5080." The number "I" is marked on the top of the ledge inside the front seat rail.

Notes: The side seat rails are tenoned through the stiles and wedged. The front of the right front corner block is a quarter-round shape with vertical grain. The left seat rail has been replaced, and the rear corner blocks have been reattached. Nail holes in the top of the seat ledge suggest the seat was nailed in place at one time. The knee brackets are held in place with single roseheaded nails. The joints of the rear seat rail and stiles are secured with two square wooden pegs. The upholstery is a modern yellow silk damask in an eighteenth-century *chinoiserie* pattern.

Woods: Mahogany; right front corner block, tulip; seat frame, white pine.

Dimensions: H. 39³⁄₁₆ in. (99.5 cm), SH. 17 in. (43.2 cm). Seat rails: W. 16 in. (40.6 cm), MW. 20⅞ in. (53.0 cm), D. 16⁷⁄₁₆ in. (41.8 cm; measured to the left of carving).

Provenance: William W. Smith, Hartford, Conn.; Charles W. Lyon, New York, N.Y.; Francis P. Garvan, New York, N.Y.; The Mabel Brady Garvan Collection, 1930.2496.

[1] Downs, *Am. Furn.,* no. 123.—[2] *Sack Coll.,* 1957–72, I, no. 18.—[3] Acc. no. 29.497.—[4] *Antiques,* 62 (Nov. 1952), inside front cover; *Antiques,* 64 (Dec. 1953), p. 425.

130

130a

131. Roundabout Chair

Possibly New York, 1775–1800

Chairs with somewhat similar features have often been attributed to New York cabinetmakers. One such example is a roundabout chair at Winterthur with the same unusual crescent-shaped crest rail.[1] The combination of walnut and hard pine also suggests an origin in the Middle Colonies or further south.

Description: The semi-circular arm rail and crescent-shaped crest on this roundabout chair are supported by three columnar-shaped arm supports. Splats with three elongated voids above a heart-shaped opening fill the space in the back. The square legs are braced by four rectangular stretchers.

Notes: The joints of the slip seat frame are pinned. The crest rail is attached with old screws. The seat ledges are attached with roseheaded nails. Each joint of the seat rails and stretchers with the legs is secured with one squared wooden peg. The two halves of the arm rail are lapped at the center. The arm supports are pinned to the arm rail from the rear with square wooden pegs. The right end of the crest rail has been cracked. The upholstery is a modern figured cotton cloth.

Woods: American black walnut; rear seat ledges and slip seat frame, pine of the *taeda* group.

Dimensions: H. 32 in. (81.3 cm), SH. 17⅝ in. (44.8 cm). Seat rails: W. 18½ in. (47.0 cm), D. 18$\frac{7}{16}$ in. (46.8 cm).

Provenance: Walter and Draper, Poughkeepsie, N.Y.; Francis P. Garvan, New York, N.Y. (1924); The Mabel Brady Garvan Collection, 1930.2560.

---

[1] Downs, *Am. Furn.*, no. 69.

131

132

132. Side Chair

Connecticut, 1775–1800

This side chair was purchased by Mrs. Archer Smith sometime before 1919. Her daughter-in-law, Mrs. Julius B. Smith, was told by Mrs. Smith that it had once belonged to Timothy Dwight (1752–1817), the eighth president of Yale College. A simplified interpretation of a pierced splat chair, it is made of cherry, a wood popular with Connecticut cabinetmakers. A similar chair is included in the 1969 exhibition of Litchfield County furniture and two other Connecticut examples cited in the catalogue of that exhibition have long histories of ownership in Litchfield.[1]

Description: A vase-shaped splat with prominent handles and lancet and diamond-shaped openings ornaments the back of this chair. The flared ears of the crest rail continue the upward line of the flat-faced stiles. Four stretchers brace the square legs.

Inscriptions: A red and white paper label inside the right rear stile just below the seat frame reads: "Timothy Dwight / 1790 / Pres. Yale."

Notes: The crest rail is pinned to the stiles. The side stretchers and side seat rails are tenoned through the rear stiles. Each through tenon has two wooden wedges. Single wooden pegs were used to secure the seat rails and stretchers to the legs. The seat frame is made without corner blocks. The tack holes on the upper edges of the seat rails have been filled. The slip seat frame is new. The upholstery is an English roller-printed cotton chintz with a polychrome floral pattern on a brown mill and die ground, ca. 1835–40.

Wood: Cherry.

Dimensions: H. 39 in. (99.1 cm), SH. 17⅜ in. (44.2 cm). Seat rails: W. 15⅝ in. (39.7 cm), MW. 19⅝ in. (49.9 cm), D. 15⅝ in. (39.7 cm).

Provenance: According to tradition, owned by Timothy Dwight (1752–1817), New Haven, Conn.; purchased before 1919 by Mrs. Archer Smith (d. 1958); Gift of Mr. and Mrs. Julius B. Smith, Waterbury, Connecticut, 1969.39.1.

---

[1] *Litchfield Furn.*, no. 13.

The Federal Era

IN THE YEARS following the close of the American Revolution, Americans adopted a new fashion in furniture design. Called "neoclassical," the style took its inspiration from recent discoveries of Roman antiquities at Pompeii and Herculaneum; the style was introduced in England during the 1760's by Robert Adam and his brothers. Books illustrating Adam's engravings for architecture and furniture were issued in the 1770's as the new style gained wider currency. The publication in 1788 of *The Cabinet-Makers' London Book of Prices* and Hepplewhite's *The Cabinet-Maker and Upholsterer's Guide* was significant for the American interpretation of the fashion, as was the appearance a few years later of Thomas Sheraton's *The Cabinet-Maker and Upholsterer's Drawing-Book.*

The Federal era is one of the few periods in the history of American furniture on which a major scholarly work has been published. Charles F. Montgomery's catalogue of this furniture at the Henry Francis du Pont Winterthur Museum, *American Furniture: The Federal Period* (1966) is the basic source of information on furniture made in America between 1788 and 1825, and this present work relies heavily upon it. Dates and places of regional origin are assigned to the Federal period furniture at Winterthur with an accuracy hitherto unknown in the study of American furniture. The business of cabinetmaking was undergoing very great changes in this period. With the nation's increasing wealth and population, there was greater demand for furniture, and cabinetmaking grew from a craft to a business. Production became increasingly specialized. Price books set standards for wages and design; London editions and American ones based on them insured that the manufacture and design of American furniture in this period was closely tied to English sources, perhaps even more so than at any previous time.

At its height the new taste produced chairs whose appearance is profoundly different from those preceding. The overall effect is less plastic. The cabriole legs, the fluted and molded stiles, the interwoven strapwork, and the naturalistic carving of the rococo era are gone. The new vision is more austere, but no less elegant. Tapered or turned legs, square or shield-shaped backs, lighter forms, and reeding or low relief carving of classical and stylized natural motifs usually constitute the new vocabulary of ornament. As with any shift in style the transitions are gradual, and at the beginning and end of the period there are special types that adhere less closely to the mode just described. The ladder or slat-back chairs at the beginning of this section (nos. 133–135) reflect the new delicacy of neoclassical taste, but they also can be linked with the preceding era in their proportions, shape of the crest rail, or other details. Likewise in the second half of the period a growing interest in the antique is apparent in chairs whose forms rely more closely on Grecian sources (nos. 154–161).

133. Side Chair

Massachusetts, 1775–1810

Between the years 1780 and 1800—a period which marked the decline of the rococo style and the establishment of the neoclassical—chairs called "slatt backs" or "splatt backs" were popular.[1] On these chairs elements of the two stylistic periods are combined. The molded stiles, serpentine crest rail, and square molded legs of this example can be found on other chairs made between 1760 and 1780. The pierced slats with their serpentine outlines are not clearly influenced by the new taste, but lend a feeling

133 134 135

of lightness and delicacy to the design. The soft maple seat rails and the carved ears like those on Massachusetts chairs at Winterthur[2] and at the Museum of Fine Arts, Boston,[3] suggest that this chair was also made in Massachusetts. Its concave front seat rail, called a "hollowed seat," and fine carving on the slats make it a superior example of its kind.

Description: The interlaced centers of the four slats are enhanced by carving, as are the ears at the tops of the molded stiles. The front seat rail is hollowed. The square seat is supported by square molded legs, with four rectangular stretchers bracing the understructure.

Notes: The top rail is worn on the back edge. The seat frame is made without corner blocks. The upholstery is old leather, but not original.

Woods: Mahogany; front and side seat rails, soft maple.

Dimensions: H. 37⅛ in. (94.3 cm), SH. 15⅜ in. (39.1 cm). Seat rails: W. 16½ in. (41.9 cm), MW. 20½ in. (52.1 cm), D. 17³⁄₁₆ in. (43.7 cm).

Provenance: Jacob Margolis, New York, N.Y.; Francis P. Garvan, New York, N.Y. (1924); The Mabel Brady Garvan Collection, 1930.2039b.

[1] Montgomery, no. 11.—[2] *Ibid.*, nos. 11–13.—[3] Randall, no. 156.

134. Side Chair

Philadelphia, 1785–1800

Neoclassical taste is more evident on this chair than on no. 133. Here the pierced slats with anthemions at the center resemble drapery festoons. Rosettes ornament the ears, and the front legs are tapered. Chairs with draped openwork slats are thought to have been made only in Philadelphia.[1] Examples such as this one have often been associated with the name of Daniel Trotter, but other shops may also have made them.[2]

Description: Anthemions ornament the centers of the slats pierced with elongated openings. The slats are supported by molded stiles ending in carved rosettes. The slip seat rests in a seat frame with a serpentine front. The front legs are slightly tapered and molded. The four stretchers are rectangular.

Inscription: The number "II" is marked on the top edge of the ledge on the front seat rail and on the inside of the back seat rail.

Notes: The side seat rails are tenoned through the stiles. The quarter-round corner blocks have vertical grain; those at the front are made of two pieces. The slip seat frame is new. The center stretcher is dovetailed to the side stretchers. The upholstery is a late eighteenth-century striped silk, probably French.

Woods: Mahogany; corner blocks, pine of the *taeda* group.

Dimensions: H. 37⅞ in. (96.2 cm), SH. 16¾ in. (42.5 cm). Seat rails: W. 17 7/16 in. (44.3 cm), MW. 21 3/16 in. (53.8 cm), D. 18¼ in. (46.4 cm).

Provenance: Henry V. Weil, New York, N.Y.; Francis P. Garvan, New York, N.Y. (1923); The Mabel Brady Garvan Collection, 1930.2038 b.

[1] Montgomery, p. 137, no. 82.—[2] Hornor, pp. 222, 224 (illus. p. 187 and pl. 368).

135. Side Chair

Connecticut, 1775–1790

The minimal use of decoration on the front legs, rear stiles, and slats of this side chair suggest it is a provincial interpretation. Its plainness, coupled with its traditional history of ownership by Ezra Stiles (1727–95) of New Haven, suggests a Connecticut origin, as does the use of cherry and red gum—woods popular with Connecticut cabinetmakers.

Description: The four slats retain the outline of those on no. 133, but have been stripped of ornamental detail. The stiles are only slightly molded, as are the top edges of the seat frame. The square front legs and four rectangular stretchers are plain.

Inscriptions: A typewritten label on the inner face of the front seat rail reads: "These chairs were owned by Ezra B. Stiles / of New Haven, Conn. He was born in North Haven, / Conn. Nov. 29, 1727. Was Graduated from Yale / College in 1746 and became President of Yale / in 1778. He died May 12, 1795." The number "XI" is marked on the top of the ledge on the front seat rail, and "II" is marked on the slip seat frame.

Notes: The right front corner block is quarter-round in shape, made up of two pieces of wood with vertical grain. Small blocks of wood remain between the rear corner blocks and the rear seat rail. All the joints of the seat rails and stretchers with the legs are secured with single wooden pegs. The center stretcher is dovetailed to the side stretchers. The upholstery is a modern figured horsehair.

Woods: Mahogany; rear seat rail, cherry; corner blocks, white pine; small pieces of wood between rear corner blocks and rear seat rail, white pine; slip seat frame, red gum.

Dimensions: H. 36 7/16 in. (92.6 cm), SH. 16⅝ in. (42.2 cm). Seat rails: W. 17 5/16 in. (44.0 cm), MW. 21⅛ in. (53.7 cm), D. 17⅛ in. (43.5 cm).

Exhibitions: Conn. Furn., p. 136, no. 247.

Provenance: According to tradition, owned by Ezra Stiles (1727–95), New Haven, Conn.; Gift of Mrs. Edward S. Harkness, New York, N.Y., to Sterling Memorial Library; transferred to the Yale University Art Gallery, 1968.10b.

Pedestal-Back Chairs

FEDERAL PERIOD pedestal-back chairs have pierced splats whose outlines are not far removed from their rococo period predecessors. The splat and the flanking stiles are carryovers from the preceding era, but the serpentine crest rail, neoclassical carved ornament, tapered legs, and general lightening of the members indicate the influence of the new taste. Chairmakers in New England favored this form whose understructure is usually braced with thin, rectangular stretchers.

136. Side Chair

Connecticut or Rhode Island, about 1795

The problem of assigning a place of origin remains unresolved with chairs of this type, which appear to have been made in Rhode Island, Connecticut, and possibly Massachusetts. The attribution of examples to Connecticut is based on a set of six chairs sold by the Hartford, Connecticut, cabinetmakers Samuel Kneeland and Lemuel Adams to a Mrs. Dickerson in 1793.[1] The Providence cabinetmaker Robert Burrough is said to have made a birch example of the type between 1800 and 1810.[2] The details of the Yale chair are not really comparable to either of these documented examples. The Hartford chair has carved volutes rather than rosettes on the splat; its urn appears to be broader and is supported on a cove-shaped pedestal with thin base and top moldings, unlike the enlarged molding under the urn on the Yale chair. On the Providence example, the pointed petals are not doubled as they are on the Yale chair, and the wedge under the urn is pierced.

Description: The outer edges of the stiles, crest rail, and splat are outlined with fine beading. The splat has an elongated, S-shaped outline and is pierced to form five ribs, the outer two ending in small rosettes. An inner pair of ribs frames an urn with a surface of carved, pointed petals. The square seat frame is supported by slightly tapered front legs. Four rectangular stretchers brace the understructure.

Notes: The corner blocks and slip seat frame are new. A 6-inch strip of wood has been inset in the front of the splat shoe. The piece of wood on the splat shoe immediately in front of the splat is a replacement. Both side stretchers have been repaired where they join the central stretcher. Breaks in the right piece of the ribbon and in the left outer rib of the splat near the ribbon have been repaired. The upholstery is a modern striped silk.

Wood: Mahogany.

Dimensions: H. 38 1/16 in. (96.7 cm), SH. 16 3/4 in. (42.5 cm). Seat rails: W. 16 13/16 in. (42.7 cm), MW. 20 9/16 in. (52.2 cm), D. 16 5/8 in. (42.2 cm).

Provenance: Paul N. and Olive L. Dann, New Haven, Conn.; Bequest of Miss Olive Louise Dann, 1962.31.8.

---

[1] The chairs were advertised in *Antiques,* 91 (April 1967), p. 404, and have since been acquired by the Winterthur Museum. See Nancy E. Richards, "Furniture of the Lower Connecticut River Valley: The Hartford Area, 1785–1810," *Winterthur Portfolio 4* (Charlottesville, Va., 1968), p. 9 (illus.).—[2] Ott, fig. 16.

137. Side Chair

Connecticut or Rhode Island, about 1795

See comments, no. 136.

Description: Although this chair has much in common with no. 136, its details are somewhat different: the pointed petals of the carved rosettes do not surround a circular depression and the central rib beneath the urn is pierced. The seat rails are also upholstered over the rails.

Notes: Holes from the original open corner braces remain on the tops of the front and side seat rails. The splat is housed in the rear seat rail and passes behind the shoe. The left front leg is repaired at the junction with the seat. The corner blocks are new. The joints of the crest rail and stiles are strengthened by dowels driven in from the top of the crest rail. The modern yellow silk upholstery illustrated has been replaced by early nineteenth-century green patterned horsehair.

Woods: Mahogany; seat rails, soft maple.

Dimensions: H. 37 9/16 in. (95.4 cm), SH. 17 1/16 in. (43.3 cm). Seat rails: W. 16 7/16 in. (41.8 cm), MW. 20 5/8 in. (52.4 cm), D. 17 9/16 in. (44.6 cm).

136

137

Provenance: Paul N. and Olive L. Dann, New Haven, Conn.; Bequest of Miss Olive Louise Dann, 1962.31.9.

138. Side Chair

Connecticut, about 1795

This cherry Connecticut side chair makes an interesting contrast with its two mahogany counterparts (nos. 136 and 137). Taller by almost 3 inches than no. 136, it presents the same decorative scheme in inlays of light wood that its counterparts displayed in carving. The chair is said to have been originally owned by Noah Webster (1758–1843), who lived in both Hartford and New Haven.

Description: A fine bead outlines the edges of the stiles, crest rail, and splat of this chair. Above a deep straight-sided base the splat is pierced with elongated voids. Near the top an urn is inlaid in light-colored woods; below the urn small pieces of light-colored wood give the effect of a ribbon interlaced between the ribs. The square seat frame is supported at the front corners with slightly tapered front legs. The legs are braced by four rectangular stretchers.

Inscription: The number "V" is marked on the inside of the front seat rail and slip seat frame.

Notes: The corner blocks are triangular. Those at the front are made of two pieces of wood. A small piece of wood is used between the block and rear seat rail. The legs are chamfered on the inside edge in the same way as no. 135 and other Connecticut chairs. Each joint of the seat rails and legs is secured with a single wooden peg. The side and rear stretchers are pinned to the legs. The splat shoe is nailed to the rear seat rail. The center stretcher is dovetailed to the side stretchers. The upholstery is an early nineteenth-century striped silk.

138a

138b

138

Woods: Mahogany; rear seat rail, cherry; corner blocks, white pine and cherry; slip seat frame, elm and tulip.

Dimensions: H. $40\frac{15}{16}$ in. (104.0 cm), SH. $16\frac{3}{4}$ in. (42.5 cm). Seat rails: W. 17 in. (43.2 cm), MW. $21\frac{1}{2}$ in. (54.6 cm), D. $17\frac{1}{8}$ in. (43.5 cm).

Provenance: According to tradition, owned by Noah Webster (1758–1843), Hartford and New Haven, Conn.; Stowe family, Middlefield, Conn.; Charles W. Lyon, New York, N.Y.; Francis P. Garvan, New York, N.Y. (1929); The Mabel Brady Garvan Collection, 1930.2405.

139. Side Chair

Rhode Island, about 1795

Although neither Hepplewhite nor Sheraton shows this splat design, the back is illustrated and called a pedestal-back chair in *The London Chair-Makers' and Carvers' Book of Prices for Workmanship* of 1802.[1] Chairs of this design are generally thought to have originated in Rhode Island. Samuel McIntire's drawing of a similar design, preserved at the Essex Institute, Salem, testifies to their popularity in that city.[2] In Rhode Island chairs, as here, a carved shell surmounts the urn. Festoons of narrow leaves are substituted for drapery, and a carved lunette takes the place of the basket found on Massachusetts chairs.[3]

Description: The stiles and crest rail are molded. The splat features a footed cup framed within an oval and supported by five narrow ribs upon a lunette-carved base. Festoons are draped from rosettes on the frame and a ring at the lip of the cup. The front of the square seat frame is serpentine-shaped. The front legs are molded, and four rectangular stretchers brace the understructure.

Notes: The side seat rails are tenoned through the stiles and are wedged. Open braces are found at the corners of the seat frame. Mahogany veneer faces the rear seat rail. The corner blocks are new. The rear and side seat rails are pinned to the rear stiles. The stretchers are nailed to the legs. A wedge-shaped piece has been added to the base of the right rear leg. The upholstery is a modern bronze-colored plain woven silk.

Woods: Mahogany; right seat rail, birch; rear seat rail, hard maple; open braces, mahogany and hard maple.

Dimensions: H. 37 15/16 in. (96.4 cm), SH. 15 11/16 in. (39.9 cm). Seat rails: W. 14 9/16 in. (37.0 cm), MW. 20 7/16 in. (51.9 cm), D. 18 3/16 in. (46.2 cm).

139

139a

Provenance: Israel Sack, Inc., New York, N.Y.; The Mabel Brady Garvan Collection, 1963.12.

[1] Montgomery, no. 42.—[2] Hipkiss, Supplement 102.—[3] Montgomery, no. 45; Ott, fig. 18; *Sack Coll.*, 1957–72, I, no. 346, and II, nos. 851 and 1096; Nutting, *Treasury*, no. 2339.

Shield-Back Chairs

TODAY the term "shield-back" is applied to chairs which in the late eighteenth and early nineteenth centuries were called "vase" or "urn" backs. These terms indicate that the ornament was inspired by the antique. Sheraton in his *Cabinet Dictionary* (1803) noted that the term "vase" was "frequently used for ancient vessels dug from underground."[1] Designs for shield- or vase-back chairs appeared in both Hepplewhite's *Guide* and Sheraton's *Drawing-Book* and were probably introduced in America about 1790. The shape, which embodies the essence of the neoclassical style, was used in most of the major centers of American cabinetmaking.

[1] Thomas Sheraton, *The Cabinet Dictionary* (New York, reprinted 1970), II, p. 328.

140. Side Chair

Charleston, South Carolina, 1795–1800

Most shield-back chairs carved with drapery swags and plumes are associated with Massachusetts and New York. This beautiful example, however, with a narrow shield and oblong rosette in the center of the back, was probably made in Charleston, South Carolina, since it bears close similarity to known Charleston chairs.[1] In keeping with the slim, attenuated lines of the back are the bold serpentine shape of the front seat rail and the dramatic taper of the legs.

Description: The shield-shaped back is outlined with a concave molding. The ribs at the center of the back support drapery swags and a plume of feathers. The seat is upholstered over the rails and is supported by tapered legs braced by medial and side stretchers.

Notes: The rear seat rail is veneered on the face with mahogany. The corner blocks are new. The left rib has been cracked and repaired near the lunette. A new piece of wood has been inserted into the swag near the left rib. The modern silk upholstery illustrated has been replaced by reproduction diamond-patterned horsehair (Peter Schneider's Sons, Inc., N.Y., black diamond horsehair).

Woods: Mahogany; seat rails, ash.

Dimensions: H. 38¼ in. (97.2 cm), SH. 15⅝ in. (39.7 cm). Seat rails: W. 13¾ in. (34.9 cm), MW. 21⅛ in. (53.7 cm), D. 17¾ in. (45.1 cm).

140

140a

Bibliography: Nutting, *Treasury,* no. 2349; Joseph Downs, "Some English and American Furniture in the Inaugural Exhibition," *The Pennsylvania Museum Bulletin,* 23 (May 1928), p. 19, fig. N; Comstock, no. 425; Meyric R. Rogers, "Garvan Furniture at Yale," *The Connoisseur Year Book* 1960, p. 60, no. 14.

Provenance: Wallace Nutting, Framingham, Mass. (sale New York, Wanamaker's, Sept. 1918 [no. 1409?]); Francis P. Garvan, New York, N.Y.; The Mabel Brady Garvan Collection, 1930.2490b.

[1] Burton, figs. 123, 125–27.

141. Armchair

Massachusetts, 1790–1800

The small pointed shield-shape back and a serpentine-shaped arm resting on a serpentine support are frequently found on Massachusetts chairs. A set of very similar chairs has been said to come from Salem.[1] A survey of documented neoclassical furniture at Winterthur shows that soft maple was used quite commonly as a secondary wood on furniture made in northeastern Massachusetts, southern New Hampshire, and the Connecticut Valley.[2] Here the rear seat rail is soft maple, and birch appears in the following side chair, from the same set, no. 142. The interplay of molded surfaces in the ribs of the back, the stiles, arm supports, and front legs gives a harmony and excitement to these relatively simple but substantial chairs.

141

Description: Radiating from the lunette at the base of the vase-back are five ribs with beaded edges and flared tops. The back is supported by molded extensions of the stiles. The serpentine arms rest on arm supports with molded front faces. The seat is upholstered over the rails. The tapered front legs are molded.

Inscription: Painted in white on the outside face of the rear seat rail is the following inscription: "IN MEMORY OF / JAMES D. LEWIS, B.A. 1828 and his grandson GEORGE A. WELCH, B.A. 1901 / Gift of Miss Caroline B. Welch."

Notes: The corner blocks are new. The top rail and lunette are cracked. The side seat rails have been repaired. The front legs have open corner braces. Mahogany veneer appears on the rear seat rail. The center stretcher is mortised and tenoned rather than dovetailed. The arms are pinned to the stiles from the rear. A piece of wood about 7 inches long has been inserted into the left rear stile where it joins the arm. The upholstery is a nineteenth-century black diamond-patterned horsehair.

Woods: Mahogany; rear seat rail, soft maple; front and side seat rails, ash; left front open corner brace, birch.

Dimensions: H. 39 5/16 in. (99.9 cm), SH. 17 1/16 in. (43.3 cm). Seat rails: W. 15 7/16 in. (39.2 cm), MW. 22 in. (55.9 cm), D. 18 1/2 in. (47.0 cm).

Provenance: Gift of Caroline B. Welch, Berea, Ky., 1942.22a.

---

[1] *Sack Coll.*, 1957–72, II, no. 886; see also Nutting, *Treasury*, nos. 2354 and 2361.—[2] Montgomery, p. 37.

142. Side Chair

Massachusetts, 1790–1800

See comments for no. 141, part of the same set.

Description: See no. 141.

Inscription: See no. 141.

Notes: A 1/8-inch mahogany facing is used on the rear seat rail. The corner blocks are new, but open braces remain at the front corners. The lunette has been repaired. The center stretcher is mortised and tenoned to the side stretchers. A 1 1/2-inch piece of wood has been added to the back of the top of the stiles where they join the crest rail. The upholstery is a nineteenth-century black diamond-patterned horsehair.

Woods: Mahogany; seat rails and open braces, birch.

Dimensions: H. 37 5/8 in. (95.6 cm), SH. 16 11/16 in. (42.4 cm). Seat rails: W. 14 7/8 in. (37.8 cm), MW. 21 1/16 in. (53.5 cm), D. 17 9/16 in. (44.6 cm).

Provenance: Gift of Caroline B. Welch, Berea, Ky., 1942.22b.

143. Side Chair

New York, 1790–1800

A variant of Plate 2 of Hepplewhite's *Guide*, this chair is related to a set of chairs formerly in the Glen Sanders House in Scotia, New York. Those chairs are attributed to the New York cabinetmaker Robert Carter, and two similar armchairs once owned by George Washington have been ascribed to Thomas Burling of New York. Such chairs, derived from a readily available design, were apparently made in many New York shops and are well represented in several collections.[1] Their quality varies widely. The Yale chair is average in execution.

Description: Unlike the shields of the preceding chairs, which end in a point, the base of this shield is rounded. Radiating from the petal-carved lunette are four fluted and imbricated ribs. A molded piece of mahogany stretches between the two stiles at the back of the seat. The seat is upholstered over the rails. The front legs are reeded and end in spade, or therm, feet.

Notes: The front and rear corner blocks are new, but open corner braces remain. The bottom edges of the side seat rails are restored. The chair has been refinished and reupholstered. The modern silk damask illustrated has been replaced by a late eighteenth-century striped silk (Gift of Lloyd Hyde, 1972. 126.7).

Woods: Mahogany; seat rails, American ash; open corner braces, red oak; rear corner blocks, white pine.

Dimensions: H. 38 1/2 in. (97.8 cm), SH. 16 13/16 in. (42.7 cm). Seat rails: W. 14 5/16 in. (36.4 cm), MW. 21 7/8 in. (55.6 cm), D. 18 3/8 in. (47.3 cm).

Provenance: Harry Arons, Ansonia, Conn.; Francis P. Garvan, New York, N.Y.; The Mabel Brady Garvan Collection, 1930.2625.

---

[1] Nutting, *Treasury*, nos. 2352 and 2360; Hipkiss, no. 100; Lockwood, II, fig. 587.

144. Side Chair

Maryland, about 1800

This chair was said to have belonged to Charles Carroll, Barrister and cousin of the signer of the Declaration of Independence; however, since Carroll died in 1783 and the chair was probably not made before 1790, at the earliest, the tradition is somewhat doubt-

142

143

144

145

ful. The chair may have been part of the same set as an example at the St. John's College Museum, Annapolis.[1] Mates to the Yale chair are now at Winterthur.[2] Other examples of the type are the set of twelve chairs at Hampton, home of the Ridgely family in Baltimore County, Maryland,[3] and those illustrated in Nutting[4] and in the Sack Collection.[5]

Description: The back is a modified shield form with the bottom edge assuming a double-serpentine shape. The edges of the back are beaded, not molded as on the four preceding examples. Three ribs with wavy outlines and carrot-shaped voids fill the back. An inlaid patera is on the center rib. The seat is upholstered over the rails. The front legs taper slightly and are braced by rectangular stretchers.

Notes: Open braces remain at the four corners. The rear seat rail is of unusual depth. The center stretcher is mortised and tenoned to the side stretchers. The upholstery is a modern rose-colored rep.

Woods: Mahogany; side and front seat rails, white oak; open braces, pine of the *taeda* group.

Dimensions: H. 38³⁄16 in. (97.0 cm), SH. 16¾ in. (42.5 cm). Seat rails: W. 15⁵⁄16 in. (38.9 cm), MW. 20 in. (50.8 cm), D. 17¹³⁄16 in. (45.2 cm).

Bibliography: "Antiques in Domestic Settings," *Antiques,* 41 (June 1942), p. 360, fig. 4; Kirk, *Early Am. Furn.,* fig. 2.

Provenance: Purchased from the descendants of Charles Carroll (1723–83), Annapolis and Baltimore, Maryland, by R. T. Haines Halsey, New York, N.Y.; Francis P. Garvan, New York, N.Y.; The Mabel Brady Garvan Collection, 1930.2850.

[1] *Antiques* 18 (Sept. 1930), p. 208.—[2] Montgomery, fig. 104.—[3] *Baltimore Furniture,* fig. 60.—[4] *Treasury,* nos. 2329 and 2357–58.—[5] *Sack Coll.,* 1957–72, II, no. 1259.

145. Side Chair

Possibly Annapolis, Maryland, 1790–1800

This chair is attributed to Maryland on the basis of provenance, as it is thought to have been in the Upton Scott House in Annapolis, home of Dr. Upton Scott who emigrated from Ireland in 1753 and who began to build his fine home about 1760. The use of red gum and southern yellow pine as secondary wood points to an origin south of New York.

Description: A fine bead outlines both the inner and outer edges of the shield back. The splat is pierced with four elongated openings; at the center, small pieces of wood give the effect of linking the ribs of the splat together like ribbon. The front legs are slightly tapered, and four rectangular stretchers brace the base.

Inscription: The number "II" is marked on the inside of the rear seat rail and on the slip seat frame.

Notes: The seat frame is made without corner blocks. A ¼-inch mahogany facing has been added to the top edge of the rear seat rail. A mahogany veneer appears on the back edge of the rear seat rail. Each joint of the seat rails and legs is secured with a single wooden peg; wooden pegs secure the joint of the center stretcher to the side stretchers. The upholstery is a modern brocade.

Woods: Mahogany; rear seat rail, sweet gum; slip seat frame, southern pine of the *taeda* group.

Dimensions: H. 38⁵⁄16 in. (97.3 cm), SH. 16¾ in. (42.5 cm). Seat rails: W. 14⅛ in. (35.9 cm), MW. 19¾ in. (50.2 cm), D. 16¹³⁄16 in. (42.7 cm).

Provenance: According to tradition, owned by Upton Scott (1722–1814), Annapolis, Md.; R. T. Haines Halsey, New York, N.Y.; Francis P. Garvan, New York, N.Y.; The Mabel Brady Garvan Collection, 1930.2761a.

Square-Back Chairs

BOTH Hepplewhite's *Guide* and Sheraton's *Drawing-Book* show the square-back chair as an alternative choice to the shield-back chair. They are usually shorter and more delicate than chairs of the rococo era, and the elements that fill in the back are distributed across the whole space, as on the shield-back chairs. Square-back chairs were made in most centers of American cabinetmaking, and since the designs were readily available in published English sources, they probably appeared at the same time as their shield-back counterparts.

146. Side Chair

New York, about 1800

Many chairs of this design, related to the square-back chair from the 1794 edition of Sheraton's *Drawing-Book* (Plate 36, No. 1), have been found in New York State, but they vary greatly in the quality of their carving and proportions.[1] Here, the execution of the back is of the finest workmanship; the carving is precise and a balance exists among the various classi-

146

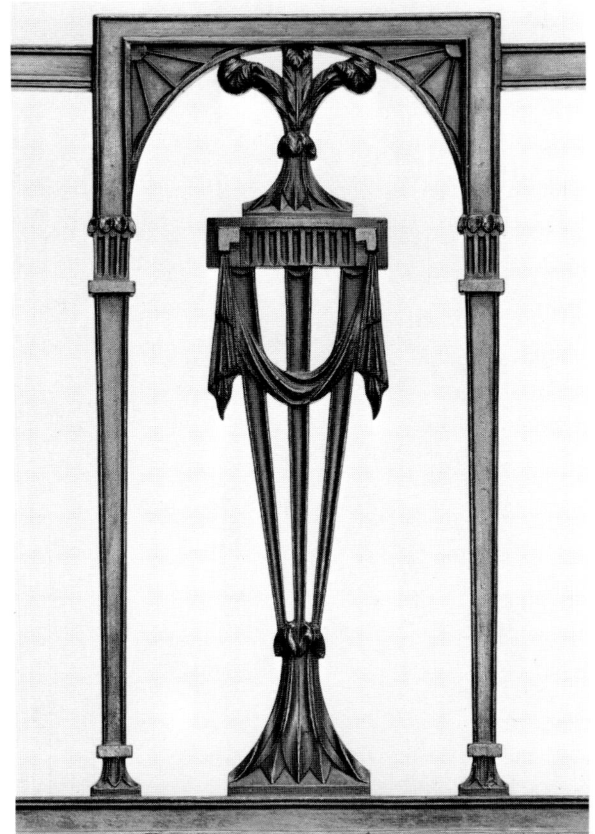

146a

cal motifs contained within the beaded frame. Related chairs are known on which the details of the design of the back are worked in light-colored wood inlays rather than in carving.[2] Other characteristic New York features of this chair are the curved cherry medial seat braces and the reeded legs with therm feet.

Description: The central portion of the back, whose top edge is raised slightly above the rest of the crest rail, encloses a pierced urn festooned with a drapery swag and crowned with plumed feathers. The top corners of this central pavilion are filled with paterae. The upholstery extends over the seat rails. The seat is supported at the front corners with reeded legs that end in therm feet.

Notes: Two medial braces are connected to the front and rear seat rails with dovetails. The corner blocks are new. The modern silk upholstery illustrated has been replaced by a reproduction black diamond-patterned horsehair (Peter Schneider's Sons, Inc., black diamond horsehair).

Woods: Mahogany; seat frame, ash; medial braces, cherry.

Dimensions: H. 36¼ in. (92.1 cm), SH. 17½ in. (44.4 cm). Seat rails: W. 15 in. (38.1 cm), MW. 21 in. (53.3 cm), D. 17$^{11}/_{16}$ in. (44.9 cm).

Provenance: Myers-Peters family, New York and New Jersey; Israel Sack, Inc., New York, N.Y.; The Mabel Brady Garvan Collection, 1964.47.

[1] As Randall notes in describing a similar chair (no. 175) at the Museum of Fine Arts, Boston, the design also appeared in the 1802 edition of the *Drawing-Book,* Plate 36. Numerous illustrations of comparable chairs appear in the literature: see Hipkiss, no. 107; Nutting, *Treasury,* no. 2391; Lockwood, II, fig. 599; Miller, I, nos. 255 and 256; Bishop, *Am. Chairs,* no. 327; *Sack Coll.,* 1957–72, I, no. 706 and III, P3470 (p. 805); Montgomery, nos. 58 and 59.—[2] Montgomery, no. 59; Hipkiss, no. 108.

147. Side Chair

New York, about 1800

This fine chair is based on a design in Sheraton's *Drawing-Book* (1802 edition, Plate 36, No. 2), which shows a chair back composed of an urn, on a base of carved leaves, flanked by two curved ribs and festoons of drapery. Here the design has been rendered to create an elegant, delicately carved chair further enhanced by the addition of plumes on top of the urn. Such an interpretation is not common in American furniture. The reeded front legs, ash seat rails, and cherry medial braces are features found on New York chairs, suggesting that this example was made there.

147

Description: On this square-back chair the corners of the crest are hollow. The top of the central section is slightly arched to accommodate the plumed feathers that rise from the urn at the center of the back, from which volutes and drapery festoons are suspended. The upholstery extends over the seat rails. The seat is supported by reeded front legs with therm feet.

Notes: The structure of the seat is strengthened by two curved medial braces. The front corner blocks are new, but the rear corner blocks are quarter-round and have vertical grain. The rear seat rail is covered with mahogany veneer. A 1½-inch piece at the base of the stiles was restored in 1962. Some height has been lost from the therm feet. The outside edges of the front and side seat rails had to be restored before the last reupholstering. The wood is split where the drapery and the right banister join. The modern silk damask upholstery illustrated has been replaced by a

147a

reproduction black diamond-patterned horsehair (Peter Schneider's Sons, Inc., black diamond horsehair).

Woods: Mahogany; rear corner blocks, white pine; seat frame, ash; medial braces, cherry.

Dimensions: H. 37 in. (94.0 cm), SH. 15 11/16 in. (39.4 cm). Seat rails: W. 15 in. (38.1 cm), MW. 20 5/8 in. (52.4 cm), D. 17 1/2 in. (44.4 cm).

Provenance: Francis P. Garvan, New York, N.Y.; The Mabel Brady Garvan Collection, 1930.2463.

148. Side Chair

New York City or Albany, about 1800

The reeded legs, the therm feet, and the medial braces of cherry are like those on no. 147 and once more suggest a New York origin. The design of the back is precise and the execution of the carving on the urn is rather stiff. Another example has been illustrated by Nutting.[1]

Description: A bead outlines the edges of the square back. The crest rail has two peaks which correspond to the tops of the flared ribs. Above the pierced urn, whose top is draped with festoons, is an oval patera. The upholstery extends over the seat rails. The seat is supported by reeded legs with therm feet.

Notes: A single, curved medial brace is attached to the front and rear seat rails with blind dovetails. The front corner blocks are quarter-round, made up of two pieces of wood with vertical grain. The rear corner blocks are of one piece. Open braces are also found in each corner. The rear seat rail is covered with a mahogany veneer. The upholstery is a beige voided velvet.

Woods: Mahogany; corner blocks, pine; seat frame, ash; open braces and medial brace, cherry.

Dimensions: H. 35 3/4 in. (90.8 cm), SH. 16 5/16 in. (41.4 cm). Seat rails: W. 14 5/16 in. (36.4 cm), MW. 19 3/16 in. (48.7 cm), D. 17 3/16 in. (43.7 cm).

Provenance: Irving W. Lyon, Hartford, Conn.; Francis P. Garvan, New York, N.Y.; The Mabel Brady Garvan Collection, 1930.2084b.

---

[1] *Treasury,* no. 2389.

149. Side Chair

New York, 1800–1810
Possibly by Abraham Slover
and Jacob Taylor (active 1802–1805)

Chairs like this one are often said to be of the Slover and Taylor school, based upon their similarity to a labeled example.[1] Abraham Slover and Jacob Taylor were in partnership in New York City between the years 1802 and 1805.[2] In writing about a similar chair at Winterthur, Montgomery cited the account book of Fenwick Lyell, in which there is evidence that Lyell made chair frames for Slover and Taylor, and noted that such information weakens attributions based on purely stylistic grounds.[3] Chairs of this type and their variants are numerous in the literature on American furniture and probably did not come from the same shop. The superbly carved double row of petals of the

148 149 150

lunette on the Yale chair is different from the single row found on most examples.

Description: Small rosettes within squares are found at the four corners of the back of this chair, whose square outline is broken by the tablet at the center of the crest (carved with a petaled lunette and paterae in the upper corners). Four thin, fluted colonnettes with ribbed and flared tops form a series of pointed arches across the back. The over-upholstered seat is supported at the front corners by reeded legs terminating in spade feet.

Notes: The seat rails are strengthened by two curved medial braces. The corner blocks are new. A mahogany veneer is applied to the rear seat rail. The lower three-quarters of the spade feet and bottoms of the rear stiles have been restored. The upholstery is a modern silk damask.

Woods: Mahogany; seat frame, ash; medial braces, American black cherry.

Dimensions: H. 36 13/16 in. (93.5 cm), SH. 17 9/16 in. (44.6 cm). Seat rails: W. 16 1/8 in. (40.8 cm), MW. 20 3/4 in. (52.7 cm), D. 17 3/4 in. (45.1 cm).

Provenance: Unknown; 1900.42e.

[1] *Antiques,* 4 (Nov. 1923), p. 215.—[2] Phelps Warren ("Setting the Record Straight: Slover and Taylor, New York Cabinetmakers," *Antiques,* 80 [Oct. 1961], pp. 350–51) established the identity of these two men. The discovery of an account book of Fenwick Lyell in the Monmouth County Historical Association (Elizabeth L. Frelinghuyen, "Collector's Notes", *Antiques,* 97 [Jan. 1970], pp. 119–20) brought to light Taylor's first name and evidence to confirm the terminal date of his partnership with Slover.—[3] Montgomery, no. 62.

150. Side Chair

Possibly Maryland, 1800–1810

This chair, whose unusual design is illustrated in the third edition of Hepplewhite's *Guide* (Plate 9), was owned by the Ghiselin family of Annapolis, Maryland. A related example, also owned in Annapolis, strengthens the supposition that this chair was made in that area.[1] However, the present state of knowledge concerning Maryland furniture is limited, and any attribution to that region must be tentative. Indeed, several features of the chair are characteristic of Philadelphia workmanship: the tapered leg with a wide reel turning at the top, the turned spade foot, and the carved rosettes in the corners of the back are all executed in the Philadelphia manner.[2] The use of cross braces, generally associated with New York, is not common in Philadelphia or Maryland.

Description: The rear stiles are decorated with round turning and carved rosettes on the plinths. A peaked, tent-like ornament decorates the center of the crest rail. Above the four narrow ribs (decorated at mid-point with small rosettes) are four rings with drapery looped between them. A tassel hangs from each of the two center rings. The seat is upholstered over the rails. The front legs are turned and tapered.

Notes: The corner blocks are quarter-round in shape with beveled faces. Those on the front are of two pieces of wood with vertical grain. The modern silk striped upholstery illustrated has been replaced by an early nineteenth-century green patterned horsehair.

Woods: Mahogany; seat frame, black ash; medial braces, pine of the *taeda* group; corner blocks, tulip.

Dimensions: H. 37⅜ in. (94.9 cm), SH. 17 7/16 in. (44.3 cm). Seat rails: W. 14 15/16 in. (37.9 cm), MW. 20 in. (50.8 cm), D. 16 9/16 in. (42.1 cm).

Bibliography: "Annapolis Windows," *Antiques,* 17 (May 1930), p. 429 (illus.).

Provenance: Reverdy Ghiselin family, Annapolis, Md.; Henry Berkeley, Annapolis, Md.; R. T. Haines Halsey, New York, N.Y.; Francis P. Garvan, New York, N.Y.; The Mabel Brady Garvan Collection, 1930.2676a.

[1] Letter from William Voss Elder III, Curator of Decorative Arts, The Baltimore Museum of Art (Jan. 11, 1967).—[2] Montgomery, no. 82.

151. Side Chair

Philadelphia, about 1800

The maker of this chair drew closely on the design in Sheraton's *Drawing-Book* (1802 edition, Plate 28, lower left). Together with no. 152, the chair exhibits the stocky proportions of many Philadelphia chairs made about 1800, and the molded front legs and rectangular stretchers also suggest a Philadelphia origin. Variants of the back are found on both Philadelphia and New York chairs. Other comparable chairs are known.[1]

Description: At the center of the crest rail is a thin projecting block carved with leaves. Between two tapering beaded ribs is a looped ornament from whose center seven ribs radiate toward the crest rail. Below the radiating ribs are three carved husks. Molded front legs support the seat, whose upholstery extends over the rails. Four rectangular stretchers brace the understructure.

Notes: A 3/16-inch mahogany veneer is applied to the rear seat rail. The corner blocks are new. A crack and small repair appears in the left rear leg at the junction with the seat rail. A crack appears near the apex of the loop in the splat. The inside of the right front leg has what appears to be a filled mortise near the base, but there is no corresponding mortise on the left leg. Nails driven into the rear stiles secure the joints of the seat rails and stiles. The inside of the right stretcher has been repaired at the joint with the central stretcher. The purple nineteenth-century silk damask illustrated has been replaced by a reproduction black diamond-patterned horsehair (Peter Schneider's Sons, Inc., black diamond horsehair).

Woods: Mahogany; seat rails, American ash.

Dimensions: H. 36¾ in. (93.3 cm), SH. 17⅜ in. (44.1 cm). Seat rails: W. 14¾ in. (37.5 cm), MW. 20½ in. (52.1 cm), D. 17 7/16 in. (44.3 cm).

Provenance: Gift of the Estate of Henry Stanley Knight, New Haven, Conn., 1947.437.

[1] Montgomery, no. 105; Nutting, *Treasury,* nos. 2375 and 2376; Lockwood, II, no. 602; Miller, no. 261; *Sack Coll.,* 1957–72, II, no. 878.

152. Side Chair

Philadelphia, about 1800

The design of the back of this chair combines the drapery festoons of no. 147 and the radiating ribs of no. 151. Such a reintegration of elements is a step away from reliance upon design books; however, the handling of detail is not as refined as on the two preceding chairs. An attribution to Philadelphia is supported by this chair's history: it was part of a set once owned by Dr. Philip Syng, a physician and grandson of the Philadelphia silversmith.[1] A set with tapered and inlaid legs has been illustrated.[2]

Description: This chair is similar to no. 151, but the side ribs end in waterleaf carving and a drapery festoon is

151

152

suspended between them. The splat also lacks the elongated loop of the other example.

Notes: The corner blocks are quarter-round in shape; those at the front are made of two pieces of wood with vertical grain. The front left corner block is a replacement. A 3/8-inch mahogany facing is applied to the rear seat rail. The splat is cracked. The upholstery is a modern striped silk in two shades of gray.

Woods: Mahogany; front and side seat rails, ash; rear seat rail, oak; corner blocks, white pine.

Dimensions: H. 35½ in. (90.2 cm), SH. 16¼ in. (41.3 cm). Seat rails: W. 15 in. (38.1 cm), MW. 21¼ in. (54.0 cm), D. 17⅜ in. (44.1 cm).

Bibliography: Nutting, *Treasury,* no. 2395; Joseph Downs, "Some English and American Furniture in the Inaugural Exhibition," *The Pennsylvania Museum Bulletin,* 23 (May 1928), fig. L.

Provenance: Dr. Philip Syng, Philadelphia, Pa.; Commodore O'Connor, Octorara, Md.; Francis P. Garvan, New York, N.Y.; The Mabel Brady Garvan Collection, 1930.2680f.

[1] Downs (see Bibliography above).—[2] *Sack Coll.,* 1957–72, II, no. 1107.

153. Side Chair

Salem, about 1800

The Gothic design of this chair back is based on Plate 9 of Hepplewhite's *Guide* (third edition). The basket of fruit on the crest rail tablet is carved in the delicate manner of Samuel McIntire of Salem; the ground surrounding it is plain, without the usual punchwork. The Museum of Fine Arts, Boston, owns two very similar chairs, and Randall indicates that many sets with this back exist, such as those in the Pierce-Nichols House and the Sage-Webb-Wilkins House in Salem.[1]

Description: The square back has elliptical corners. Between the beaded edges of the frame, eight concave-faced ribs intersect in an arched pattern. The upholstery extends over the front rails. The seat is supported at the front corner with plain tapered legs.

Notes: Triangular, horizontally grained front corner blocks have been reattached, but the rear corner blocks are missing. A mahogany veneer is applied to the rear seat rail.

153a

Two wooden pegs secure the joints of the side seat rails and rear stiles. Single wooden pegs secure the joints of the rear seat rail and stiles. The chair has been refinished. The striped silk upholstery illustrated has been replaced by a reproduction black diamond-patterned horsehair (Peter Schneider's Sons, Inc., black diamond horsehair).

Woods: Mahogany; front seat rail, ash; side seat rails, birch; rear seat rail, beech; front corner blocks, white pine.

Dimensions: H. 38 in. (96.5 cm), SH. 17 7/16 in. (44.3 cm). Seat rails: W. 14 5/8 in. (37.1 cm), MW. 20 7/8 in. (53.0 cm), D. 17 7/8 in. (45.4 cm).

Bibliography: "American Furniture . . . ," *Handbook of the Gallery of Fine Arts* (Associates in Fine Arts at Yale University), 5 (1931), p. 59 (illus.); Miller, I, p. 203 (illus. p. 202, no. 271).

Provenance: Charles W. Lyon, New York, N.Y.; Francis P. Garvan, New York, N.Y.; The Mabel Brady Garvan Collection, 1930.2227.

---

[1] Randall, nos. 169 and 170.

153

Chairs in the Grecian Manner

IN THE PERIOD between 1791, when Thomas Sheraton's *The Cabinet-Maker and Upholsterer's Drawing-Book* began to appear serially, and 1803, when his *Cabinet Dictionary* was published, an intensified interest in antique prototypes and decoration influenced English furniture design. Chair and sofa designs were labeled "Grecian," a term Sheraton defined: "GRECIAN, properly, is one born in Greece, or that is skilled in the Greek language. I, however, here use it adjectively, to signify any thing executed or shaped in imitation of the taste of the Greeks."[1] *The London Chair-Makers' and Carvers' Book of Prices for Workmanship* of 1802 and its supplement of 1808 probably were the immediate source for the style in America; they include details for chairs with the scroll backs whose sinuous, sweeping lines remained popular well into the century (as no. 161 illustrates). The outflaring front legs reveal a slight influence of the Grecian taste, which becomes more evident on the klismos chairs following in this sequence.

[1] Thomas Sheraton, *The Cabinet Dictionary* (New York, rpt. 1970), II, p. 245.

154. Side Chair

Boston, about 1805
Possibly by John Seymour (b. about 1738–d. about 1818) and / or Thomas Seymour (1771–1848)

Chairs of this design can probably be dated in the first years of the nineteenth century. *The London Chair-Makers' and Carvers' Book of Prices for Workmanship* of 1802 lists prices for many details for scroll-back chairs, including that for finishing them with a veneer on a straight back rail. Prices are also listed for veneering "tablets in tops" of such chairs. Exquisitely crafted examples of this design have often been attributed to the Boston cabinetmakers John and Thomas Seymour. The application of birch veneer to the front seat rail, the stiles, and the rails in the back adds to the brilliance of these chairs, which are among the most graceful and elegant examples of seating furniture produced in America during the Federal period.[1]

Description: The tops of the stiles, curved backward above the seat, are reeded and carved with rosettes where they meet the lower and middle ribs in the back. At the center of the turned crest is a birch veneered tablet; below it are two curved and reeded ribs. They echo the pattern of

154

155a

the four reeded pieces which form a large lozenge shape in the lower back. The seat is upholstered half overthe rails, and is supported at the front corners by flared legs, veneered with birch on two-thirds of the front face and reeded below.

Notes: Corner blocks have been added and the front legs have been repaired at the junction with the seat. The modern yellow striped silk upholstery illustrated has been replaced by a reproduction black diamond-patterned horsehair (Peter Schneider's Sons, Inc., black diamond horsehair).

Woods: Mahogany; rear seat rail, beech; front and side seat rails, birch.

Dimensions: H. 34½ in. (87.6 cm), SH. 16¾ in. (42.5 cm). Seat rails: W. 17¾ in. (45.1 cm), MW. 18⅞ in. (47.9 cm), D. 16⅝ in. (42.2 cm).

Provenance: According to tradition purchased about 1870 from a house on Follen Street in Cambridge, Mass., by the mother of Miss Elizabeth Tower of Cambridge; bequeathed by Miss Tower to A. F. Hayden (Boston?); Museum of Fine Arts, Boston; The Mabel Brady Garvan Collection, 1963.18.1.

[1] See also Montgomery, no. 38, and Hipkiss, no. 116.

155. Side Chair

New York, 1810–1820

Of all the scroll-back chairs in this collection, none has lines that flow so effortlessly and gracefully as those on this chair. The vigorous carving of the eagle provides a visual foil to the otherwise streamlined form. A set of virtually identical chairs is at Winterthur,[1] and other sets also exist, but the design source is unknown.

Description: Beaded edges form a continuously curving line from the rear stiles through the side seat rails and front legs. Supported between the beaded stiles is a splat carved with an eagle with outstretched wings. The crest above the

155

156

156a

eagle is a tablet outlined with beading. The front seat rail is outlined with beading, and the legs are saber-shaped.

Inscription: The number "IIII" is marked on the top of the rear seat rail.

Notes: A 1/4-inch mahogany facing covers the front seat rail. A mahogany veneer is applied to the rear seat rail. The junction of the back and side rails has been repaired. The scrolled top of the left stile has been replaced; the scrolled top of the right stile has been repaired. The silk upholstery illustrated has been replaced by a green silk (Scalamandré, 96158–6) and a rose and gold braid (Scalamandré, V 280–3).

Woods: Mahogany; front seat rail, cherry; rear seat rail and sides of slip seat frame, ash; back and front of slip seat frame, soft maple.

Dimensions: H. 33 1/16 in. (84.0 cm), SH. 16 11/16 in. (42.4 cm). Seat rails: W. 15 1/16 in. (38.3 cm), MW. 17 13/16 in. (45.2 cm), D. 15 3/8 in. (39.1 cm).

Bibliography: Kirk, *Early Am. Furn.*, p. 82, fig. 66.

Provenance: Francis P. Garvan, New York, N.Y.; The Mabel Brady Garvan Collection, 1930.2624a.

---

[1] Montgomery, no. 76.

156. Side Chair

New York, 1810–1820

The unbroken line of the seat rail and stiles of this scroll-back chair are inspired by the *klismos* chair and show the influence of such classical Greek design on furniture of the early nineteenth century. The adaptation of the antique is further noticeable in the furry legs and lion's-paw feet. The reeding, which becomes narrower as it moves from the seat to the crest rail, enhances the sweep of the side rails. These chairs may have been made as early as 1810, but the earliest documentation of their design is the sketches made by Duncan Phyfe for Charles Bancker in 1815 or 1816 and the design for the stay rail (splat) illustrated in *The New-York Book of Prices for Manufacturing Cabinet and Chair Work* for 1817. In the latter, the stay rail is described as having double Prince of Wales feathers tied with a Gothic molding (D, Plate 6).[1]

Pl. 11—*Federal chair installation at the Yale University Art Gallery; Mabel Brady Garvan Galleries.*

Pl. 12—*Square-back side chair, New York, about 1800 (no. 146).*

Pl. 13—*Fancy-painted side chair, New York, about 1800 (no. 162).*

Pl. 14—*Side chair in the Grecian manner, New York, 1810–1820 (no. 155).*

157

157a

Description: The stiles and side seat rails are reeded with lines that taper as the pattern reaches the crest rail. The veneered crest is bowed and bordered by a bead. Pairs of C-scrolls bound together at the center support the oval at the center of the splat. Below the reeded front seat rail, the curved tops of the legs are squared. The front faces are veneered within the framing border. The lower shafts are carved in a hairy pattern and terminate in small paw feet.

Inscription: The number "VIII" is marked on the inside of the rear seat rail.

Notes: A mahogany facing covers the front seat rail. A mahogany veneer is applied to the rear seat rail. Metal corner braces strengthen the junction of the seat frame and stiles. The backs of the tops of the stiles have been repaired where they join the crest rail. The nineteenth-century silk damask illustrated has been replaced by a green silk (Scalamandré, 96158–6) and a rose and gold braid (Scalamandré, V 280–3).

Woods: Mahogany; front and rear seat rails, American black ash; slip seat frame, cherry.

Dimensions: H. 32⅛ in. (81.6 cm), SH. 15⅞ in. (40.3 cm). Seat rails: W. 14⅞ in. (37.8 cm), MW. 17 in. (43.2 cm), D. 16⅛ in. (41.0 cm).

Bibliography: Kirk, *Early Am. Furn.*, p. 56, fig. 41.

Provenance: R. T. Haines Halsey, New York, N.Y.; Francis P. Garvan, New York, N.Y.; The Mabel Brady Garvan Collection, 1930.2693b.

---

[1] Montgomery, p. 104.

157. Side Chair

New York, 1810–1820

Of all the scroll-back chairs produced in New York during the Federal period, those with lyres in their backs are illustrated most frequently in the literature. A design for such a chair is in *The New-York Book of Prices for Manufacturing Cabinet and Chair Work* for 1817 (E, Plate 6).[1] On most examples of the form, the carving on the lyres is of water leaves, with raised petals attached to a vertical rib.[2] The swirling movement of those raised petals and the curved tips on the branches of the lyres give the design a flow not achieved by the double-petaled leaves and rosettes of this example. A lyre-back chair at Winterthur also has a double row of petals, but its scale is smaller.[3]

Description: The reeding on the stiles and side seat rails is confined within a framing border. The treatment of the crest is similar to that on no. 156, but the back is filled with a carved lyre resting on a reeded rail. Below the plain front seat rail, the tops of the front legs are ornamented with waterleaf carving, and the lower shafts are carved in a hairy pattern terminating in paw feet.

Inscription: The number "II" is marked on top of the front seat rail.

Notes: The slip seat frame, which is probably a replacement, is pegged to the front and rear seat rails. The corner blocks are new. Slight repairs have been made to the lyre. The chair was repaired by Jacob Margolis in 1934. The top of the left stile at the junction with the crest rail has been repaired with glue and a wooden peg. The lyre is pegged through the lower rail in the back. The nineteenth-century silk damask illustrated has been replaced by a green silk (Scalamandré, 96158–6) and a rose and gold braid (Scalamandré, V 280–3).

Wood: Mahogany.

Dimensions: H. 32 7/16 in. (82.4 cm), SH. 15 3/4 in. (40.0 cm). Seat rails: W. 15 3/8 in. (39.1 cm), MW. 17 5/8 in. (44.8 cm), D. 16 3/4 in. (42.5 cm).

Bibliography: Charles Nagel, Jr., "A Chair of the Early Nineteenth Century," *BAFA,* 6 (June 1935), p. 59 (illus.); Kirk, *Early Am. Furn.,* p. 59, fig. 42.

Provenance: Gift of Henrietta C. Bartlett, New Haven, Conn., 1934.46.

[1] Montgomery, no. 73.—[2] *Sack Coll.,* 1957–72, II, no. 374.—[3] Montgomery, no. 73.

158. Side Chair

New York, 1810–1820

A great part of the success of scroll-back side chairs depends upon the beauty of their stance. This example does not compete with others in the collection, principally because the front legs—which are decorated only with fine beading on their outer edges—do not project at the base far beyond the front line of the chair. Unusual here are the oak leaves and acorns carved on the crest rail; they are rarely found on New York chairs, which generally display the popular reeds, or swags and bowknots.

Description: The reeding on the stiles and side seat rails does not taper as energetically as that on no. 156. Carved oak leaves and acorns decorate the crest rail, below which two C-shaped ribs are joined together laterally with a carved rosette. The bottom rail in the back is also reeded. Coarse reeding appears on the front seat rail, and the saber front legs are plain.

Notes: Slight cracks appear in the banister; the seat frame is a replacement. Round applied bosses are missing from the sides of the tops of the front legs. The upholstery is old yellow silk damask.

Woods: Mahogany; front and rear seat rails, ash.

Dimensions: H. 32 1/16 in. (81.4 cm), SH. 15 7/16 in. (39.2 cm). Seat rails: W. 15 in. (38.1 cm), MW. 17 1/4 in. (43.8 cm), D. 16 in. (40.6 cm).

Bibliography: Miller, I, p. 222, no. 323; McClelland, p. 176, pl. 160.

Provenance: R. T. Haines Halsey, New York, N.Y.;

158

158a

Francis P. Garvan, New York, N.Y.; The Mabel Brady Garvan Collection, 1930.2007.

159. Side Chair

New York, 1815–1825

This side chair is but a shadow of its former self. The crest rail, front seat rail, and legs were once decorated with gilt stenciling like other chairs of this type.[1] American cabinetmakers often chose this ornamentation in place of the more expensive brass mounts popular in France. The carved cornucopia splat, acanthus leaves at the tops of the uprights, and the paws have been gilded with a powder applied to wet paint (which in this case was green). A thin squab probably once covered the caned seat and filled the drop between the side rails and the cane. Information in the Garvan files states that this chair was purchased from a Mrs. Copperthwaite, whose grandfather maintained a residence and shop across the street from Duncan Phyfe. A John K. Cowperthwaite had a "Fancy Chair Store" at No. 4 Chatham Square, New York City, in 1816.[2]

Description: Two cornucopias, joined at the center by grape leaves and grapes, ornament the back of this chair. The tops of the stiles flanking the deep crest rail are decorated with waterleaf carving. Round gilt bosses are found at the ends of the front seat rail. The squared front saber legs are carved near the floor with hairy shanks and terminate in paw feet.

Notes: Gold stenciling on the crest and front seat rail of the chair has been covered with new black paint. The cane and side caning rails have been replaced. Pieces have been glued onto the bottoms of the front legs to give sufficient depth for the sides of the paws to be carved.

Woods: Rear seat rail, hard maple; right side seat rail, birch.

159

Dimensions: H. 31 5/8 in. (80.3 cm), SH. 16 9/16 in. (42.1 cm). Seat rails: W. 14 15/16 in. (37.9 cm), MW. 17 7/8 in. (45.4 cm), D. 16 in. (40.6 cm).

Provenance: Mrs. Copperthwaite; Francis P. Garvan, New York, N.Y.; The Mabel Brady Garvan Collection, 1931.315a.

---

[1] *Classical America,* no. 51.—[2] Montgomery, no. 468.

160. Side Chair

New York, 1815–1825

The form of this scroll-back chair is different from that of the preceding examples. In this case the veneered crest rail is fitted over the stiles rather than being enclosed between them. The figure of richly colored dark wood serves as ornament instead of carving and gilt. The solid curved splat is probably stronger and more comfortably contoured to the back than the carved splats of nos. 155–159. The beading and the rear legs are slightly thicker than normal.

160

Description: This *klismos*-type side chair from a set of eight dining chairs has a contoured crest rail whose top edge ends in small scrolls. The rectangular, slightly contoured slat at the center of the back is veneered. The front face of the stiles above the seat has beaded edges which continue onto the side seat rails and tops of the front legs. A coarser bead is found on the edges of the front seat rails. The lower part of the front legs are ornamented with hairy carving and terminate in pad feet.

Notes: A crack in the end of the right seat rail just before it joins the stile has been repaired. A crack also appears along the inner edge of the right seat rail. The upholstery is a nineteenth-century figured horsehair.

Woods: Mahogany; front and rear seat rails, ash.

Dimensions: H. 32 1/8 in. (81.6 cm), SH. 16 1/2 in. (41.9 cm). Seat rails: W. 15 1/4 in. (38.7 cm), MW. 17 7/8 in. (45.4 cm), D. 20 in. (50.8 cm).

Provenance: Bequest of Miss Olive Louise Dann, New Haven, Conn., 1962.31.71c.

161. Side Chair

American, about 1830–1850

Of the four styles of furniture discussed by J. C. Loudon in his *Encyclopaedia of Cottage, Farm, and Villa Architecture* (London, 1833), "the Grecian or modern style" was given the most importance.[1] Chairs such as this example continued the "antique" influence established by designs like those seen on nos. 155–160 well into the nineteenth century. The line that flows downward from the crest rail is still present here, although there is a strange disjuncture at the front of the seat rail before the curve is picked up again by the saber-shaped leg. The splat is a neoclassical urn form, and the scrolled ends of the crest are reminiscent of volutes on Ionic columns. Like much furniture in the Empire style, this chair relies on dark, exotically figured mahogany for much of its visual impact.

Description: The mahogany veneered crest rail has rounded ends and is scrolled backward at the top. Between it and the urn-shaped splat is a slightly arched, torus-shaped molding. The stiles which are attached to the back of the crest rail are squared and rake back as they near the floor. Their sweeping line is continued visually from above the seat into the side seat rails. The front legs are saber shaped, and the front seat rail is veneered.

Notes: About a 2-inch long repair has been made to the veneer in the front seat rail. The joint of the left front leg and side seat rail has been repaired. The joints of the stiles and crest rail have been repaired. The upholstery is a modern red cotton velvet.

Woods: Mahogany; slip seat frame, yellow poplar.

Dimensions: H. 34 in. (86.3 cm), SH. 16¾ in. (42.6 cm). Seat rails: W. 17¾ in. (45.1 cm), D. 16¾ in. (42.5 cm).

Provenance: Purchased a few years ago as part of the furnishings of the Department of Statistics' offices in the Dana House, Yale University.

---

[1] John C. Freeman, ed., *Furniture for the Victorian Home* (American Life Foundation, 1968), p. 143.

161

Fancy-Painted Seating Furniture

AFTER 1800, paint, along with inlay and carving, served as a principal means of decorating the most elegant furniture. Hepplewhite noted in 1788: "For chairs, a new and very elegant fashion has arisen within these years, of finishing them with painted or japanned work, which gives a rich and splendid appearance to the minuter parts of the ornaments, which are generally thrown in by the painter."[1] Nos. 162 and 163 in this catalogue are among the very high-style American chairs of the early part of the Federal era that reflect the fashionable English taste. Outstanding examples of the type are rare; they include the oval-back chairs owned by the Derby family, the white-and-gold painted chairs owned by Joseph and Anna DeLancey Yates of Albany,[2] and a chair with a dark-colored background traditionally said to have been made by John Seymour of Boston.[3] Less elegant but more common are the chairs in the turner's tradition (made from parts turned on a lathe and put together without mortise and tenon joints for the most part), many of which were probably made by craftsmen who also made windsor chairs. Perhaps the richest examples of this mode extant in American furniture are the productions of Hugh and John Finlay and their competitors in Baltimore.[4] Nos. 165–168 in this catalogue are humbler examples of the type.

162

[1] George Hepplewhite, *The Cabinet-Maker and Upholsterer's Guide* (New York, rpt. of 3rd. ed. 1969), p. 2.—[2] Dean A. Fales, Jr. *American Painted Furniture 1660–1880* (New York, 1972), p. 103, no. 172.—[3] *Ibid.*, p. 110, no. 183.—[4] William Voss Elder, III, *Baltimore Painted Furniture 1800–1840* (Baltimore, 1972), p. 28, no. 6.

162. Side Chair

New York, about 1800

Few neoclassical chairs of prettier design or appearance survive than this painted specimen. An identical pair of chairs and matching settee in The Metropolitan Museum of Art were originally owned by John Carter of New York City and helped to establish a place of origin for this example.[1] A New York attribution is further substantiated by the cherry cross-braced construction of the seat. In terms of its color scheme this chair can be compared to an example attributed to John Seymour of Boston in the collection of Mr. and Mrs. Bertram K. Little.[2]

Description: The black painted surface of this square-back chair is decorated with yellow painted flowers and stripes. At the center of the back, flanked by two pairs of molded ribs, is a vase with a floral bouquet. The seat is upholstered over the rails.

Notes: Two curved medial braces are dovetailed to the front and rear seat rails. The left medial brace is a replacement. The paint is slightly abraded. The top rail has been cracked above the splat, and the neck of the vase is cracked and reinforced at the rear with a metal plate. The joints of the side seat rails and stiles are secured with two dowels. The modern printed cotton chintz upholstery illustrated has been replaced by a green moiré silk (Brunschwig & Fils, 359044).

Woods: Stiles and front legs, black ash; back rails, seat rails, and medial braces, cherry; corner blocks, white pine.

Dimensions: H. 34 15/16 in. (88.7 cm), SH. 16 5/8 in. (42.2 cm). Seat rails: W. 14 1/16 in. (35.7 cm), MW. 18 3/4 in. (47.6 cm), D. 16 7/8 in. (42.9 cm).

Provenance: Wallace Nutting, Framingham, Mass. (sale New York, Wanamaker's, Sept. 1918); Francis P. Garvan, New York, N.Y.; The Mabel Brady Garvan Collection, 1930.2724.

[1] *The Metropolitan Museum of Art Guide to the Collections,* 1961, p. 32, no. 52.—[2] Vernon C. Stoneman, *John and Thomas Seymour Cabinetmakers in Boston, 1794–1816* (Boston, 1959), pp. 318–19, no. 215.

163. Side Chair

Boston, patented in 1808
Samuel Gragg (active about 1800–1830)

163

This fancy chair branded "S. Gragg / Boston / Patent" on the front and rear seat rails was made in the shop of the Boston chairmaker Samuel Gragg, to whom a patent for "An elastic chair" was issued on August 31, 1808.[1] Gragg's use of bent wood for virtually all the parts of the chair in order to recreate the sinuous lines of Grecian designs is a unique and ingenious achievement in early nineteenth-century American furniture design. Gragg also advertised that he made windsor chairs. Undoubtedly his knowledge of the techniques and methods of bending wood essential in the manufacture of windsor furniture provided him with the technological skill necessary to shape his materials in an original way to meet the requirements of high-style design. The fact that Gragg patented his "elastic chair" suggests that he knew his idea was innovative, and it preceded by many years the use of bent wood by nineteenth-century furniture makers such as Michael Thonet and John Belter. He made two types of bentwood chairs, all examples of which have painted peacock feathers. One model had stiles and seat rails of one piece of bent wood, like this example. The other had a continuous stile, seat rail, and front leg of bent wood. Three sets of bentwood furniture branded with Gragg's mark are known. No. 163 was part of a set of eight side and two arm chairs and a settee; other pieces of the set are now at Win-

163a

163b

terthur and the Art Institute of Chicago; another set is privately owned; a third is divided among Winterthur, Gore Place, Waltham, Massachusetts, the Museum of Fine Arts, Boston, the Society for the Preservation of New England Antiquities, and the collection of Mr. and Mrs. Bertram K. Little.

Description: The surface of this fancy chair is painted a light yellow, with brown and tan stripes, peacock plumes at the center of the back, and green leaves at the tops of the rear stiles, front legs, and center of the front seat rail. Bent pieces of wood form a continuous curved line from the scrolled crest rail to the front seat rail. The round front and rear legs flare out near the floor. The ends of the front legs are carved to resemble hoof feet. Round stretchers brace the legs—those in front being bent to a concave shape.

Notes: The slats that form the seat are dovetailed to the front and rear seat rails. The paint is chipped and worn. The filler covering the screws that secure the side seat rails to the rear seat rail is missing.

Woods: Slats, stiles, side seat rails, legs, oak; rear seat rail, American ash; front seat rail and rear stretcher, soft maple; top front stretcher, beech.

Dimensions: H. 33½ in. (85.1 cm), SH. 17⅜ in. (44.2 cm). Seat rails: W. 15¼ in. (38.7 cm), MW. 17½ in. (44.5 cm), D. 14¼ in. (36.3 cm).

Bibliography: Patricia E. Kane, "Samuel Gragg: His Bentwood Fancy Chairs," *Yale University Art Gallery Bulletin,* XXXIII, 2 (Autumn 1971), p. 26, fig. 1.

Provenance: Harry Arons, Bridgeport, Conn.; Gift of Mr. and Mrs. Charles F. Montgomery, New Haven, Conn., 1968.98.

[1] *A List of Patents Granted by the United States from April 10, 1790 to December 31, 1836* (Washington, D.C., 1872), p. 67.

164

164. Settee

New York, 1815–1825

This settee, grained to resemble bird's-eye maple and painted with landscape scenes, is a fine example of fancy furniture, though somewhat less high-style than nos. 162 and 163. Its possible place of origin is New York, and the small summer house painted on the right panel of the back and the landscape on the center panel may depict the Hudson River Valley. The design of the panel at the left with castellated towers and a Gothic building appears to have been derived from a print. A chair with similar painting once owned by the Van Rensselaer family is now at Winterthur.[1]

Description: The surface is grained to resemble bird's-eye maple and is decorated with black painted stripes. Four turned stiles with flattened front faces divide the back into three sections with three graduated slats in each. The top slats are painted with landscape scenes. The serpentine-shaped arms have scrolled handholds and rest on ring-, vase-, and ball-turned arm supports. The seat has rounded front corners. Below the seat rails are ball-and-ring-turned front legs with ball front feet. The three front stretchers are flat and the medial and rear stretchers are turned round.

Notes: The three painted panels were covered with beeswax in 1963. The cushion is covered in a modern striped silk in two shades of gray.

Woods: Rear stiles, front legs, and stretchers, soft maple; slats in back, medial braces, and seat rails, cherry; braces between rear stiles, mahogany; band over seat rails, basswood.

164a

164b

164c

Dimensions: H. 34⅛ in. (86.7 cm), SH. 17½ in. (44.4 cm). Seat rails: W. 68 in. (172.7 cm), MW. 73³⁄₁₆ in. (185.9 cm), D. 20½ in. (52.1 cm).

Provenance: R. T. Haines Halsey, New York, N.Y.; Francis P. Garvan, New York, N.Y. (1929); The Mabel Brady Garvan Collection, 1930.2246.

[1] Montgomery, no. 469.

165 166

165. Side Chair

Possibly New England, 1810–1820

Feathery, gold-painted leaves appear in the blocks of the stretcher and back rails of this fancy chair. The round rear stiles are bent back above the seat and end in nipple-like knobs, a treatment comparable to three chairs in the Winterthur Collection.[1] The front legs with their bulb feet cuffed by reel turnings are executed with more detail than is usually found on fancy-painted furniture. The shape of the foot is like those found on New England card tables and is the basis for the tentative suggestion of a New England origin.

Description: The round posts of this fancy chair, painted black and gold, curve backward above the rush seat. They are joined by three turned-and-blocked back rungs with an oval ornament between the upper two, and four ball-turned and tapered spindles between the lower. The vase-and-reel-turned front legs terminate in bulb feet. Two plain stretchers are found on each side, one at the rear, and a turned-and-blocked stretcher at the front.

Notes: The paint and gilded decoration are worn.

Wood: Birch.

Dimensions: H. 34¼ in. (87.0 cm), BPH. 35½ in. (90.2 cm), SH. 18⅜ in. (46.7 cm). Seat rails: W. 14¼ in. (36.2 cm), MW. 17⁵⁄₁₆ in. (44.0 cm), D. 16¼ in. (41.3 cm).

Provenance: Francis P. Garvan, New York, N.Y.; Mabel Brady Garvan, New York, N.Y. (1937); The Mabel Brady Garvan Collection, 1950.713.

[1] Montgomery, nos. 486, 487, and 488.

166. Side Chair

New England, 1810–1820

Gold-painted sprays of leaves interspersed with snaking tendrils ornament the flattened faces of the stiles and blocked rails on the back of this fancy-painted chair—ornament so individual that ultimately it may enable a more specific place of origin to be assigned to the chair. The legs, the strip of wood facing the seat front, and the spindles are painted with more conventional leaves. The turnings on the front legs are not as successful as those on no. 165.

Description: This fancy chair is painted black and has

gold decoration. The stiles have flattened front faces. The blocked-and-turned back rails support three flat-faced spindles. The tops of the front legs have a small tapered turning. The stretchers are round with the exception of the front one, which is blocked and turned.

Notes: The finish and decoration are probably original. The center spindle has been split and repaired.

Wood: Soft maple.

Dimensions: H. 34¾ in. (88.3 cm), BPH. 35⅝ in. (90.5 cm), SH. 18¼ in. (46.4 cm). Seat rails: W. 14¼ in. (36.2 cm), MW. 17½ in. (44.4 cm), D. 14⁵⁄₁₆ in. (36.4 cm).

Provenance: Francis P. Garvan, New York, N.Y.; Mabel Brady Garvan, New York, N.Y. (1937); The Mabel Brady Garvan Collection, 1950.716.

167. Rocking Chair

American, 1810–1820

Although this child's rocking chair is not decorated with ornamental painting, it is included here since its form owes much to fancy chairs, such as no. 166. Like that chair, the stiles bend backward above the seat and are flattened on the front faces. The front stretcher is blocked and turned. The tulip rockers suggest that the chair was made south of Massachusetts.

167

Description: This chair is painted black, and above the seat the front faces of the stiles are flattened. The two rungs in the back support two flattened ball-and-taper-turned spindles. The turned arms rest on lemon-shaped arm supports. Below the rush seat the front legs and the rear and side stretchers are round. The front stretcher has a block at the center. The legs rest on rockers.

Notes: The rockers are pegged to mortises in the stiles and front legs. Old black paint covers yellow. Small nails driven from the side strengthen the joints of the arms and stiles.

Woods: Maple; rockers, tulip.

Dimensions: H. 17¾ in. (45.1 cm), BPH. 18⅝ in. (47.3 cm), SH. 6¾ in. (17.1 cm). Seat rails: W. 9¼ in. (23.5 cm), MW. 11⅝ in. (29.5 cm), D. 9¹⁄₁₆ in. (23.0 cm).

Provenance: Francis P. Garvan, New York, N.Y.; The Mabel Brady Garvan Collection, 1931.1212.

168. Side Chair

Portland, Maine, about 1850
Walter Corey (d. 1889)

The fashion for graining furniture to imitate rosewood arose in the 1820's. Painters often chose furniture in the Grecian style, such as this chair, on which to display their skillful handiwork. This example, which was made in an era when the American furniture-making trades were radically changing, was the product of the prolific chair factory of Walter Corey in Portland, Maine. Corey went from Massachusetts to Portland in 1836, and there bought the furniture shop of Nathaniel Ellsworth. He eventually built his business into a large furniture factory, six stories high, with machinery run by a sixty-horse-power engine, and employed over one hundred men.[1] By 1875 the factory system had revolutionized the furniture business, however, and Corey's business felt the changes. In that year, Edward H. Elwell wrote: "No retailer or jobber in furniture can now manufacture his own goods, being unable to compete with factories where each branch of the business is made a specialty, and the cost of production reduced, by system, to the lowest figures. . . . Thus it has come about that the house of Walter Corey & Co. has relinquished the manufacture of furniture, and now confines itself to a distributing business."[2] Another

168a

chair from Corey's factory has been illustrated.[3]

Description: Gold lines define the various parts of this side chair, which is grained to imitate rosewood. Above the inverted vase-shaped splat a scrolled crest rail is supported on curved stiles. The seat rail at the front of the caned seat is scrolled. Saber-shaped legs support the front of the seat. The rectangular front stretcher (bent to a concave shape) is complemented at the sides and rear by round stretchers.

Inscription: "W. COREY. PORTLAND, ME." is stenciled on the rear seat rail.

Notes: The crazed surface has been restored without disturbing the rosewood graining. The flat front stretcher is fastened to the front legs with machine-cut nails. The stiles are nailed to the rear seat rail from the sides. Two round plugged holes at the top of each stile conceal the method used for attaching the crest rail.

Wood: Hard maple.

Dimensions: H. 33½ in. (85.1 cm), SH. 17¼ in. (43.8 cm). Seat rails: W. 14¾ in. (37.5 cm), MW. 18¼ in. (46.3 cm), D. 17⅜ in. (44.1 cm); overall W. 18½ in. (47.0 cm), overall D. 20⅝ in. (52.4 cm).

Provenance: Found in Falmouth Foreside, Maine; Dean A. Fales, Jr., Kennebunkport, Maine; Gift of Mr. and Mrs. Charles F. Montgomery, New Haven, Conn., 1970.70.

168

---

[1] Edward H. Elwell, *The Successful Business Houses of Portland* (Portland: W. S. Jones, 1875), p. 99.—[2] *Ibid.*, pp. 100–01.—[3] Fales, *Am. Painted Furn.*, p. 202, fig. 325.

Figs. 4a and b—"*The Beardsley Limner.*" Dr. and Mrs. Hezekiah Beardsley. *Oil on canvas, ca. 1788–1790. Yale University Art Gallery; gift of Gwendolen Jones Giddings.*

Windsor Seating Furniture

THE WINDSOR CHAIR was constructed from a variety of woods, the properties of each suitable for its particular role. The turned members were generally of maple, a hard wood which could be crisply turned. The spindles and crest rail were usually of ash, oak, or hickory—woods with wiry strength which could be easily bent. The seat was most often of pine or tulip—soft, easily shaped woods which, because of their great tendency to shrink, held the legs secure. The various grains and colors were masked with paint—green was the virtually unanimous choice until the last decade of the eighteenth century.

Nancy Goyne Evans, the most recent scholar of windsor chairs, notes that no one has offered a satisfactory explanation of the term windsor as applied to furniture, or suggested a specific time and place of origin for the prototype.[1] References to windsors can be found in England in the 1720's, and the form probably began to be made in America in the 1740's.[2] The structure of a windsor chair has no precedent in any of the examples in this catalogue. Instead of stiles from floor to crest rail, it has as its main structural element a thick plank seat into which all other parts fit.

Windsor chairs are truly universal. Their painted surfaces made them impervious to weather and thus ideal for outdoor use. To judge by the number of portraits from the mid-eighteenth to the early nineteenth century whose subjects are shown seated in these chairs, those who could not afford or did not choose to buy mahogany or upholstered furniture selected windsor chairs for common household seating.

[1] Goyne, p. 541.—[2] *Ibid.*, p. 538.

169. Low-Back Windsor Armchair

American, 1755–1775

One of the earliest forms of windsor chairs referred to in contemporary records was the "low back'd" type.[1] The provenance of this low-back chair might prompt an attribution to a craftsman in the Newport area; however, some of its features have been identified as characteristics of Pennsylvania craftsmanship: the cylindrical lower section of the legs, ball-shaped feet (badly worn), a wide U-shaped seat, and attenuated vase-shaped arm supports.[2] America's first center of windsor chairmaking was Philadelphia, and

169

from that city large numbers of "Philadelphia chairs" were exported.[3] This chair may easily have found its way from Philadelphia to Newport in the coastal trade.

Description: This low-back armchair is painted brown and has a semi-circular crest rail applied to the arm rail. Two very thin arm supports with vase turnings and nine spindles support the arm and crest rails. The semi-circular seat has a small peak at the center of the front. The upper part of the raked legs are vase-and-reel-turned, with a straight-sided cylinder below. The rings are found at the bottom of the legs. The two side stretchers have bulbous centers, and the medial stretcher has a double-ring turning at the center.

Notes: Holes were bored through the seat for the legs and through the arm rail for the six side spindles and two arm supports. Traces of reddish paint remain. There is worm damage, particularly on the seat. The bottoms of the feet are missing. The three center back spindles and the fourth spindle from the right are pinned to the arm rail with square wooden pegs. Both the arm supports and the spindles, with the exception of the third and fifth from the left and fifth from the right, are pinned to the seat with square wooden pegs. The stretchers are nailed to the legs with modern nails. The center stretcher is nailed to the side stretchers. The crest rail is nailed to the arm rail with roseheaded nails.

Woods: Spindles, oak; crest rail, seat, legs, stretchers, soft maple.

Dimensions: H. 27⅝ in. (70.2 cm), SH. 15¼ in. (38.7 cm). Seat: W. 21⅞ in. (55.6 cm), D. 14¾ in. (37.5 cm).

Provenance: From a house near Newport, R.I.; Vernon's Antique Shop, Newport, R.I.; Gift of D. Bryson Delavan, New York, N.Y., 1941.119.

---

[1] Goyne, p. 538.—[2] *Ibid.*, p. 538.—[3] *Ibid.*, p. 540.

170. High-Back Windsor Armchair

Pennsylvania, 1755–1775

Along with the low-back windsor chair, the "high back'd" windsor was among the early examples of the type made in America. The form was apparently introduced to America from England in the 1740's, and their early manufacture centered in Philadelphia.[1] On this example the turned legs with cylindrical lower sections and ball-shaped feet are the identifying features of Pennsylvania workmanship.

Description: The serpentine crest rail ends in carved volutes and rests on nine tapered spindles that pierce the semi-circular arm rail. Each end of the arm rail rests on three short spindles and a vase-and-reel-turned arm supports. The arm rail echoes the shape of the seat. Four splayed vase-and-reel-shaped legs end in partial bulb feet. The side stretchers have bulbous centers, and the bar-like medial stretcher is probably a replacement.

Notes: Holes were bored through the seat for the legs and through the arm rail for the spindles and arm supports.

170

The chair has been refinished, but traces of red and green paint remain. The feet are very worn. Screws secure the medial stretcher to the side stretchers and the side stretchers to the legs. Cut nails secure the tops of the legs and the base of the right arm support to the seat. The tops of the arm supports, the outer back spindles and the center back spindle are nailed to the arm rail. The outer back spindles and center back spindle were also nailed to the crest rail, although only the nail in the left spindle remains.

Woods: Crest rail, spindles, and arm rail, white oak; seat, tulip; arm supports, legs, and stretchers, soft maple.

Dimensions: H. 45 15/16 in. (116.7 cm), SH. 17 3/16 in. (43.7 cm). Seat: W. 24 7/8 in. (63.2 cm), D. 16 3/8 in. (41.6 cm).

Provenance: Mrs. Elizabeth Coale, New York, N.Y.; Francis P. Garvan, New York, N.Y. (1929); The Mabel Brady Garvan Collection, 1930.2367.

[1] Goyne, p. 538.

171

171. High-Back Windsor High Chair

Pennsylvania, 1755–1775

In many respects this high chair, a relatively rare form in windsor furniture, is similar to no. 170. Nutting illustrates this chair and describes it as "a good Pennsylvania baby high chair, but not equal to No. 2507," another example once in his collection.[1] Although the latter does have bolder turnings and thicker parts, the Yale chair, despite its restorations, is a fine example of a form not commonly found.

Description: The design is very like that of no. 170, except that the front line of this seat is shaped to a peak and the turnings of the legs are more elongated.

Notes: Holes were bored through the arm rail for the spindles and arm supports. Red and green paint is found under the modern black. The right rear leg and right stretcher were replaced many years ago, since they are painted red like the rest of the chair. The seat has been cracked and was once repaired by braces (since removed) into which all the legs were fitted. Holes in the seat for the legs have been filled. The right arm support and outer back spindles are replacements. Holes for the latter in the arm rail have been filled. A retaining bar originally went through the tops of the arm supports. The stretchers are nailed to the legs, and the spindles and stiles are pinned to the crest rail.

Woods: Crest rail, spindles, and arm rail, white oak; seat, sycamore; arm supports, legs, and stretchers, hickory.

Dimensions: H. 38 3/4 in. (98.4 cm), SH. 19 7/8 in. (50.5 cm). Seat: W. 14 3/8 in. (36.5 cm), D. 10 1/4 in. (26.0 cm).

Bibliography: Nutting, *Windsor Handbook,* p. 100; Nutting, *Treasury,* no. 2530.

Provenance: Wallace Nutting, Framingham, Mass. (sale New York, Wanamaker's, Sept. 1918); Francis P. Garvan, New York, N.Y.; The Mabel Brady Garvan Collection, 1930.2364.

[1] Nutting, *Treasury,* no. 2530.

172

172. High-Back Windsor Armchair

Connecticut, 1755–1775

Basically, this chair is like a low-back windsor, but with additional spindles and crest resting on the arm rail. Found in the town of Lebanon, Connecticut in the late nineteenth century by Dr. Irving W. Lyon, it is similar to one in the collection of Mr. and Mrs. Samuel H. Wax which comes from nearby Rhode Island.[1] Another example with similar feet and crossed stretchers is also said to be from Rhode Island.[2] This example has some features unusual on American windsor chairs—the legs slightly swelled just below the seat and above the stretchers, the feet that appear to imitate the hoof shape, and the crossed stretchers—but these are common on English windsor chairs.

Description: The spindles are shaped like the stretchers of New England Queen Anne style chairs—slightly bulbous at the center and with turned, tapered ends. The shape of the seat is similar to that of no. 169, but the side edges are bluntly beveled. Four cylindrical legs, squeezed at the bottom by a ring turning, are braced by crossed stretchers. The ends of the stretchers are turned like the spindles and the centers are block-shaped.

Notes: The chair has been refinished, but traces of light green paint remain. Cracks in the right section of the arm rail and its crest have been repaired. The outer, second, and fourth spindles from the right are nailed to the arm rail. The outer and second top spindles from the right are also nailed to the crest rail. The right arm support is nailed to the seat from the side. The stretchers are pinned to the legs with square wooden pegs.

Woods: Lower back spindles, maple; upper back spindles, oak; seat, soft maple.

Dimensions: H. 44 in. (111.8 cm), SH. 15 11/16 in. (39.8 cm). Seat: W. 22 5/8 in. (57.5 cm), D. 14 9/16 in. (37.0 cm).

Bibliography: Lyon, p. 184 (illus. opp. p. 202, fig. 82).

Provenance: Found in Lebanon, Connecticut, by Irving W. Lyon, Hartford, Conn. (1878); Francis P. Garvan, New York, N.Y.; The Mabel Brady Garvan Collection, 1930.2378.

1 "Wethersfield: Living with Antiques, The Home of Mr. and Mrs. Samuel H. Wax," *Antiques*, 86 (Oct. 1964), p. 463.—2 *Sack Coll.*, 1957–72, II, no. 719.

173. Writing-Arm Windsor Chair

Lisbon, Connecticut, about 1765–1785
Ebenezer Tracy (1744–1803)

In combining desk and chair, this windsor branded by Ebenezer Tracy displays the ingenuity of Yankee craftsmen. It is one of the monumental examples of its type. The huge balloon-shaped writing arm, supported by very full vase-shaped turnings, has beneath it a small drawer and a locking device on the candle-slide. The massive chestnut seat supports a drawer hung on side runners. The underside of the seat has the chisel mark "1"; higher numbers have been observed on other Tracy writing-arm windsors, and it has been suggested that perhaps Tracy numbered these models. As with the other branded Tracy chair at Yale, no. 189, the spindle area is not isolated by an incised line. An example at Williamsburg also is

branded by Tracy but lacks the crest,[1] and Nutting illustrates a closely related version.[2]

Description: Heavy vase-and-reel-turned legs and stretchers with bulbous centers and ogee ends support the thick, semi-circular seat. Both the bottom and the top edges of the front of the seat are peaked at the center. A projection on the right side provides a base for the pair of ogee-and-vase-turnings that support the writing arm. Six spindles with bulbous shapes in their lower portions pierce the arm rail and support a serpentine-outlined crest with rounded ends. Shorter bulbous spindles support the ends of the arm rail. A drawer is suspended beneath the seat, and a drawer and candleslide are suspended under the writing arm.

Inscriptions: Branded once on underside of seat: "EB: TRACY"; twice superimposed: "TRACY". Chiseled mark "I" also on underside of seat.

Notes: Holes were bored through the arm rail for the four right arm spindles and right arm support. The chair has been refinished, but traces of red and green paint remain. The supports on the undersides of the seat and the writing arm for the drawers are probably new. The outer back spindles and the third spindle from the right are pinned to the crest rail. The center arm spindle is pinned to the arm rail from the back.

Woods: Crest rail, legs, drawer supports, right arm, soft maple; small drawer, sides and front of large drawer, tulip; bottom of large drawer, white pine; seat, chestnut; spindles and stretchers, white oak.

Dimensions: H. 43 in. (109.2 cm), SH. 15 15/16 in. (40.5 cm). Seat: W. 27 in. (68.6 cm), D. 18½ in. (47.0 cm).

Exhibitions: Conn. Furn., p. 137, no. 249; Minor Myers, Jr., and Edgar de N. Mayhew, *New London County Furniture* (New London, 1974), p. 65, no. 74.

Bibliography: Kirk, *Early Am. Furn.*, fig. 25.

Provenance: Bequest of Janet Smith Johnson, New York, N.Y., in memory of her husband, Frederick Morgan Johnson (class of 1891), 1955.33.3.

---

[1] Greenlaw, no. 159.—[2] *Treasury*, no. 2630–31.

174. Writing-Arm Windsor Chair

Probably Connecticut, 1785–1800

174

This writing-arm windsor is light and delicate compared with no. 173. The bamboo turnings on the arm supports suggest a date no earlier than the 1780's, while the retention of the vase-shaped turnings of the legs indicates that it probably was not made much after 1800. The provenance and the shape of the crest rail, like that on no. 175, a Connecticut chair, is the basis for assigning Connecticut as the place of origin. Nutting shows a similar chair with vase-turned arm supports.[1]

Description: The vase-turned legs are not as stocky as on no. 173, and the seat, which is beveled to a single line at the front, is much sleeker. Three tapered spindles support the large upward-tilting writing arm. The ends of the thin arm rail rest on two bamboo-turned arm supports and tapered spindles. Seven tall spindles pierce the arm rail and support a serpentine-outlined crest with upward thrusting ends.

Notes: Holes were bored through the seat for the legs and through the arm rail for the two right spindles and right arm support. Brown paint covers old black paint. A crack appears in the writing arm at the junction with the back spindle. Later rockers have been removed, and the notches at the base of the feet have been filled. Holes on the underside indicate that the writing arm was upholstered at one time. The end of the arm rail is screwed to the underside of the writing arm. The outer back spindles and center back spindle are pinned to the stiles.

Woods: Crest rail, arm rail and spindles, red oak; writing arm, tulip; seat, basswood; legs and stretchers, soft maple.

Dimensions: H. 44¾ in. (113.7 cm), SH. 16½ in. (41.9 cm). Seat: W. 24⁵⁄₁₆ in. (61.8 cm), D. 16⅛ in. (41.0 cm).

Exhibition: Conn. Furn., p. 137, no. 250.

Provenance: E. B. Leete, Guilford, Conn.; Henry H. Taylor, Bridgeport, Conn.; Francis P. Garvan, New York, N.Y.; The Mabel Brady Garvan Collection, 1930.2368.

[1] *Treasury*, no. 2615.

175. High-Back Windsor Armchair

Connecticut, 1775–1800

In the portraits of Dr. and Mrs. Hezekiah Beardsley of New Haven, painted by an unknown artist about 1788–1790, the subjects sit on green windsor chairs very similar to this example. The evidence offered by the portraits and by the chair's history of ownership in the Munson family of Southbury, Connecticut, provides a fairly sound basis for assigning it a Connecticut origin. Chairs of a similar design were made in 1796 by John Wadsworth of Hartford for the Connecticut State House.[1]

175

Description: The seven tall tapered spindles pierce the arm rail and support a serpentine-shaped crest rail with upward thrusting ears. The splayed ends of the arms rest on short spindles and vase-shaped arm supports which join the seat with straight tapered ends. The seat rises to a gentle peak in the front and an incised line isolates the spindle area. The four legs are vase-and-reel turned, and the stretchers have bulbous centers.

Notes: Holes were bored through the seat for the legs and through the arm rail for the spindles and arm supports. The chair has been refinished, but traces of green and red paint remain. The center and outside spindles are nailed to the crest rail from the front.

Woods: Crest rail, spindles, and arm rail, red oak; seat, white pine; arm supports, legs, and stretchers, soft maple.

Dimensions: H. 36¼ in. (92.1 cm), SH. 16⅜ in. (41.6 cm). Seat: W. 16¼ in. (41.3 cm), D. 16⁹⁄₁₆ in. (42.1 cm).

Bibliography: "Gallery Notes," *BAFA*, 3 (Dec. 1928), p. 32 (illus.); Leslie Richardson, "An Early Connecticut Interior," *Antiques*, 16 (Dec. 1929), p. 501, fig. 2.

Provenance: Munson family, Southbury, Conn.; George and Ben Arons, Ansonia, Conn.; Frank McCarthy, Longmeadow, Mass.; Francis P. Garvan, New York, N.Y.; The Mabel Brady Garvan Collection, 1930.2050f.

[1] "Connecticut Cabinetmakers: Part II," *The Connecticut Historical Society Bulletin*, 33 (Jan. 1968), p. 27.

176. Sack-Back Windsor Armchair

American, 1765–1795

Windsor chairs of this type, with their arm rails topped by a hoop-shaped piece of bent wood, are called "sack-back" and were popular until the end of the eighteenth century. The similarity of this chair to branded examples by the Philadelphia windsor chairmakers John Wire[1] and Joseph Henzey,[2] the provenance, and the combination of tulip and red gum suggest that Philadelphia might be the place of

176

origin. However, the incurved line at the bottom of the legs is associated with Rhode Island windsor chairs—thus the difficulty in assigning many windsor chairs a specific place of origin. The construction of the handholds should be noted: a piece of beech was attached to the underside of the arm rail and a piece of maple to the outer edge. Sufficient thickness was thus attained so that the chairmaker could carve the finely knuckled handholds.

Description: Above the elliptical seat whose front edge is peaked at the center, seven tapered spindles pierce the semi-circular arm rail and the curved rail rising above it. The ends of the arm rail terminate in knuckled handholds and rest on vase-turned arm supports and two short spindles. Raked, vase-turned legs are braced by two side stretchers with bulbous centers and a medial stretcher with both bulbous center and tapered ends.

Inscription: Illegible chalk inscription on bottom of seat; pencil inscription may possibly read "Dan. [Wilson] or [Welsted] / white & Stripe."

Notes: Holes were bored through the seat for the legs and through the rails for the spindles and arm supports. The outer edges and bottom halves of the handholds are applied. The outer edge of the handhold is pinned to the end of the arm rail by round wooden pegs about halfway between the arm supports and the first arm spindles. The reddish-brown varnish and gilding covers coats of red, green, and white paint. Small nails reinforce the joints of the arm spindles and arm rail. The outside and center back spindles are also nailed to the top rail.

Woods: Top rail, arm rail and spindles, American hickory; bottom of scrolled handholds, beech; seat, tulip; arm supports, outsides of handholds, red gum; legs and stretchers, soft maple.

Dimensions: H. $37\frac{5}{16}$ in. (94.8 cm), SH. $17\frac{3}{8}$ in. (44.1 cm). Seat: W. $20\frac{1}{8}$ in. (51.0 cm), D. $16\frac{7}{16}$ in. (41.8 cm).

Provenance: M. G. Ramsey, York, Pa.; Francis P. Garvan, New York, N.Y.; The Mabel Brady Garvan Collection, 1930.2373.

[1] Hornor, pl. 465 (opp. p. 301).—[2] Goyne, p. 539.

177. Sack-Back Windsor Armchair

American, 1765–1795

This sack-back windsor armchair is markedly less animated than no. 176. An immediately noticeable difference is the variation in the scrolled handholds. Here they are much shallower, and, interestingly enough, they are carved from the solid end of the arm rail; additional depth was not supplied by applying pieces of wood as on the other chair. Although the form of the chairs is very similar, a Pennsylvania origin is less certain for this one, since white pine and birch—woods generally associated with New England furniture—were used here.

Description: This chair closely resembles no. 176, but

the knuckled handholds are not as well formed, the seat is not so boldly peaked, and the turnings are not as full.

Notes: Holes were bored through the rails for the spindles and arm supports. The reddish-brown varnish is not original and traces of green paint remain. Small nails driven from the outside reinforce the joints of the top rail, the back center spindle, and the right arm support with the arm rail. The left arm support was nailed at one time from the inside of the arm rail.

Woods: Top rail, arm rail, and spindles, white oak; seat, white pine; legs, stretchers, arm supports, birch.

Dimensions: H. 37 in. (94.0 cm), SH. 18 1/16 in. (45.9 cm). Seat: W. 21 11/16 in. (55.1 cm), D. 15 5/16 in. (38.9 cm).

Bibliography: Ayer Coll., p. 33, no. 154.

Provenance: Fred Wellington Ayer, Bangor, Me.; Francis P. Garvan, New York, N.Y.; The Mabel Brady Garvan Collection, 1930.2350.

177

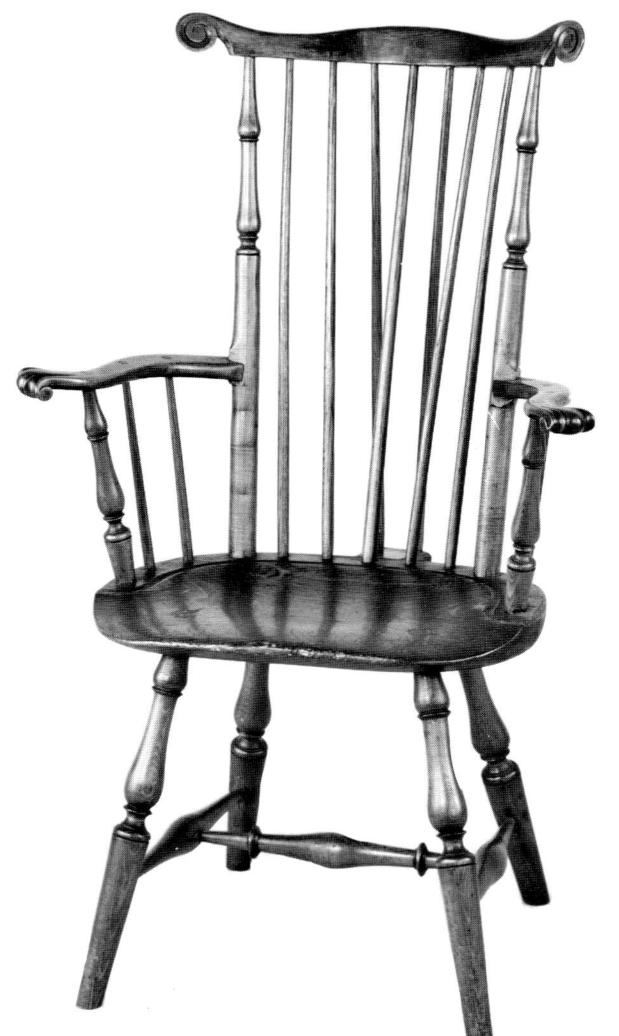

178

178. Fan-Back Windsor Armchair

Massachusetts, 1780–1800

"Fan-back" is the term generally applied to chairs with tall spindles flanked by stiles to which the arms are fastened. On this classic New England fan-back, the features are unmistakable: the very tall back is strengthened by bracing spindles; the snaking arms with well-knuckled handholds are attached to the unusually long, round section of the stiles. The seat is even more oval than those on the sack-back chairs. This chair is typical of many examples attributed to New England. In this case, an attribution to Massachusetts is perhaps warranted, since the chair, according to family tradition, was originally owned by Obediah Pease (1743–1831) of Edgartown.

Description: The serpentine crest rail with carved volute ears rests on five tapered back spindles, two bracing spindles, and stiles with vase-and-reel-turned tops. The snakelike arms thrust out laterally and terminate in knuckled handholds; vase-and-reel-turned arm supports and tapered spindles support them. On the oval seat, a projection at the back supports the bracing spindles and an incised line isolates the spindle area. The raked legs are vase-and-reel turned and are braced by two side stretchers with bulbous centers and a central stretcher with rings and a bulbous center.

Notes: Holes were bored through the seat for the legs and through the arms for the spindles and arm supports. The arms were doweled through the stiles and pinned. The chair has been refinished, but traces of red and black paint remain. The left ear and the seat have been cracked and repaired. The stretchers are fastened to the legs with wooden pegs which appear to be new, but they may replace what was there originally. The stiles have been repinned to the crest rail and seat. The center back spindle has been nailed to the crest rail.

Woods: Crest rail, spindles, white oak; seat, white pine; stiles, arms, arm supports, legs, and stretchers, beech.

Dimensions: H. 43¼ in. (109.9 cm), SH. 17¼ in. (43.8 cm). Seat: W. 21¼ in. (54.0 cm), D. 20 in. (50.8 cm).

Bibliography: Meyric R. Rogers, "The Mabel Brady Garvan Collection of Furniture," *Yale Alumni Magazine,* 25 (Jan. 1962), p. 13 (illus.); Kirk, *Early Am. Furn.,* fig. 144.

Provenance: According to tradition, owned by Captain Obediah Pease (1743–1831), Edgartown, Mass.; descended to Maria Thurston Pease; Laura M. Pease; Charles W. Lyon, New York, N.Y.; Francis P. Garvan, New York, N.Y. (1919); The Mabel Brady Garvan Collection, 1930.2360.

179. Fan-Back Windsor Armchair

Massachusetts, 1780–1800

In many ways this chair is so like no. 178 that it is conceivable that they originated in the same shop, or at least in the same area. A comparison of their details reveals that this seat is much broader and that the spindles and braces are spaced much further apart.

Description: The proportions of this chair are larger than those of no. 178, but many of the details are similarly executed. The peak at the front of the saddle seat of this chair is bolder.

Notes: Holes were bored through the seat for the legs and through the arms for the spindles and arm supports. The arms are pinned at the rear of the stiles. Traces of green and red paint remain. The center stretcher is pinned to the side stretchers. The stiles, the projection for the

179

Pl. 15—*Sofa, Salem, 1800–1810 (no. 226).*

Pl. 16—*Rococo revival side chair, New York, 1850–1860 (no. 244).*

Pl. 17—*Couch, New York, 1820–1830 (no. 223).*

Pl. 18—*Soft pad chair (no. 283), designed by Charles Eames in 1969, installed at the Yale University Art Gallery, with Eames chair bases on the wall and other Eames chairs (nos. 268 and 280) in the background.*

bracing spindles, the two spindles on each side of the central spindle, and the arm supports are pinned to the seat with wooden pegs. All the back spindles and the stiles with the exception of the bracing spindles and the second spindle from the right are pinned to the crest rail.

Woods: Crest rail, spindles, white oak; seat, white pine; right side stretcher, beech.

Dimensions: H. 45¼ in. (114.9 cm), SH. 16$^{15}/_{16}$ in. (43.0 cm). Seat: W. 24$^{5}/_{16}$ in. (61.8 cm), D. 22¾ in. (57.8 cm).

Bibliography: *BAFA,* 4 (Dec. 1930) (illus. inside front cover); Kirk, *Early Am. Furn.,* fig. 145.

Provenance: Francis P. Garvan, New York, N.Y.; The Mabel Brady Garvan Collection, 1930.2603.

180. Fan-Back Windsor Armchair

Connecticut, 1780–1800

Although it is usually difficult to assign a specific place of origin to windsor chairs, this chair offers some clues. According to a label once on the underside of the seat, it was purchased in Southington, Connecticut, and it may well have been made in that area. The plausibility of a Connecticut origin is further strengthened by the fact that the arms are made from cherry, a wood favored in that state. The repetition of the eight vase-turned parts—on the stiles, arm supports, and legs—contributes to the chair's vivacious appearance.

Description: The serpentine crest rail with rounded ears rests on slightly swelled back spindles and two vase-and-reel-turned stiles. The downward sloping arms terminate in scrolled handholds and rest on slightly swelled arm spindles and vase-and-reel-turned arm supports. On the saddle seat an incised line isolates the spindle area. The seat is supported by vase-and-reel-turned legs and swelled stretchers.

Inscription: A label at one time on the underside of the seat and now lost read: "This unusually made Windsor chair I bought from Mr. Rodney Langdon in Southington, Connecticut. September 26, 1877 I. W. Lyon."

Notes: The arms are tenoned through the stiles. Holes were bored through the arms for the spindles and arm supports. Traces of black and green paint remain. The stiles and center back spindle are pinned to the crest rail with square wooden pegs. The arm supports and the stiles are pinned to the seat from the side with larger square wooden pegs.

Woods: Crest rail, white oak; spindles, hickory; seat, tulip; arms, American black cherry; stiles, arm supports, legs, and stretchers, soft maple.

180

Dimensions: H. 39 in. (99.1 cm), SH. 18 in. (45.7 cm). Seat: W. 17¼ in. (43.8 cm), D. 18 in. (45.7 cm).

Provenance: Rodney Langdon, Southington, Conn.; Irving W. Lyon, Hartford, Conn. (1877); Francis P. Garvan, New York, N.Y.; The Mabel Brady Garvan Collection, 1930.2374.

181. Fan-Back Windsor Side Chair

American, 1790–1800

Windsor side chairs were probably not produced in America until the 1770's, and the earliest examples may have been chairs in the fan-back style.[1] Regional attribution of these chairs is very difficult; similar

181

examples bear the brand of Francis Trumble,[2] of William Cox and Lawrence Allwine of Philadelphia,[3] and of Ansel Goodrich of Northampton, Massachusetts.[4]

Description: The ends of the serpentine crest rail are undercut to form scrolled ears. Elongated vase-turned stiles and slightly tapered spindles support the crest. The boxy saddle seat has a slight peak on its front edge and a faint incised line isolating the spindle area. Robust vase-, reel-, and flattened-ball-turned legs support the seat. The side stretchers have bulbous centers and the medial stretcher has turned rings and a bulbous center.

Inscription: "J. M. Pease" is written in chalk on the underside of the seat.

Notes: Holes were bored through the seat for the legs. Black paint covers a gray-green paint. The center of the crest rail was once decorated with a gilded bowknot. Square-headed nails reinforce the joints of the center stretcher to the side stretchers and the side stretchers to the legs. The stiles, the two outermost back spindles, and the center back spindle are nailed to the seat. The stiles are pinned to the crest rail. The first, third, fifth, and seventh back spindles from the left are nailed to the crest rail.

Woods: Crest rail, ash; spindles, oak; seat, white pine; stiles, legs, and stretchers, maple.

Dimensions: H. 37½ in. (95.2 cm), SH. 17½ in. (44.4 cm). Seat: W. 16$\frac{1}{16}$ in. (40.8 cm), D. 16$\frac{3}{16}$ in. (41.1 cm).

Provenance: Charles W. Lyon, New York, N.Y.; Francis P. Garvan, New York, N.Y.; The Mabel Brady Garvan Collection, 1930.2358.

---

[1] Goyne, p. 539.—[2] *Ibid.*, fig. 4.—[3] Hornor, pl. 489 and 490.—[4] *Antiques*, 18 (July 1930), p. 38.

182. Fan-Back Windsor Side Chair

American, 1795–1805

The design of this chair is very similar to no. 181, but all the contours are softer, and the proportions of the legs to the seat and back are not quite so individual.

Description: In contrast to no. 181, on which the ends of the serpentine-shaped crest rail are undercut to form scrolls, these rounded ears turn upward. The turnings of the stiles are like those of no. 181, yet thinner. The saddle seat is beautifully shaped and is supported by vase-and-reel-turned legs. The three stretchers have bulbous centers.

Notes: The chair has been refinished, but traces of black and green paint remain. The stiles and the second, fourth, and sixth spindles from the left are pinned to the crest rail. The bases of the stiles are nailed to the seat from the side with cut nails. The center stretcher is nailed to the side stretchers, and the side stretchers are nailed to the legs with cut nails.

Woods: Crest rail, spindles and stiles, ash; seat, basswood; legs and stretchers, soft maple.

Dimensions: H. 36¾ in. (93.3 cm), SH. 17$\frac{11}{16}$ in. (44.9 cm). Seat: W. 15$\frac{1}{16}$ in. (38.3 cm), D. 15¾ in. (40.0 cm).

Provenance: Francis P. Garvan, New York, N.Y.; The Mabel Brady Garvan Collection, 1930.2697a.

182 183

183. Fan-Back Windsor Side Chair

American, 1785–1800

Bamboo turnings made their appearance on windsor chairs during the 1780's.[1] On this fan-back chair they are used on the stiles, legs, and stretchers.

Description: The curve on the crest rail of this chair is not as animated as that on no. 182. The bamboo-turned stiles flank seven slightly tapered spindles. The saddle seat is slightly peaked at the front, and on it an incised line isolates the spindle area. The widely splayed legs and the stretchers are bamboo turned.

Notes: Holes were bored through the seat for the legs. The black paint is modern. Angle-iron braces support the joints of the legs and seat. The stiles are pinned from the side of the seat with square wooden pegs. The stiles and center back spindle are pinned to the crest rail.

Woods: Crest rail, spindles, and stiles, white oak; seat, tulip; legs and stretchers, birch.

Dimensions: H. 38⅞ in. (86.0 cm), SH. 16¾ in. (42.5 cm). Seat: W. 15 in. (38.1 cm), D. 14¹³⁄₁₆ in. (37.6 cm).

Provenance: Gift of Sarah Bigelow Reid, Brooklyn, N.Y., 1933.17b.

---

[1] Goyne, p. 540.

184. Fan-Back Windsor Side Chair

Connecticut, 1795–1810

The fresh, unusual design of this chair, whose total effect is one of great animation, possibly suggests an origin in a Connecticut shop, where furniture of great individuality was often produced. The maker of this chair exaggerated his designs: the straddle of the legs is as wide as possible, and the braces stretch across the back almost to the very ends of the crest rail. The figure-eight-shaped seat is made of curly maple—a rare feature on windsor chairs, since the seats were usually of a soft wood that could be easily shaped.

184

Description: A double serpentine-shaped crest rail with upward thrusting ends is supported by vase-turned stiles, six tapered spindles, and two tapered bracing spindles. Exaggerated curves define the sides of the saddle seat, which is sharply peaked in front. Widely splayed, vase-and-reel-turned legs are braced by three stretchers with bulbous centers.

Inscription: An old inscription in chalk on the underside of the seat reads: "Mrs. D".

Notes: Holes were bored through the seat for the legs. Traces of red, white, and green can be found under the black paint. The stiles are pinned to the crest rail. The left bracing spindle is nailed to the crest rail.

Wood: Soft maple.

Dimensions: H. 34 in. (86.4 cm), SH. 17⅝ in. (44.8 cm). Seat: W. 15¹⁄₁₆ in. (38.3 cm), D. 18½ in. (47.0 cm).

Exhibitions: Girl Scouts Exhibition, no. 527; *Conn. Furn.,* p. 138, no. 251.

Bibliography: Miller, I, p. 264 (illus. p. 265, no. 456).

Provenance: Charles W. Lyon, New York, N.Y.; Francis P. Garvan, New York, N.Y.; The Mabel Brady Garvan Collection, 1930.2267.

185. Fan-Back Windsor Side Chair

Connecticut, possibly the Westbrook area, 1775–1795

The intricacy of the ornamentation on this windsor chair probably from the Westbrook area of Connecticut typifies the best and most imaginative Connecticut craftsmanship.[1] The scalloped bottom edge and domed top edge of the crest rail are arrestingly different from the more orthodox interpretations of the fan-back chair (no. 181).

Description: The crest rail is scalloped along the bottom edge, and has large round ears, two cupped indentations and a large, semi-circular dome shape at the center. Stiles with ball-, reel-, and urn-shaped turnings and nine tapered spindles support the crest. The thick but narrow saddle seat is peaked at the front. On it a faint incised line isolates the spindle area. Ball-, reel-, and vase-turned legs are braced by side stretchers with bulbous centers and an unusual medial stretcher in the form of a double vase with reels flanking the central ball.

Notes: The gold decoration on the black paint may or may not be original. The paint is somewhat abraded. The left ear has been repaired. The stiles and center back spindle are nailed to the crest rail from the front. Modern wire nails were used to secure the joints of the side stretchers with the rear legs and the center stretcher with the side stretchers.

Woods: Crest rail and spindles, red oak; seat, tulip; stiles, legs, stretchers, soft maple.

Dimensions: H. 38 in. (96.5 cm), SH. 18¼ in. (46.4 cm). Seat: W. 14 in. (35.6 cm), D. 15⅝ in. (39.7 cm).

Exhibitions: Conn. Furn., p. 138, no. 252.

Bibliography: Henry B. Stoddard, "Special Windsor

185

Style Found," *American Collector,* 1 (April 19, 1934), pp. 1 and 6 (illus.); *Ornamented Chair,* p. 69, fig. 6; Kirk, *Early Am. Furn.,* fig. 166.

Provenance: Henry B. Stoddard, Fairfield, Conn.; Gift of Moreau L. Stoddard, Fairfield, Conn., 1953.33.1.

[1] Stoddard (see Bibliography above).

186. Child's Rod-Back Windsor Side Chair

American, 1800–1810

The rod-shaped crest rail on this child's chair is related to the style of rod-back windsors that became popular in the first decade of the nineteenth century.[1]

Description: The round, curved crest rail rests on bamboo-turned stiles and spindles. The seat is not peaked in front, but is beveled to a pointed ridge at the front and sides. The legs and stretchers are bamboo turned.

Notes: Holes were bored through the rail for the spindles and stiles. Traces of green and red paint remain.

Woods: Crest rail, red oak; seat, tulip; spindles, stiles, stretchers, legs, birch.

Dimensions: H. 22 13/16 in. (57.9 cm), SH. 11½ in. (29.2 cm). Seat: W. 12 in. (30.5 cm), D. 11¼ in. (28.6 cm).

Bibliography: Leslie Richardson, "An Early Connecticut Interior," *Antiques,* 16 (Dec. 1929), p. 500, fig. 1.

Provenance: Jacob Margolis, New York, N.Y.; Francis P. Garvan, New York, N.Y. (1925); The Mabel Brady Garvan Collection, 1930.2139.

[1] Goyne, p. 541.

186

187

187. Rod-Back Windsor Side Chair

Possibly Connecticut, 1815–1830

The rod-back was a variation on the windsor form introduced in the first decade of the nineteenth century. Among its distinctive features are the double rails at the top of the back and the arrangement of four stretchers replacing the traditional central and side stretchers. Parts such as the boxy seat and bamboo turnings are not well articulated in this late example of the windsor tradition. The slight swellings in the spindles—a feature of earlier Connecticut windsor chairs—and the fact that this chair was found in the Sterling Memorial Library at Yale are the basis for a tentative suggestion of a Connecticut origin.

Description: Above the very square seat with edges beveled inward, stiles with faint bamboo turnings support two rods at the top of the back. Three of the seven slightly bulbous spindles pierce the lower rod and join the top one. The raked legs have faint bamboo turnings. A bamboo-turned stretcher is between each pair of legs.

Notes: The chair was first painted white, then green, then reddish-brown. The stiles are pinned to the seat from the side with square wooden pegs. Holes are bored through the seat for the legs. Faint grooves mark the placement of the two back rails and stretchers. The two top rails are nailed to the stiles with small rectangular nails driven from the sides.

Woods: Crest rail, spindles, and rear stiles, hickory; seat, tulip; legs and stretchers, soft maple.

Dimensions: H. 33¼ in. (85.2 cm), BPH. 34¼ in. (87.8 cm), SH. 17½ in. (44.9 cm). Seat: W. 17¼ in. (44.2 cm), D. 15¼ in. (39.1 cm).

Provenance: Sterling Memorial Library transfer, 1971.104.

188. Bow-Back Windsor Armchair

New York or Southern New England, 1785–1800

The daring construction of the continuous bow-back chair is a great achievement of the windsor chairmaker's craft, but because of its inherent weaknesses, the rail often breaks where it is bent to form the arms. Bow-backs often bear brands or labels of New York and southern New England chairmakers.[1] An identical chair was labeled in 1790 by Henry Locke of New York.[2]

Description: The continuous bowed crest rail has a bead on the edges that ends where the wood is bent forward to form the flat, slightly enlarged handholds. Nine tall, tapered spindles fill the back, with two shorter ones on each side just behind the vase-and-reel-turned arm supports. The saddle seat is peaked at the front and on it an incised line isolates the area of the spindles and arm supports. Four vase-and-reel-turned legs rake at an extreme angle and are braced by two side stretchers with bulbous centers and a central stretcher with a bulbous center and rings.

Notes: Holes for the legs, spindles, and arm supports were bored all the way through the seat. The legs and spindles are wedged from the top. Traces of old green and red paint can be found. Small nails were driven from the inner edge of the bowed crest rail. On the two spindles

188

flanking the central back spindle the nails were driven from the rear.

Woods: Crest rail and spindles, American ash; seat, tulip; arm supports, legs, stretchers, soft maple.

Dimensions: H. 36½ in. (92.7 cm), SH. 18¹⁄₁₆ in. (45.9 cm). Seat: W. 17¾ in. (45.1 cm), D. 16½ in. (41.9 cm).

Bibliography: Kirk, *Early Am. Furn.*, fig. 142.

Provenance: Gift of C. Sanford Bull, Middlebury, Conn., 1953.50.7b.

[1] Downs, *N.Y. State Furniture*, p. 9, no. 73 (illus.).—[2] DAPC.

189. Bow-Back Windsor Armchair

Lisbon, Connecticut, 1785–1795
Ebenezer Tracy (1744–1803)

This bow-back chair by Ebenezer Tracy has beautiful turnings, but unlike no. 188, whose nine spindles are spaced regularly, the even number of spindles used here leaves a gap that divides the back into two halves. The line formed by the continuous bow is also not executed smoothly—the incised lines end abruptly just above the arm spindles and the bow scoops into the arms. The spindles have swelled turnings at the center, characteristic of Connecticut windsor chairs. This feature appears on the writing

189

armchair also by Tracy (no. 173) and on other published examples by such Connecticut makers as Amos Denison Allen, who apprenticed with Tracy.[1] The two Tracy chairs in this catalogue also share other unusual details: the seats are chestnut, a hard wood which was not easy to shape, and they do not have incised lines isolating the spindle arms.

Description: The bowed crest rail has beaded edges that stop where the taller back spindles end and the wood sweeps forward to form the arms and handholds. The back spindles, two bracing spindles and arm spindles have distinctive swellings at the middle. They are arranged in a less regular pattern than those on no. 188, to accommodate the bracing spindles and the taller back. Contrary to usual practice, an incised line does not isolate the spindle area. The turnings are similar to those on the preceding chair, except that the central stretcher lacks rings.

Inscription: Branded on underside of seat: "EB: TRACY."

Notes: Holes were bored through the crest rail for the four center back spindles, the two bracing spindles, the four arm spindles, and the two arm supports. Wooden pegs were used to secure the two center back spindles and the two inner arm spindles to the crest rail. The second arm spindle on the right side and the first arm spindle on the left side are pegged to the seat from the side. Both bracing spindles are pegged to the extension of the seat from the side. Traces of green paint remain. The bracing spindles are spliced at the lower end.

Woods: Crest rail, spindles, arm supports, and stretchers, white oak; seat, chestnut; legs, hard maple.

Dimensions: H. 38⅝ in. (98.1 cm), SH. 17⅝ in. (44.8 cm). Seat: W. 17¼ in. (43.8 cm), D. 20 in. (50.8 cm).

Bibliography: Kirk, *Early Am. Furn.*, fig. 143.

Provenance: Irving W. Lyon, Hartford, Conn.; Francis P. Garvan, New York, N.Y.; The Mabel Brady Garvan Collection, 1930.2377.

[1] Goyne, p. 541.

190

190. Bow-Back Windsor Armchair

Rhode Island, 1790–1805

In America windsor chairs were used in formal settings. This example with two unusual refinements—the mahogany arms and the vase-turned spindles—may well have graced a drawing room or front hall. Nutting illustrated this chair, or one identical to it, and assigned it a Rhode Island origin.[1] Other examples with the distinctive vase-turned spindles are thought to have been made there, such as the set branded "A. G. Case," which was owned by a colonial Rhode Island family.[2] However, similar chairs with the label of Thomas and William Ash of New York are also known, and thus complicate the problem of assigning chairs of this type a strictly Rhode Island origin.[3] A chair with similar spindles was also made by Ebenezer Tracy in nearby eastern Connecticut.[4] Many of the chairs attributed to Rhode Island have ash seats, an unusual feature also present on this example. Green paint originally covered all surfaces of this chair with the exception of the arms.

Description: The bowed back is decorated with a beaded edge and surrounds seven vase-turned spindles and two bracing spindles. Downward sloping mahogany arms with scrolled handholds are attached to the bowed back and are supported by arm spindles with vase turnings and larger arm supports. The saddle seat is slightly peaked at the front and has an incised line isolating the spindle area. The leg and stretcher turnings are fuller on this example than on nos. 188 and 189, and the ends of the legs have an incurved taper.

Notes: Holes were bored through the seat for the legs and through the crest rail for the back spindles. Traces of old green, red, and white paint remain. Nail holes in the seat from upholstery have been filled. The two outer back spindles, the two bracing spindles, and the three center back spindles are nailed to the crest rail from the back with cut nails. The arms are pinned to the tops of the arm supports, and the arm spindles with square wooden pegs are driven in from the side. The scrolled end of the right arm is a replacement.

Woods: Crest rail, spindles, and arm supports, American hickory; arms, mahogany; seat, American ash; legs and stretchers, soft maple.

Dimensions: H. 39 13/16 in. (101.1 cm), SH. 17 1/2 in. (44.4 cm). Seat: W. 17 3/16 in. (43.7 cm), D. 19 3/4 in. (50.2 cm).

Provenance: Louis Guerineau Myers, New York, N.Y.; Francis P. Garvan, New York, N.Y.; The Mabel Brady Garvan Collection, 1930.2354.

[1] Nutting, *Treasury*, no. 2696.—[2] Goyne, p. 542, fig. 10; *Antiques*, 96 (Oct. 1969), p. 453.—[3] *Antiques*, 16 (Aug. 1929), p. 147.—[4] DAPC.

191. Bow-Back Windsor Side Chair

American, 1785–1800

Like the three preceding armchairs, this chair is called a "bow-back" today, but it was known as an "oval-back" when the style made its appearance during the 1780's.[1] With its boldly peaked seat and back rail curving inward where it joins the seat, this chair has a quite vigorous design. Two bracing spindles were added, as was often done, to reinforce the fragile construction of the back, and the rail was pinned to the sides of the seat with square wooden pegs.

Description: The beaded, bowed back surrounds seven tapered back spindles and two tapered bracing spindles. The saddle seat is peaked at the front and has an incised line to isolate the spindle area. The turned legs and stretchers are similar to those on no. 188, but are a little fuller.

Inscriptions: The name "Bert" is painted in black on the underside of the seat; a red and white paper label reads: "Property of / Millicent Bingham".

Notes: The chair was first painted gray and then had at least two coats of black paint. The right rear leg has been broken and repaired in the narrow section of the vase turning. The center stretcher is nailed to the side stretchers. The bowed-back rail is pinned to the sides of the seat with square wooden pegs. Holes were bored through the seat for the legs and through the top rail for the three center spindles.

Woods: Crest rail, oak; seat, tulip; right front leg, soft maple.

Dimensions: H. 36 3/4 in. (93.3 cm), SH. 18 1/2 in. (47.0 cm). Seat: W. 15 3/4 in. (40.0 cm), D. 20 3/4 in. (52.7 cm).

Provenance: Bequest of Millicent Todd Bingham, Washington, D.C., 1969.42.1.

[1] Goyne, p. 539.

192. Bow-Back Windsor Side Chair

American, 1785–1800

The tack holes on the seat indicate that this chair was upholstered at one time, as many windsor chairs were, and it is important to note the shape of this seat—the deep, thick edge and lack of a peak at the center may indicate a seat designed especially for upholstery. The bold turnings on the legs and stretchers, particularly the grooved contours of the bulbous ring turnings on the medial stretcher, are perhaps this chair's finest features.

Description: Nine spindles are found on the back of this chair, rather than seven as on no. 191. This example is also different in other respects: the seat is not saddled and its edges are quite thick. The ring turnings on the medial stretcher enclose a flattened ball.

Inscription: Branded twice on underside of seat: "MRS. E. HART".

Notes: Holes were bored through the seat for the two front legs and through the back rail for the spindles. Traces of green paint remain. Nail holes from upholstery tacks have been filled just in front of the groove along the back of the seat and along its front face. Square wooden pegs driven from the sides secure the bowed crest rail and the two bracing spindles to the seat. The two bracing spindles and the center back spindle are nailed to the crest rail from the back with small nails.

Woods: Crest rail and spindles, American hickory; seat, tulip; legs and stretchers, soft maple.

191

192

193

194

Dimensions: H. 38 in. (36.5 cm), SH. 15 13/16 in. (40.2 cm). Seat: W. 15 7/8 in (40.3 cm), D. 18 5/16 in. (46.5 cm).

Provenance: Irving W. Lyon, Hartford, Conn.; Francis P. Garvan, New York, N.Y.; The Mabel Brady Garvan Collection, 1930.2053.

193. Child's Bow-Back Windsor Side Chair

American, 1785–1800

This child's chair is very like no. 191. The turnings on the right front leg differ from those on the other legs, indicating that the leg may be a replacement.

Description: This chair is a miniature version of no. 191, except that the back is not braced.

Notes: Holes were bored through the seat for the legs and through the back rail for the two back spindles flanking the center back spindle. Traces of green and gray paint remain.

Woods: Crest rail and spindles, white oak; seat, tulip; legs and stretchers, soft maple.

Dimensions: H. 25 3/8 in. (64.5 cm), SH. 11 1/16 in. (28.1 cm). Seat: W. 11 11/16 in. (29.7 cm), D. 11 1/4 in. (28.6 cm).

Provenance: Charles W. Lyon, New York, N.Y.; Francis P. Garvan, New York, N.Y.; The Mabel Brady Garvan Collection, 1930.2351.

194. Child's Bow-Back Windsor Side Chair

American, 1785–1800

During the 1780's, when the bow-back chair was introduced, a change took place in the style of turnings: bamboo turnings replaced the baluster. The turnings of the legs and stretchers of this small-sized windsor chair reflect the newer style.

Description: The bowed back is curved inward as it reaches the rather elongated saddle seat. Five tapered spindles are found in the back. The short, raked legs are bamboo turned and the bulbous stretchers have grooves at the center.

Notes: Holes were bored through the seat for the legs and through the back rail for the spindles. The chair has been refinished, but traces of red and green paint remain. The center back spindle is nailed to the crest rail with a small nail driven from the back.

Woods: Top rail and spindles, American hickory; seat, tulip; legs and stretchers, maple.

Dimensions: H. 19 3/8 in. (64.5 cm), SH. 7 7/16 in. (18.9 cm). Seat: W. 10 in. (25.4 cm), D. 9 3/4 in. (24.8 cm).

Bibliography: Reifsnyder Coll., p. 171, no. 587.

Provenance: Howard Reifsnyder, Philadelphia, Pa.; Francis P. Garvan, New York, N.Y.; The Mabel Brady Garvan Collection, 1930.2383b.

195. Bow-Back Windsor Side Chair

Possibly Philadelphia, about 1810

According to Fred Tuck of Pinehurst, North Carolina, who purchased the chairs from descendants of the Wing family, this chair was made for Henry Wing of Wayne, Maine, about 1810. The Henry Wing family also owned a similar windsor settee (no. 196), branded by the Philadelphia windsor chairmakers

195

Gilbert and Robert Gaw. If, indeed, the furniture was purchased *en suite* by the Wings, it seems likely that this chair was also imported from Philadelphia.

Description: Both edges of the bowed back are beaded, and the wood is bent inward as it reaches the seat. Seven tapered spindles brace the back. The front edge of the seat is ridged and the corners are rounded; an incised line isolates the spindle area. Four raked, bamboo-turned legs are braced by bamboo-turned stretchers.

Notes: Holes were bored through the seat for the legs and through the back rail for the spindles. Traces of red, gray, and green paint remain under the black. The continuous bowed back rail is pegged to the seat from the side with square wooden pegs.

Woods: Crest rail and spindles, ash; seat, basswood; legs and stretchers, soft maple.

Dimensions: H. 38 9/16 in. (97.9 cm), SH. 18 1/2 in. (47.0 cm). Seat: W. 16 9/16 in. (42.1 cm), D. 16 7/16 in. (41.8 cm).

Bibliography: Kirk, *Early Am. Furn.*, fig. 169.

Provenance: Henry Wing family, Wayne, Me.; descended to Dr. Hackett's grandchildren, Kennebunk, Me.; Fred Tuck, Pinehurst, N.C.; Henry H. Taylor, Bridgeport, Conn.; Francis P. Garvan, New York, N.Y.; The Mabel Brady Garvan Collection, 1930.2352a.

196. Windsor Settee

Philadelphia, about 1810

Gilbert and Robert Gaw (active late eighteenth and early nineteenth centuries)

This windsor settee has been heavily restored, but the brand of the Philadelphia windsor chairmakers Gilbert and Robert Gaw on the underside of the seat makes it still an important part of the Yale collection. Gilbert Gaw's shop was on the south side of Drinker's Alley before 1795 and long after.[1] The dates of the partnership of Gilbert and Robert Gaw are not certain, although in 1796 they billed George Washington forty-four dollars for twenty-four "ovel Back Chairs."[2] The family history of this settee suggests that it was bought by the Henry Wing family of Wayne, Maine, in 1810. A side chair from the same family (no. 195) may have originally accompanied the settee.

Description: The crest has a straight top edge and rounded corners. Twenty-five tapered bamboo-turned spindles are found in the back. Three short spindles and a larger bamboo-turned arm support are under each downward sloping arm with scrolled handhold. The side edges of the front corners of the seat are indented. The eight legs and the three stretchers parallel to the front are bamboo turned. The stretchers running from front to back have bulbous centers.

Inscription: Branded three times on underside of seat: "G and R Gaw".

196a

Notes: Holes were bored through the seat for the legs and through the rail for some of the back spindles. Several coats of paint have been applied over the original red. Both arms, the arm supports, the arm spindles, the left back leg, and 3 inches at the base of all the other legs have been replaced. The crest rail is split at the center.

Woods: Crest rail and spindles, ash; seat, tulip; legs, stretchers, arms, and arm supports, soft maple.

Dimensions: H. 36 5/8 in. (93.0 cm), SH. 17 1/8 in. (43.5 cm). Seat: W. 74 9/16 in. (189.4 cm), D. 20 1/2 in. (52.1 cm).

Provenance: Henry Wing family, Wayne, Me.; descended to Dr. Hackett's grandchildren, Kennebunk, Me.; Fred Tuck, Pinehurst, N.C.; Henry H. Taylor, Bridgeport, Conn.; Francis P. Garvan, New York, N.Y.; The Mabel Brady Garvan Collection, 1930.2033.

[1] Hornor, p. 307.—[2] *Ibid.*, p. 303.

197. Windsor Settee

Probably Pennsylvania, 1785–1800

The elongated, serpentine crest rail perches lightly on the spindles and stiles of this windsor settee. Its sinuous line reflects the style of neoclassical seating furniture. Bamboo turnings, introduced in the 1780's, are used extensively—for the legs, stretchers, spindles, and even at the tops of the vase-shaped arm supports. The Pennsylvania origin is assigned on the basis of provenance.

Description: The serpentine crest rail is supported at the

196

197

middle by a beaded brace and at the ends by serpentine-shaped stiles. Tightly spaced bamboo-turned spindles support the crest rail and the arms. The ends of the arms terminate in scrolls just beyond vase-and-cone-turned arm supports. The front corners of the seat are scooped out with a beaded edge that continues from the sides. The treatment of the base is similar to that on no. 196.

Notes: Holes were bored through the seat for the legs, through the arms for the arm spindles and arm supports, and through the rail for some of the back spindles. A shrinkage crack appears in the seat. The reddish-brown paint covers old red and green paint.

198

Woods: Spindles, crest rail, and arms, oak; seat, tulip; legs, stretchers, and rear stiles, soft maple.

Dimensions: H. 36 in. (91.4 cm), SH. 16⅛ in. (41.0 cm). Seat: W. 75⅛ in. (190.8 cm), D. 21¾ in. (55.2 cm).

Provenance: Samuel Whitaker Pennypacker (1843–1916), Philadelphia, Pa.; Pennypacker Sale, 1930; Jacob Margolis, New York, N.Y. (1930); Francis P. Garvan, New York, N.Y.; The Mabel Brady Garvan Collection, 1930.2379.

198. Rod-Back Windsor Settee

American, about 1810

During the first decade of the nineteenth century a new style of windsor chair, known as the rod-back, was introduced (see no. 187). Windsor furniture in this style bears a close relationship to the fancy-painted furniture popular at about the same time, particularly because of the use of oval medallions. Traces of paint on this rod-back settee suggest that it may once have been colored red and green.

Description: The double rod at the top is supported by bamboo-turned spindles, five of which pierce the lower rod. A large oval medallion appears at the center of the top rail, two smaller ones are between the spindles that pierce the lower rail, and a medium-sized one is on the central back spindle. The serpentine-shaped arms with knuckled handholds rest on bamboo-turned spindles and arm supports. The thick plank seat has an incised line along its front edge and isolating the spindles. The eight bamboo-turned legs are braced by bamboo-turned stretchers.

Notes: Holes were bored through the seat for the legs, through the top rails for the spindles, through the arms for the arm spindles and arm supports, and through the stiles for the lower top rail. The settee has been refinished, but traces of red and green paint remain. The base of the left rear foot was repaired in 1947. The right scrolled handhold has been restored. Orange shellac was removed in 1964.

Woods: Crest rail, spindles, and legs, hickory; seat, tulip; rear stiles, arms, arm supports, and stretchers, soft maple.

Dimensions: H. 32¹¹⁄₁₆ in. (83.0 cm), SH. 17⁵⁄₁₆ in. (44.0 cm). Seat: W. 80⅞ in. (205.4 cm), D. 17½ in. (44.4 cm).

Bibliography: Nutting, *Treasury,* no. 1652; *Reifsnyder Coll.,* p. 162, no. 558.

Provenance: Howard Reifsnyder, Philadelphia, Pa.; Francis P. Garvan, New York, N.Y.; The Mabel Brady Garvan Collection, 1930.2381.

Stools

STOOLS are pieces without arms or backs, usually made for sitting, but sometimes designed as footrests. They have been made in America from the seventeenth century to the present time, but during this period their role has changed. From medieval times to the seventeenth century in Europe stools—along with their extended form, the backless bench—were a more common form of seating furniture than chairs. This may also have been the case in seventeenth-century American households. By the eighteenth century, according to the evidence of inventories, stools were no longer an essential seating form, but as small, handy pieces of furniture, they have continued to be produced to serve many purposes.

199. Joint Stool

New England, 1690–1715

The name "joint stool" is derived from the jointed, mortise-and-tenon method of construction. With its wide overhanging top and bold turnings, this stool dating from near the end of the seventeenth century is a fine example of the form. Although the turnings are boldly executed, their reel, disc, and vase shapes are more comparable to turnings found on the stretchers of early eighteenth-century chairs (no. 40) than to seventeenth-century baluster forms. The similarity of the turnings to those found on New England chairs and the use of soft maple suggest a New England origin. A closely related stool is owned by the Metropolitan Museum of Art.[1]

Description: The rectangular top of this joint stool has a thumbnail-molded edge, and the bottom edges of the framing are also molded. The four raked legs have a vase turning above a deep reel, and feet with thin necks and bulbous bases. Rectangular stretchers are pinned to the blocks in the legs.

Notes: The stool has been refinished, but traces of black and gray paint remain. The feet are worn at the base and one foot has been replaced. The top is pegged to the frame.

Wood: Soft maple.

Dimensions: H. 21¼ in. (54.0 cm). Seat rails: W. 16⅛ in. (41.0 cm), MW. 22⅛ in. (56.2 cm), D. 13½ in. (34.3 cm), FD. 10¼ in. (26.0 cm).

Bibliography: "Living With Antiques," *Antiques,* 45 (April 1944) (illus. p. 190).

199

Provenance: Gift of C. Sanford Bull, Middlebury, Conn., 1949.245.

[1] R. T. H. Halsey and Charles O. Cornelius, *A Handbook of the American Wing*, 6th ed., rev. by Joseph Downs (New York, 1938), fig. 14.

200. Stool

Probably Canadian, 1750–1800

The bulbous turnings on the legs and stretchers of this stool are separated by sharp-edged, paired rings—not a typical feature of American regional designs. But such turnings on the base of an armchair from Quebec, Canada[1] may provide a clue to the place of origin of this example.

Description: The square top rests on a frame supported at the four corners by raked legs decorated with ridged ring turnings. Below the blocks into which the stretchers fit is a ring-and-reel turning and a bulbous foot. The stretchers are similar in profile to the legs, but the center turnings are decorated with grooves.

Notes: The top is nailed to the frame. Traces of green, red, and white paint remain.

200

Woods: Top, seat rails, white pine; stretchers, beech and oak; legs, white oak and birch.

Dimensions: H. 18⅞ in. (47.9 cm), W. 10½ in. (26.7 cm), D. 10½ in. (26.7 cm).

Provenance: Jacob Margolis, New York, N.Y.; Francis P. Garvan, New York, N.Y. (1925); The Mabel Brady Garvan Collection, 1930.2135b.

[1] Jean Palardy, *The Early Furniture of French Canada* (Toronto and New York, 1965), fig. 315.

201. Stool

Probably Salem, Massachusetts, 1810–1815

Seating furniture with "Grecian cross" legs (such as a side chair at Winterthur[1] and sofas at Yale [no. 230] and the Metropolitan Museum of Art) has as yet been found only in New York, and it is often associated with Duncan Phyfe, to whom this handsome curule stool with reeded and carved legs has formerly been attributed.[2] The execution of the water leaf carving here is, however, more comparable to the motif as it is found on square-back Salem sofas than to the same motif on furniture from New York. The outline of the water leaves, like that on the two Salem sofas in this collection (nos. 226 and 227), is soft and wavy, with individual petals indicated by three incised lines. On the water leaves of New York examples the wavy edge corresponds to the raised ribs which radiate from the central stem (see no. 157). The handling of the carving casts doubt upon a New York attribution and raises the possibility that the stool may have been made in Salem.

Description: The "hollowed" seat is upholstered and supported on reeded "Grecian cross" legs. A raised rosette ornaments their junction, and from it laurel leaves curve along the upper legs and water leaves along the lower pair. A double, reeded, urn-shaped stretcher joins the two pairs of legs, which terminate in carved paw feet.

Notes: The center sections of the rear legs have been repaired. The red satin upholstery illustrated has been replaced by a red satin with a yellow medallion in the French Empire style of the early nineteenth century (Gift of Lloyd Hyde, 1972.126.17).

Woods: Mahogany; seat rails, American ash.

Dimensions: H. 15¼ in. (38.7 cm), W. 19¼ in. (48.9 cm), D. 15⁹⁄₁₆ in. (39.5 cm).

Bibliography: McClelland, p. 94, pl. 85.

Provenance: Frank McCarthy, Longmeadow, Mass.; Francis P. Garvan, New York, N.Y. (1929); The Mabel Brady Garvan Collection, 1930.2008.

[1] Montgomery, no. 72.—[2] McClelland, p. 94, pl. 85.

201

202. Stool

American, 1835–1845

The burled wood and C-scrolls used in this stool are characteristic features of the French Restauration style which became popular in the late 1820's and the 1830's. A broadside printed in 1833 for the New York cabinetmaking firm of Joseph Meeks and Sons illustrates furniture with stylistic details similar to those found on this stool. The information available thus far on Restauration style furniture does not provide a sufficient basis for assigning the stool a specific place of origin.

Description: The rails are curved so that the ends are higher than the center; the side rails give the effect of a double cylinder form. The pair of opposed C-scrolls that constitute the base merge at the center. Small buttons form the feet and are also placed between the legs and seat, providing a transition. Two ogee-and-cylinder-turned stretchers brace the legs.

Notes: Two of the button feet have been replaced. The cane is new. Minor cracks in the legs have been repaired. The stool has been refinished.

Wood: Hard maple.

Dimensions: H. 14 in. (35.6 cm), W. 29⅞ in. (79.5 cm), D. 17 7/16 in. (44.4 cm).

Provenance: Francis P. Garvan, New York, N.Y.; The Mabel Brady Garvan Collection, 1950.709.

202

203. Footstool

Albany, New York, about 1840–50

J. W. Netterville, active about 1833–1867

A paper label glued to the underside of this stool identifies it as having been made by J. W. Netterville of Albany, New York. An entry in *Hoffman's Albany Directory* of 1841–2 shows a John W. Netterville, cabinetmaker and undertaker, at the same Church Street address as appears on the label. John had been preceded at 21 Church Street by Thomas Netterville, perhaps a relative; John's earlier address was 103 Green Street.[1] A reference to J. W. Netterville, cabinetmaker and undertaker, occurs in the Albany directories as late as 1867. The combination of cabinetmaking and undertaking was not uncommon, and since the earliest days in America cabinetmakers

203

had been called upon to make coffins. John W. Netterville proudly advertised that he supplied "Shrouds, Coffins and Furniture of the highest quality," also a "refrigerator for preserving deceased persons."[2]

Description: The rectangular upholstered top is covered with black horsehair worked at the center with a *petit-point* wreath of flowers and at the corners with small floral-like motifs. The sides of the stool are large ogee-shaped moldings. The corners are supported by four ogee-bracket feet.

Inscription: A paper label glued to the underside reads: "FROM / J. W. NETTERVILLE'S / CABINET WARE HOUSE / 17, 19 & 21 Church-st. / ALBANY."

203a

Notes: One foot has been replaced. The bottom edges of the ogee-shaped moldings are badly marred. The moldings are of tulip veneered with mahogany and attached to the square inner frame of cherry.

Woods: Mahogany; tulip and cherry.

Dimensions: H. 7¼ in. (18.3 cm), W. 14¾ in. (37.8 cm), D. 13¾ in. (35.2 cm).

Provenance: Gift of Mr. and Mrs. Richard Stiner, B.A. 1945W, 1975.24.2.

[1] *Child's Albany Directory*, 1833/4.—[2] *Albany Directory for the Year 1867* (Samson Davenport & Co., 1867).

204

204. Footstool

American, 1850–1870

The needlework top which appears to be original to this footstool is a virtuoso example of the art that became so popular in the nineteenth century. The multi-colored floral pattern is embellished with white, brown and clear glass beads. The whole is supported on a curvilinear frame whose C-scroll and floral carving reflects the elaborate richness of the rococo-revival style.

Description: The top is worked with a pattern of beaded roses and sprays of other flowers against a red *gros-point* ground with large leaves worked in shades of green and gold. The front and rear serpentine-shaped seat rails have a carved foliated C-scroll with pendant foliage. The short cabriole legs are ornamented with a single flower bud on a stalk with leaves. The legs terminate in French scroll feet.

Notes: The top of one leg is cracked. A modern composition board on the underside of the seat suggests that the stuffing in the cushion may have been restored.

Wood: Mahogany.

Dimensions: H. 11¼ in. (28.8 cm), W. 14½ in. (37.1 cm), D. 11¼ in. (28.8 cm).

Provenance: Gift of Mr. and Mrs. Richard Stiner, B.A. 1945W, 1975.24.1.

205. Footstool

Boston, 1862–1875
George W. Ware and Company (1862–1875)

This stool, the smallest in the Yale collection, was designed as a rest for the feet and not as a seat. The simple torus molding and the feet with outer edges reminiscent of saber-shaped legs demonstrate the persistence of Grecian design well into the nineteenth century. The stool bears the label of Geo. W. Ware and Company; George W. Ware is listed in *Stimpson's Boston Directory* of 1860–61 as a member of Blake, Ware & Co., Furniture Dealers. In 1862 he formed his own firm, George W. Ware & Co., which lasted until 1875, according to the *Boston Almanac and Business Directories* of 1862 and 1875.

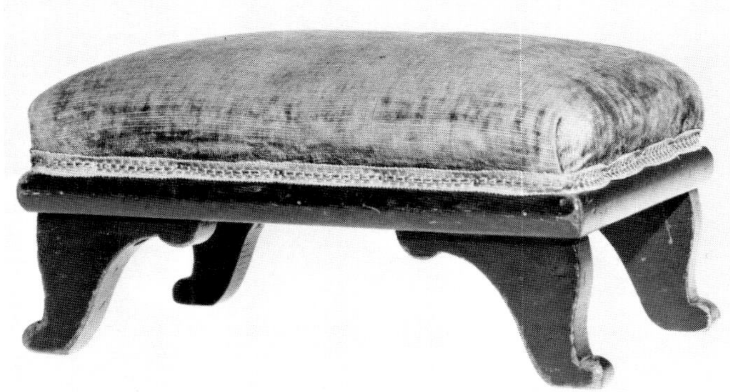

205

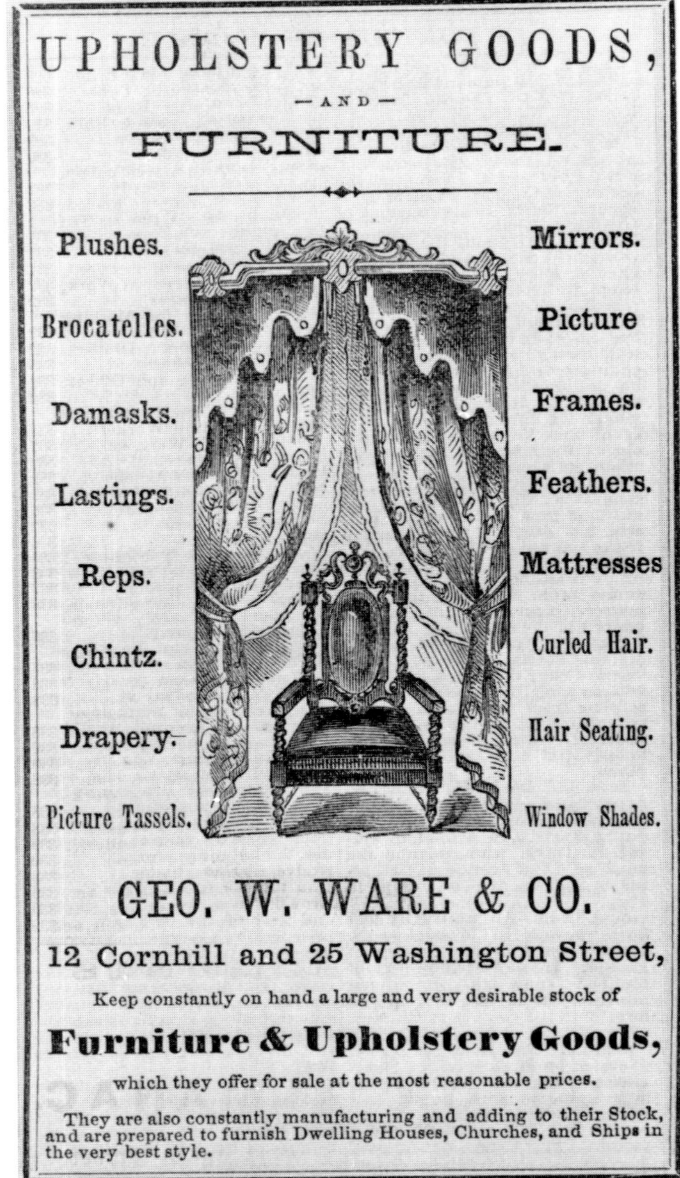

Fig. 5—*Advertisement of George W. Ware and Company, from* The Boston Almanac and Business Directory *of 1862.*

Description: The footstool is rectangular in shape, and is supported on four legs with serpentine outlines that end in small scrolled feet. Worn green velvet upholstery trimmed with gold-colored braid covers the cushion resting on a torus-shaped molding.

Inscription: A label on the bottom of the footstool reads: "GEO. W. WARE & CO. / Manufacturers and Dealers in / FURNITURE, / Looking-Glasses and Upholstery Goods, / PLUSHES, DAMASKS & BROCATELLES, / No. 12 Cornhill, and 26 Washington Street, / BOSTON."

Notes: The legs are held in place by screws, one being strengthened by several nails. The legs and feet are quite worn.

Woods: Mahogany; white pine; ash.

Dimensions: H. 5½ in. (14.0 cm), W. 8½ in. (21.5 cm), D. 12⅝ in. (31.3 cm).

Provenance: Gift of Mr. and Mrs. Charles F. Montgomery, New Haven, Conn., 1974.88.

205a

Upholstered Armchairs and Lolling Chairs

THE EARLIEST known American upholstered armchairs are in the Queen Anne style. Judging by the small number that survive today and by the scattered references to them in household inventories, they were not common in the eighteenth century. The additional cost of having backs and seats covered with wool damasks or needlework undoubtedly put open armchairs beyond the reach of all but well-to-do colonial Americans. In the portraits of the Boston aristocracy by John Singleton Copley, women are often shown seated in them. Unlike easy chairs, which were apparently reserved for the use of the sick and infirm, eighteenth-century upholstered armchairs and their successors, "lolling" chairs (as the form was called in the Federal period),[1] were elegant and comfortable pieces of furniture for use in the principal rooms. The form underwent few real changes in the Federal period other than to acquire the details of neoclassical design. As later entries in this catalogue indicate, it did not go out of fashion with the close of the Federal period.

[1] Montgomery, p. 155.

Fig. 6—*John Singleton Copley,* Mrs. Isaac Smith. *Oil on canvas, 1769. Yale University Art Gallery; gift of Maitland Fuller Briggs, B.A. 1896.*

206. Upholstered Armchair

Massachusetts, 1730–1760

The rounded, inviting contours of the serpentine-shaped arms and their slender curved supports are superb features of this early New England armchair, which has few peers. A construction feature found here is typical of New England upholstered armchairs and easy chairs: the front legs are walnut, but the rear legs are maple stained to look like walnut to avoid wasting expensive wood on that part of the stile cov-

206

ered by upholstery. When mahogany was the primary wood, such as in no. 207, the mahogany rear legs were usually grafted onto a maple frame; apparently maple could not be stained convincingly to match mahogany. Chairs related to this one include an example at Winterthur with a slightly hollowed crest rail, and another in the same collection with a straight crest.[1] A comparable example with a serpentine-shaped crest rail has also been illustrated.[2]

Description: The upholstered back of this armchair ends in a gentle arc. Short S-shaped arms are cantilevered from the stiles and rest on C-shaped arm supports attached to the side seat rails. Ridged cabriole legs terminating in pad feet support the front of the seat. The rear legs rake back slightly, and the understructure is braced by block-and-spindle stretchers.

Notes: The corner blocks have been replaced. Because the stiles are made of maple they are of one piece of wood. The modern upholstery illustrated has been replaced with a modern rose-colored moreen (Scalamandré, 1946–4; trim, Brunschwig & Fils, 17/57).

Woods: Front legs, walnut; seat rails, rear legs, stretchers, soft maple.

Dimensions: H. $39\frac{9}{16}$ in. (100.5 cm), SH. $12\frac{11}{16}$ in. (32.2 cm). Seat rails: W. $19\frac{7}{16}$ in. (49.4 cm), MW. $23\frac{1}{8}$ in. (58.7 cm), D. 19 in. (48.3 cm).

Bibliography: *Antiques,* 41 (Feb. 1942), inside front cover.

Provenance: Paul N. and Olive L. Dann, New Haven, Conn.; Bequest of Olive Louise Dann, 1962.31.2.

[1] Downs, *Am. Furn.,* nos. 19 and 20.—[2] *Antiques,* 88 (Dec. 1965), p. 732.

207. Upholstered Armchair

Probably Massachusetts, 1760–1780

When Ezra Stiles (1727–95), the seventh president of Yale College, died in New Haven, his inventory contained "1 worked arm chair" (with "easy chair" crossed off) valued at £6.[1] In all likelihood the reference was to the armchair pictured here, which according to tradition belonged to him. Upholstered chairs were not common in Connecticut households, but Stiles was a prominent person and would probably have owned one. The skilled workmanship and the mahogany primary wood suggest an origin outside of Connecticut, possibly Massachusetts. The use of mahogany and the straight legs braced by rectangular stretchers also account for the fact that this chair is assigned a later date than no. 206. Its square, broad proportions are also in keeping with its mid-eighteenth-century date and can also be observed on another chair illustrated in the literature.[2]

Description: The short, broad back is finished with a serpentine-shaped crest. The square upholstered arms, attached midway to the stiles, rest on C-shaped mahogany arm supports. The square front legs are plain in contrast with the rectangular stretchers, molded on their top outer edges.

Notes: When the chair was stripped of its upholstery the following observations could be made about its structure. The mahogany rear legs are mortised and tenoned to the seat frame. Above the seat frame the mahogany is cut at an angle to provide a strong joint with the frontward sloping maple frame of the back (the two pieces are held with glue and screws). The top and bottom back rails are mortised and tenoned to the maple stiles. The ends of the arms are mortised through the stiles, and the fronts of the arms are screwed to the tops of the arm supports. Thin corner braces are glued to slots in the seat rails. The absence of brass shafts or round impressions on the seat rails indicates that the chair was never trimmed with brass tacks. The chair has recently been upholstered in red moreen (Brunschwig & Fils, 38691.01).

Woods: Mahogany; seat rails, back frame, arms, soft maple.

Dimensions: H. 38⅜ in. (97.5 cm), SH. 14½ in. (36.8 cm). Seat rails: W. 23¼ in. (59.1 cm), MW. 26¾ in. (67.9 cm), D. 23⅛ in. (58.7 cm).

Provenance: According to tradition, owned by Ezra Stiles, New Haven, Conn.; Sterling Memorial Library transfer to the Yale University Art Gallery, 1969.52.1.

[1] Ezra Stiles's probate papers are on file at the Connecticut State Library, Hartford, Docket no. 9904.—[2] Nutting, *Treasury*, no. 2305.

208

207

208. Upholstered Armchair

Massachusetts, 1760–1785

In the mid-1760's John Singleton Copley painted a portrait of Mrs. Isaac Smith sitting in an armchair similar to this example. Her chair was covered with a rich gold damask textile and was trimmed with brass tacks; this chair is presently covered in a glorious eighteenth-century Italian yellow silk damask of similar effect. The molding on the arm supports and legs was a treatment that continued into the Federal period. A related chair has been illustrated by Nutting.[1]

Description: This armchair is similar to no. 207 in its overall form, but not in detail. The back is almost four inches taller; the arm supports are molded, not plain, and join the side seat rails about four inches from the corner. The molding is repeated on the front legs, and the rectangular stretchers have slightly rounded top edges. Brass tacks trim the edges of the chair.

Notes: Cracks in the medial stretcher and right rear leg

have been repaired. The upholstery is an eighteenth-century Italian yellow silk damask (Gift of Lloyd Hyde, 1972.126.9).

Woods: Mahogany; seat rails, soft maple.

Dimensions: H. 42½ in. (107.9 cm), SH. 13⅝ in. (34.6 cm). Seat rails: W. 22⅛ in. (56.2 cm), MW. 26 7/16 in. (67.2 cm), D. 23¼ in. (59.1 cm).

Bibliography: Kirk, *Early Am. Furn.*, fig. 117.

Provenance: Francis P. Garvan, New York, N.Y.; The Mabel Brady Garvan Collection, 1930.2106.

[1] *Treasury*, no. 2304.

209. Lolling Chair

Massachusetts, 1790–1800

The term "Martha Washington," often applied to chairs of this type today, is of recent coinage; in his catalogue of the Federal period furniture at Winterthur, Montgomery established that their contemporary name was "lolling" chair.[1] Evidence of the neoclassical style emerges in this variation of the Massachusetts upholstered armchair whose molded front legs and arm supports taper to give the chair a lighter appearance. Other examples of Massachusetts Federal period lolling chairs have tapered and molded arm supports and front legs like this one, but none of

209

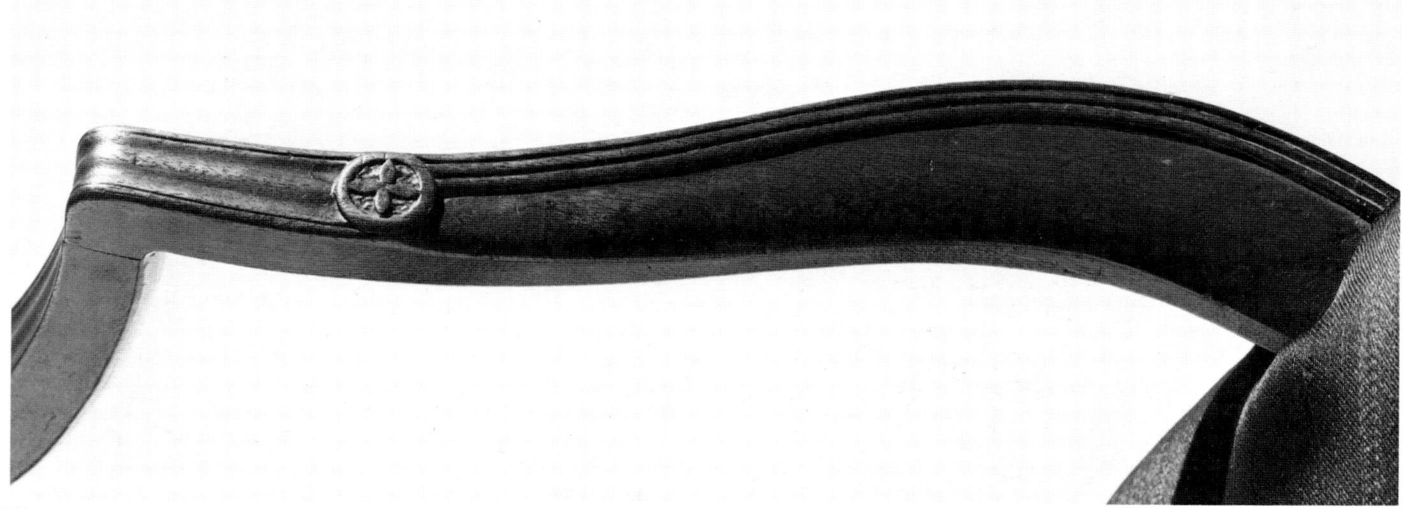

209a

the chairs illustrated in the literature has the extra detail of a rosette and triple bead found on the arm of this example.[2]

Description: Behind the molding, at the very end of the arm, is a small roundel enclosing a rosette. A triple bead emphasizes the sweep of the arm's curved outer edge. The rectangular stretchers are square on the top edge.

Notes: All the legs are rounded at the base and were once fitted with casters. The front corner blocks are new. The seat rails show considerable worm damage. The chair is upholstered with a modern black horsehair.

Woods: Mahogany; seat rails and frame, soft maple.

Dimensions: H. 39¾ in. (101.0 cm), SH. 13½ in. (34.3 cm). Seat rails: W. 19 15/16 in. (50.6 cm), MW. 24 7/16 in. (62.1 cm), D. 21⅜ in. (54.3 cm).

Provenance: Francis P. Garvan, New York, N.Y.; The Mabel Brady Garvan Collection, 1930.2108.

[1] Montgomery, p. 155.—[2] See Montgomery, no. 111; Bishop, *Am. Chairs*, no. 415; Greenlaw, no. 63; Randall, no. 179; *Sack Coll.*, 1957–72, I, no. 131, and II, no. 1257.

210. Lolling Chair

Rhode Island, about 1795

Stop-fluting, which ornaments the arm supports and front legs of this chair, is generally associated with Newport furniture of the 1760's to 1780's, although in the Federal period it was occasionally used in the Boston area. On a lolling chair at Winterthur made by Stephen Badlam of Dorchester, stop-fluting is combined with garlands of floral carving and neatly cuffed feet.[1] These extra features are not found on the Yale chair, and their absence might justify a Rhode Island origin. Various motifs are repeated in the design of the chair: the pronounced curve of the crest rail is caught again in the sweep of the arms, and the stop-fluting on the legs is echoed in the arm supports.

Description: The pronounced serpentine-curve of the crest rail and the perceptible inward taper of the stiles are individual features of this lolling chair. The boldly serpentine-shaped upholstered arms rest on C-shaped arm supports. Stop-fluting is used on the arm supports and tapered front legs. The understructure is braced by four rectangular stretchers with slightly rounded top edges.

Notes: The left arm support has been repaired and the corner blocks are new. The modern floral striped upholstery illustrated has been replaced by a green silk moiré (Brunschwig & Fils, 359044) with gold and green silk fringe (Brunschwig & Fils, 90256–3).

210

Woods: Mahogany; seat rails, soft maple.

Dimensions: H. 42¼ in. (107.3 cm), SH. 13½ in. (34.3 cm). Seat rails: W. 20⅜ in. (51.8 cm), MW. 26⅛ in. (66.4 cm), D. 22 5/16 in. (56.7 cm).

Bibliography: Antiques, 34 (Oct. 1928), illus. inside front cover.

Provenance: Joe Kindig, Jr., York, Pa.; Paul N. and Olive L. Dann, New Haven, Conn.; Bequest of Olive Louise Dann, 1962.31.24.

[1] Montgomery, no. 110.

211

211. Lolling Chair

Boston, about 1805
Probably by Lemuel Churchill (working 1805 to about 1828)

Whereas Chippendale-style precedents provided the form for the preceding chairs, this chair has a significant new overall shape. The outline of the back is flared and the rear legs rake at an angle. The rounded seat and soft contours of the beaded front legs, arm supports, and arms are inviting. Both the form and detail can be linked to a known chairmaker—Lemuel Churchill. The beading on the legs, which forms a small arch at the top of the arm support, is a feature found on a chair[1] labeled by Churchill, who probably made this example.

Description: The straight-topped, hollowed back flares from the seat and is supported by square rear legs set at an angle. The tapered front legs and serpentine arm supports are of one piece. Their beaded edges end in a small arch at the front of the contoured and curving arms.

Notes: The corner blocks are new. The upholstery is a modern striped material in cream, gray, and red.

Woods: Mahogany; seat rails, birch.

Dimensions: H. 42 in. (106.7 cm), SH. 14 in. (35.6 cm). Seat rails: W. 21 in. (53.3 cm), MW. 23⅜ in. (59.4 cm), D. 21⅜ in. (54.3 cm).

Provenance: Paul N. and Olive L. Dann, New Haven, Conn.; Bequest of Olive Louise Dann, 1962.31.33.

---

[1] Montgomery, no. 116.

Easy Chairs

READERS of eighteenth-century inventories have often noted with some surprise that easy chairs are generally found in upstairs bed chambers. That fact, however, is compatible with their original use by aged or sick persons—a practice far removed from our twentieth-century concept of the easy chair as lounge chair. In his brief but informative catalogue on early American easy chairs, Morrison Hecksher states that most easy chairs were originally made with "close stools" or frames to hold chamber pots (see no. 218 in this catalogue).[1] Their upholstered surfaces and high backs and wings also must have provided comfort and protection against cold drafts. One of the few eighteenth-century American portraits to show an easy chair is John Singleton Copley's painting of Mrs. John Powell, in which the widow sits enclosed by the high back and wings of her crimson upholstered easy chair.[2]

Fig. 7—*John Singleton Copley,* Mrs. John Powell. *Oil on canvas, about 1764. Yale University Art Gallery; bequest of Stephen Carlton Clark, B.A. 1903.*

[1] *In Quest of Comfort: The Easy Chair in America* (Metropolitan Museum of Art, n.d.), p. 10.—[2] The Yale University Art Gallery, Bequest of Stephen Carlton Clarke, B.A., 1903 (1961.18.13).

212. Easy Chair

New England, 1740–1790

The classic New England easy chair generally has the features found on this example: wings whose front edges curve downward to vertical cone-shaped arms; a seat frame with rounded front corners and flattened front edge; cabriole front legs terminating in pad feet; and block-and-spindle stretchers. The construction of the seat frame is typical of New England chairs with rounded front corners. The horizontal rails are mortised and tenoned together at the front corners, and the tops of the short cabriole legs are fitted into them with a dovetail tenon.[1] The structure of the back legs is similar to that observed on the upholstered armchair in this collection (no. 206), whose rear stiles are of single pieces of maple.

Description: From the ends of the gently arched crest the serpentine line of the wings flows forward to the arms, which end in vertical scrolled cones. At the rounded front corners are cabriole legs having pointed knee brackets and terminating in pad feet. The rear legs are squared and rake

212

backward. Block-and-spindle stretchers brace the understructure.

Notes: The rear stretcher and the right rear corner block have been replaced. The eighteenth-century blue silk damask illustrated has been replaced by a modern rose-colored moreen (Scalamandré, 1946–4; trim, Brunschwig & Fils, 17/57).

Woods: Front legs, medial and side stretchers, American black walnut; back legs, seat rails, soft maple.

Dimensions: H. 45¼ in. (114.9 cm), SH. 12½ in. (31.7 cm). Seat rails: W. 24⅜ in. (61.9 cm), MW. 29$\frac{5}{16}$ in. (74.5 cm), D. 21¾ in. (55.2 cm).

Bibliography: Charles Nagel, Jr., "Room from the Joel Clark House . . . ," *BAFA* 4 (Oct. 1932) (illus. p. 139).

Provenance: Francis P. Garvan, New York, N.Y.; The Mabel Brady Garvan Collection, 1930.2107.

---

[1] Morrison H. Heckscher, "Form and Frame: New Thoughts on the American Easy Chair," *Antiques,* 100 (Dec. 1971), pp. 890–92.

213. Easy Chair

New England, 1765–1795

Stylistically, this chair with its serpentine-shaped crest rail is later than no. 212. It is difficult to assign a specific place of origin to classic New England easy chairs. In this case, the provenance may be misleading, since it suggests a Connecticut origin, but the particular features found here—the shape of the cabriole legs and block-and-spindle stretchers—are shared by so many counterparts that a general assignment to New England seems better justified than a Connecticut attribution. The structure of the seat frame on this example is like that on no. 212.

Description: This easy chair is quite similar to no. 212, although the crest rail is serpentine and the front feet have very deep pads.

Notes: The rear stretcher and right rear foot have been repaired. The front legs have triangular corner blocks nailed to the seat rails. The side stretchers are pinned to the rear legs with a single wooden peg. The upholstery is a modern brocaded material.

Woods: Front legs and stretchers, American black walnut; back legs, corner blocks, seat rails, soft maple.

Dimensions: H. 46 in. (116.8 cm), SH. 13 in. (33.0 cm). Seat rails: W. 24⅜ in. (61.9 cm), MW. 30⅜ in. (77.2 cm), D. 22¼ in. (56.5 cm).

213

Provenance: Hillhouse family, New Haven, Conn.; descended to James Hillhouse, New Haven, Conn. (B.A. Yale 1875), to his widow Hildegarde Speyers Hillhouse (1938), to his brother Francis Hillhouse, New Haven, Conn. (1942); Paul N. and Olive L. Dann, New Haven, Conn.; Bequest of Olive Louise Dann, 1962.31.6.

214. Easy Chair

Philadelphia, 1755–1775

The hospitable and comfortable appearance of this easy chair is emphasized by the fullness of the rounded front seat rail and the horizontally rolled arms. These arms with their C-scrolled ends usually indicate a Philadelphia origin, especially when they appear in conjunction with well-knuckled claw-and-ball feet, knees with carved cartouches, and stump rear legs. An illustration of a similar easy chair, stripped of its upholstery, reveals the probable struc-

214

ture of this example.[1] Philadelphia chairmakers were able to achieve the sweeping bowed shapes of their seat rails by using wide horizontal boards mortised and tenoned together in the manner of Queen Anne style chairs, with the legs fitted into a dovetail housing at the front.[2]

Description: Curving downward from the gently arched crest of this easy chair are serpentine-shaped wings. The horizontally rolled arms have C-shaped ends fastened to the side seat rails with a short vertical cone. The seat rails, curved on the front and sides, are supported by cabriole front legs with claw-and-ball feet. A bead outlines the upper parts of the legs, which also have a carved cartouche and foliate pendant. The rear legs are oval in cross section.

Notes: The side seat rails and rear brackets are tenoned through the back posts. The front and side seat rails form a deep square, mortised and tenoned together. The tops of the front legs are fitted into the underside of the front seat rail. The right knee brackets on both front legs have been replaced. The eighteenth-century rose silk damask illustrated has been replaced by an eighteenth-century Italian rose silk damask (Gift of Lloyd Hyde, 1972.126.13).

Woods: American black walnut; seat rails, white oak.

Dimensions: H. 44 5/16 in. (112.6 cm), SH. 13 1/4 in. (33.7 cm). Seat rails: W. 24 in. (61.0 cm), MW. 27 3/8 in. (69.5 cm), D. 24 3/8 in. (61.9 cm).

Provenance: Paul N. and Olive L. Dann, New Haven, Conn.; Bequest of Olive Louise Dann, 1962.31.25.

[1] Morrison H. Hecksher, "Form and Frame: New Thoughts on the American Easy Chair," *Antiques,* 100 (Dec. 1971), fig. 4.—[2] *Ibid.,* p. 890.

215. Easy Chair

Probably New England, 1788–1800

George Hepplewhite in his *Cabinet-Maker and Upholsterer's Guide* (1788) illustrated an easy chair with a separate wing attached to an arm that extended all the way back to the stile (see no. 216). Chairs of this type, however, tend to retain the generous proportions and

215

straight molded legs of the Chippendale era. Although a similar example at Winterthur[1] is said to have been made in Philadelphia, others have been assigned a New England or Massachusetts origin.[2] The presence of hard maple and birch as secondary woods supports a New England origin for this chair. The absence of a loose cushion tends to distort the height of the arms and depth of the seat.

Description: This generously proportioned chair has a flamboyant, serpentine-curved crest and wings with a serpentine profile. The arms extend back to the stiles. The front corners of the square seat are supported by square, molded legs. The rear legs rake backward, and the understructure is braced by four rectangular stretchers with slightly rounded top edges.

Notes: The chair has been upholstered without a cushion in a modern damask-weave textile. The corners of the seat frame are strengthened by four open corner braces.

Woods: Mahogany; seat rails, birch; corner braces, hard maple.

Dimensions: H. 48 in. (121.9 cm), SH. 13 7/16 in. (34.1 cm). Seat rails: W. 24 5/16 in. (61.8 cm), MW. 30 9/16 in. (77.6 cm), D. 25 1/8 in. (63.8 cm).

Provenance: R. S. Somerville, New York, N.Y.; Francis P. Garvan, New York, N.Y. (1929); The Mabel Brady Garvan Collection, 1930.2032.

---

[1] Downs, *Am. Furn.*, no. 93.—[2] *Sack Coll.*, 1957–72, I, nos. 138, 455, 557, 665, II, no. 961, and III, p. 749, P3373.

216

216. Easy Chair

Possibly Baltimore, 1790–1805

This easy chair stripped of its upholstery reveals the new arrangement of arm and wing of the Federal period, already seen in no. 215. The materials may indicate a Baltimore origin for this example. Usually seating furniture was made with seat rails of hard wood which gave the extra strength needed for this critical structural part, but here the seat rails are of *taeda* pine, also used on the seat rails of an easy chair at Winterthur which is thought to have been made in Baltimore.[1] The Yale chair additionally shares with that example tapered legs braced by rectangular stretchers and a sloping arm (although here the pitch is not so steep). Since this latter feature seems to be peculiar to easy chairs made in that city, it is further evidence that the Yale chair may be of Baltimore origin.

Description: The arms are constructed as in no. 215. The sloping surface on the front face of the arm continues to the tops of the tapered front legs. Rectangular stretchers brace the understructure.

Notes: The medial stretcher was replaced in 1965.

Woods: Legs and stretchers, mahogany; seat rails, frame of back, ends of arms, pine of the *taeda* group; arms, tulip; arm braces, white pine.

Dimensions: H. 44 1/4 in. (112.4 cm), SH. 14 11/16 in. (37.3 cm). Seat rails: W. 21 1/4 in. (54.0 cm), MW. 28 11/16 in. (72.9 cm), D. 25 in. (63.5 cm).

Provenance: Irving W. Lyon, Hartford, Conn.; Francis P. Garvan, New York, N.Y.; The Mabel Brady Garvan Collection, 1930.2689.

---

[1] Montgomery, no. 127.

217

217. Easy Chair

Possibly Baltimore, 1790–1805

Like no. 216, the seat rails of this easy chair are of a soft wood—tulip. Baltimore is again suggested as the possible place of origin. The arms are slightly sloped like those on no. 216, but more importantly the peculiar rounded and upward thrusting corners of the wings are also found on two chairs said to be from Baltimore.[1]

Description: The front legs of this easy chair taper and there are no stretchers.

Notes: The chair has been upholstered without a cushion in a modern blue rep.

Woods: Mahogany; seat rails, tulip.

Dimensions: H. 45¼ in. (114.9 cm), SH. 13⅝ in. (34.6 cm). Seat rails: W. 24$^{3}/_{16}$ in. (61.4 cm), MW. 27½ in. (69.8 cm), D. 25¼ in. (64.1 cm).

Provenance: Irving W. Lyon, Hartford, Conn.; Mrs. John P. Penney (Mamie P. Lyon), Pittsburgh, Pa.; Francis P. Garvan, New York, N.Y.; The Mabel Brady Garvan Collection, 1930.2031.

[1] Montgomery, no. 127; *Baltimore Furniture,* no. 66.

218. Easy Chair

Possibly Annapolis, Maryland, 1810–1820

This easy chair is said to have come from Annapolis. The form remains much the same as it appeared on earlier examples (nos. 216 and 217), but the heavy turnings of the legs account for the late date assigned. Perhaps the chair's most interesting feature is its support for a chamber pot, an accessory that many easy

218

219

220

chairs probably had originally. English and American price books of the period list as an option "a close stool . . . slider clamp'd."[1]

Description: The legs are turned rather than tapered. The top of the leg is composed of three rings below which is a cone form above a deep reel turning. The bottoms of the legs are fitted with brass casters.

Notes: The underside of this chair is fitted with a board to accommodate a chamber pot.

Woods: Mahogany; seat rails, tulip; platform, white pine; tracks for the board to support the chamber pot, white oak.

Dimensions: H. 47¼ in. (120.0 cm), SH. 15 in. (38.1 cm). Seat rails: W. 23 in. (58.4 cm), MW. 27 in. (68.6 cm), D. 23 in. (58.4 cm).

Provenance: R. T. Haines Halsey, New York, N.Y.; Francis P. Garvan, New York, N.Y.; The Mabel Brady Garvan Collection, 1930.2529.

[1] Montgomery, p. 168.

219. Easy Chair, Bergère Type

American, about 1820–1840

Chairs described as the "bergère" type are usually smaller than full-sized easy chairs and have hollowed backs with rounded top rails, as opposed to wings. On this example the crest is outlined in wood which continues down the edges of the arms to form scrolled handholds. The shape of the turnings on the front legs is somewhat similar to those on no. 218, but here the forms have become fuller. This chair appears to have been made *en suite* with no. 220, which has a higher back.

Description: The barrel-shaped back is outlined with a band of mahogany extended at the front to form scrolled handholds, resting above arm supports with serpentine front faces. A quarter-round molding along the front edge of the seat rests on the front seat rail, veneered with mahogany. A mahogany band extends around the side and rear seat rails of the chair. The back legs swing out in a modified serpentine shape and end in brass casters. The heavy turned front legs have a flattened ball flanked by rings at the top, and a ring turning above the caster at the base.

Notes: The right rear leg is repaired with a metal brace. Both ends of the crest rail have been cracked and repaired. Minor repairs have been made to the veneer.

Woods: Mahogany; seat rails, cherry.

Dimensions: H. 32¾ in. (83.2 cm), SH. 13¼ in. (33.6 cm). Seat rails: W. 22 in. (55.8 cm), D. 21 in. (53.3 cm).

Provenance: This chair is now in the second-floor reception area of Woodbridge Hall, Yale University (donor unknown).

220. Easy Chair, Bergère Type

American, about 1820–1840

See comments, no. 219.

Description: This example is very similar to no. 219, except that the back is taller and a small variation occurs in the turning of the front leg, where an extra ogee form is added below the top reel.

Notes: The tops of both stiles have been broken and repaired. Minor repairs have been made to the veneer.

Woods: Mahogany; seat rails, cherry.

Dimensions: H. 40 in. (101.6 cm), SH. 13⅜ in. (34.0 cm). Seat rails: W. 22⅝ in. (57.4 cm), D. 22¼ in. (56.5 cm).

Provenance: This chair is used in the second-floor reception area of Woodbridge Hall, Yale University (donor unknown).

Couches and Daybeds

THE WORD COUCH is derived from the French verb *coucher,* "to lie down," and the furniture forms bearing this name were intended for repose. In their attempt to define the form, the authors of the *Dictionary of English Furniture* state that distinctions between couch, daybed, and sofa are difficult to draw.[1] The terms may have been used interchangeably with no strict distinction made between pieces for lying down and those for sitting. In America the word "couch" is found sometimes in inventories; the term may have referred to the form now generally called a daybed. Singleton quotes the 1653 inventory of Captain William Tinge, which mentioned "one green couch laid with a case, £2-10-0."[2] Hornor states that in Philadelphia "throughout the initial century and a half daybeds were called couches."[3]

The height of popularity for couches probably occurred in the era of caned chairs—in the late seventeenth and early eighteenth centuries. Samuel Sewall's daughter Judith ordered a couch and walnut chairs from England in 1720.[4] The earliest example in this collection (no. 221) is American made and probably dates a few years later. The custom of owning a couch never entirely died out in the eighteenth century, and examples with later eighteenth-century stylistic features are known.

By the early years of the nineteenth century the stylistic model for the couch form was that of antiquity. Sheraton refers to a piece similar to nos. 222 and 223 as a "Grecian Couch,"[5] inspired by the manner of "lying at meat amongst the Romans and Greeks."[6]

[1] Macquoid and Edwards, II, p. 157.—[2] Singleton, I, pt. 3, p. 189.—[3] Hornor, p. 57.—[4] Thomas M. Halsey, ed., *Diary of Samuel Sewall 1674–1729* (New York, 1973), II, p. 954.—[5] Thomas Sheraton, *The Cabinet Dictionary* (1803; reprinted New York: Praeger Publishers, 1970, 2 vols.), II, pl. 49.—[6] *Ibid.;* see the entry "Grecian," pp. 245–48.

221. Daybed or Couch

Massachusetts, 1720–1735

American-made daybeds from the first years of the eighteenth century have survived in fewer numbers than caned examples imported from England. Although this daybed or couch—whose details relate to those of "Boston" chairs (no. 40)—has few counterparts, similar daybeds are owned by Winterthur and the Metropolitan Museum of Art,[1] and two others have been illustrated.[2]

Description: On this brown painted daybed the stationary backrest is supported by raked back stiles, capped by urn-and-ball finials. The arched top of the upholstered backrest and the stiles are beaded in the manner of "Boston" chairs. The frame for the cushion rests on three pairs of ogee-turned legs braced by six double-ball-and-ring-turned side stretchers and four double-ball-(without ring) turned medial stretchers.

Notes: The brown paint appears to be old. The front stretcher has been damaged. New corner braces have been added to reinforce the junction of the stiles and side seat rails. The rear stretcher is badly worn. The brown cotton upholstery illustrated has been replaced by blue green wool velvet (Brunschwig & Fils, 3648.00/7) and silk fringe (Scalamandré, FL 531–13).

Wood: Soft maple.

Dimensions: H. 35 in. (88.9 cm), BPH. 36½ in. (92.7 cm), SH. 15 in. (38.1 cm). Seat rails: W. 21 11/16 in. (55.1 cm), D. 61 7/16 in. (156.1 cm).

Provenance: Charles W. Lyon, New York, N.Y.; Francis P. Garvan, New York, N.Y.; The Mabel Brady Garvan Collection, 1930.2572.

[1] Nutting, *Treasury,* no. 1591.—[2] See Herbert Cescinsky and George Leland Hunter, *English and American Furniture* (Garden City, New York, 1929), p. 74 (top), and *Antiques,* 55 (April 1949), p. 262 (lower right).

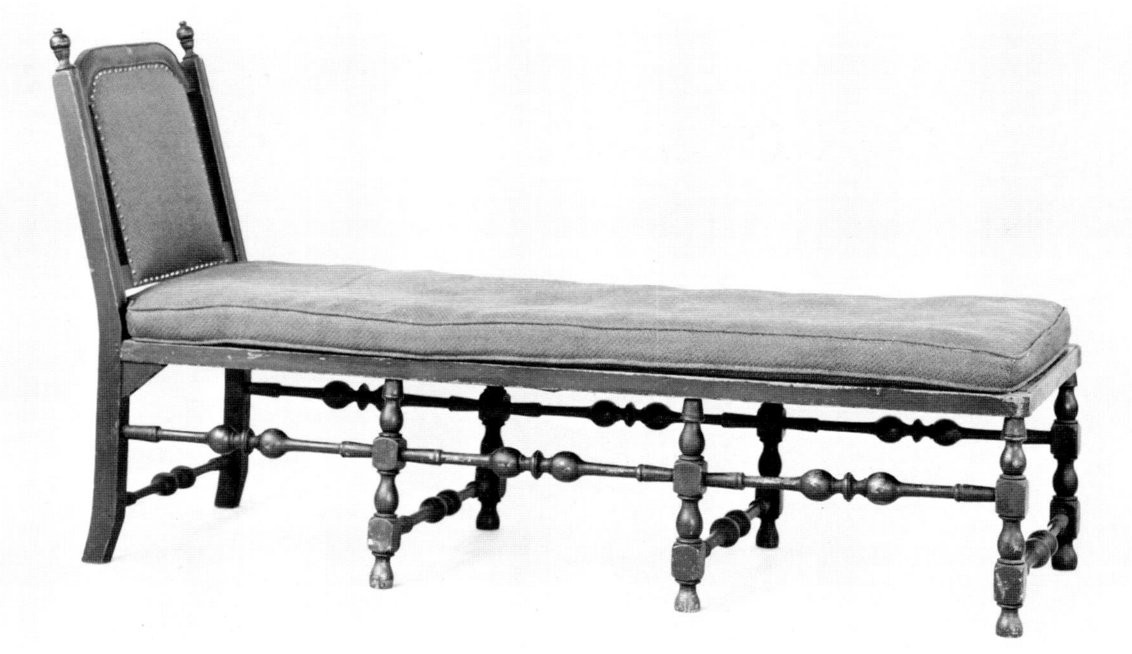

221

222

222. Couch

Baltimore, 1810–1820

The higher left end of this example indicates that it was designed for reclining rather than for sitting; the word "couch" is therefore applied to distinguish it from a sofa. A design for a "Grecian couch" is illustrated in Plate 6 of Thomas Sheraton's *Cabinet-Maker, Upholsterer, and General Artists' Encyclopedia* (1804–1808).[1] The fine, sinuous lines and delicate carving and reeding of this example probably warrant dating it in the second decade of the nineteenth century. Baltimore is the probable place of origin. A couch with virtually identical details, except for reeded rather than acanthus-carved legs, was made in that city for the Biddle family.[2]

Description: The left end is higher than the right; to the higher end a back is attached which extends two-thirds of the length of the couch. A thin border of mahogany outlines the back, and the end of the top edge is a scroll with carved rosette. The scrolled ends of the couch are faced with reeded mahogany terminating in carved rosettes. The cornucopia-shaped feet are decorated with flat leaf carving and end in elaborate brass casters.

Notes: Minor repairs have been made to the front feet. The upholstery is a modern yellow silk damask.

Woods: Mahogany; side rails and medial brace, tulip.

Dimensions: H. 31 13/16 in. (80.8 cm), SH. 11 1/8 in. (28.3 cm). Seat rails: W. 26 in. (66.0 cm), D. 61 1/4 in. (155.6 cm).

Provenance: Bequest of Charles Stetson, Boston, Mass., 1954.37.25.

[1] Harris, fig. 44.—[2] *New York Times,* Nov. 10, 1969, p. 52.

223. Couch

New York, 1820–1830

In comparison with the restrained design of no. 222, this "Grecian couch"—replete with flamboyant gilt decoration and muscular carving—epitomizes the exuberance of high-style furniture in the Empire taste. Little work has yet been done to distinguish the regional origins of furniture of that period, but the presence of tulip and cherry, the very fine stenciling, and overall excellence of the workmanship prompt an attribution to New York, a major furniture producing center.

Description: The upholstered back is outlined with a thin black painted border stenciled with anthemions. The top edge curls into a scroll just past the middle of the back and then sweeps down to an elongated serpentine curve to meet the scrolled lower end of the couch. The higher end repeats the form of the cornucopia stenciled on its front face. Above the paw feet with their scrolled and leaf-carved brackets are tablets with carved rosettes. The carved tablets support the stenciled tablets at the ends of the convex front seat rail. The feet, tablets, and seat rail are all decorated with gold stenciling.

Notes: The paint and stenciling are original. The bottom of the sofa is a large board. The feet are ash, with a facing of fine-grained wood applied to the front for the carving. The yellow silk upholstery with a Greek-key trim illustrated has been replaced by yellow wool (Brunschwig & Fils, 38693) and red and gold braid (Conso, 77187–13).

Woods: Backboard, white pine; front and rear seat rails and paw feet, ash; medial braces, tulip; front of left arm, cherry.

Dimensions: H. 29 15/16 in. (76.0 cm), MH. 33 1/8 in. (84.1 cm), SH. (taken at long side) 12 5/8 in. (32.1 cm). Seat rails: W. 20 3/4 in. (52.7 cm), D. 60 in. (152.4 cm).

Exhibitions: Furn. by N.Y. Cabinetmakers, p. 79, no. 130; *Classical America,* p. 60, no. 52.

Bibliography: Aronson, 3rd ed., p. 402, fig. 1139; Robert C. Smith, "Late Classical Furniture in the United States, 1820–1850," *Antiques,* 74 (Dec. 1958), p. 520 (illus.); Harris, no. 192; Comstock, no. 538; Bishop, p. 286.

Provenance: Francis P. Garvan, New York, N.Y.; The Mabel Brady Garvan Collection, 1930.2622.

223

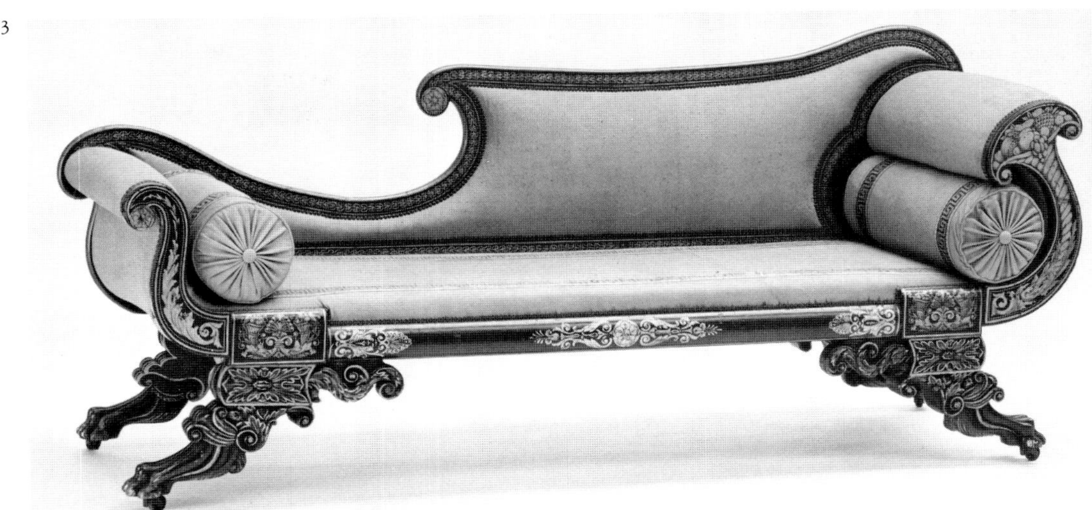

224

225

Sofas

SOFAS are seating forms designed for sitting rather than lying down, but in introducing designs for sofas (Plates XXIX and XXX) in the *Director,* Thomas Chippendale noted that "when made large, they have a Bolster and Pillow at each End, and Cushions at the Back, which may be laid down occasionally, and form a Mattrass."[1]

In household inventories the distinction between couches, sofas, and settees may not have been strictly drawn. Without doubt they were luxury objects in the eighteenth and early nineteenth centuries, although by 1830 when "Grecian sofas" came into vogue, many more homes appear to have been furnished with these large upholstered pieces (see no. 234).

[1] Thomas Chippendale, *The Gentleman & Cabinet-Maker's Director* (1762; rpt., New York: Dover, 1966), p. 4.

224. Sofa

Probably Philadelphia, 1785–1795

With its bold serpentine-curved crest rail and steeply pitched rolled arms, this sofa typifies the best examples of the Chippendale style, but the tapered front legs and spade feet suggest a date at the beginning of the neoclassical period. A similar sofa in the Henry Ford Museum[1] has been assigned a New York origin. However, Joe Kindig, Jr., who sold this sofa in 1934, thought it had originated in Philadelphia, and a related example with reeded legs at Winterhur also has been assigned tentatively to Philadelphia.[2] The character of the spade feet on that sofa has been compared to the work of Daniel Trotter, Adam Haines, Jonathan Gostelowe, and other Philadelphia cabinetmakers. Philadelphia furniture often has tulip and oak as secondary woods.

Description: Scrolled arms slope forward from the ends of the serpentine-shaped crest rail. The C-shaped front faces of the arms curve to meet the tops of the square front legs. The front seat rail is serpentine shaped. The rear legs rake backward and the tapered front legs end in spade feet. Thin rectangular stretchers brace the understructure.

Notes: The silk damask upholstery illustrated has been replaced by a reproduction yellow wool damask (F. Schumacher, Peyton Randolph damask).

Woods: Mahogany; side rails, red oak; front and rear rails, tulip.

Dimensions: H. 40 11/16 in. (103.3 cm), SH. 14 15/16 in. (37.9 cm). Seat rails: W. 70 13/16 in. (179.9 cm), MW. 76 1/8 in. (193.4 cm), D. 28 1/8 in. (71.4 cm).

Bibliography: Antiques, 25 (March 1934), p. 81 (illus.).

Provenance: Joe Kindig, Jr., York, Pa.; Paul N. and Olive L. Dann, New Haven, Conn.; Bequest of Olive Louise Dann, 1962.31.13.

[1] Comstock, no. 349.—[2] Montgomery, no. 261.

225. Sofa

Massachusetts or New Hampshire, 1790–1800

Framed by fine reeding which sweeps around at the ends of the arms to join the tops of the arm supports with carved floral rosettes, this New England square-back sofa is exceptionally delicate. The inlaid tablet of light wood and narrow reeding of the crest rail and arms relate it directly to a number of chairs made in Boston during the late eighteenth and early nineteenth century.[1] In all likelihood this sofa was made either in Boston, in one of the north shore towns, or possibly even in Portsmouth, New Hampshire, where a chair with similar latticed inlay was found.[2]

Description: A border of fine reeding outlines the square

back and sloped upper surfaces of the arms. At the center of the crest is a tablet veneered with light wood crisscrossed with black inlaid lines. The arm supports, molded on the front surfaces, have serpentine-shaped inner edges and join the ends of the arms with small rosettes. The outer front legs are tapered and inlaid with a lozenge, bellflower, and drop. The two inner legs have only a bellflower and drop. The front legs terminate in tapered brass cups and casters. The square rear legs have casters without cups.

Notes: The large triangular-shaped corner blocks are replacements. Smaller triangular-shaped blocks have been used to reinforce the joints of the center front and rear legs with the curved medial braces. The upholstery is a modern floral striped silk.

Woods: Mahogany; seat rails and cross-braces, ash; light and dark wood inlays.

Dimensions: H. 38 in. (96.5 cm), SH. 14 7/16 in. (36.7 cm). Seat rails: W. 74 3/16 in. (188.4 cm), MW. 74 1/8 in. (188.3 cm), D. 25 in. (63.5 cm).

Bibliography: Burroughs, p. 163 (illus. p. 179, bottom of pl. XV).

Provenance: Bequest of Charles Stetson, Boston, Mass., 1954.37.29.

[1] Randall, nos. 171, 172, 174, 184.—[2] Richard Randall, Jr., *The Decorative Arts of New Hampshire 1725–1825* (Manchester, New Hampshire, Currier Gallery of Art, 1964), no. 69 (illus.).

226. Sofa

Salem, 1800–1810

The design for a "square sofa," whose arm supports are a continuation of the front legs, was introduced in Sheraton's *Drawing-Book* in 1793, while the exact outline came from a 1791 plate.[1] With its basket of fruits and flowers, star-punched background, and borders of rosettes and fluting, this square-back sofa is recognizable as a finely carved example of the Salem school. Many examples of Salem furniture are attributed to Samuel McIntire, whose only documented furniture work, carving on the double chest made by William Lemon for Madame Elizabeth Derby West, reveals that he was a carver of superb skill.[2] A comparison of the carving on the Lemon chest and on this sofa shows that the detail here is not as delicate, making an attribution to McIntire's hand unlikely. This Salem sofa in the Yale Collection is nonetheless an exceptional example of the form, having few peers with swags and fruit flanking a carved basket, and reeded legs.

Description: The tablet at the center of the crest rail on

226

this square-back sofa is a carved basket of fruit and flowers flanked by drapery festoons bearing bunches of fruits and flowers. The brackets flanking the tablet have similar swags, and the background of all this carving is punched with a star motif. The tablet and brackets rest on a frieze of alternating flutes and rosettes. Larger rosettes within squares are at the ends of the crest. The tops of the sloped arms and handholds have water leaf carving. Volutes enclosing a rosette and a pair of leaves with buds are carved on the sides of the handholds, which rest on urn-and-vase-turned arm supports. The urn and top of the support have carved pointed leaves. The seat rail is veneered on the front, outlined by beading, and supported on four tapered and reeded legs. The rear legs are square and rake back slightly.

Notes: A crack in the right handhold has been repaired. The original canvas and rope supports for the cushion are still in place. The threadbare pink moiré material illustrated has been replaced by a modern red, green and cream striped silk (Scalamandré, 1235–8).

226a

226b

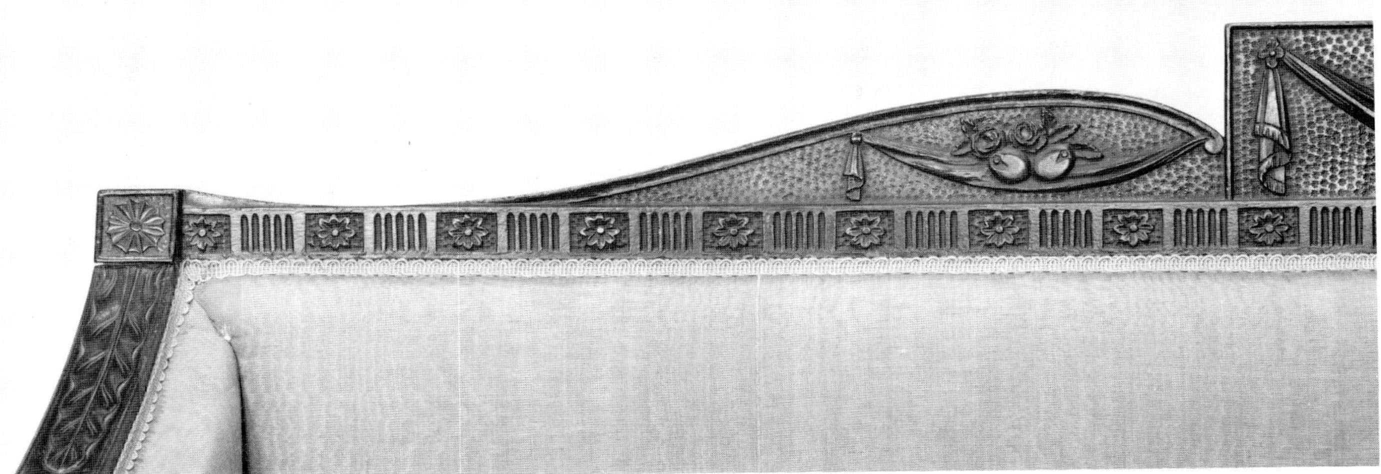

226c

Woods: Mahogany; rails and medial braces, birch; corner blocks, white pine.

Dimensions: H. 38 9/16 in. (97.9 cm), SH. 14 1/16 in. (35.7 cm). Seat rails: W. 79 1/4 in. (201.3 cm), MW. 81 7/8 in. (208.0 cm), D. 25 1/4 in. (64.1 cm).

Bibliography: Bigelow Coll., p. 84, no. 135; Nutting, *Treasury,* no. 1706; Joseph Downs, "Some English and American Furniture in the Inaugural Exhibition," *The Pennsylvania Museum Bulletin,* 23 (May 1928), p. 110, fig. J.; Fiske Kimball, "Furniture Carvings by Samuel McIntire," *Antiques,* 18 (Dec. 1930), p. 498, figs. 1, 1a; Kirk, *Early Am. Furn.,* fig. 40.

Provenance: This sofa was owned by the White family of Salem, Massachusetts, and was bought at the sale of the effects of Captain Joseph White; Francis Hill Bigelow, Cambridge, Mass.; Francis P. Garvan, New York, N.Y. (1924); The Mabel Brady Garvan Collection, 1930.2509.

---

[1] Montgomery, no. 269.—[2] Hipkiss, no. 41.

227. Sofa

Salem, 1800–1810

This sofa is very similar to no. 226, but the lower angle from which the plaited basket is viewed and the small leaves and berries streaming from it give the carving on the tablet a lighter appearance. Salem sofas

227

227a

227b

with similar carving are at Winterthur,[1] in the Karolik Collection,[2] and in the Bayou Bend Collection.[3]

Description: Though close to no. 226, many details of this sofa are executed differently. The basket is viewed from a lower angle so that its contents are less visible, and a vine rather than swags flank it. The front rail is upholstered and the front legs are not reeded.

Notes: The medial braces have been replaced. The upholstery is a modern floral stripe material.

Woods: Mahogany; rails, hard maple.

Dimensions: H. 37 7/16 in. (95.1 cm), SH. 12 15/16 in. (32.9 cm). Seat rails: W. 72 3/8 in. (183.8 cm), MW. 76 in. (193.0 cm), D. 25 9/16 in. (64.9 cm).

Exhibitions: Girl Scouts Exhibition, no. 727.

Bibliography: "Long Text and Brief Sermon," *Antiques,* 16 (Nov. 1929), p. 369 [illus.]; Fiske Kimball, "Furniture Carvings by Samuel McIntire," *Antiques,* 18 (Dec. 1930),

227c

p. 499, fig. 2; *Garvan Coll.*, p. 262, no. 386; Miller, I, p. 315 [illus. p. 317, no. 564]; Nagel, pl. 27b; Meyric R. Rogers, "Garvan Furniture at Yale," *The Connoisseur Year Book* 1960, p. 63, no. 19; Kirk, *Early Am. Furn.*, fig. 39.

Provenance: Clifford Crowninshield, Salem, Mass.; his sister, Mrs. James Devereux, Salem, Mass.; her great-granddaughter, Mary Devereux Waters, Salem, Mass.; Brooks Reed, Boston, Mass.; Francis P. Garvan, New York, N.Y.; The Mabel Brady Garvan Collection, 1931.310.

[1] Montgomery, no. 269.—[2] Hipkiss, no. 121.—[3] Bishop, no. 369.

228. Sofa

New York, 1805–1815
Possibly by Duncan Phyfe (1768–1854)

Sofas of this type—decorated with carved swags, bowknots, reeds, or ears of wheat, and having serpentine-shaped ends and reeded seat rails and legs—are generally highly prized and are often attributed to the workshop of Duncan Phyfe. The tentative attribution of this example is based upon five sofas closely linked to Phyfe's shop.[1] Furniture documented as having been made by Phyfe is decorated with this carving, and to date no other New York cabinetmakers can be shown to have used this vocabulary of ornament. Of the sofas illustrated in the literature, the examples once owned by Mrs. Giles Whiting[2] and Edward Delafield[3] are similar to this one in having ears of wheat tied with a bowknot in the central panel of the back rail flanked by swags and bowknots on either side. Of the two, the Delafield sofa is most comparable to the Yale example, since the tops of the arm supports are reeded rather than vase shaped. The stiff ears of wheat in the central panel of the Yale example are indicative of the quality of its carving, which is somewhat less graceful than most other examples.

Description: The crest rail scrolls backward and is divided into three sections. Ears of wheat tied with a bowknot are carved in the middle section, and there are festoons of drapery with swags and tassels on either side. The ends of the sofa are serpentine shaped and the reeding on the upper edges continues into the scrolled handholds. The latter rest on arm supports of an urn with carved, pointed leaves and a reeded cone-shaped section. The lower edges of the side and front seat rails are reeded. Following the shape of the serpentine ends, the side seat rails curve into rounded front corners. Four tapered and reeded legs support the front of the sofa. The rear legs are square and rake back slightly.

Notes: The three medial braces are missing. The corner blocks have been replaced. The right front center leg has been reattached. The front center legs are reeded only on the outside faces.

Woods: Mahogany; rails, soft maple; medial braces, cherry.

Dimensions: H. 37⅝ in. (95.6 cm), SH. 13¾ in. (34.9 cm). Seat rails: W. 74¼ in. (188.6 cm), MW. 78⅞ in. (200.3 cm), D. 26 in. (66.0 cm).

Provenance: R. T. Haines Halsey, New York, N.Y.; Francis P. Garvan, New York, N.Y.; The Mabel Brady Garvan Collection, 1930.2027.

[1] McClelland, pls. 236, 237, 257, 264, 281.—[2] *Ibid.*, pl. 144.—[3] *Ibid.*, pl. 257.

229. Sofa

New York, 1805–1815
Possibly by Duncan Phyfe (1768–1854)

Caned sofas of this type may possibly also have been made in the shop of Duncan Phyfe. The slim drapery festoons and the lively, fluttering ribbons on the bowknots are more ably carved on this caned sofa than the similar motifs found on the preceding upholstered example. Although this example lacks the "sweeping elbows," as the added refinement of the serpentine-shaped arms was called,[1] the caned sofa form is rare and can be compared with examples at Winterthur[2] and in the Karolik Collection.[3] A smaller scale example was illustrated by McClelland[4] and one with the same pattern of carving as the Yale example has been illustrated.[5] A loose cushion may originally have been used on the seat.

Description: The ends, seat, and three back panels of this sofa are caned. The crest rail scrolls backward and is divided into three sections. Reeds, tied with a bowknot, are found in the center section, and festoons with bowknots and tassels on either side. The reeded upper parts of the stiles divide the sections of the back. The lower back rail is also reeded. From the ends of the crest rail the arms, reeded on their upper edges, slope forward to scrolled

228

229

handholds. The tapered and reeded arm supports are ornamented at the bottom with a flared, carved collar above ring turnings. The outer edges of the side and front seat rails are reeded. The front edge of the front seat rail curves forward. Four slightly tapered, reeded legs with bulb-shaped feet support the front of the sofa.

Notes: The four original medial braces are missing and have been replaced with two new iron medial braces. The front legs are reeded only on the outside faces.

Wood: Mahogany.

Dimensions: H. 36¾ in. (93.3 cm), SH. 15^15^⁄16 in. (38.9 cm). Seat rails: W. 71^11^⁄16 in. (182.1 cm), MW. 72⅛ in. (183.2 cm), D. 22^5^⁄16 in. (56.7 cm).

Exhibition: Philadelphia, Pa., Pennsylvania Museum of Art, Jan. 8–Feb. 26, 1931.

Bibliography: "Exhibition of Georgian Art," *The Pennsylvania Museum Bulletin* (Jan. 1931) (illus. p. 14); Miller, I, p. 287 (illus. p. 289, no. 513).

Provenance: R. T. Haines Halsey, New York, N.Y.; Francis P. Garvan, New York, N.Y.; The Mabel Brady Garvan Collection, 1930.2006.

[1] Montgomery, no. 277.—[2] *Ibid.,* no. 278.—[3] Hipkiss, no. 123.—[4] Pl. 146.—[5] *Antiques,* 91 (March 1967), p. 264.

230. Sofa

New York, 1810–1815
Possibly by Duncan Phyfe (1768–1854)

Of the three Duncan Phyfe–type sofas in this collection which share the same vocabulary of carved ornament, this small example supported on "Grecian cross" legs is the most unusual. Although a few sofas with pairs of crossed legs have been illustrated in the literature,[1] to date this is the only known version supported by a single pair of legs. The design for the legs was derived from the Roman curule chair and probably began to be made in New York shops following the publication of "Chairs with Grecian Cross Fronts" in the 1808 *Supplement to the London Chair-Makers' and Carvers' Book of Prices.*[2] The beautifully carved drapery festoons and bowknots, and the tapering of the reeding to emphasize the flow and sweep of the lines place this sofa among the finest.

Description: The pair of "Grecian cross" legs terminate in carved paw feet. Reeding, becoming narrower as it reaches the small turned bosses on the ends of the arms, emphasizes the flow and sweep of the crossed leg design. The back, seat, and ends of the sofa are caned. The crest rail scrolls backward and is divided into three sections. Festoons, bowknots, and tassels are carved in the middle section, and reeds tied with a bowknot appear on both sides. The latter motif was also used on the tablets at the tops of the arms.

Notes: The right rear seat rail and the junction of the right arm and back have been repaired. The upholstery is a modern burgundy-colored satin.

Wood: Mahogany.

Dimensions: H. 34^11^⁄16 in. (88.1 cm), SH. 15⅜ in. (39.1 cm). Seat rails: W. 46⅞ in. (119.1 cm), MW. 46¾ in. (118.7 cm), D. 21¼ in. (54.0 cm).

Bibliography: Lockwood, II, p. 162, fig. 665; McClelland, p. 166, pl. 147; Meyric R. Rogers, "The Mabel Brady Garvan Collection of Furniture," *Yale Alumni Magazine,* 25 (Jan. 1962), p. 14 (illus.).

Provenance: Mrs. Frank M. Bosworth, New York, N.Y.; Francis P. Garvan, New York, N.Y.; The Mabel Brady Garvan Collection, 1930.2633.

[1] See Hipkiss, no. 124; McClelland, pls. 169, 280.—[2] Montgomery, no. 72.

231. Sofa

Northeastern Massachusetts or Portsmouth, New Hampshire, 1800–1810

Sofas with bulbous, reeded front legs continuing into arm supports of similar shape and joined to a downward curving "crane-neck" handle are generally thought to come from the area of Boston or the north shore of Massachusetts. The echoing of the shape of the reeded legs in the arm supports and the tapering of the reeds under the reel turnings here are refinements of the sort found on the better examples. The horizontally scrolled handholds are a most unusual feature. Highly figured veneer sometimes outlines the gently sweeping backs of these sofas, but on this example the crest rail is simply upholstered.

Description: The crest rail of this sofa is gently arched and the top edges of the arms slope downward in a modified serpentine curve. Cantilevered from the ends of the upholstery are short arms that curve in toward the center of the sofa. The arms rest on reeded, vase-shaped arm supports. The vase is repeated on the four front legs, although it is somewhat more truncated.

230

230a

231

Notes: The right rear leg has been repaired. The feet have been cut, possibly ½ or ¾ inch. Minor damage occurs on the surface of the legs. The upholstery is a modern brocaded material.

Woods: Mahogany; maple.

Dimensions: H. 34¼ in. (87.0 cm), SH. 13½ in. (34.3 cm). Seat rails: W. 71½ in. (181.6 cm), D. 25 in. (63.5 cm).

Provenance: E. F. Sanderson, Moor's End, Nantucket, Mass. (sale New York, B. Altman and Co., Oct. 1928); Francis P. Garvan, New York, N.Y.; The Mabel Brady Garvan Collection, 1930.2092.

232. Sofa

Possibly Salem, 1800–1810

This diminutive sofa shows features frequently found on examples made in Salem—the use of the central tablet on the crest rail, flanked by veneered brackets with serpentine upper edges; the reeded, bulbous arm supports; and the tapered legs. A similar sofa with a satinwood tablet has also been assigned to Salem.[1] The tight, highly stylized carving on the crest rail of this example, no. 232, is comparatively rare, and it is unlike the delicate, free-flowing motifs of well-known Salem work—with one exception: the border of a Salem oval-back chair owned by the Derby family is carved with similar three-pronged leaves.[2] This relationship also supports the possibility of a Salem origin.

Description: The tablet at the center of the crest rail on this "square sofa" has four carved leaves arranged in a cross pattern with paterae in the corners. Flanking the tablet, the crest rail is veneered and has serpentine-shaped upper edges. From the ends of the crest rail the molded arms slope forward, their scrolled handholds resting on reeded, vase-shaped arm supports. The three front legs are tapered and reeded.

Notes: Tack holes appear on the rear legs below the

232

232a

present upholstery. The corner blocks have been replaced. The seat rails are strengthened by one medial brace.

Woods: Mahogany; seat rails, cherry.

Dimensions: H. 36¾ in. (93.4 cm), SH. 13¾ in. (35.0 cm). Seat rails: W. 47¾ in. (121.4 cm), D. 25 in. (63.5 cm).

Provenance: Charles W. Lyon, New York, N.Y.; Francis P. Garvan, New York, N.Y.; The Mabel Brady Garvan Collection, 1930.2094a.

[1] *Sack Coll.*, 1957–72, I, no. 469.—[2] Montgomery, no. 16.

233. Sofa

Massachusetts, about 1820

The pattern of the legs on this sofa, a series of rings with an ogee and vase form above a ring-and-ball foot, is similar to the legs on two chamber tables made by William Hook of Salem,[1] and to the legs on a desk and sofa thought to have been made in Boston about 1820.[2] Also indicative of a Massachusetts origin is the reeded front seat rail, which appears on a couch labeled by the Salem cabinetmaker Thomas Needham.[3] Hints of Empire taste can be observed in the wide band of dark veneer on the crest rail, and in the scrolled handholds. Another example with a similar outline and arm supports stood for many years in the Old Manse at Concord, Massachusetts.[4]

Description: The deep crest rail is veneered. The beaded tops of the arms begin at its lower edge. The line of the arm is stepped and then curves into a scrolled handhold supported by a carved pineapple arm support. The front edge of the seat rail is decorated with coarse reeding. The leg is composed of a series of ring turnings, an ogee turning, and a vase form above a ring-and-ball foot.

Notes: The left scrolled handhold has been repaired. The right rear corner block has been replaced. The upholstery is a reproduction beige silk damask in a nineteenth-century pattern.

Woods: Mahogany; seat rails and medial braces, birch.

Dimensions: H. 37 7/16 in. (95.1 cm), SH. 14 3/16 in. (36.0 cm). Seat rails: W. 72⅛ in. (183.2 cm), MW. 76 in. (193.0 cm), D. 23¾ in. (60.3 cm).

Provenance: Irving W. Lyon, Hartford, Conn.; Mrs. John P. Penney (Mamie P. Lyon), Pittsburgh, Pa.; Francis P. Garvan, New York, N.Y.; The Mabel Brady Garvan Collection, 1931.1229.

[1] *Essex County Furn.*, figs. 17 and 19.—[2] Montgomery, nos. 201 and 273.—[3] *Ibid.*, no. 282.—[4] Moore, p. 88, fig. 36.

234. Sofa

American, 1820–1840

Sofas with crest rails capped by a cylindrical bar terminating in volutes, serpentine-shaped ends, and animal paw feet may have been introduced about 1820. The most elegant example of the form is the dolphin-end sofa at the Metropolitan Museum of Art.[1] The Yale example is not executed with the finesse of the former example, but the dolphins on the arms and the detailed carving of the hairy paws are features which elevate it above the ordinary. Sofas of this form survive in greater numbers than those of the earlier period, and their popularity continued well into the nineteenth century.

Description: The veneered, cylindrical crest rail ends in volutes decorated with leaf carving. The edges of the back curve down from under the volutes and join the upholstered serpentine ends of the sofa. Scaled dolphins with twisted tails ornament the ends of the arms and face the veneered front seat rail. The front legs are hairy lions' paws below cornucopia-shaped brackets filled with fruit.

Notes: The bosses on the volutes may not be original. The veneer on the crest rail has been damaged. The upholstery is a modern rust-colored cotton velvet.

Woods: Mahogany; seat rails, soft maple.

Dimensions: H. 34 in. (86.3 cm), SH. 14¾ in. (37.5 cm). Seat rails: W. 86 in. (218.5 cm), D. 25¼ in. (64.1 cm).

Provenance: This sofa is presently used in the second-floor reception area in Woodbridge Hall, Yale University (donor unknown).

[1] Marilynn Johnson, Marvin D. Schwartz and Suzanne Boorsch, *19th-Century America: Furniture and Other Decorative Arts* (New York, 1970), no. 45.

235. Miniature Sofa

Probably New York, 1820–1830

Much debate surrounds the question of the purpose of miniature furniture. Were these small replicas of full-sized forms made as toys, cabinetmakers' models, or as apprentices' masterpieces? While evidence does not show that cabinetmakers made them as models for prospective customers, a desk at Winterthur with the label of Philadelphia toymaker Abraham Forst suggests they were made as toys,[1] and a chest of

233

234

235

drawers at Yale with the inscription "Built by Henry Seem when an apprentice at Sam Hogland and Dan Pitenger in Easton—in the year 1856" shows that apprentices may have made such small objects as a way of trying their hands at completed forms.[2] This rare miniature sofa is a small-scale version of no. 234 except for eagle brackets in place of cornucopias. The use of cherry and white pine as secondary woods plus the finely detailed hairy paw feet suggest New York as the place of origin.

Description: The form of this miniature sofa is similar to that of no. 234. The scrolls on the crest rail end in rosettes, and eagles' heads are found above the hairy paw feet. The ends of the arms and the front seat rail are veneered.

Notes: The outside toes of the right rear foot have been restored. The two lower feathers are missing from the eagle on the right front foot. The horsehair and brass tacks appear to be original. The junction of back and arms has been repaired. A horizontal crack appears in the back. The carved eagles are applied to the front legs. The reat seat rail is veneered.

Woods: Mahogany; side rails and cross braces, American cherry; corner blocks, white pine.

Dimensions: H. 14¾ in. (37.5 cm), SH. 7 in. (17.8 cm). Seat rails: W. 21 in. (53.3 cm), MW. 21¼ in. (54.0 cm), D. 9⅛ in. (23.2 cm).

Exhibitions: Classical America, p. 57, no. 45.

Bibliography: Aronson, p. 185, fig. 542; Schiffer, p. 230, fig. 232.

Provenance: Francis P. Garvan, New York, N.Y.; The Mabel Brady Garvan Collection, 1930.2097.

[1] Schiffer, p. 189, no. 194.—[2] *Ibid.,* p. 122, no. 132.

236. Sofa

American, 1830–1850

Although the dimensions of this sofa are practically the same as those on no. 234, this example gives the

236

appearance of being much larger. When Empire forms can be characterized as more robust and flamboyant, the general assumption is that they should be given a somewhat later date. Whereas the feet on no. 234 sit squarely under the sofa, on this example they jut out in the manner of illustration number 39 in the well-known broadside issued in 1833 by Joseph Meeks and Sons, cabinetmakers in New York.

Description: The basic design is similar to that of no. 233, but certain details are executed differently. The thin serpentine line of the arms is now shaped like the cornucopia carving which faces it. Bolsters fill the hollow spaces formed at the ends of the sofa. The convex front seat rail is flanked by long veneered tablets. Paw feet jut out beneath cornucopia-shaped brackets filled with fruits and scrolling leaves.

Notes: The sofa has recently been refinished and reupholstered with a floral stripe voided velvet.

Woods: Mahogany; seat rails, maple.

Dimensions: H. 34⅛ in. (86.5 cm), SH. 15¼ in. (38.7 cm). Seat rails: W. 86 in. (218.4 cm), D. 22¾ in. (57.8 cm).

Provenance: The sofa was purchased a few years ago as part of the furnishings of the Department of Statistics' offices in the Dana House, Yale University.

237. Miniature Sofa

American, 1835–1845

Figure 139 in *The Cabinet Makers' Assistant*, published by John Hall in Baltimore in 1840, shows a design for a sofa with scroll ends whose form is not unlike this miniature sofa at Yale. Here a series of carved leaves on the crest rail replaces the veneer shown in the Hall design. Rather than the exuberant animal and foliate carving found on the three preceding examples, this sofa displays the subtle curves, scroll feet, and wide bands of rich veneer characteristic of the French Restauration style, which made its influence felt in America in the late 1820's and 1830's.

Description: A series of leaves is carved along the straight crest rail. The scrolled arms are veneered with mahogany on their front faces, and have small, peaked mahogany appliqués near the bases. A mahogany veneer covers the lower edges of the side seat rails. The rounded edge of the front seat rail is flanked by blocks veneered with mahogany. The front feet are rounded scrolls that curve into points as the feet near the seat rail.

237

Notes: Minor repairs have been made to the veneer. The seat is made as a loose slip seat. The plain muslin upholstery illustrated has been covered with an early nineteenth-century green patterned horsehair.

Woods: Mahogany; white pine.

Dimensions: H. 10¼ in. (26.0 cm), SH. 3$\frac{9}{16}$ in. (9.0 cm). Seat rails: W. 21 in. (53.3 cm), D. 6$\frac{7}{16}$ in. (16.4 cm).

Provenance: Francis P. Garvan, New York, N.Y.; The Mabel Brady Garvan Collection, 1931.313.

238. Sofa

American, 1850–1870

The shape of this sofa is similar to examples by John Henry Belter of New York, but the ornament is much simpler than the richly carved and pierced decoration and laminated rosewood backs of Belter's sofas.[1] This example conveys the elaborate elegance of rococo-revival taste with its sweeping lines, pierced crest, and large shell at the center of the rosewood seat rail.

Description: The serpentine-shaped back sweeps around in curved ends. A carved ornament at the center of the top rail is pierced at the center with C-scrolls and leaves trail-

238

ing to the sides. The short wooden arms in front of the upholstered ends have reeded top edges, scrolled handholds, and beaded front faces terminating in volutes near the base. The short cabriole front legs end in small scrolls and their beaded edges continue along the rosewood front seat rail. On the bottom edge of the seat rail the bead is interrupted by elongated S-scrolls that flank a carved shell. The rear legs are turned.

Notes: The sofa has been refinished and reupholstered with a floral stripe voided velvet.

Woods: Rosewood; seat rails, white oak.

Dimensions: H. 42¼ in. (107.4 cm), SH. 12¾ in. (32.4 cm). Seat rails: W. 83⅛ in. (211.1 cm), D. 25 in. (63.5 cm).

Provenance: This sofa was purchased a few years ago as part of the furnishings of the Department of Statistics' offices in the Dana House, Yale University.

---

[1] Marilynn Johnson, Marvin D. Schwartz and Suzanne Boorsch, *19th-Century America: Furniture and Other Decorative Arts* (New York, 1970), no. 126.

Seating Furniture of Board Construction

BOARD CONSTRUCTION—that is, construction using pieces of wood fitted together with rabbeted joints fastened with nails, as opposed to that using pegged mortise-and-tenon joints—was the easiest and least expensive way of making early American furniture. Woodworkers with the most rudimental skills could and did make furniture in this manner from the seventeenth century into the nineteenth. It was a kind of construction used primarily for simple chests and similar case pieces, rarely for seating furniture, with the exception of the few forms found in this section—children's rocking chairs, chair-tables, and settles. Most of the objects thus constructed are thought to have come from rural areas.

239. Child's Rocking Chair

American, 1750–1800

With its board sides and back, this child's rocking chair, like the settle (no. 241), may have provided extra protection against cold drafts during the winter months. Most of the examples of the form have fairly simple decoration, which makes them difficult to date and place regionally.[1] The tin hearts on both the front and back of this example are an unusual feature.

Description: Constructed of six boards, this chair has tin hearts nailed to the front and rear of the top back edge. Beginning at the crest rail, the sides are shaped with a gentle arch. The line which defines the edges of the sides curves upward again to form the handholds. Attached to bottoms of the sides are rockers with serpentine-shaped ends.

Notes: The chair retains traces of old black and brown paint. The left rocker has been pinned to the side with two square wooden pegs. The molding around the edges of the back is held in place with small sprigs.

Woods: Back, tulip; sides and seat, white pine; rockers, soft maple.

239

Dimensions: H. 21 1/16 in. (53.5 cm), SH. 5 11/16 in. (14.4 cm). Seat rails: MW. 9 11/16 in. (24.6 cm), D. 9 3/4 in. (24.8 cm).

Bibliography: Schiffer, p. 68, fig. 38.

Provenance: Irving W. Lyon, Hartford, Conn.; Francis P. Garvan, New York, N.Y.; The Mabel Brady Garvan Collection, 1930.2293.

[1] See Nutting, *Treasury*, nos. 2488, 2490, 2491, and 2495; *Colonial Antiques*, no. 30.

240. Chair-Table

Hudson River Valley or New Jersey, about 1800

The chair-table is another form of seating furniture often of board construction. Unlike the seventeenth-century representatives of the form whose turned frames usually support a drawer under the seat (see no. 7), chair-tables made from boards usually have a storage box with a hinged lid instead. Although some examples of the form are more elaborately ornamented with serpentine curves, such as one illustrated by Nutting,[1] this plainer chair-table exhibits a pleasing geometric play of circular shapes. Many trestle-foot tables of this form have been found in New Jersey and in the Hudson Valley.

240

Description: The round top pivots on two cleats attached to the underside. When opened, the hinged lid of the storage box on the base serves also as the seat. The edges of the boards below the box are shaped with semi-circular cut-outs. The boards fit into trestle feet with rounded ends.

Notes: The chair-table has been refinished, but traces of red paint remain. The pin hinge, right foot, and left brace under the box have been replaced. The left foot has been damaged by worms and has minor restorations. Shrinkage cracks appear in the top.

Wood: Birch.

Dimensions: H. 28 1/2 in. (72.4 cm), Diam. 43 in. (109.2 cm), W. 14 15/16 in. (37.9 cm), D. 12 1/2 in. (31.7 cm).

Provenance: Walter and Draper, Poughkeepsie, New York; Francis P. Garvan, New York, N.Y.; The Mabel Brady Garvan Collection, 1930.2146.

[1] *Treasury*, no. 1770.

241. Settle

American, 1750–1800

The settle is a furniture form going back to medieval times. High-backed and not readily movable, it is a type of seating which seems closer to architecture than to casual, portable furniture. The boards in the back of this example, one of which has beaded edges, are reminiscent of the sheathing in eighteenth-century houses. With their high-backed construction, settles undoubtedly provided protection against winter drafts; this example has the further protection of a hood. Because they were made over a long period of time and are usually of the simplest construction, they are difficult to date and to place regionally. This example has been included in an exhibition of Connecticut furniture, but the evidence

241

for a Connecticut attribution is unknown to the author.[1]

Description: The back of this hooded settle is made of three tapered boards—the center one having beaded edges. The back board below the seat rakes at an angle, and the end boards are cut accordingly to accommodate it. The end boards are shaped so that a 6-inch-deep projection frames the back above the arm rest. The end boards broaden to their full width a foot above the seat, and the front edges have a short serpentine curve below round, upright handholds. The lower edges of the end boards are cut to form ogee arches. Below the seat a front rail is nailed to rabbets in the end boards.

Notes: Pieces have been added to the bases of the front feet. Traces of brown paint remain on the front and back. The seat fits into mortises in the end boards. The back boards are fitted together with a tongue and groove.

Wood: Atlantic white cedar.

Dimensions: H. 56¾ in. (114.1 cm), SH. 16¾ in. (42.5 cm), D. 17¾ in. (45.1 cm), W. 74⅝ in. (189.6 cm).

Exhibitions: *Conn. Furn.*, p. 144, no. 261.

Provenance: C. M. Traver Co., New York, N.Y. (sale New York, Anderson Galleries Inc., April 17–18, 1925, p. 66, no. 314); Francis P. Garvan, New York, N.Y.; The Mabel Brady Garvan Collection, 1930.2382.

[1] *Conn. Furn.*, p. 144, no. 261.

Revival Styles and the Arts and Crafts Movement

DURING the nineteenth century the American furniture-making industry underwent enormous changes both in the way furniture was made, and in the sources of its designs. Beginning with such enterprises as Lambert Hitchcock's chair factory in Hitchcocksville, Connecticut, in the second decade of the century, the trend in the industry was to supplant hand tools with water-powered or steam-powered tools, and in so doing to standardize and increase the volume of production. Furniture-making establishments became larger and a greater part of their wares were produced for distant markets. East coast furniture centers, such as New York, continued to be important, but as the population spread westward during the course of the century, large factories in major midwestern cities such as Cincinnati and Chicago supplied new and strong competition.

An assortment of eclectic historic revival styles dominated furniture design in the nineteenth century. The Gothic taste, which had never really died in England since medieval times, underwent a resurgence in the 1830's. In 1833 J. C. Loudon, in his *Encyclopedia of Cottage, Farm, and Villa Architecture and Furniture,* described the principal furniture styles as "the Grecian or modern style, which is by far the most prevalent; the Gothic or perpendicular style, which imitates the lines and angles of the Tudor Gothic Architecture; the Elizabethan style, which combines the Gothic with the Roman or Italian manner; and the style of Louis XIV, or the florid Italian, which is characterized by curved lines and excess of curvilinear ornament."[1] The inspiration for American furniture designs continued to come from abroad, particularly from England and France, and this transatlantic link was fostered in the nineteenth century by the great international exhibitions. Just past mid-century a reaction to excessive ornamentation, particularly that badly produced by mechanical means, was pioneered by English designers such as William Morris and Bruce J. Talbert. Called the Arts and Crafts Movement, it followed the credo set forth by Charles Eastlake in *Hints on Household Taste* (1868), and it stressed rectangular outlines and simple honest construction in furniture design. Among the American furniture makers who produced designs following these tenets was Gustav Stickley, whose stark, functional Craftsman furniture (no. 262) stands in sharp contrast to the highly ornamented styles of mid-century.

[1] J. C. Loudon, *An Encyclopedia of Cottage, Farm and Villa Architecture and Furniture* (London, 1833), p. 1039.

242. Side Chair

New York City, about 1850

The eclecticism in the interpretation of historic styles in the nineteenth century is evident in the design of this chair, on which a Gothic pointed arch edged by crockets on the crest is combined with spool-turned stiles, spindles, and legs reminiscent of the Jacobean era. On the front seat rail the pendants and round-headed arches introduce some of the influence of Moorish taste. The chair might have been called "Gothic" or "Elizabethan" in the nineteenth century. Its history of ownership in New York suggests it was

242

243

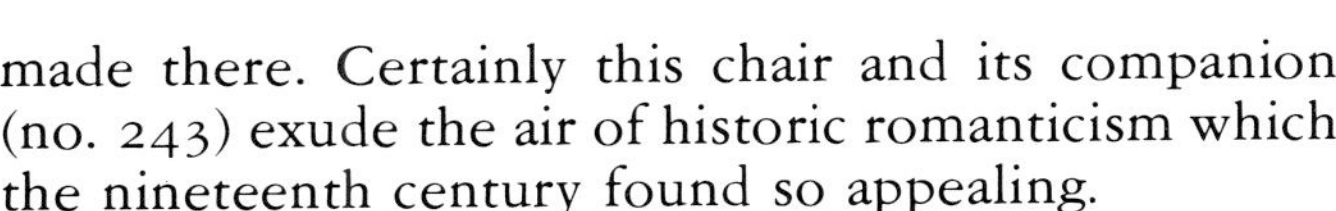

made there. Certainly this chair and its companion (no. 243) exude the air of historic romanticism which the nineteenth century found so appealing.

Description: The stiles, spindles, and front legs are decorated with spool turnings. The pierced crest is in the shape of a pointed arch with crockets along its top edge. The stiles end in urn-shaped finials with steeple tops. Along the lower edge of the seat upholstered halfway over the rails are four arches with pointed drops suspended between them and a beaded band above them.

Inscription: The upholstery tag on black scrim underneath the seat reads: "C. L. VIETOR / 1170 FIFTH AVENUE / Remade and Renovated by / FRANK BROTHERS / 1309 MADISON AVENUE."

Notes: Two of the drops and some of the beading on the front seat rail have been replaced. In the reupholstering process pieces of mahogany were replaced in the tacking areas on the seat rails.

Wood: Mahogany.

Dimensions: H. 44⅛ in. (112.1 cm), SH. 14 in. (35.6 cm). Seat rails: W. 15⅝ in. (39.7 cm), MW. 18 in. (45.7 cm), D. 18⅛ in. (46.0 cm).

Provenance: Alexander Knox, Jr., New York, N.Y.; Mrs. Carl L. Vietor; Gift of Mr. and Mrs. Alexander O. Vietor, New Haven, Conn., 1973.83.1.

243. Side Chair

New York City, about 1850

See comments, no. 242.

Description: This chair came to Yale with no. 242 and is very like it. The chief difference between them is that the crest rail here is composed of three whorls topped by two pierced heart shapes on the sides and a tear shape at the center.

Inscription: An upholstery tag on the black scrim underneath the seat reads: "C. L. VIETOR / 1170 FIFTH AV-

ENUE / Remade and Renovated by / FRANK BROTHERS / 1309 MADISON AVENUE."

Notes: A crack appears in the left side of the crest rail where it joins the stile. One drop and 2¼ inches of beading have been replaced on the front seat rail. When the chair was reupholstered pieces of mahogany were replaced in the tacking areas on the seat rails.

Wood: Mahogany.

Dimensions: H. 44⅜ in. (112.7 cm), SH. 14⅛ in. (35.9 cm). Seat rails: W. 15½ in. (39.4 cm), MW. 17¼ in. (43.8 cm), D. 16⅞ in. (42.9 cm).

Provenance: Alexander Knox, Jr., New York, N.Y.; Mrs. Carl L. Vietor; Gift of Mr. and Mrs. Alexander O. Vietor, New Haven, Conn., 1973.83.2.

244. Upholstered Side Chair

New York, 1850–1860

Rococo parlor chairs with contoured backs of laminated sheets of rosewood are often attributed to John Belter of New York, a German immigrant who took out a series of patents between 1847 and 1858.[1] However, other New York cabinetmakers, such as Charles Baudoine, the firm of Joseph Meeks and Son, and Charles Klein, as well as Ignatius Lutz of Philadelphia, were competing with Belter in the production of fine rococo revival furniture. An attribution of this small chair to a specific shop is therefore impossible. The back of the chair is made of five laminated layers of wood; the rosewood basket of flowers on the crest, carved from the solid, is fitted to the top. In an article on Belter's patent furniture, Clare Vincent points out that the grapevines, floral motifs, and C-scrolls were probably inspired by English design books published in the 1840's, but that the technique of bending wood relates to German developments. Belter's creations and those of his competitors are the richest expressions in furniture of the rococo revival in America.

Description: The hollowed back is upholstered at the center and is bordered by pierced grapevine carving. At the top of the back is a carved basket of flowers. The bowed upholstered seat has a serpentine-shaped front edge which is repeated in the rosewood seat rail below it. A four-petaled flower and leaves are at the center of the rail. Shells with foliated streamers ornament the tops of the cabriole legs, which terminate in French feet with carved leaves. The square rear legs swing out at an angle and end in small scrolled feet.

244

Notes: The back is made up of five plys of rosewood, the front ply being greater in depth. A two-ply rosewood veneer was used on the side rails, and a ⅜-inch rosewood facing on the front seat rail. The toes of the front feet have been replaced; they were copied from a chair in the Brooklyn Museum (illustrated in Comstock, no. 647). The casters have also been replaced. The brocaded material illustrated has been replaced by a reproduction brocatelle (Scalamandré, 97099–1) and braid (Scalamandré, V127–22).

Woods: Rosewood; mahogany; seat rails, ash.

Dimensions: H. 37¼ in. (94.6 cm), SH. 13$^{11}/_{16}$ in. (34.8 cm). Seat rails: W. 18¼ in. (46.4 cm), D. 17⅛ in. (43.5 cm).

Provenance: Phillip Sewell Staats, Staatsburg, N.Y.; George W. Staats, Springfield, Mass.; The Mabel Brady Garvan Collection, 1965.31.

[1] See Clare Vincent, "John Henry Belter's Patent Parlour Furniture," *Furniture History*, III, 1967, pp. 92–99.

245. Armchair

American, about 1860

This armchair, a mate, and ten accompanying side chairs (all at Yale; see no. 246) were probably used as a parlor suite. Although they are not as richly ornamented as the Belter-type chair, no. 244, their sweeping curvilinear lines, elegantly framed oval backs, and carved crest rails embody the essence of the rococo revival taste. Rosewood was chosen for the most expensive nineteenth-century furniture, but on these chairs and the majority of their contemporaries, black walnut was used instead.

Description: The oval upholstered medallion in the back is supported at the sides with the elongated S-shaped ends of the stiles. The top of the oval is ornamented with a garland of fruit and leaves. The short arms are covered with a small upholstered pad and rest at the front on curvilinear arm supports. The front, side, and rear seat rails are bowed and upholstered half over the rails. The soft grooves molding the short cabriole front legs are continued onto the front seat rail. The front legs rest on casters; the rear legs are square and swing out as they reach the floor.

Notes: The front of the front seat rail is a walnut facing applied to the ash. A thin walnut veneer is applied all the way around the exposed lower edge of the rear and side seat rails. The blocks supporting the joints of the stiles and arm supports with the seat rails are attached with cut nails and glue. The veneer is cracked in back of the left rear leg. Small breaks at the bottom of the oval have been repaired. The bottoms of both front legs have been shattered—a repair that often occurs on chairs of this type, whose delicate feet had to bear the stress caused by the casters. The chair has been upholstered with a modern silk brocatelle (Scalamandré, 96196–4) and braid (Scalamandré, V127–13).

Woods: Walnut; seat rails and blocks (supporting the joints of the rear stiles and the arm supports to the seat rails), ash.

Dimensions: H. 38½ in. (97.8 cm), SH. 13⅞ in. (35.2 cm). Seat rails: W. 17¼ in. (43.8 cm), MW. 23¼ in. (59.1 cm), D. 21½ in. (54.7 cm).

Provenance: Donor unknown; Yale University Art Gallery, 1970.98.7a.

245

246

246. Side Chair

American, about 1860

See comments, no. 245.

Description: This side chair is one of ten that accompanies the preceding armchair and has similar details.

Notes: The blocks supporting the joint of the stiles and seat rails were replaced long ago and have been added to recently. The bottoms of both front feet have been broken. The veneer on the seat rails behind both rear legs has been cracked. Small repairs have been made to the joints at the bottom of the oval. The chair has been upholstered with a modern silk brocatelle (Scalamandré, 96196–4) and braid (Scalamandré, V127–13).

Woods: Walnut; seat rails, ash.

Dimensions: H. 35½ in. (90.2 cm), SH. 15½ in. (39.3 cm). Seat rails: W. 15¼ in. (38.8 cm), MW. 18¼ in. (46.4 cm), D. 18⅜ in. (46.6 cm).

Provenance: See no. 245; Yale University Art Gallery, 1970.98.7g.

247

247. Side Chair

American, 1850–1880

This balloon-back rococo revival chair is of the type often sold as parts of a "parlor suit," as the advertisement from *Mason's Monthly Budget* illustrates. In describing "Drawing-Room Chairs"—the English name for the form—Blackie and Sons' *Victorian Cabinet-Maker's Assistant* noted that these chairs "should be smaller and decidedly lighter in character than chairs intended for dining-room purposes—grace and elegance being requisite in the one case, solidity and strength essential in the other."[1] Robert C. Smith has observed that the balloon-back chair is named for the rounded shape of the back, which is thought to have developed from the prominent volutes on the crest rails of late classical scroll-back chairs of the 1830's.[2] By the mid to late 1840's, the transition to the balloon-back shape was evident. Once the design was established, the chair became one of the most popular of the mid-nineteenth century rococo revival. Well-suited to new techniques in mass production, they were manufactured in enormous quantities. Although the height of the popularity of the balloon-back was during the 1850's and 1860's, they were still being produced and sold as late as the 1880's.

Description: This side chair has a curvilinear front seat rail and cabriole front legs ending in modified French scroll feet. At the joints of the stiles and crest rail are small areas of leaf carving. The sweeping line of the back is continued through the small braces that span the space between the stiles and the side seat rails. Bowed side and rear seat rails complement the serpentine front seat rail and are upholstered half over the rails. The rear stiles, square below the seat, rake backward but curve in again just as they reach the floor.

Notes: The chair bears evidence of nineteenth-century production methods. Circular-saw marks appear on the front corner blocks, and band-saw marks are found on the seat rails. The triangular front corner blocks of ash are fastened with glue and cut nails. The thin rear corner braces of walnut are dovetailed to the side and rear seat rails. The brocaded silk material covers older velvet upholstery.

Woods: American walnut; front seat rail and corner blocks, ash; side and back seat rails, beech.

Dimensions: H. 34¼ in. (87.8 cm), SH. 17¾ in. (45.5 cm). Seat rails: W. 13¾ in. (35.0 cm), MW. 17 in. (43.2 cm), D. 18¼ in. (46.4 cm).

16 Mason's Monthlv Budget.

$60 for this BLACK WALNUT PARLOR SUIT,
(Haircloth or Reps. Seven Pieces.)
CONSISTING OF
Tete-a-Tete Arm-chair, Reception Chair and four Chairs,
AT
MASON'S Wholesale and Retail Manufacturing Warehouse,
101, 103, 105 & 107 Myrtle Ave., and 292 & 249 Bridge St.,
BROOKLYN.

Fig. 8—Mason's Monthly Budget, *about 1860*.

Provenance: Provost's House, 35 Hillhouse Avenue, New Haven (previous provenance unknown); Yale University Art Gallery, 1974.64.2.

[1] Reprinted by Dover Publications, Inc., 1970, p. 47.—[2] Robert C. Smith, "Rococo revival furniture, 1850–1870," *Antiques*, 75 (May 1959), p. 474.

248. Upholstered Rocking Chair

American, about 1840–1870

The shape of the stiles and legs of this rocking chair and the upholstery are similar to those in a drawing made by an English traveler, James Frewin, during a visit to the United States in 1838. Of rocking chairs Frewin wrote: "In America it is considered a compliment to give the stranger the rocking-chair as a seat; and when there is more than one in the house, the stranger is always presented with the best."[1] Numerous examples of rocking chairs like this one survive today. They were probably produced in great quantities during the nineteenth century by means of new methods of mass production, as the mechanical character of the carving on the crest suggests.

Description: The tall, wavy stiles of this rocking chair support a round cornered crest, which is carved at the center with three plumed or leaf-like forms flanked by

248

249 A

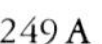

249 B

raised moldings. The back enclosed by this frame is upholstered, as is the seat cushion. The mahogany arms, upholstered on the top edges, rest on arm supports in the form of a scrolling vine with blossom ends. On the upper edge of the veneered front seat rail is a quarter-round molding. The short, saber-shaped front legs and the rear legs are mortised into the curved rockers.

Notes: The top right corner of the front seat rail has been broken and repaired. The crest rail has been broken from the stiles. The chair has recently been upholstered with a beige velvet.

Woods: Mahogany; plank seat, white pine; seat rails, ash.

Dimensions: H. 32 in. (81.3 cm), SH. 15¼ in. (38.7 cm). Seat rails: W. 24⅞ in. (63.4 cm), D. 35¼ in. (89.5 cm).

Provenance: This chair was purchased a few years ago as part of the furnishings of the Department of Statistics' offices in the Dana House, Yale University.

[1] John Gloag, "The Rocking Chair in Victorian England," *Antiques*, 99 (Feb. 1971), p. 241.

249 A and B. Upholstered Armchairs

American, 1880–1900

Few pieces of nineteenth-century American furniture strive for such an aura of baronial splendor as do these chairs. With heads of an eagle and a dog carved on the crest rails, they are more massive than the rococo and Renaissance revival chairs that were widely produced by American furniture makers. In their book of accounts for chairs covering the period 1883–88, the English firm of Gillow introduced a design with a similar treatment of the stretchers and front leg.[1] This evidence may provide a basis for dating the American example.

Description: The tall backs have a round-cornered top rail above which is a pierced crest of grapes and leaves with an eagle's head at the center of one chair (a), and a dog's head at the center of the other (b). The serpentine-shaped lower rail is ornamented with leaves and a vine. Palmette leaves are carved on the stiles just above the seat rails. Double-ball turnings link the arms, upholstered on their top edges, to the rear stiles. At the front the arms rest on octagonally faceted arm supports. The seats are upholstered half over the rails. The faceted, trumpet-form legs have bulbous gadroons at the top. Crossed stretchers of an exaggerated serpentine shape, with a turned boss at the center, brace the legs.

Notes: Recently an old, opaque, flaking finish was removed. The upholstery is red liege mohair velvet (Arthur H. Lee and Jofa No. J324020), and red silk braid (Scalamandré, V 65–27).

Woods: Walnut; ash blocks reinforce the joints of the arm supports and rear stiles with the side seat rails.

Dimensions: H. 51¼ in. (130.2 cm), SH. 17⅜ in. (44.1 cm). Seat rails: W. 21 in. (53.4 cm), MW. 23¾ in. (60.4 cm), D. 22½ in. (57.1 cm).

Provenance: Yale University Art Gallery, 1970.98.6 a and b.

[1] *Gillow's Estimate Book*, Chairs, nos. 580–770, 1883–88, pp. 677 and 679 (microfilm of the records of the Gillow firm of Lancaster, England).

250. Rocking Chair

American, about 1908

In the last quarter of the nineteenth century furniture in so-called colonial styles appeared on the market. As Americans developed a curiosity about their past and collected the housewares of their forefathers, furniture manufacturers capitalized upon the desire for styles reminiscent of the colonial era. Most pieces of "colonial" furniture were not faithful reproductions, but combined a variety of stylistic details from the past—as this chair does, with its modified shield-back form of the Federal era and the knuckled handholds of earlier eighteenth-century chairs. A date in the first decade of the twentieth century can be suggested for this rocking chair on the basis of its similarity to a design by H. Schaubel of Allentown, Pennsylvania, of about 1908.[1]

Description: The chair has a modified shield-shaped back, curved arms with knuckled handholds, and saber-shaped front legs. The banister at the center of the back is pierced with elongated cut-outs. The top edge of the square seat frame is molded and the curved rockers have serpentine-shaped ends.

250

Notes: The slip seat frame has been reupholstered with a blue-green wool velvet (Brunschwig & Fils, 3648.00/7).

Woods: Mahogany; slip seat frame, white pine.

Dimensions: H. 39 in. (100.0 cm), SH. 16½ in. (42.3 cm). Seat rails. W. 26¼ in. (67.3 cm), MW. 22⅛ in. (56.2 cm), D. 35¾ in. (91.6 cm).

Provenance: Bequest of Millicent Todd Bingham (d. 1969), Washington, D.C., 1969.42.22.

[1] N. I. Bienenstock, *A History of American Furniture* (New York, Furniture World, 1970), p. 107.

251. Side Chair

Framingham, Massachusetts, 1917–1936
Wallace Nutting (1861–1941)

Beginning in 1917, Wallace Nutting operated a com-

251

pany in Framingham, Massachusetts, making reproductions of Pilgrim and eighteenth-century furniture. This slat-back chair bears Nutting's brand. Like many colonial revival productions, however, it is by no means faithful to the original. Perhaps the model Nutting had in mind was a New England slat-back chair, such as no. 9 in this catalogue, but the scale here is much larger. While scale may be the most immediate and striking difference, the outline of the splats and the combination of a ball-and-ring-turned front stretcher with sausage-turned side stretchers are also not in accord with eighteenth-century practice. The tendency to exaggerate and re-create forms in more monumental scale is indicative of the basic romanticism of the colonial revival movement.

Description: The thick stiles and front legs are decorated with ball turnings outlined by soft hollows. The stiles end in ball-and-double-reel finials. Between the stiles are five arched slats, the top one of which has serpentine curved ends. Below the rush seat a double baluster and ring-turned front stretcher contrasts with the sausage-turned stretchers at the sides and the plain rear stretchers.

Inscription: Branded on the underside of the rear stretcher: "WALLACE NUTTING".

Woods: Maple and ash.

Dimensions: H. 46⅞ in. (119.1 cm), BPH. 49¾ in. (126.4 cm), SH. 18⅛ in. (46.0 cm). Seat rails: W. 16⅛ in. (41.0 cm), MW. 21⅞ in. (55.6 cm), D. 16½ in. (41.9 cm).

Provenance: Bequest of Shepherd Stevens, B.A. 1922 (d. 1962), New Haven, Conn., 1963.28.9.

Factory Chairs

AS THE BROADSIDE of the Lewisburg Furniture Company (Fig. 9, about 1895) suggests, chairs were produced in great numbers in many late nineteenth- and early twentieth-century factories. The trend toward mass production began in the second quarter of the nineteenth century with enterprises such as Lambert Hitchcock's chair factories in Connecticut, and grew as the century progressed. Perhaps the most ingenious innovation of the period was Michael Thonet's bentwood seating furniture, created in Austria at mid-century. These beautiful chairs were put together with screws, and hence could be reduced to compact pieces for easy transport; Thonet was thus able to capture a world market. The other factory chairs shown here along with Thonet's creations are not as elegant nor as technologically innovative, but

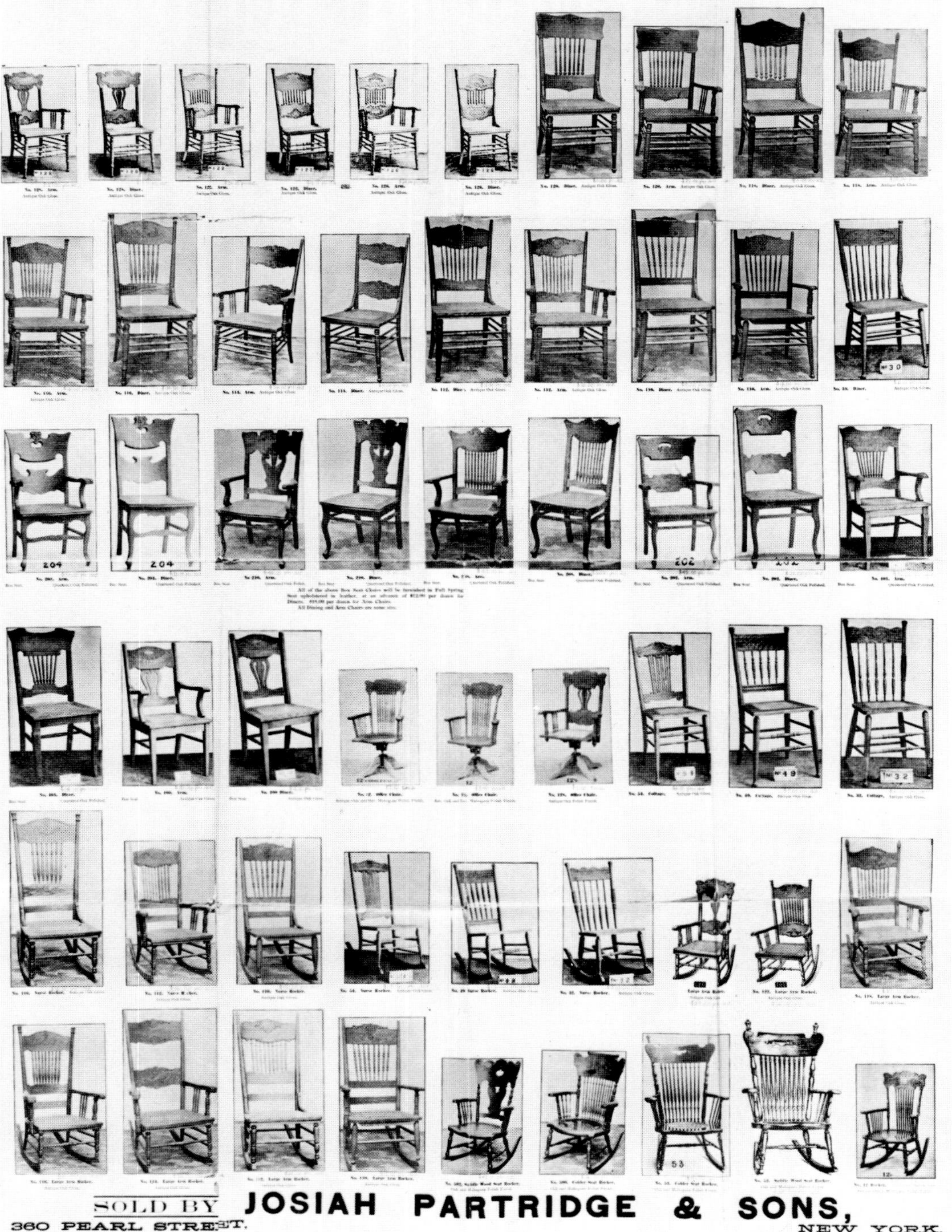

Fig. 9—*Advertisement of Josiah Partridge and Sons, New York, about 1893–1897.*

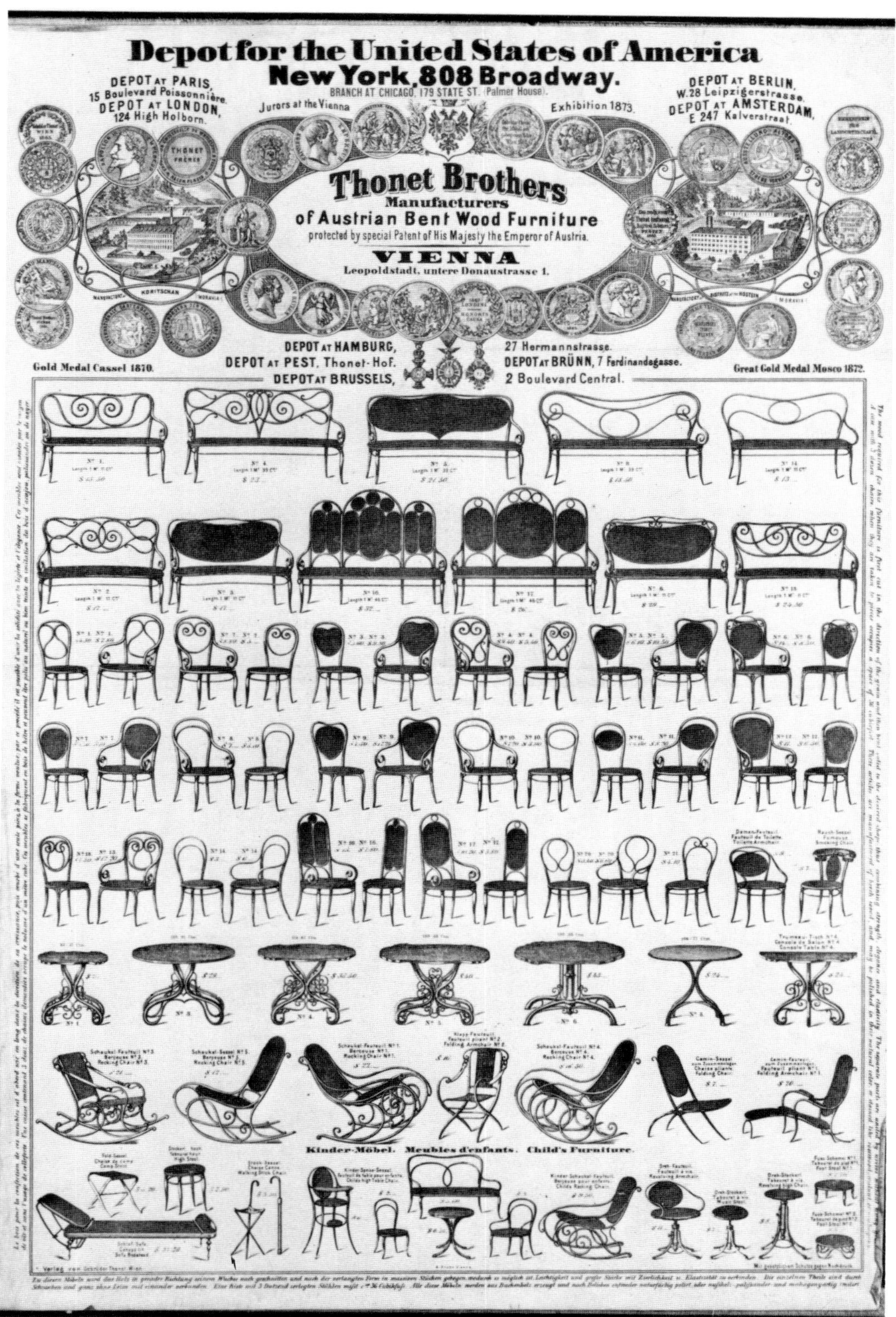

Fig. 10—*Advertisement of the Thonet Brothers, New York, about 1874. The New-York Historical Society; Landaver Collection.*

they share the characteristics of being made of easily produced and assembled parts. Some (no. 255) reflect the forms of earlier American furniture, and others (nos. 257–260) draw their inspiration from the English Arts and Crafts movement.

252. Rocking Chair No. 5

Austria, about 1876
Thonet Brothers, Manufacturers

In 1830 Michael Thonet began experimenting with bending wood, and by the 1840's his bentwood furniture was receiving much attention and praise. By the time of his death in 1871, his designs were so popular that four large factories were in operation, in Germany, Austria, Hungary, and Poland, and showrooms were open in many major cities throughout the world. The Thonet Brothers firm aimed their furniture at a truly international market. Their 1874 broadside (Fig. 10) advertising the stock available at the New York showroom, 808 Broadway, is printed in three languages, German, French, and English, and includes this information along the right border: "The wood required for this furniture is first cut in the direction of the grain and then bent solid to the desired shape, thus combining strength, elegance and elasticity. The separate parts are united by screws without using glue. A case with 3 dozen chairs, when they are taken to pieces, occupies a space of 36 cubic feet. These articles are manufactured of beech wood, and may be polished in their natural color, or stained like rosewood, walnut or mahogany." The first bentwood rocking chair was produced in 1860, and a rocking chair like this example appears on the broadside as "Rocking Chair No. 5" with a price of twelve dollars. Thonet Brothers displayed their furniture at the Philadelphia Centennial in 1876, where Walton Agnew reportedly bought this example.

Description: The individual bent beechwood sections create a sinuous, sleigh-like form. The rockers are long pieces of wood curved up at the front to form tear-shaped openings overlapped on the top edges by the ends of the stiles. The seat and upper back section are caned. The three elliptically shaped sections of the seat and back are screwed to the stiles. Two plain round stretchers screwed to the rockers where they touch the floor and near their ends give stability to the form.

252

Inscription: Branded "THONET" on the inner face of the bottom of the back frame.

Notes: The chair has been recaned.

Wood: Beech.

Dimensions: H. 41 in. (105.1 cm), SH. 18½ in. (47.4 cm), OW. 19 in. (48.7 cm), OD. 43 in. (110.3 cm).

Provenance: Walton Agnew (1825–1913), Kennett Square, Pa., purchased at the International Centennial Exhibition, Philadelphia (1876), according to David Stockwell; Gift of Mr. and Mrs. David Stockwell, Wilmington, Del., 1972.5.

253

253. 2890–54 Bentwood Armchair

Poland, about 1963
Introduced by Thonet Brothers in 1870 and still manufactured by Thonet Industries.

In the 1874 broadside of the Thonet furniture available at the New York showroom (Fig. 10), a chair of this type appears as "No. 14" at the price of six dollars. The model is still produced by the Thonet firm and was chosen as the seating furniture for the Library of the Yale University School of Art and Architecture, which opened in 1963. This model has often been associated with the architect Le Corbusier, who found its curvilinear lines compatible with many of his designs. Le Corbusier furnished his Pavillon de l'Esprit Nouveau at the 1925 Exposition des Arts Décoratifs in Paris with these chairs and said of them: "We have introduced the humble Thonet chair of steamed wood, certainly the most common as well as the most costly of chairs. And we believe that this chair, whose millions of representatives are used on the Continent and in the two Americas, possesses nobility."[1]

Description: The interplay of round and curvilinear forms characterizes the design. The stiles in the back are formed of a continuous piece of wood whose balloon-shaped top joins the arm rail bent to form hoop-shaped arms. The ends of the arm rail are attached to the round wooden seat. A circular piece of bent wood about three inches below the seat braces the legs. The two round, slightly flared front legs are doweled into the underside of the seat frame.

Inscription: A paper label glued to the underside of the seat reads: "THONET / ONE PARK AVENUE / NEW YORK / FOUNDED 1830".

Materials: Bent beech; nylon glides.

Dimensions: H. 32 in. (81.3 cm), OW. 22¼ in. (56.5 cm), OD. 23⅛ in. (58.7 cm).

Provenance: Purchased as seating furniture for the Library in the Yale University School of Art and Architecture.

[1] Greta Daniel, "Thonet Furniture," *Interiors* (Sept. 1953), p. 157.

254. Armchair

American, about 1850

During the nineteenth century the manufacture of furniture became increasingly mechanized. Factories in all parts of the country began to produce large numbers of useful, comfortable chairs such as this example. Like many of its counterparts, this one is made of stained walnut and has a caned seat. Certain features, such as the turnings on the legs, continue the decorative tradition of earlier "fancy" painted chairs.

Description: Nine vase-and-ring-turned spindles fit between the wooden bands outlining the cane seat and arm rail. The arm rail is bent to a semi-circular shape at the back, and curves forward at the front to join the seat. Attached to the back of the arm rail is a crest with a slightly arched top and an oblong cut-out at the center. The turned rear legs taper at both ends. The tops of the front legs are ogee-turned above a flattened ball and rings. A reel-and-ring turning also appears at the bottom of the leg about 3 inches above the button-like foot. The front stretchers

254

repeat some of the turnings on the spindles, and the side and rear stretchers are plain.

Wood: Walnut.

Dimensions: H. 29⅜ in. (74.6 cm), SH. 17 in. (43.2 cm). Seat rails: W. 21¼ in. (54.0 cm), D. 17¾ in. (45.1 cm).

Provenance: The chair is part of the furnishings of the office of the College Treasurer, Yale University.

255. Side Chair

Gardner, Massachusetts, about 1880
S. Bent & Brothers Inc. (est. 1867)

This small chair owes much to windsor seating furniture, a type Americans have perpetuated to the present time. Like eighteenth-century windsor chairs, it follows the principle of fitting legs and back into a plank seat. The strength of this structure was not left to chance: typical of the nineteenth-century fascination with technological gadgets are the metal rods which brace the whole. The bowed oak crest, spindles, and contoured plank seat are details borrowed from the earlier form. On this example, however, paint was not used to mask the different grains of the wood.

Description: The legs and back of this chair are fitted into a plank seat in the manner of earlier windsor chairs. The structure is strengthened by two steel rod devices. One is fitted from the crest rail through the seat, bolted on the underside. The second is attached to a brace screwed to the underside of the seat and is hooked to crossed rods from the legs. Four ball and flattened vase-shaped spindles are found in the back between the bowed oak crest. The front legs and four stretchers are ornamented with ring turnings, and the side and rear stretchers are plain.

Inscriptions: A paper label glued to the underside of the seat reads: "PROGRESSIVE CHAIRMA. . . / S. BENT & BROTHERS INC / GARDNER, MASS." A cartouche at the bottom has streamers on either side reading: "EST. / 1867", and in the center is written "26X". Written in black paint

255

on the bottom of the seat is "O.W. 31–32" and on the back edge of the seat " '3 [numeral obliterated] O.W. '32".

Woods: Legs and stretchers, birch; seat, ash; crest and spindles, oak.

Dimensions: H. 32⅞ in. (83.5 cm), OW. 16$^{15}/_{16}$ in. (43.0 cm), OD. 19⅝ in. (49.9 cm).

Provenance: Numerous chairs of this type can be found in Yale University buildings, suggesting that in the nineteenth century large numbers must have been purchased as general seating furniture; Yale University Art Gallery, 1975.5.

256. Armchair

American, about 1870–1890

An 1875 advertisement for the Philander Derby Company of Gardner, Massachusetts, shows "cane seat chairs" of this type, which owes some of its inspiration to rococo revival furniture.[1] On this example the curved crest with beading and small areas of leaf carving imitates the lines of balloon-back chairs (no. 247). The rear legs and the front feet sweep outward with more than the usual degree of gracefulness.

256

Description: The back and seat are caned. The rounded corners of the crest are outlined by a beaded edge, and the arched top is flanked by small pieces of foliated carving. Sinuous, bent arms slope downward from the stiles to the tops of the flattened-ball and taper-turned arm supports. Two ogee-and-ball-turned spindles brace each arm. The tops of the front legs are decorated with reels, and ring-and-reel turnings are found just above the tapered and curved feet. The ends of the rear stiles also swing out to the sides. The side and rear stretchers are plain, and the front stretcher is decorated with ring-and-reel turnings.

Inscription: A metal plaque on the crest reads: "President Porter's Chair."

Wood: Black walnut.

Dimensions: H. 38¼ in. (97.1 cm), SH. 17½ in. (44.5 cm). Seat rails: W. 20⅞ in. (53.0 cm), D. 18¼ in. (46.4 cm).

Provenance: This chair was used by Noah Porter, President of Yale from 1871 to 1886, and now stands in the Corporation Room at Woodbridge Hall.

[1] Bishop, no. 678.

257. Armchair

American, about 1900

The term "Arts and Crafts Movement" is often loosely applied to nineteenth- and early twentieth-century furniture that reveals a variety of stylistic trends, from the designs of Charles Eastlake to the "Craftsman" furniture of Gustav Stickley (see no. 262). This armchair and its accompanying side chair, no. 258, are related to this aesthetic. The wood is oak, valued for its appearance and durability. The forms are straightforward, unencumbered by the elaborate ornamentation that characterized many of the revival styles of the nineteenth century. The ornament used—the spindles in the back reminiscent of windsor chairs and the ring turnings at the tops of the

257

258

Fig. 11—*Oak extension dining table, part of the set with nos. 257 and 258.*

legs recalling "fancy" painted chairs—reaches back to the handcraft era.

Description: Ten thin, tightly spaced spindles supported by two rails ornament the center of the back. Above the spindles is a crest whose upper edge is embellished with a pair of serpentine scrolls with serrated, leaf-like ends. The scrolled arms are supported by inverted vase-shaped turnings, and the center of the square seat is caned. Two pairs of rings divided by a flattened ball appear at the tops of the turned front legs. Three tapered stretchers are between the front legs, and single stretchers are at the sides and rear.

Notes: Round-headed screws fasten the arms to the stiles and the arm supports to the seat. The seat frame is screwed to the seat rails from the underside of the seat rails. The joints of the stiles and seat rails are concealed with a turned oak button.

Wood: Oak.

Dimensions: H. 38¾ in. (101.9 cm), BPH. 41½ in.

(106.4 cm), SH. 18¹⁄₁₆ in. (45.7 cm). Seat rails: W. 17⁹⁄₁₆ in. (44.5 cm), MW. 18⁷⁄₈ in. (47.6 cm), D. 18⁵⁄₈ in. (47.2 cm).

Provenance: This armchair, a mate, six side chairs, and a dining table were transferred from the old Yale Infirmary, which was built in 1892 and enlarged in 1906, to the Yale University Art Gallery, 1973.123.2a.

258. Side Chair

American, about 1900

See comments, no. 257.

Description: The side chair matches the design of the arm chair, except that it has two front stretchers and only nine back spindles.

Notes: The oak buttons on the backs of the stiles, covering the screw holes of the joint of the seat rails and stiles, have been replaced.

Wood: Oak.

Dimensions: H. 37³⁄₄ in. (96.8 cm), BPH. 39¹⁄₂ in. (101.3 cm), SH. 17¹⁵⁄₁₆ in. (45.4 cm). Seat rails: W. 14¹⁄₁₆ in. (35.5 cm), MW. 15³⁄₄ in. (40.0 cm), D. 16¹⁄₁₆ in. (40.7 cm).

Provenance: Transferred from the old Yale Infirmary, which was built in 1892 and enlarged in 1906, to the Yale University Art Gallery, 1973.123.3c.

259

259. Side Chair

American, 1900

Although of the same type as the preceding examples, this chair is different in its details. The rounded and flared stiles, the elongated finials, and the tightly spaced spindles give the design greater visual impact.

Description: Eleven tapered, tightly spaced spindles fill the back. The tall rounded stiles, which flare out at the base, end in bullet-shaped finials. The crest rail between the stiles has two slight serpentine curves at the ends of its upper edge. Below the square seat, caned in the center, are two round front legs with a series of ring turnings at the top. Three rounded stretchers, slightly thickened at the center, brace the front legs, two are at the sides, and one is at the rear.

Notes: As on the two preceding chairs, screws are used to fasten the seat rails to the stiles and to the seat frame. The seat has been re-caned.

Wood: Oak.

Dimensions: H. 41 in. (104.1 cm), BPH. 47 in. (119.4 cm), SH. 18 in. (46.0 cm). Seat rails: W. 14³⁄₄ in. (37.5 cm), MW. 17⁵⁄₈ in. (45.0 cm), D. 17¹⁄₄ in. (44.0 cm).

Provenance: Miss Gertrude Klein (d. 1951), Philadelphia, Pa.; Gift of Mr. and Mrs. John E. Loeb, New Haven, Conn., 1974.39.

260. Armchair

American, about 1913

This huge armchair must have been specially ordered for its original owner, William Howard Taft, a man of great size. Although the turnings of the stretchers and the legs borrow much of their inspiration from the earlier "fancy" painted chairs, the use of oak, the broad scrolled crest, and the square spindles are related to the designs of Frank Lloyd Wright and the general mode of the Arts and Crafts Movement.[1] Manufacturers of mass-produced furniture such as this chair quickly picked up features of the Arts and Crafts style and began incorporating them into their wares.

Description: Below the deep oak crest rail whose upper edge is scrolled backward are nineteen tightly spaced rectangular spindles. The large elliptical plank seat has an indentation starting at the arm supports isolating the spindle area. The angular, slightly curved arms with scrolled handholds rest on vase-turned arm supports ending in ball pendants. The round, tapered front legs flare out near the floor and have ball-and-ring-turned tops. The side and rear stretchers are plain rounds, but the two front stretchers have a ball flanked by ring turnings at the center.

Inscription: A metal plaque attached to the crest rail reads: "THIS CHAIR WAS USED BY / WILLIAM HOWARD TAFT / FROM 1913 TO 1923."

Notes: The seat is constructed of four planks fastened together on the underside by two oak braces screwed to the boards. Metal braces are screwed to the ends of the arm supports and the underside of the seat.

Wood: Oak.

Dimensions: H. 35⅝ in. (90.5 cm), SH. 18 in. (45.7 cm), W. 30¼ in. (76.8 cm), D. 21½ in. (54.6 cm).

Provenance: William Howard Taft (B.A. 1878) probably used this chair while professor of law at Yale between 1913 and 1921. The chair is now in the Corporation Room of Yale University.

[1] Robert J. Clark, ed., *The Arts and Crafts Movement in America* (Princeton, 1972), no. 88.

261. Desk Chair

Gardner, Massachusetts, about 1931

P. Derby Co.

When the Sterling Law Buildings were completed at Yale in 1931, oak desk chairs like this one were

260

261

purchased as part of their original furnishings. This model demonstrates the persistence of the aesthetic of the Arts and Crafts Movement in America. The use of the contoured square spindles in the back is a modification of the straight spindles found in much late nineteenth-century furniture. In keeping with its intended use, the chair was constructed of rugged and durable oak.

Description: This desk chair without arms sits on a revolving, sprung, four-legged pedestal base with casters. The thick oak seat has a contoured surface. To its back edge are attached the contoured stiles which curve in slightly and broaden as they near the crest rail. The latter has rounded upper corners and is arched on the lower edge. Below it are six curved spindles which fan out slightly from the seat.

Inscription: An impressed roundel on the back edge of the seat reads: "P. DERBY CO. GARDNER MASS."

Notes: The second spindle from the left is cracked and loose. The seat is split. The side of the right stile has been scraped. The ends of the pedestal are well worn.

Wood: Oak.

Dimensions: H. 34 in. (86.3 cm), SH. 17⅝ in. (44.8 cm). Seat: W. 17¾ in. (45.1 cm), D. 16⅜ in. (41.6 cm).

Provenance: Part of the original furnishings of the Sterling Law Buildings of the Yale Law School; Yale University Art Gallery, 1974.62.

The Arts and Crafts Movement

FOLLOWING the Philadelphia Centennial in 1876, some American furniture manufacturers began to produce wares influenced by the English Arts and Crafts Movement, a growing force since the 1860s. Until recently this furniture had elicited only minor interest from furniture historians and collectors, but in the decade of the 1970's two major exhibitions have fostered new awareness of this stark, geometric furniture. The first, *19th-Century America,* an exhibition in celebration of the hundredth anniversary of the Metropolitan Museum of Art (1970), showed furniture by Frank Lloyd Wright, George W. Maher, Gustav Stickley, and the brothers Charles and Henry Greene. That landmark exhibition, covering a hitherto little studied era of American art, spawned at least one other major exhibition, *The Arts and Crafts Movement in America 1876–1916*, organized by the Art Museum, Princeton University, and the Art Institute of Chicago (1972–73). Since the catalogue of that show includes an even greater variety of American Arts and Crafts Movement furniture, it is an invaluable guide to the plain, rectangular furniture created by followers of the movement such as Gustav Stickley.

262. Reclining Chair

Eastwood, New York, about 1910
Gustav Stickley (1857–1942)

The furniture of Gustav Stickley and his ideas as expressed in his publication, *The Craftsman,* were crucial to the last major phase of the Arts and Crafts Movement in America. Stickley was employed in the furniture-making business for a number of years before he concentrated his efforts on stark, geometric oak furniture. He showed a major selection of it at the Pan-American International Exposition in Buffalo in 1901. This reclining chair is of mahogany rather than oak, but its square legs and severe lines reveal all the earmarks of Stickley's Craftsman style. The creation of the form with a hinged back for greater com-

262

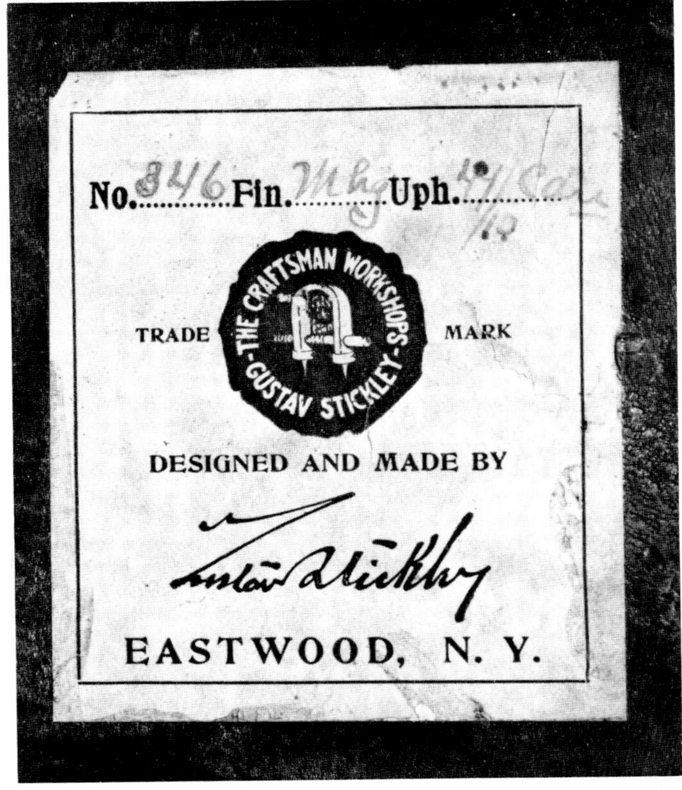

262a

fort is attributed to one of the founders of the Arts and Crafts Movement in England, William Morris, and is sometimes referred to as a "Morris chair." Stickley's catalogues of 1909 and 1913 describe chair no. 346 as a "reclining chair with spring seat cushion," available in sheepskin, velour, or cotton velvet for $24 or in Craftsman canvas for $20.[1] The handwritten letters "can" on the label reveal that this chair was originally upholstered in canvas.

Description: The horizontal slat back pivots at the base and rests against adjustable supports fitted to holes in the ends of the arms. All four square legs pierce the flat arms, and are braced by corbel-like supports. Loose cushions rest against the back and seat.

Inscriptions: A paper label attached to the front seat rail reads: "No. 346, Fin. Mhg. Uph. 44/10 can." In the center of the label is the Craftsman Trade Mark, a medallion with the words "THE CRAFTSMAN WORKSHOPS—GUSTAV STICKLEY" surrounding a joiner's compass with the words '*Als ik kan*" ("As I can"). Below the medallion are the words: "DESIGNED AND MADE BY / Gustav Stickley / EASTWOOD, N.Y."

Notes: The original support for the seat has been replaced with plywood. A 1⅛-inch high piece of pine has been added to the top of the front seat rail.

Woods: Mahogany; plywood base and supports for seat (replacements).

Dimensions: H. 41¼ in. (105.8 cm), SH. 13½ in. (34.3 cm). Seat rails: 23¼ in. (59.1 cm), MW. 23⅜ in. (59.4 cm), D. 24 in. (60.1 cm).

Provenance: Rev. Benjamin S. Winchester, D. D.; Gift of Miss Alice Winchester, Newton, Conn., 1972.68.

---

[1] *Craftsman Furniture Made by Gustav Stickley at the Craftsman Workshops Eastwood, New York,* January, 1909, p. 22; Sept., 1913, p. 13.

The Bauhaus

FIFTY YEARS after its creation, the furniture designed by Marcel Breuer and Mies van der Rohe of the Bauhaus still remains an effective symbol of modernity in interior design. Marcel Breuer's Wassily chair (no. 263) was the first chair to use nickel-plated tubular steel, and Mies van der Rohe's MR chair (no. 266) followed by a few months Mart Stam's design for a cantilevered chair in 1926. Such innovative designs were the fulfillment of Walter Gropius's plan for the Bauhaus. Appointed the head of the school in 1919, Gropius brought together artists and technicians to collaborate on designs fit for industrial production. The seating furniture of Marcel Breuer and Mies van der Rohe has become an integral part of the twentieth-century American landscape; Knoll Associates have reproduced the furniture of Mies since 1948; Breuer's furniture became available through Knoll with the acquisition of the Gavina Group in 1969.

263. Wassily Lounge Chair

Milan, Italy, about 1971
Designed by Marcel Breuer (b. 1902) in 1925;
reproduced by Gavina S.p.A., Milan, Italy, since 1965

The Wassily chair is named after the artist Wassily Kandinsky and was used in furnishing his house on the Bauhaus campus at Dessau, Germany, in 1925–26. The chair was designed by Marcel Breuer, a Hungarian trained at the Bauhaus from 1920 to 1924 and head of the furniture workshops there from 1924 to 1928. In his early tubular metal furniture, Breuer was attempting to create forms that had both visual and physical lightness and that were comfortable without being encumbered by thick upholstery. Unlike their forerunners in the Arts and Crafts Movement, the designers of the Bauhaus embraced modern technology. Breuer has said of this furniture: "Mass production and standardization had already made me interested in polished metal, in shiny and impeccable lines in space as new components for our interiors. I considered such polished and curved lines not only symbolic of our modern technology, but actually technology itself."[1] The original versions were produced for the Bauhaus by Mannesmann Steel, then with Standard-Möbel of Berlin, and were upholstered in canvas. Shortly thereafter Thonet Brothers obtained the rights to produce this chair. In 1965

263

Gavina of Milan began making reproductions, of which this chair is an example. Gavina was acquired by the American firm of Knoll Associates in 1968, and the Wassily lounge chair subsequently became available in the Knoll Collection as a part of the Gavina Group.

Description: The bent, tubular steel frame is composed of three units—legs, seat, and back—bolted together. Strips of cowhide stretched across the frame form the back, seat, and arm rests.

Inscription: A paper label on the underside of the seat frame reads: "GAVINA N. 4443 / mod Wassily dis. M. Breuer / Made in Italy."

Materials: Polished tubular steel and black cowhide.

Dimensions: H. 28¾ in. (73.0 cm), SH. 16⅞ in. (42.9 cm), OW. 31 in. (78.8 cm), OD. 27¼ in. (69.2 cm).

Provenance: Knoll International, New York, N.Y.; Millicent Todd Bingham Fund, 1971.67.1.

[1] *Marcel Breuer Buildings and Projects 1921–1961* (New York, 1962), p. 234.

264

264. Cesca Side Chair

Milan, Italy, about 1971
Designed by Marcel Breuer (b. 1902) in 1928; reproduced by Gavina S.p.A., Milan, Italy, from 1965

Marcel Breuer's classic tubular steel chairs are named after Wassily Kandinsky's daughter, Cesca. The chair was first designed in 1928, and like the Wassily chair, the originals were produced in conjunction with Mannesmann Steel, then Standard-Möbel of Berlin. As with the Wassily chair, Thonet Brothers obtained the rights to produce this chair (and in modified forms the design is produced by many other manufacturers). Since 1965 Gavina of Milan has reproduced it. That company was acquired by Knoll Associates in 1968, and since 1969 the Cesca chair has been a part of its Gavina Group.

Description: The polished steel frame is bent in such a way that the U-shaped base and straight front legs support a cantilevered seat and back panel. The oblong frame of the back panel (in natural beechwood) is caned, as is the seat frame, which has rounded back corners and a straight front.

Inscription: A label on the underside of the front seat rail reads: "GAVINA S.p.A. / Reg. TRADE MARK / Made in Italy."

Materials: Polished tubular steel, beech, cane.

Dimensions: H. 31½ in. (80.0 cm), SH. 18⅛ in. (46.0 cm), OW. 18½ in. (47.0 cm), OD. 25⅝ in. (65.1 cm).

Provenance: Knoll International, New York, N.Y.; Millicent Todd Bingham Fund, 1971.67.2.

265. Cesca Armchair

Milan, Italy, about 1971
Designed by Marcel Breuer (b. 1902) in 1928; reproduced by Gavina S.p.A., Milan, Italy, from 1965

See comments, no. 264.

Description: The polished steel frame is bent in such a way that the U-shaped base and straight front legs support

265

a cantilevered seat and back panel. An extension of the tubular steel around the edges of the back panel forms the arms, whose upper surfaces are fitted with black wooden arm rests. The oblong frame of the back panel is caned, as is the seat.

Inscription: A label on the underside of the front seat rail reads: "GAVINA S.p.A. / Mod. Cesca-dis: M. Breuer / Made in Italy."

Materials: Polished tubular steel, black painted beechwood, cane.

Dimensions: H. 31½ in. (80.0 cm), SH. 18⅛ in. (46.0 cm), OW. 23⅝ in. (60.0 cm), OD. 23⅝ in. (60.0 cm).

Provenance: Knoll International, New York, N.Y.; Millicent Todd Bingham Fund, 1971.67.3.

266. MR Dining Chair

East Greenville, Pennsylvania, about 1973
Designed by Ludwig Mies van der Rohe (1886–1969) in 1926; manufactured by Knoll International, Inc.

Ludwig Mies van der Rohe, an architect without formal training, learned the principles of design and construction from his father, a master stone mason. In Germany he had a long career as an architect before coming to America in 1938 to direct the School of Architecture at the Illinois Institute in Chicago. His MR chair, designed in 1926, was shown at the Werkbund Exhibition in Stuttgart and at the Exposition de la Mode in Paris in 1927. Mies patented the chair's principle of a resilient cantilever, which can be related to the cantilevered principles employed in many of his architectural designs.

266

Description: The continuous, tubular stainless steel frame curves forward and downward from the bar-like top rail to form the uprights and side seat rails. Beyond the black leather upholstery of the seat, the legs arc in a generous curve that flows into a U-shaped base.

Notes: The upholstery strips are laced on the back and underside. A removable metal bar beneath the leather seat spans the side seat rails.

Materials: Polished tubular stainless steel, black cowhide.

Dimensions: H. 31 in. (78.7 cm), SH. 15½ in. (39.5 cm), OW. 19½ in. (49.5 cm), OD. 27¼ in. (69.2 cm).

Provenance: James Furniture, Palisades Park, N.J.; Mrs. James C. Greenway Fund, 1973.77.6.

267

267. Spoleto Chair

East Greenville, Pennsylvania, 1973
Designed by Marcel Breuer (b. 1902);
manufactured by Knoll International, Inc.

Among the reproductions of early twentieth-century designs appearing on the market recently is Marcel Breuer's Spoleto chair. The chair corresponds in feeling, though not in detail, to Breuer's designs of the 1920's; its bent chrome-plated frame and taut black leather upholstery strips are related to the design of the Wassily chair (no. 263). Its form is also indebted to Mart Stam's cantilevered chair in tubular steel of 1926, but the upholstery strips are not seamed to form sleeves around the metal as they were in that early design.

Description: The bent chrome-plated steel tubes support a cantilevered seat and back upholstered in black leather. The chair is similar to no. 266, but the legs in front are straight rather than rounded.

Inscription: A gummed paper label on the underside of the seat reads: "Knoll International / 320 Park Ave. / New York, N.Y. 10022" and has a red dot with a large white "K" in the center at the right. Stamped on the label is "JUL 17 1973".

Materials: Chrome-plated steel; black leather upholstery.

Dimensions: H. 31 in. (78.8 cm), SH. 18¼ in. (46.4 cm), W. 20 in. (50.8 cm), D. 24½ in. (62.2 cm).

Provenance: James Furniture, Palisades Park, N.J.; The Mabel Brady Garvan Collection, 1975.4a.

The Post-War Era

ONE OF THE MOST IMPORTANT INFLUENCES in American chair design since World War II has been the work of Charles and Ray Eames. Their designs have moved away from the machine aesthetic to what Peter Smithson has described as the "Eames aesthetic." "Before Eames, no chairs (of the modern canon) were many coloured, or really light in weight, or not fundamentally rectangular in plan (i.e., the chairs of Rietveld, Stam, Breuer, Le Corbusier, Mies, Aalto). Eames' chairs . . . belong to the occupants, not to the building."[1] The Eames molded plywood chairs, which the Herman Miller Company began to produce in 1947, filled a great need for quality furniture available to a large market.

In post–World War II America the traditional concept of a chair as four legs supporting a seat frame was frequently abandoned, and innovations emerged in the utilization of materials. Wood, the traditional material of furniture makers, was manipulated in different ways (nos. 268–269), as in the Eames chairs. Wire, an old material, assumed new importance (nos. 272–278). Man-made fabrics allowed inventive uses of upholstery and an unprecedented role for color in furniture design (nos. 283–284). And perhaps most revolutionary of all was the potential for new forms inherent in newly developed molded glass fiber and plastics (nos. 285–289).

This section of the catalogue also makes clear the international character of furniture design in our era. From the time of its creation after World War II, the Knoll Company has been making European designs available in America. Chiefly as a result of Knoll's acquisition in 1968 of the Gavina Company of Milan, reproductions of early twentieth-century furniture designs are now being marketed. Within the last decade Italy has taken the lead in furniture design. As the major exhibition "Italy: The New Domestic Landscape" held at The Museum of Modern Art, New York, in 1972 made clear, Italian designers were creating the most innovative seating furniture in the 1960's.

[1] Peter Smithson, "Just a Few Chairs and a House," *Architectural Design*, 36 (September 1966), p. 446, and quoted in *Modern Chairs 1918–1970* (London, 1970), no. 30.

268. DCW Chair

Detroit, Michigan, and Venice, California, 1946
Designed by Charles Eames (b. 1907); manufactured by Evans Products Co.

Known by the initials DCW ("dining chair wood"), this chair by Charles Eames is one of the most famous and innovative of the century. The design was innovative not only because the molded panels of the back and seat were bent in more than one direction, but also because a rubber shockmount system was used to give the chair resiliency. The shockmounts were screwed to the bracing piece, but the use of newly developed glues made it possible to glue the rubber to the back and seat panel so that the joint was not visible on the front surfaces. This shockmount system typifies Eames's interest in and careful attention to working out the technological details of his designs. The back and seat panels of this example are identical to those on the DCM chair (no. 269), but the supporting structure is of slightly thicker plywood, bent in only one plane.

Charles Eames, born in St. Louis in 1907, studied architecture at Washington University and opened his own architectural office in 1930. In 1936 he was awarded a fellowship, and later a teaching post, at

268

Cranbrook Academy. Among his colleagues there was Eero Saarinen, with whom Eames submitted a joint entry to the exhibition "Organic Design in Home Furnishings" held at the Museum of Modern Art in 1940. Their chair design based on shells of plywood molded in more than one direction was awarded first prize. In 1941 Eames married Ray Kaiser, a colleague at Cranbrook who had helped Eames and Saarinen prepare the designs for the competition. After moving to southern California in 1941, the Eameses worked on developing low-cost methods for laminating and molding plywood, but World War II prevented putting molded plywood chairs into production. By 1946 production was begun, and a small exhibition at the Museum of Modern Art was devoted to them. The underside of the seat of this chair bears the label of Evans Products Company, which produced the plywood for Eames chairs for a brief period before their manufacture was taken over by the Herman Miller Company in 1947.

Description: The plywood seat and back panels of this dining chair, one of a pair, are molded in compound curves. They are supported by an understructure composed of a pair of U-shaped legs—the front ones slightly taller than the back ones. A C-shaped piece of heavier molded plywood bent in only two dimensions links the back and seat panels and the legs.

Inscription: A label on the underside of the seat reads: "EVANS [crossed with another EVANS; both share the A] / MOLDED PLYWOOD DIVISION / EVANS PRODUCTS COMPANY."

Materials: Ash plywood; rubber shockmounts.

Dimensions: H. 29½ in. (74.9 cm), SH. 16 in. (40.6 cm), OW. 19½ in. (49.5 cm), OD. 21 in. (53.3 cm).

Provenance: Gift of Mr. and Mrs. Valerian Lada-Mocarski, New Haven, Conn., 1973.104b.

269. DCM Chair

Zeeland, Michigan, about 1973
Designed by Charles Eames (b. 1907) in 1946; manufactured by Herman Miller, Inc., since 1947

The Eames molded plywood chair introduced a new trend in seating furniture. The chairs did not adhere to a rectilinear shape; they were lightweight and could be moved around easily. Their hardware—the rubber shockmounts at the junctures of the plywood panels and the understructure—was readily visible. The DCM chair ("dining chair metal") was the most popular variant of the molded plywood design, and it is still manufactured by the Herman Miller Company, which began making the chairs in 1947. The self-leveling nylon glides seen at the base of the legs of this chair supplanted the rubber and chrome tips on the original models.

Description: The molded plywood seat and back panel of this chair are bent in compound curves. They are supported by an understructure composed of a pair of U-shaped legs of tubular steel—the front ones slightly taller than the back ones. A C-shaped piece of steel tubing links the back and seat panels with the legs.

Inscription: A black paper label with silver writing under the seat reads: "herman miller" preceded by an M-shaped logo.

269

Materials: Chromium-plated tubular steel frame; plywood seat and back with walnut veneer.

Dimensions: H. 29¾ in. (75.6 cm), SH. 15½ in. (39.5 cm), OW. 19⅞ in. (50.5 cm), OD. 20⅞ in. (53.1 cm).

Provenance: Gift of Herman Miller, Inc., Zeeland, Mich., 1973.106.3.

270. Armchair

Copenhagen, Denmark, about 1971

Designed by Hans Wegner (b. 1914) in 1949; manufactured by Johannes Hansen, Copenhagen

In Scandinavian furniture such as this armchair, the aesthetics of eighteenth- and nineteenth-century furniture design are continued. The warmth and color of wood and the beautiful ways it can be shaped with hand tools are important in this example. Although the Wegner chair and the Eames chair (no. 268) both use wood in a very sculptural way, this one evokes a more traditional response than its machine-produced counterpart. Not surprisingly, the designer, like his eighteenth-century predecessors, drew some of his inspiration from Oriental sources. At a retrospective exhibition of Wegner's work held at Georg Jensen (New York) in 1965, the classic Wegner chair was displayed along with a 1943 reproduction of a Chinese child's chair, from which it had evolved.[1]

In 1969 Knoll International secured exclusive distribution rights to the designs of Hans Wegner manufactured by his master cabinetmaker, Johannes Hansen. Wegner was trained at the Copenhagen School of Arts and Crafts, where he taught from 1946 to 1953; Hansen was the founder of the Copenhagen Cabinetmakers' Guild.

Description: The sculptural arm rail, composed of three pieces of wood fastened with a saw-tooth joint, is sup-

270

ported on four tapered legs. The woven cane seat is attached to the seat rails, whose front and back are slightly bowed.

Inscriptions: A label on the medial brace reads: "Made for / Knoll International / by Johannes Hansen, Denmark / Designed by Hans Wegner." Branded on the right side of medial brace: "JOHANNES HANSEN / COPENHAGEN / DENMARK."

Materials: Teak and woven cane.

Dimensions: H. 30 in. (76.2 cm), SH. 17 in. (43.0 cm). Seat rails: W. 19¼ in. (50.0 cm), MW. 22¼ in. (57.0 cm), D. 18⅛ in. (46.0 cm).

Provenance: Knoll International, Inc., New York, N.Y.; Millicent Todd Bingham Fund, 1971.67.4a.

---

1 Rita Reif, "Show Honors Work of Hans Wegner," *The New York Times* (May 5, 1965), p. 40c.

271. Side Chair

East Greenville, Pennsylvania, about 1973
Designed by William Stephens (b. 1922) in 1967; manufactured by Knoll International, Inc.

271

With the rear stile, side seat rail, and front leg made of a single curving piece of bent wood, this chair departs radically in concept from traditional chairmaking. A forerunner is the "elastic" chair patented by Samuel Gragg of Boston in 1808 (no. 163). Here this structural method creates a chair with an unusually fluid and graceful line. William Stephens, its designer, joined the Knoll International Design Development Group in 1960, five years after his graduation from the Philadelphia College of Art with a degree in Industrial Design. Since 1971, when he replaced Don Albinson as manager, Stephens has headed the group—a small team of professional designers based in an outgrown Knoll factory in Greenville, Pennsylvania, whose task it is to find ways to duplicate each prototype in quality and then to produce it in quantity. The methods of production are often unorthodox and frequently require specially built machines and tools. All members of the group contribute original designs to the Knoll Collection from time to time. The design and development of the Stephens chair followed the research and tooling of a design by another member of the group—the laminated wood chair by Don Pettit. Stephens made the first sketches and models for his own chair in 1965, and it appeared on the market in 1968.

Description: The one-piece seat and back, a naugahyde upholstered unit, is cradled in a walnut frame. Laminated, bent pieces are molded in a continuous curve from the crest, along the sides of the seat, through the front legs to the floor. The rectangular rear legs merge with these pieces just above the seat.

Materials: Laminated walnut veneer; blue naugahyde upholstery.

Dimensions: H. 32 in. (81.3 cm), SH. 15¾ in. (40.0 cm), OW. 19½ in. (49.5 cm), OD. 22½ in. (57.1 cm).

Provenance: James Furniture, Palisades Park, N.J.; Mrs. James C. Greenway Fund, 1973.77.7.

272. Side Chair

East Greenville, Pennsylvania, about 1973
Designed by Harry Bertoia (b. Italy, 1915) in 1952; manufactured by Knoll International, Inc.

The Italian-born sculptor Harry Bertoia emigrated to America in 1930, studied at the Detroit School of Arts and Crafts, and then at the Cranbrook Academy, where he later taught metalwork. In 1950 Hans Knoll encouraged him to experiment, and in 1952 his series of wire shell seating furniture was introduced. Bertoia's chairs may be thought of as a functional extension of his metal sculpture. Their shells of welded steel wire seem to float on steel rod bases. The deep, cupped lozenge shape of the lounge chairs (nos. 274 and 275) are even more exotic. Both Bertoia's and Eames's wire chairs (no. 276), developed at about the same time, use a similar lattice wire construction that may have been influenced by new developments in rapid spot welding techniques and by the production of the now-ordinary plastic and wire kitchen dish drainer. Wire was not used again as the principal material in American furniture design until Warren Platner's furniture of 1966, which uses wire in a very different way.

272

Description: The vinyl-coated, lattice wire shell of this side chair is supported on a two-piece black-painted steel rod base. The upper section of the base is a cradle bolted to the seat and welded to a pair of U-shaped legs.

Inscription: A gummed paper label on the underside of the seat reads: "Knoll International / 320 Park Avenue / New York, N.Y. 10022." To the right is a red dot with a white "K" in the center.

Materials: Vinyl-coated steel wire; seat pad, elastic naugahyde (Knoll design, 1956).

Dimensions: H. 30 in. (76.2 cm), SH. 17¾ in. (45.0 cm), OW. 21 in. (53.3 cm), OD. 22½ in. (57.2 cm).

Provenance: James Furniture, Palisades Park, N.J.; Mrs. James C. Greenway Fund, 1973.77.2.

273. Side Chair

East Greenville, Pennsylvania, about 1971
Designed by Harry Bertoia (b. Italy, 1915) in 1952; manufactured by Knoll International, Inc.

See comments, no. 272.

Description: The lattice wire shell of this side chair, similar to that of no. 272, is covered with a skin of dark green cotton upholstery. The rod and wire is chromium plated rather than vinyl coated and black painted.

Inscriptions: A gummed paper label on the underside of the seat reads: "Knoll International / 320 Park Avenue / New York, N.Y. 10022" and has at the right a red dot with a white "K" in the center. On the front seat rail is another tag which reads: "Do Not Remove / COMMONWEALTH / OF / PENNSYLVANIA / DEPT. OF LABOR & / INDUSTRY / SOLD BY / Sep 24 1971 / Date of Deliv / Distrib by / Knoll Int., Inc. / 320 Park Ave. / N.Y., N.Y."

273

Materials: Chromium-plated steel rod frame with welded lattice wire shell; dark green cotton upholstery (Tony Prestini design).

Dimensions: H. 30 in. (76.2 cm), SH. 17½ in. (44.5 cm), OW. 21 in. (53.3 cm), OD. 22½ in. (57.2 cm).

Provenance: Knoll International, Inc., New York, N.Y.; Millicent Todd Bingham Fund, 1972.52.2.

274. Small Diamond Chair

East Greenville, Pennsylvania, about 1973
Designed by Harry Bertoia (b. Italy, 1915) in 1952; manufactured by Knoll International, Inc.

See comments, no. 272.

Description: The diamond-shaped lattice wire shell of this lounge chair is concave at the center and forms the seat. Over the upper surface of the shell is stretched a skin of brown upholstery with a lateral seam. The two-piece steel rod base, painted black, consists of a cradle bolted to the lattice wire shell and a pair of raked legs.

Inscription: A paper label attached to the front seat rail reads: "DO NOT REMOVE / COMMONWEALTH / OF / PENNSYLVANIA / DEPT. OF LABOR & / INDUSTRY / SOLD BY / Date of Deliv / Distrib. by / Knoll Int., Inc. / 320 Park Avenue / N.Y., N.Y."

Materials: Vinyl-coated steel wire; black painted steel wire; brown cotton upholstery (Tony Prestini design).

Dimensions: H. 30½ in. (77.4 cm), SH. 15⅛ in. (38.5 cm), OW. 33¾ in. (85.7 cm), OD. 28 in. (71.1 cm).

Provenance: James Furniture, Palisades Park, N.J.; Mrs. James C. Greenway Fund, 1973.77.3.

274

275

275. **Large Diamond Chair and Ottoman**

East Greenville, Pennsylvania, about 1973
Designed by Harry Bertoia (b. Italy, 1915) in 1952; manufactured by Knoll International, Inc.

See comments, no. 272.

Description: This lounge chair is a larger version of no. 274. The ottoman is supported on a similarly shaped base. The top of the ottoman is an oblong form with bowed sides of lattice wire upholstered to match the chair.

Inscription: A small white rectangular label on the underside of the chair seat reads: "Knoll International / 320 Park Avenue / New York, N.Y. 10022" and has a red dot to the right with a white "K" in the center. An identical label appears on the ottoman.

Materials: Vinyl-coated steel wire; black painted steel wire; red cotton upholstery (Tony Prestini design).

Dimensions: Chair: H. 27¾ in. (70.5 cm), SH. 14½ in. (36.8 cm), OW. 45 in. (114.3 cm), OD. 32¾ in. (83.2 cm). Ottoman: H. 14¾ in. (37.4 cm), SH. 13¼ in. (33.6 cm), OW. 24 in. (60.9 cm), OD. 17¼ in. (43.8 cm).

Provenance: James Furniture, Palisades Park, N.J.; Mrs. James C. Greenway Fund, 1973.77.4 a,b.

276. **DKR Chair**

Zeeland, Michigan, about 1955
Designed by Charles Eames (b. 1907) in 1952; manufactured by Herman Miller Co., Inc.

Charles Eames's DKR chair was developed in 1952. In contrast to Bertoia's series, in which the floating shapes created by the wire evoke a romantic response, Eames's chair is much more straightforward and less fanciful, qualities in keeping with the Eames aesthetic. The strut-like bracing system of the legs, which reminds one of airplane technology, is illustrative of Eames's interest in the direct expression of structural technique. As with most Eames designs, various shells and bases can be used interchangeably on this chair. This shell was also available as plain wire and with partial upholstery.

Description: The lattice wire unit has a contoured seat and tapered back covered with a skin of gray naugahyde upholstery. The raked legs terminate in nylon glides and are bolted to a square (with two cut-out corners) of tubular steel attached to the underside of the lattice wire shell. Welded to the legs is a wire bracing structure. Meeting in a square under the seat are two short, wing-like pieces of bent wire directed upward to the legs. Two longer, similarly shaped pieces point downward.

276

Materials: Steel lattice wire shell and tubular steel base; gray naugahyde upholstery; nylon glides.

Dimensions: H. 31¼ in. (79.4 cm), OW. 18¾ in. (47.6 cm), OD. 22⅜ in. (57.0 cm).

Provenance: Sillman and McNair Associates, New Haven, Conn. Purchased (1955) as part of the original furnishings of Louis Kahn's addition to the Yale University Art Gallery, 1975.7.

277

277. Dining Chair

East Greenville, Pennsylvania, about 1971
Designed by Warren Platner (b. 1919) in 1966; manufactured by Knoll International, Inc.

Architect Warren Platner collaborated with Knoll International on his wire furniture from 1963 to 1967. The steel wire collection represents the first of his designs to be created for production in quantity. In 1961 he began welding metal wires to metal rings to obtain " . . . a small-scale detail related to over-all form. This was the important thing—like people who are forms with details: hair, eyebrows, noses, etc., I wanted the furniture to be all one form, not just a furniture of tops and bottoms, which is the usual thing."[1] With the completion of each prototype, the Knoll Design Development Group developed the tooling necessary to duplicate Platner's original. The lattice wire chairs of Bertoia (nos. 272–275) and Eames (no. 276) are the forerunners of Platner's creations, but unlike the earlier chairs, the entire form of Platner's is of wire, and there are fewer welds because of the vertical wires.

Platner's wire collection includes a large easy chair, a sofa, lounge and dining chairs, an ottoman, and side, coffee, and dining tables. The patented construction of continuous vertical wires, tied like sheaves of wheat rather than meshed, comes in two finishes—a dark, patinated copper oxide and a silver-like nickel finish. The collection was introduced at an American Institute of Architects convention in 1966, where it drew an immediate favorable response.

Warren Platner has pursued his interests in both architecture and design throughout his career. He presently heads his own architectural firm, Warren Platner and Associates, which he founded in 1968. He received his B. Arch. from Cornell in 1941; in 1955 he won the Rome Prize in Architecture, in 1956 an Advanced Fulbright Award in Architecture, and in 1963 a Graham Foundation Award in Furniture Design which allowed him to develop his wire chairs.

Description: Tightly spaced vertical wires, flaring out into a cup-shaped seat above the cone-shaped pedestal, form the frame. Three rings in the base and a perimeter wire around the seat and back (to which the vertical wires are welded) give the form stability. An arch of black upholstery covers the top edge of the back and a cushion fills the base of the seat.

Materials: Nickel-finish steel rod; black woolen upholstery.

Dimensions: H. 29 in. (73.7 cm), SH. 15⅜ in. (39.1 cm; measured to the top edge of the wire shell), OW. 26½ in. (67.3 cm), OD. 22 in. (55.9 cm).

Provenance: Gift of Knoll International, Inc., New York, N.Y., 1971.44.2.

---

[1] *Progressive Architecture,* XLVII (July 1966), 7, p. 166.

278

279

278. Lounge Chair

East Greenville, Pennsylvania, about 1971
Designed by Warren Platner (b. 1919) in 1966; manufactured by Knoll International, Inc.

See comments, no. 277.

Description: The frame of this lounge chair is similar to that of no. 277, but the cupped seat and back are covered with upholstery wrapped around the edges of the frame.

Materials: Dark patinated copper oxide on steel rod; white woolen upholstery.

Dimensions: H. 30½ in. (77.5 cm), SH. 14½ in. (36.8 cm; measured to the edge of wire shell), OW. 36½ in. (92.7 cm), D. 25½ in. (64.8 cm).

Provenance: Gift of Knoll International, Inc., New York, N.Y., 1971.44.1.

279. GF 40/4 Stacking Chair

Youngstown, Ohio, about 1973
Developed by David Rowland, 1956–1964; manufactured by the General Fireproofing Company

The sight of forty GF 40/4 chairs stacked in their wheeled dolly is a wonder to behold. Tilted at a forty-five-degree angle, compact beyond all imagination, they more closely resemble an abstract wire sculpture than forty stacked chairs. Their creator, industrial designer David Rowland, trained at the Cranbrook Academy of Art, developed the concept over an eight year period, from 1956 to 1964. In 1965 the chairs won the American Interior Design International Award, and in 1968 they received a Gold Medal at the Third International Furniture Exhibition in Vienna. When stacked, forty chairs are only four feet high—this density is not approached by any other stacking chairs on the market.

Description: The rectangular back and seat panels in black vinyl-finished metal are supported by a chromium-plated tubular steel base. A continuous piece of metal is bent to form the uprights that support the back panel, and develops into the rear legs, floor brace, front legs, and side seat rails. The rear seat rail and front stretcher are separate.

Inscription: A gummed paper label on the underside of the seat reads: "GF / BUSINESS FURNITURE / 40/4 / CHAIR / designed by / David Rowland / U.S. Patents No. 3,080,194 / D-202,775; D-200,107; 3,254, 362 / Other U.S. and

Foreign Patents Pending / Forest City, North Carolina Division / The General Fireproofing Company / Youngstown, Ohio 44501 / No. B28265 Color."

Materials: Chromium-plated steel frame; seat and back stamped from vinyl-covered sheet metal.

Dimensions: H. 29½ in. (74.9 cm), OW. 20⅛ in. (51.1 cm), OD. 22 in. (55.9 cm).

Provenance: The GF 40/4 stacking chair is used in many parts of Yale University.

280. 670/671 Lounge Chair and Ottoman

Zeeland, Michigan, about 1973

Designed by Charles Eames (b. 1907) in 1956; manufactured by Herman Miller, Inc., since 1956

The mode established by the severe, taut upholstery of the chairs designed in the 1920's by Marcel Breuer and Mies van der Rohe was unmistakably altered by the introduction in 1956 of Charles Eames's 670/671 lounge chair and ottoman. The chair has been described as a reversion to an English club chair.[1] The plump, tufted leather-covered cushions exude an aura of comfort. The extraordinary feature of the 670/671 ensemble is that the upholstery cushions are completely detachable by a system of gromets, hooks, and snaps, and can easily be reversed or changed. This concept is startlingly different from the traditional one of tacking upholstery to a wooden frame and reveals Eames as a master of technological advances in modern furniture design.

Description: The lounge chair is composed of three sections of molded rosewood plywood upholstered with leather-covered latex and down. The leather-upholstered molded arms bridge the gap between the seat and lower section of the back. A five-pronged swiveling pedestal base

280

of cast aluminum, polished on the upper surfaces, supports the whole. The cushion of the ottoman echoes the sections of the chair and is supported on a four-pronged base.

Inscription: A black paper label with silver writing under the seat of both pieces reads "herman miller" preceded by an M-shaped logo.

Materials: Molded plywood and rosewood veneers, cast aluminum, black leather-covered latex foam and down upholstery.

Dimensions: Chair: OH. 33½ in. (85.1 cm), SH. 11½ in. (29.5 cm; measured to top of wooden frame), OW. 33½ in. (85.1 cm), OD. 31¾ in. (80.7 cm). Ottoman: OH. 16¾ in. (42.6 cm), SH. 10¾ in. (27.5 cm; measured to top of wooden frame), OW. 25¾ in. (65.4 cm), OD. 20¾ in. (52.7 cm).

Provenance: Gift of Herman Miller, Inc., Zeeland, Mich., 1973.106.4a,b.

[1] Peter Smithson, "Just a Few Chairs and a House," *Architectural Design* 36 (Sept. 1966), p. 446.

281. 72U Chair

East Greenville, Pennsylvania, about 1973
Designed by Eero Saarinen (1910–1961) in 1948; manufactured by Knoll International, Inc.

The "chair with the hole in the back" (as it is known internationally) is a direct descendant of the prize-winning designs Eero Saarinen developed with Charles Eames for The Museum of Modern Art's "Organic Design in Home Furnishings" exhibition in 1940 (see no. 268). Instead of using molded plywood for the contoured back, however, Saarinen employed a new material, molded plastic, which had become available by the time this chair was brought out in 1951. Saarinen, born in Finland, emigrated to America at the age of thirteen. He returned to Europe to study sculpture in Paris for one year before attending the Yale School of Architecture. He worked with his father, Eliel Saarinen, at the Cranbrook Academy of Art, where he met Charles Eames.

Description: The 72U's crescent-shaped back forms a lunette-like opening where its lower edge is arched before joining the edges of the seat cushion. The thick-edged seat is supported by two pairs of slightly raked metal legs on disc-shaped nylon-tipped glides.

Inscription: A small white rectangular label on the underside of the seat reads: "Knoll International / 320 Park Avenue / New York, N.Y. 10022" and has a red dot to the right with a white "K" in the center.

281

Materials: Polished tubular steel; molded plastic shell reinforced with fiber glass nylon stretch fabric.

Dimensions: H. 31¾ in. (80.7 cm), OW. 21½ in. (54.6 cm), OD. 20 in. (50.8 cm).

Provenance: James Furniture, Palisades Park, N.J.; The Mabel Brady Garvan Collection, 1975.6a.

282. Swivel Armchair

East Greenville, Pennsylvania, about 1973
Designed by Charles Pollock (b. 1930) in 1965; manufactured by Knoll International, Inc.

Charles Pollock, a member of the Knoll Design Development Group, completed work on his group of executive office chairs between 1962 and 1965. Although the designer may not have drawn directly

282

upon Eames's 670/671 lounge chair and ottoman (no. 280), this swiveling office chair shares with its predecessor comfortable-looking tufted leather upholstery. Just as Eames's lounge chair was daring in introducing cushy upholstery to a design audience that had favored trim, impeccable lines since the 1920's, so Pollock's swivel chair is a radical departure in office seating. Even Eames's swiveling office chair (no. 283) does not make so bold a statement about being comfortable at work. Pollock's chair was awarded first prize at the convention of the American Institute of Architects held in Washington, D.C., in 1965.

Description: The cup-like seat is outlined by a band of polished aluminum. The black leather upholstery cushions on the back and seat are gently tufted and buttoned. Hoop-shaped black arms fit into the curve of the seat and back. A round polished shaft with a swivel and height adjustment at the top supports the seating unit. The four prongs of the pedestal base have polished upper surfaces and sit on casters.

Inscription: A gummed paper label on the underside of the seat reads: "Knoll International / 320 Park Avenue / New York, N.Y. 10022" and has a red dot with a large white "K" in the center at the right.

Materials: Molded plastic, polished aluminum and steel, leather upholstery.

Dimensions: H. 31 in. (78.7 cm), OW. 26¼ in. (66.7 cm), OD. 28¼ in. (71.7 cm).

Provenance: Knoll International, New York, N.Y.; The Mabel Brady Garvan Collection, 1974.129.

283. Soft Pad Chair

Zeeland, Michigan, about 1973
Designed by Charles Eames (b. 1907) in 1969; manufactured by Herman Miller, Inc., since 1969

This tilt-and-swivel chair is one of the so-called aluminum group, which consists of chairs with diecast aluminum frames resting on pedestal bases.

283

These chairs were first produced in 1958 as single seating and a variation was produced in 1962 as tandem seating for airport terminals. This lounge chair is one of the "soft pad," a later development of the aluminium group, introduced in 1969 by Herman Miller in which back and seat cushions filled with polyester foam are sewn to the supporting fabric stretched between the top and front cylinders. In his catalogue of the 1973 exhibition of Charles Eames's furniture at The Museum of Modern Art, Arthur Drexler explained the complex method of attaching the upholstery pad to the cast aluminum side ribs: "Cast in one piece, the side rib is modelled to form a bar and flange, and terminates at each end with a cylinder. Slipped into the flanges and secured in place with concealed brass nails, the seat pad wraps around the cylinders but is not itself stiffened across its top and bottom edges by any internal metal construction."[1] In this variation of the soft pad group, the mechanism beneath the seat for the tilt and swivel and the addition of arms detracts from the sleekness of the design evident in the less complex models.

Description: Slung between the two cast aluminum side ribs is a one-piece upholstery pad supplemented by three horizontal back cushions and a seat cushion. Hoop-shaped arms of cast aluminum are attached to the side ribs. Below the black-finished height adjustment mechanism is a cylindrical stem with black steel inset. A four-pronged cast aluminum pedestal forms the supporting base.

Inscription: A paper label under the seat reads: "Under Penalty of Law / This Tag Not to be Removed / Except by Consumer / All New Material / Consisting of / Polyester Fiber 50% / Urethane Foam 50% / Reg. No. Conn. 2097 (MICH.) / Certification is made / by the manufacturer that the / materials in this article / are described in / accordance with law. / Made by / HERMAN MILLER, INC. / ZEELAND, MICHIGAN. 49464 / GARDENA, CALIF. 90247/7148/EA-419."

Materials: Cast aluminum frame, steel swiveling base, polyester fiber, urethane foam.

Dimensions: OH. 38¾ in. (98.4 cm), SH. 17 in. (43.0 cm), OW. 23½ in. (59.7 cm), OD. 23 in. (58.4 cm).

Provenance: Gift of Herman Miller, Inc., Zeeland, Mich., 1973.106.2.

[1] Arthur Drexler, *Charles Eames: Furniture from the Design Collection* (The Museum of Modern Art, New York, 1973), p. 42.

284

284. Suzanne Double Lounge Chair

Milan, Italy, about 1971
Designed by Kazuhide Takahama in 1969; manufactured by Gavina S.p.A., Milan, Italy

The repetition of a single design element and the purity of the tightly stretched synthetic fabric give this double lounge chair a look of streamlined, modern elegance. Kazuhide Takahama is a Japanese architect now living in Italy. His lounge chair was included in the Knoll Associates' introduction of the Gavina Group furnishings in New York in 1969.

Description: One shape, a round-topped rectangle, is repeated in the upholstered back, seats, and polished steel cross beams of this double lounge chair.

Inscription: A label on the underside reads: "Made in Italy / by Gavina S.p.A."

Materials: Polished tubular steel; synthetic stretch fabric.

Dimensions: H. 26¾ in. (67.9 cm), SH. 13¾ in. (34.9 cm), OW. 29⅞ in. (75.9 cm), OD. 58⅝ in. (148.9 cm).

Provenance: Gift of Knoll International, Inc., New York, N.Y., 1971.55.

285. Armchair

East Greenville, Pennsylvania, about 1970
Designed by Eero Saarinen (1910–1961) in 1956; manufactured by Knoll International, Inc.

Commonly referred to as the "tulip pedestal chair," this design remains the most elegant of Eero Saarinen's creations. It is said that Saarinen was disappointed not to be able to cast his chair in one piece. The present cast aluminum stems, necessary for the slender, delicate lines of the pedestal, violated his intention. Of his pedestal furniture the designer himself said: "The undercarriage of chairs and tables in a typical interior makes an ugly, confusing, unrestful world. I wanted to clear up the slum of legs. I wanted to make the chair all one thing again. All the great furniture of the past from Tutankhamun's chair to Thomas Chippendale's have always been a structural total. With our excitement over plastic and plywood shells, we grew away from this structural total. As now manufactured, the pedestal furniture is half-plastic, half-metal. I look forward to the day when the plastic industry has advanced to the point where the chair will be one material as designed."[1]

Description: From the large round foot rises a thin pedestal which flares as it meets the base of the plastic seating unit. The edges of the white contoured seating unit curl and broaden to form the elbow rests. The line of the back ascends above the elbow rests and is slightly hollowed at the center of its upper edge.

Inscription: Cast into the underside of the base: "BR 50".

Materials: Cast aluminum with fused plastic finish; molded plastic shell; blue plain-woven seat cushion.

Dimensions: H. 31½ in. (80.8 cm), MH. 32 in. (82.5 cm), SH. 16 in. (41.0 cm), measured to top of plastic shell, OW. 25½ in. (65.3 cm), OD. 23½ in. (60.2 cm).

Provenance: The Yale Center for British Art and British Studies, New Haven.

[1] Aline Saarinen, ed., *Eero Saarinen on His Work* (New Haven and London, 1962), p. 68.

285

286. Panton Stacking Chair

Zeeland, Michigan, about 1973
Designed by Verner Panton (b. 1926) in 1960; manufactured by Herman Miller, Inc., since 1967

The DAR chair, developed by Charles Eames and other designers in collaboration with the Engineering Department of the University of California (Los Angeles Campus) for the International Competition for Low-Cost Furniture Design sponsored by The Museum of Modern Art, New York, in 1948, was the first chair to have a seat of molded glass fiber supported on metal legs. In the same exhibition Robert Lewis and James Prestin entered a one-piece molded glass fiber chair, but the production of it proved too costly. It was not until 1967, when Herman Miller began producing Verner Panton's stacking chair, that the concept was made economically feasible. Panton, a Danish-born designer now living in Switzerland, had first conceived of his design in 1960.

Description: The upper surface of this chair's single piece of glass fiber is molded to varying degrees of concavity, the

286

287

greatest being the deep depression at the base which provides the stabilizing foot for the cantilevered seat and back. The back tapers to a rounded top and the edges of the sides are folded over.

Materials: Orange molded glass fiber.

Dimensions: H. 32¾ in. (83.2 cm), OW. 20¾ in. (52.7 cm), OD. 23¾ in. (60.3 cm).

Provenance: Gift of Herman Miller, Inc., Zeeland, Mich., 1973.106.1.

287. Plia Folding Chair

Bologna, Italy, about 1973

Designed by Giancarlo Piretti in 1969; manufactured by Anonima Castelli Company, Bologna; distributed in U.S.A. by Krueger Metal Products, Inc., Green Bay, Wisconsin

The designer of this chair used joints cleverly. Its three essential parts fold in two positions for convenient storage; the side pivots allow the chair to be folded completely flat or stacked partially open. In the same series are the Plona folding armchair (1970) with a leather seat and the Platone folding desk (1971). Giancarlo Piretti is a professor of design at the Bologna School of Art and Director of Research and Design for the Anonima Castelli Company in Bologna, one of Italy's largest producers of wood and steel office furniture.[1]

Description: The folding chair is composed of three hinged parts: one is an open aluminum rectangle with rounded corners forming the front feet and supporting the back rest, a piece of plastic 5¼-inches deep with a semicircular indentation; the second is the U-shaped rear legs; and the third the square clear plastic seat with a circular indentation in the center and an aluminum frame.

Materials: Clear plastic and aluminum.

Dimensions: H. 29¼ in. (74.3 cm), SH. 17¼ in. (43.8 cm), OW. 18¼ in. (46.3 cm), OD. 19⅝ in. (49.8 cm).

Provenance: James Furniture, Palisades Park, N.J.; Mrs. James C. Greenway Fund, 1973.77.5.

[1] *Interiors*, 130 (Jan. 1971), p. 34.

288. Solar Lounge Chair

Milan, Italy, about 1973

Designed by Carlo Bartoli (b. 1931) in 1967; manufactured in Italy for Stendig Inc.

Carlo Bartoli, trained at Milan Polytechnic, began work as an architect and furniture and industrial designer in his own Milan office in 1959. His interest in the use of plastic materials for the home began in 1966, and the following year his "Solar" chair, or "Gaia" chair as it is also known, was made by Arflex of Milan. Bartoli was attracted to plastics because of the variety of shapes they could assume and their technical possibilities, which were different from those of all traditional materials. The Solar chair is made structurally sound by the use of fiber glass to reinforce the polyester. This added strength allows the spaces between the legs to be cut out, creating a lighter, more sculptural appearance. The load-bearing ability of the frame was tested by making full-scale plaster models of the chair with wooden frames and networks. The curves conform comfortably to the human body. The chair was designed for use with or without cushioning and is produced in four colors: white, red, mustard, and dark green.

288

Description: This one-piece molded armchair has concave sides and back, and a seat that slants toward the back. Slightly rounded, arched openings are on the front, sides, and back.

Inscription: A label on the underside of the seat reads: "Original Design / Stendig / Made in Italy."

Materials: Polyester reinforced fiber glass.

Dimensions: H. 27 in. (68.6 cm), SH. 13¼ in. (33.7 cm), OW. 29¾ in. (75.6 cm), OD. 31 in. (78.7 cm).

Provenance: James Furniture, Palisades Park, N.J.; Mrs. James C. Greenway Fund, 1973.77.1.

289. Selene Chair

American, about 1973

Designed by Vico Magistretti in 1968; manufactured by Artemide, USA

First introduced in 1968, this molded fiber glass stacking chair designed by Vico Magistretti was included in the Italian Design Exhibition at the Hallmark Gallery, New York, in that year. Light and easily portable, the chair is ideal for casual seating arrangements. The Selene chair is molded from Reglar, the registered trademark of the fiber glass–reinforced plastic produced by Artemide. The deep folds in the molding of the legs is related to Magistretti's other plastic furniture, the Stadio 80 table (1968) and the Gaudi and Vicario armchairs (1971), also manufactured by Artemide. Vico Magistretti received his degree in design from Milan Polytechnic in 1945.

Description: The squarish back has edges that curl forward at the sides. Just above the seat the edge of the side widens and is bent into a deep crevice to form the rear legs. The top surface of the seat is slightly concave and the edges are curved to form a 2-inch skirt. The fiber glass is molded on the front legs in a manner similar to that on the rear legs.

Inscription: The following information is molded in the plastic: "ARTEMIDE USA / BURLINGTON HOUSE INTERNATIONAL / MODEL SELENE / DESIGNER VICO MAGISTRETTI / PATENT 793415."

Material: Red molded fiber glass.

Dimensions: H. 29¾ in. (75.5 cm), SH. 17¾ in. (45.0 cm), OW. 15⅝ in. (47.0 cm), OD. 18 in. (46.0 cm).

Provenance: Purchased as seating furniture for the multi-media lounge of the Mabel Brady Garvan Galleries, Yale University Art Gallery; The Mabel Brady Garvan Collection, 1973.172a.

289

Beds

IN SEVENTEENTH- and eighteenth-century parlance a "bedstead" was the wooden framework supporting mattress and hangings. The word "bed" meant bedstead, mattress, and hangings together. The hangings usually consisted of a top, a headcloth, a curtain at each post, and a top and bottom valance.

In a catalogue of bedsteads the curator would ideally show at least three views of each bed—one with winter drapery, or "furniture," as the hangings were termed originally, one with summer hangings, and one without hangings. Because old textiles are in such short supply, it is usually impossible for museums to present early beds authentically dressed in all their glory for the winter season. Almost without exception, beds shown in historic houses and museums approximate the simpler summer dress. Now that good reproduction materials are available and make facsimile hangings possible, we hope at some future time to dress the beds in the Yale collections with valances, bases, and voluminous hangings like those with which they were once covered. In the meantime we present them in skeletal form, which has the advantage of exposing the details of the wooden framework.

The bedsteads included do not date before the mid-eighteenth century. No American bedstead from the seventeenth century has yet been identified, and examples from the early years of the eighteenth century are likewise exceedingly rare. Generally early American households had bedsteads of two types, those with high posts to be finished with curtains, and those with low posts.

290. High Post Bedstead

New York or Rhode Island, 1765–1785

The beautifully stop-fluted foot posts of this bedstead suggest an attribution to either New York or Rhode Island where that motif was favored in the eighteenth century. A New York bedstead with stop-fluted posts is at Winterthur,[1] and a Newport example with claw-and-ball feet is owned by the Rhode Island School of Design.[2] The absence of a secondary wood (the supports for the bed slats are not original) eliminates one important feature for determining the place of origin more accurately. Although there may have been a central peak on the headboard, its scalloped outline plus the bedstead's turned rather than squared headposts contribute to a rich effect.

Description: The four columnar-turned posts above the rails terminate in Marlborough legs below. The front posts are stop-fluted. The center of the deep headboard is straight, with two downward sloping scallops on either side.

Notes: The mortise-and-tenon joints of the rails and posts have been altered. The bolt holes have been filled and the bolt hole covers are modern. Parts of the Marlborough feet have been replaced. The top of the headboard is probably missing. The upper 3½ inches of the headboard slots in the headposts have been filled. The bedstead has been refinished.

Wood: Mahogany.

Dimensions: H. 92⅛ in. (234.0 cm), W. 58¼ in. (148.0 cm), D. 77⅞ in. (197.8 cm).

Provenance: Francis P. Garvan, New York, N.Y.; The Mabel Brady Garvan Collection, 1934.363.

---

[1] Downs, *Am. Furn.*, fig. 2.—[2] Comstock, fig. 235.

290

291

291. High Post Bedstead

New England, 1785–1800

The square, plain headposts of this bedstead are characteristic of New England and New York examples, but the use of birch and white pine point to a New England origin. A date at the beginning of the neoclassical revival seems appropriate. Plate 105 of Hepplewhite's *Guide* shows bed pillars with the general contours of these footposts, even including the Marlborough feet which are reminiscent of earlier, mid-eighteenth-century styles. Plate 95 of the same design book shows a bed whose turnings are virtually identical to those on this example.

Description: The deep cornice with rounded corners is supported by tapered headposts and front posts with Marlborough legs and a reel-and-vase-turned and tapered, fluted shaft. The top edge of the headboard is cut to form two somewhat heavy scrolls.

Notes: The cornice retains old red paint, but the rest of the bedstead has been refinished. The side rails have been spliced and lengthened by 3⅞ inches. The sides of the cornice have been extended 4¼ inches and the rear rail is new. Modern mattress supports have been removed from inside the side rails. The bolt hole covers are replacements.

Woods: Yellow birch; cornice, white pine.

Dimensions: H. 87⅞ in. (223.3 cm), BPH. 82⅜ in. (209.2 cm), W. 56⅝ in. (143.9 cm), D. 77⅞ in. (197.8 cm).

Provenance: Irving W. Lyon, Hartford, Conn.; Mrs. John P. Penney (Mamie P. Lyon), Pittsburgh, Pa.; Francis P. Garvan, New York, N.Y.; The Mabel Brady Garvan Collection, 1930.2402.

292. High Post Bedstead

Charleston, South Carolina, 1790–1810

A number of stylistic features on this richly worked bedstead help establish its place of origin as Charleston, South Carolina. The headposts, unlike those on the previous examples in this catalogue, have open-ended slots into which the headboard slips. This form of construction, the mahogany rails notched for slats, and the fringed crescents at the base of the reeding on the footposts are acknowledged signs of Charleston workmanship.[1]

Description: The tapered headposts have slots into which the headboard, with serpentine-shaped ends, slides. The front posts have tapered legs terminating in spade feet. A rectangle of triple-string inlay appears on the front and side faces of the legs and inlaid ovals are found just above the rails. The upper part of the columns are turned to a double-urn shape with a reeded shaft above. The lower urn is carved with a double row of leaves and the upper one is

292

292a

fluted and carved with heads of rice.

Notes: Hooks to hold a skirt have been removed from the undersides of the bed rails and headposts. New wooden inserts have been added around the bolt holes of the footposts. The bolt hole covers and casters are missing. The bedstead has been refinished.

Woods: Mahogany; slats, pine of the *taeda* group.

Dimensions: H. 93¾ in. (238.2 cm), W. 68⅜ in. (173.7 cm), D. 79⅞ in. (202.9 cm).

Provenance: J. K. Beard, Richmond, Va.; Francis P. Garvan, New York, N.Y.; The Mabel Brady Garvan Collection, 1930.2514.

[1] Montgomery, no. 8.

293. High Post Bedstead

Charleston, South Carolina, 1810–1820

With the exception of the mahogany rails (which are not notched for slats), this bedstead shares a number of similarities with no. 292 and is also attributed to Charleston. The carving, particularly of the eagles on the posts and cornice, is brilliantly handled. A date somewhat later than that of the preceding example would seem appropriate, since the front legs are ring turned and there is a reliance solely on carved rather than inlaid decoration.

Description: See no. 292. Here the cornice has a top

293

293a

293b

molding of ring turnings and eagle-carved plaques on three sides. The upper urn on the footpost is carved with eagles and floral swags in place of the rice on no. 292. A double row of acanthus leaves is found at the top of the reeded shaft. The legs are an elongated vase form with multiple ring turnings.

Notes: The bolt holes have been repaired, and the brass bolt hole covers are old. The bed has been refinished.

Woods: Mahogany; cornice, white pine and pine of the *taeda* group.

Dimensions: H. 101⅛ in. (256.9 cm), BPH. 93 in. (236.3 cm), W. 66½ in. (168.9 cm), D. 81½ in. (207.0 cm).

Exhibitions: Classical America, p. 52, no. 36.

Bibliography: Aronson, p. 22, fig. 58; Mabel M. Swan, "Wings Over Baltimore," *Antiques*, 42 (July 1942), p. 18, fig. 8.

Provenance: R. T. Haines Halsey, New York, N.Y.; Francis P. Garvan, New York, N.Y.; The Mabel Brady Garvan Collection, 1930.2025.

294. High Post Bedstead

Middle Atlantic States, 1790–1815

Octagonally chamfered headposts, known as "pencil" posts, are primarily a feature of New England beds and are therefore unusual on this bed, thought to come from the Middle Atlantic states. Numerous decorative features (including the rear feet that taper sharply and the front feet that assume a baluster form) point to a date well within the Federal period. On the footposts the urn-and-vase-shaped turnings are thin and sinuous, as neoclassical design should be. The turned decoration at the top of the footposts is so close to the tester that it appears that the tops of the posts have been cut down.

Description: The headposts are both tapered and chamfered. The headboard has a serpentine-shaped upper edge flanked by two scallops and semi-circular cut-outs in the headboard where it joins the posts. The rails have rope pegs along their upper edge. The front legs are an elongated vase form, and above the rails an urn supports an elongated baluster.

294

Notes: The red paint is old. The bolt hole covers are missing. Several rope pegs have been broken. The tester frame is new, and the tops of the posts have been shortened.

Woods: Soft maple; headboard, tulip.

Dimensions: H. 82 in. (208.3 cm), BPH. 81 in. (205.7 cm), W. 54¾ in. (139.1 cm), D. 77½ in. (196.8 cm).

Provenance: Samuel T. Freeman and Co., Philadelphia, Pa.; Charles R. Morson, New York, N.Y.; Francis P. Garvan, New York, N.Y.; The Mabel Brady Garvan Collection, 1930.2550.

295. Fold-Up Bedstead

New England, 1790–1815

295

Although many folding bedsteads have been found in Connecticut, they were undoubtedly made throughout New England. Designed with side rails hinged just before the headposts so that the length of the bedstead could be swung back against them, these bedsteads provided an efficient means of saving space in small eighteenth-century rooms, which usually served multiple purposes. The necessary omission of footposts made full testers an impossibility; half-testers were generally used on fold-up bedsteads to support the curtains.

Description: The headposts are tapered and chamfered like those on no. 294. They support a half-tester for the curtains. The side rails are hinged in front of the headposts so that the bottom part of the bedstead can be folded against the back. The top edge of the headboard is straight and the upper corners are notched. The short front legs have cylindrical knobs at the top and are turned to a taper below the rails.

Notes: The red paint is old. The half-tester is a replacement.

Woods: Soft maple; medial brace, red oak.

Dimensions: H. 84⅝ in. (215.0 cm), W. 53¼ in. (135.3 cm), D. 74¾ in. (189.9 cm).

Provenance: Frank McCarthy, Longmeadow, Mass.; Francis P. Garvan, New York, N.Y.; The Mabel Brady Garvan Collection, 1930.2526.

296. Bedstead

American, about 1850–1870

Although the nineteenth-century design book by Blackie and Sons, *The Victorian Cabinet-Maker's Assistant* (1853), continued to show designs for bedsteads that used high posts to be finished with curtains, this rococo revival bedstead with an elaborately ornamented headboard was clearly meant to stand alone.[1] From the time of the introduction of the "French" bedstead in the early nineteenth century, designs for elaborate beds without high posts or curtains paralleled the older form. Made of solid and veneered rosewood, the most exotic nineteenth-century furniture wood, this bedstead has few peers for its richness of ornament.

Description: The bedstead consists of a headboard, footboard, two side rails, and seven slats. The headboard is supported between two end posts outlined with opposing scrolls. Its crest is richly carved with a festoon of fruits, leaves, and pods on top of a broken-arch scrolled pediment. To the sides the top edge is ornamented with a fretwork of opposed C-scrolls. A shell with streamers of leaves and tendrils decorates the space just below the pediment. The front corners of the footboard are rounded and the arched top edge is outlined by opposed C-scrolls. Rectangular moldings ending in scrolls and fleur-de-lis surround applied bosses and C-scroll carving on the side rails and end. The edges of the feet, U- or lyre-shaped in outline, are ornamented with carving.

Notes: Small pieces of molding are missing from both ends of the headboard. The French polish finish is crazed at the center of the head and footboards.

Woods: Rosewood and pine.

Dimensions: H. 68¼ in. (173.4 cm), W. 59¾ in. (151.8 cm), D. 82¼ in. (208.9 cm).

Provenance: This bed belongs to a suite of furniture now used in the President's house; Bequest of Thomas Wells Farnam (B.A. 1899) (d. 1943), New Haven, Conn., 1943.357.

[1] Blackie and Sons, *The Victorian Cabinet-Maker's Assistant* (London, 1853; Dover reprint, 1970), pl. 82.

297. Miniature Cradle

American, about 1800

Some child undoubtedly derived infinite delight from this most unusual double-hooded toy cradle. Its urn-shaped finials and vase-and-ring-turned uprights in the neoclassical style suggest its approximate date.

296

297

Maple and white pine were used throughout the northern states and so provide no firm basis for an attribution of origin.

Description: Double-serpentine trestle-like feet support the uprights and the cross-bar from which the cradle is suspended. The cradle has two hooded ends and slat sides. The uprights are turned to an elongated vase form and end in small urn-shaped finials.

Notes: The arched top rail has been cracked and repaired.

Woods: Maple; hoods, mahogany; bottom of cradle, white pine.

Dimensions: H. 18½ in. (47.0 cm), BPH. 19¼ in. (48.9 cm), W. 10³⁄₁₆ in. (25.9 cm), D. 21¹⁄₁₆ in. (53.5 cm).

Bibliography: Nutting, *Treasury*, no. 1573; Kirk, *Early Am. Furn.*, fig. 172; Schiffer, p. 158, fig. 160.

Provenance: Jacob Margolis, New York, N.Y.; Francis P. Garvan, New York, N.Y. (1925); The Mabel Brady Garvan Collection, 1930.2394.

298. Bed Steps

Possibly Charleston, South Carolina, 1790–1810

These bed steps are probably southern; they were purchased with the bed (no. 292) attributed to Charleston, although they may not have been made for it originally. White pine is generally associated with furniture made north of Pennsylvania, but is occasionally found on southern furniture. Beginning in 1810, the New York price books list bed steps with treads lined with carpet, undoubtedly once present here.[1] Among the options offered in the price books for bed steps was "preparing and hinging the top for a pot cupboard."[2] The top tread of these steps is fashioned in just that manner.

Description: The upper tread of these bed steps is hinged at the back to form the lid of a box. Rectangles of dark and light line inlay ornament the faces of the steps. The front step is flanked by two light wood rectangles, and the whole is supported on four short tapered feet. The side edges of the front feet are decorated with light string.

Notes: Tack holes on both treads indicate they once were carpeted. The front molding of the top step is a replacement. The brass hinges are old, but the wood around them has been repaired. The steps have been refinished.

Woods: Mahogany; white pine.

Dimensions: H. 18¼ in. (46.4 cm), W. 19¾ in. (50.2 cm), D. 21¹⁵⁄₁₆ in. (54.8 cm).

Provenance: J. K. Beard, Richmond, Va.; Francis P. Garvan, New York, N.Y.; The Mabel Brady Garvan Collection, 1930.2515.

---

[1] Montgomery, no. 446.—[2] *Ibid.*

298

Concordance

Accession Number	Catalogue Number
1841.1	1
1900.42e	149
1930.2006	229
1930.2007	158
1930.2008	201
1930.2025	293
1930.2027	228
1930.2029a	74
1930.2029b	75
1930.2031	217
1930.2032	215
1930.2033	196
1930.2038b	134
1930.2039b	133
1930.2040	60
1930.2042	18
1930.2046	28
1930.2050f	175
1930.2053	192
1930.2058	114
1930.2060	107
1930.2077a	64
1930.2077c	65
1930.2078	54
1930.2084b	148
1930.2086b	115
1930.2092	231
1930.2094a	232
1930.2097	235
1930.2101b	93
1930.2102b	92
1930.2103	90
1930.2104	91
1930.2105a	99
1930.2106	208
1930.2107	212
1930.2108	209
1930.2114	102
1930.2116	127
1930.2117	113
1930.2127a	124
1930.2135b	200
1930.2136a	38
1930.2139	186
1930.2146	240
1930.2160	37
1930.2179a	21
1930.2185	88
1930.2202	50
1930.2227	153
1930.2242b	103
1930.2246	164
1930.2256a	47
1930.2258a	82
1930.2267	184
1930.2269	49
1930.2289	6
1930.2290	9
1930.2291	5
1930.2292	80
1930.2293	239
1930.2294	42
1930.2295c	35
1930.2296	27
1930.2297	10
1930.2301	30
1930.2302	14
1930.2303	83
1930.2304	43
1930.2350	177
1930.2351	193
1930.2352a	195
1930.2354	190
1930.2358	181
1930.2360	178
1930.2364	171
1930.2367	170
1930.2368	174
1930.2373	176
1930.2374	180
1930.2377	189
1930.2378	172
1930.2379	197
1930.2381	198
1930.2382	241
1930.2383b	194
1930.2394	297
1930.2402	291
1930.2405	138
1930.2406	66
1930.2407d	72
1930.2409	63
1930.2411a	70
1930.2414	71
1930.2415	123
1930.2416	57
1930.2417b	51
1930.2419	59
1930.2421	41
1930.2422b	73
1930.2423	16
1930.2425	89
1930.2426	77
1930.2428	85
1930.2432	29
1930.2433	86
1930.2434	78
1930.2446	79
1930.2449b	26
1930.2450	31
1930.2453	12
1930.2463	147
1930.2467	7
1930.2477	11
1930.2478b	126
1930.2479	101
1930.2490b	140
1930.2491	67
1930.2495	108
1930.2496	130
1930.2497a	116
1930.2498	94
1930.2499e	106
1930.2500	129
1930.2501	96
1930.2502	112
1930.2509	226
1930.2514	292
1930.2515	298
1930.2516a,b	117
1930.2518	104
1930.2520	39
1930.2523	36
1930.2526	295
1930.2529	218
1930.2530	105
1930.2545	68
1930.2550	294
1930.2556a	52
1930.2559	55
1930.2560	131
1930.2561	118
1930.2562	95
1930.2563	128
1930.2565	109
1930.2566b	110
1930.2572	221
1930.2603	179
1930.2609	15
1930.2611	22
1930.2615a	81
1930.2616	20
1930.2621	17
1930.2622	223
1930.2624a	155
1930.2625	143
1930.2626e	53
1930.2633	230
1930.2635	69
1930.2658	40
1930.2663	45
1930.2676a	150
1930.2680f	152
1930.2689	216
1930.2693b	156
1930.2695	120
1930.2697a	182
1930.2712	56
1930.2724	162
1930.2738	125
1930.2761a	145
1930.2850	144
1931.310	227
1931.313	237
1931.315a	159
1931.1211	32
1931.1212	167
1931.1219	46
1931.1229	233
1933.17b	183
1934.46	157
1934.363	290
1934.405	44
1941.119	169
1942.22a	141
1942.22b	142
1943.357	296
1947.437	151

Accession Number	Catalogue Number
1949.245	199
1950.694	87
1950.709	202
1950.713	165
1950.714	23
1950.716	166
1952.20.2	61
1952.50.1	3
1953.33.1	185
1953.50.2	24
1953.50.4	122
1953.50.6	25
1953.50.7b	188
1953.50.8	76
1954.37.25	222
1954.37.29	225
1955.33.3	173
1962.31.1	100
1962.31.2	206
1962.31.6	213
1962.31.7c	160
1962.31.8	136
1962.31.9	137
1962.31.13	224

Accession Number	Catalogue Number
1962.31.24	210
1962.31.25	214
1962.31.33	211
1962.31.71c	160
1963.6	4
1963.7	19
1963.10	58
1963.11a	121
1963.12	139
1963.13	8
1963.18.1	154
1963.18.2	111
1963.28.9	251
1964.47	146
1965.3	2
1965.21	119
1965.31	244
1966.47b	84
1966.119	113
1967.26	97
1967.28.1	98
1968.10b	135
1968.98	163
1969.39.1	132
1969.42.1	191

Accession Number	Catalogue Number
1969.42.22	250
1969.52.1	207
1969.52.2	34
1970.70	168
1970.98.6a,b	249a,b
1970.98.7a	245
1970.98.7g	246
1971.15.1	48
1971.23	33
1971.44.1	278
1971.44.2	277
1971.55	284
1971.67.1	263
1971.67.2	264
1971.67.3	265
1971.67.4a	270
1971.104	187
1971.122	62
1972.5	252
1972.52.2	273
1972.68	262
1973.77.1	288
1973.77.2	272
1973.77.3	274
1973.77.4a,b	275

Accession Number	Catalogue Number
1973.77.5	287
1973.77.6	266
1973.77.7	271
1973.83.1	242
1973.83.2	243
1973.104b	268
1973.106.1	286
1973.106.2	283
1973.106.3	269
1973.106.4a,b	280
1973.123.2a	257
1973.123.3c	258
1973.172a	289
1974.39	259
1974.62	261
1974.64.2	247
1974.88	205
1974.129	282
1975.4a	267
1975.5	255
1975.6a	281
1975.7	276
1975.24.1	204
1975.24.2	203

Photograph Credits

E. Irving Blomstrann, 2, 7, 17, 37, 37a, 61a, 91a,b, 92, 92a,b,c, 93, 94, 96, 97a,b, 99, 99a,b, 101, 103, 103a, 104, 104a,b, 106–108, 111a,b, 113b, 115, 115a, 116, 116a, 117a, 118a, 124a,b, 128a, 129b, 130a,b, 139a, 140a, 146a, 147a, 156a, 164a,b,c, 196a, 198, 201–203, 203a, 204, 207, 222, 224, 225, 226, 226a,b,c, 227, 227a,b,c, 228, 229, 230a, 231, 232, 232a, 237, 240, 245, 246, 249A,B, 251, 285, 298; Color plates 2–10, 12–17

Richard Cheek, 216

Norman McGrath, Color plates 1, 11, 18

Joseph Szaszfai, 9a,b, 48, 62, 62a,b,c, 97, 98, 117, 138a,b, 160, 161, 168, 168a, 171, 187, 191, 205, 205a, 208, 209, 209a,

Joseph Szaszfai *continued*
219, 220, 234, 236, 238, 242, 243, 247, 248, 250, 253–262, 262a, 263, 266, 268, 269, 271–284, 286–289, 296; Figs. 9, 11

Charles Uht, 3–6, 8–16, 18, 19, 19a,b,c, 21–23, 25–29, 31, 32, 34, 35, 35a, 36, 36a, 40–42, 43, 43a, 44, 44a, 50–55, 56, 56a, 57, 59, 60, 63–65, 68–81, 84–87, 89, 90, 90a, 94a, 95, 100, 102, 102a,b, 105, 109, 110, 112, 112b, 113, 119, 120–126, 128, 129, 129a, 130–137, 139–153, 153a, 154, 155, 155a, 157, 157a, 158, 158a, 159, 162, 163, 163a,b,c, 165–167, 169, 170, 172–183, 185, 186, 188–190, 192–194, 199, 200, 206, 210–213, 215, 217, 218, 221, 230, 233, 235, 239, 241, 290, 291, 292, 292a, 293, 293a,b, 294, 295; Fig. 8

Index

References are to catalogue number unless they are specifically cited as page references.

C

H

I

J

K

L

M

N

O

P

Q

R

Y

Z